D0882575

Exploring
GENESIS

THE JOHN PHILLIPS COMMENTARY SERIES

Exploring
GENESIS
An Expository Commentary

JOHN PHILLIPS

Grand Rapids, MI 49501

Exploring Genesis: An Expository Commentary

Published in 2001 by Kregel Publications, a division of Kregel, Inc., P.O. Box 2607, Grand Rapids, MI 49501. For more information about Kregel Publications, visit our Web site: www.kregel.com.

Library of Congress Cataloging-in-Publication Data
Phillips, John.
Exploring Genesis: an expository commentary / by John Phillips.
p. cm.
Originally published: Chicago: Moody Press, 1980.
Includes bibliographical references.
1. Bible N.T. Genesis—Commentaries. I. Title.
BS1235.53 .P48 2001 222'.1107—dc21 2001033769
CIP

ISBN 0-8254-3488-2

Printed in the United States of America

1 2 3 / 05 04 03 02 01

Contents

PART ONE
The Beginnings of the Human Race
Primeval History

PART TWO
The Beginnings of the Hebrew Race
Patriarchal History

FOREWORD

For many years now I have been pursuing the expository approach in my preaching. On Sunday morning and again on Sunday night I prayerfully select a book of the Bible, then expound that book to my people, chapter by chapter, verse by verse. I have found that method extremely rewarding. It blesses my own life, feeds my flock, and reaches out to the unsaved.

Those who follow the expository method are aware of the need to have good expository commentaries available to enhance and illumine one's own efforts. A few years ago, while preaching through the book of Romans, I came across a volume entitled *Exploring Romans* by John Phillips. I had not heard of John Phillips, but was immediately blessed by his book. In subsequent years I obtained other volumes by him. I found *Exploring the Scriptures, Exploring Revelation,* and *Exploring Hebrews* equally helpful and inspiring.

Soon thereafter, I learned that Mr. Phillips was residing in my home state of Georgia. Through a mutual friend I was able to meet Mr. Phillips and invite him to lead a Bible conference here at Dauphin Way. I was thrilled to discover that he was even better in person than on the printed page! My people and I were marvelously fed as he ministered the Word in our midst. I consider him to be one of the finest Bible teachers in the world today.

It was with real joy that I received the news that he was preparing a book on Genesis. He was gracious enough to send me his manuscript. I have been reading his material on Genesis with amazement and gratitude. I have many books on Genesis, but none is so helpful and enriching as this one. Mr. Phillips' work is scholarly, scriptural, and simple. It attains the rare combination of being both theological and devotional. His outlines are superb. His interpretations are fresh, yet germane. His illustrations are appropriate to the truth being exposed. His use of imagination in the study of personalities throughout Genesis is the best I have ever read.

I heartily recommend this volume to pastors, evangelists, Sunday school teachers, and all who want greater insight into the book of beginnings. I predict it will become the most popular commentary on Genesis written in our time.

Jerry Vines
Pastor, Dauphin Way Baptist Church
Mobile, Alabama

PREFACE

It is a book of facts, a book of firsts, a book of faith, a book of forecasts, a book of funerals. It has been called "the seedplot of the Bible" because all the vast forests of Scripture start there as seedlings. It is said to give us the beginning of everything except God. It is the book of Genesis.

Genesis is the opening crescendo of Scripture, for God does not begin the book with a timid, tentative note or two. He begins it with the thunder of drums as worlds leap out of nowhere to populate the skies. He begins it with the crash of cymbals as the human race falls into sin. He begins it with the blare of trumpets heralding the inundation of a world.

How shall we approach this vast book? With simple faith to begin with, for the facts it sets forth are to be believed, not to be bandied about at the whims of the world. With increasing interest, as its heroes march across the page before us, as nations rise and fall, as the Hebrew people emerge thereafter to dominate the Bible to the end.

If we are going to begin a study of the Scriptures, where could we better begin than in the beginning with Genesis and with God? In *Exploring Genesis* we have mapped our course with crisp, clear outlines. We have sought to be true to the text. We have tried to bring to life again the people who crowd its pages. We have sought to exalt the Lord Jesus Christ.

May Genesis become one of your favorite books, one you will want to continually explore.

GENERAL OUTLINE

PART ONE

The Beginnings of the Human Race

Primeval History

(1:1–11:32)

CHAPTER 1–The Creation (1:1–2:25)

I. The Introduction (1:1)

II. The Narration (1:2-31)
- A. How Life Was Established on Earth (1:2-13)
  - 1. Prevailing Chaos Described (1:2)
  - 2. Prevailing Chaos Dispelled (1:3-13)
    - a. Darkness Dispelled (1:3-5)
    - b. Disorder Dispelled (1:6-10)
      - (1) The Clouds Raised (1:6-8)
      - (2) The Continents Raised (1:9-10)
    - c. Deadness Dispelled (1:11-13)
- B. How Law Was Established on Earth (1:14-31)
  - 1. The Heavenly Bodies Commanded to Rule (1:14-19)
  - 2. The Human Beings Created to Rule (1:20-31)
    - a. Man's Domains Prepared for Him (1:20-25)
    - b. Man's Domains Presented to Him (1:26-31)
      - (1) How God Created Adam (1:26-27)
      - (2) How God Crowned Adam (1:28-31)
        - (i) A Posterity (1:28*a*)
        - (ii) A Position (1:28*b*)
        - (iii) A Possession (1:29-31)

III. The Conclusion (2:1-7)
- A. God Resting (2:1-3)
  - 1. The Creation Complete (2:1)
  - 2. The Creator Content (2:2-3)
- B. God Reviewing (2:4-7)
  - 1. Astronomy Reviewed (2:4)
  - 2. Agronomy Reviewed (2:5-6)
  - 3. Anthropology Reviewed (2:7)

- IV. THE CONSUMMATION (2:8-25)
  - A. Adam's Home (2:8-17)
    - 1. Somewhere Ideal to Dwell (2:8-14)
    - 2. Something Ideal to Do (2:15-17)
      - a. A Specific Task (2:15)
      - b. A Sacred Trust (2:16-17)
        - (1) Stated as Pleasantly as Possible (2:16)
        - (2) Stated as Plainly as Possible (2:17)
  - B. Adam's Helpmeet (2:18-25)
    - 1. Adam's Desire Foreseen by God (2:18)
    - 2. Adam's Desire Fostered by God (2:19-20)
    - 3. Adam's Desire Fulfilled by God (2:21-25)
      - a. The Making of the Woman for Adam (2:21-22*a*)
      - b. The Marriage of the Woman to Adam (2:22*b*-25)
        - (1) The Marriage Vision (2:22*b*)
        - (2) The Marriage Vow (2:23-24)
        - (3) The Marriage Virtue (2:25)

CHAPTER 2—The Curse (3:1—4:15)

- I. THE FALLEN RACE (3:1-24)
  - A. Man's Fall (3:1-8)
    - 1. The Subtlety of the Serpent (3:1-6)
      - a. The Appeal to Eve's Intellect (3:1*b*-5)
        - (1) The Doubt (3:1*b*-3)
        - (2) The Denial (3:4)
        - (3) The Delusion (3:5)
      - b. The Appeal to Adam's Emotions (3:6)
        - (1) Turn the Look to Lust
        - (2) Turn the Desire to Decision
        - (3) Turn the Choice into a Chain
        - (4) Turn the Sinner into a Seducer
    - 2. The Success of the Serpent (3:7-8)
      - a. The Plight of Adam and Eve (3:7)
      - b. The Flight of Adam and Eve (3:8)
  - B. Man's Future (3:9-24)
    - 1. Adam Summoned (3:9)
    - 2. Adam Searched (3:10-13)
      - a. His Explanation (3:10)
      - b. His Excuse (3:11-12)
      - c. His Example (3:13)
    - 3. Adam Sentenced (3:14-19)
      - a. War (3:14-15)
      - b. Woe (3:16)
      - c. Work (3:17-19)

(1) Unrewarding Toil (3:17-19*a*)
(2) Unrelenting Terror (3:19*b*)
4. Adam Saved (3:20-24)
a. God's Grace on Man's Behalf (3:20-21)
(1) Adam's Confession (3:20)
(2) Adam's Covering (3:21)
b. God's Government on Man's Behalf (3:22-24)

II. The First False Religion (4:1-15)
A. The False Inference of Cain's Religion (4:1-7)
1. A Purely Human Scheme (4:1-2)
2. A Purely Human Sacrifice (4:3-4)
3. A Purely Human Satisfaction (4:5-7)
B. The Fierce Intolerance of Cain's Religion (4:8-15)
1. Characterized by Force (4:8)
2. Characterized by Falsehood (4:9)
3. Characterized by Futility (4:10-12)
4. Characterized by Fear (4:13-15)

CHAPTER 3—The Catastrophe (4:16—9:29)

I. A World Fast Ripening for Judgment (4:16—6:22)
A. God's Assessment of Those Times (4:16—6:7)
1. The Ungodly (4:16-24)
a. Their Indifference to God (4:16-17)
(1) Indifference to His Person (4:16)
(2) Indifference to His Paradise (4:17)
b. Their Independence of God (4:18-24)
(1) Moral Disorder (4:19)
(2) Marvelous Discovery (4:20-22)
(i) Marketing—Jabal (4:20)
(ii) Music—Jubal (4:21)
(iii) Metalurgy—Tubal-Cain (4:22)
(3) Militant Defiance (4:23-24)
2. The Unworldly (4:25—5:32)
a. How the New Seed Commenced (4:25—5:5)
(1) A New Birth (4:25-26)
(2) A New Book (5:1-5)
b. How the New Seed Continued (5:6-32)
(1) The Patriarchs (5:6-20)
(2) The Prophets (5:21-32)
(i) A Witness to God's Presence—Enoch (5:21-24)
(ii) A Witness to God's Patience—Methuselah (5:25-27)

(iii) A Witness to God's Peace—Lamech (5:28-31)
(iv) A Witness to God's Purposes—Noah (5:32)

3. The Unruly (6:1-7)
   a. Their Great Apostasy (6:1-3)
      (1) The Final Expression of the Perversion of Man (6:1-2)
      (2) The Final Exhaustion of the Patience of God (6:3)
   b. Their Godless Activity (6:4)
   c. Their Growing Anarchy (6:5-7)
      (1) God's Discernment (6:5)
      (2) God's Disappointment (6:6)
      (3) God's Decision (6:7)

B. God's Answer to Those Times (6:8-22)
1. A Man (6:8-13)
   a. Energized by God (6:8-10)
      (1) He Was Forgiven (6:8)
      (2) He Was Faithful (6:9)
      (3) He Was Fruitful (6:10)
   b. Enlightened by God (6:11-13)
      (1) God Reviewing the Earth (6:11-12)
      (2) God Revealing His Wrath (6:13)
2. A Plan (6:14-22)
   a. Finished Work of Christ (6:14-16)
   b. Faithful Word of God (6:17-22)

II. A WORLD FINALLY RELINQUISHED TO JUDGMENT (7:1-24)

A. The Deliverance of the Godly (7:1-9)
1. The Full Commitment Demanded of Noah (7:1)
2. The Final Commission Delivered to Noah (7:2-4)
3. The Faithful Compliance Demonstrated by Noah (7:5-9)

B. The Destruction of the Godless (7:10-24)
1. Its Timing (7:10-16)
   a. The Further Delay of the Judgment (7:10)
   b. The Final Dawning of the Judgment (7:11-16)
2. Its Totality (7:17-24)
   a. The Extent of the Flood (7:17-20)
   b. The Execution by the Flood (7:21-24)

III. A WORLD FRESHLY RECOVERED FROM JUDGMENT (8:1–9:29)

A. Noah Tarrying (8:1-5)
1. While God Remembered (8:1-2)
2. While the Flood Receded (8:3)
3. While the Ark Rested (8:4-5)

- B. Noah Testing (8:6-14)
    - 1. What Noah Sought (8:6-12)
    - 2. What Noah Saw (8:13-14)
- C. Noah Trusting (8:15–9:17)
    - 1. The Lord's Command to Noah (8:15-19)
        - a. The Command Heard (8:15-17)
        - b. The Command Heeded (8:18-19)
    - 2. The Lord's Covenant With Noah (8:20–9:17)
        - a. God Spoke Secretly (8:20-22)
        - b. God Spoke Sovereignly (9:1-17)
            - (1) The General Provisions of the Covenant (9:1-7)
            - (2) The Great Provision of the Covenant (9:8-17)
                - (a) Its Substance (9:8-12)
                - (b) Its Sign (9:13-17)
- D. Noah Toiling (9:18-23)
    - 1. Noah the Father (9:18-19)
    - 2. Noah the Farmer (9:20)
    - 3. Noah the Failure (9:21-23)
- E. Noah Testifying (9:24-29)
    - 1. By Lip (9:24-27)
    - 2. By Life (9:28-29)

CHAPTER 4—The Coalition (10:1–11:32)

- I. DIVINE GOVERNMENT (10:1–11:9)
    - A. The Completeness of Man's Dispersal (10:1-32)
        - 1. The Japhetic Races (10:1-5)
            - a. Introduction (10:1)
            - b. The Founders (10:2)
            - c. The Families (10:3-5)
        - 2. The Hamitic Races (10:6-20)
            - a. Notable Names (10:6-7)
            - b. Notorious Nimrod (10:8-12)
            - c. Near Neighbors (10:13-20)
        - 3. The Semitic Races (10:21-32)
            - a. The Royal Line (10:21-25)
            - b. The Related Line (10:26-31)
            - c. Conclusion (10:32)
    - B. The Cause of Man's Dispersal (11:1-9)
        - 1. Their Materials (11:1-3)
        - 2. Their Method (11:4*a*)
        - 3. Their Motive (11:4*b*)
        - 4. Their Mistake (11:5-9)

- II. DIVINE GRACE (11:10-32)
    - A. Abram's Family Tree (11:10-26)

- B. Abram's Family Ties (11:27-32)
  - 1. Abram the Person (11:27-30)
  - 2. Abram the Pilgrim (11:31-32)
    - a. The First Step (11:31*a*)
    - b. The First Stop (11:31*b*-32)

PART TWO

The Beginnings of the Hebrew Race

Patriarchal History

(12:1–50:26)

CHAPTER 5–The Progenitor: Abraham (12:1–25:18)

- I. THE PATH OF FAITH (12:1-20)
  - A. Abram Believing (12:1-9)
    - 1. Finding the Path of Faith (12:1-4)
      - a. A Statement of Faith (12:1-3)
      - b. A Step of Faith (12:4)
    - 2. Following the Path of Faith (12:5-8)
      - a. Abram Witnessing (12:5)
      - b. Abram Walking (12:6*a*)
      - c. Abram Waiting (12:6*b*-7)
      - d. Abram Worshiping (12:8)
    - 3. Forsaking the Path of Faith (12:9)
  - B. Abram Backsliding (12:10-20)
    - 1. Famine (12:10)
    - 2. Foreboding (12:11-12)
    - 3. Falsehood (12:13)
    - 4. Frustration (12:14-15)
    - 5. Flattery (12:16)
    - 6. Failure (12:17-20)

- II. THE PRICE OF FAITH (13:1-18)
  - A. The Marks of a Spiritual Man (13:1-4)
    - 1. Separation (13:1)
    - 2. Sanctification (13:2-3)
    - 3. Sacrifice (13:4)
  - B. The Mind of a Spiritual Man (13:5-9)
    - 1. Worrying Circumstances (13:5-6)
    - 2. Wicked Neighbors (13:7)
    - 3. Weaker Brethren (13:8-9)
      - a. Spiritual Directness (13:8*a*)
      - b. Spiritual Discernment (13:8*b*)
      - c. Spiritual Dignity (13:9)

- C. The Moves of a Spiritual Man (13:10-18)
  - 1. Restrained by God (13:10-13)
    - a. Lot's Weak Devotions
    - b. Lot's Worldly Desires (13:10)
    - c. Lot's Wrong Decisions (13:11-13)
  - 2. Reassured by God (13:14-16)
    - a. As to His Possessions (13:14-15)
    - b. As to His Posterity (13:16)
  - 3. Regulated by God (13:17-18)

III. THE POWER OF FAITH (14:1-24)

- A. The Desperate Battle (14:1-11)
  - 1. The Coalitions (14:1-2)
  - 2. The Conflict (14:3-9)
  - 3. The Collapse (14:10-11)
- B. The Deluded Brother (14:12)
- C. The Dynamic Believer (14:13-24)
  - 1. The Weakness of the Flesh (14:13)
  - 2. The Wisdom of the World (14:14-16)
    - a. Abram Acted Swiftly (14:14)
    - b. Abram Acted Sensibly (14:15)
    - c. Abram Acted Successfully (14:16)
  - 3. The Wiles of the Devil (14:17-24)
    - a. The Significant Meeting with the King of Salem (14:17-20)
    - b. The Sinister Meeting with the King of Sodom (14:21-24)
      - (1) The Subtle Temptation of Abram (14:21)
      - (2) The Simple Testimony of Abram (14:22-24)

IV. THE PLEDGE OF FAITH (15:1-21)

- A. The Building of Abram's Family (15:1-7)
  - 1. The Word of God's Power (15:1-4)
    - a. The Pledge (15:1)
    - b. The Plea (15:2-3)
    - c. The Plan (15:4)
  - 2. The Witness to God's Power (15:5-6)
  - 3. The Working of God's Power (15:7)
- B. The Basis of Abram's Faith (15:8-12)
  - 1. Calvary Shadowed: He Apprehends Its Mystery (15:8-10)
  - 2. Calvary Shared: He Apprehends Its Misery (15:11-12)
- C. The Brightness of Abram's Future (15:13-21)
  - 1. The Specific Time Involved (15:13-16)
    - a. The Permissive Will of God (15:13-14)
    - b. The Personal Will of God (15:15)
    - c. The Preordaining Will of God (15:16)

2. The Specific Territory Involved (15:17-21)
   a. The Guarantee of the Land (15:17)
   b. The Greatness of the Land (15:18-21)

V. THE PAWNING OF FAITH (16:1-16)
  A. The Test of the Silence of God (16:1-6)
    1. Abram's Double Mind (16:1-4)
      a. The Problem (16:1)
      b. The Proposal (16:2-3)
      c. The Price (16:4)
    2. Sarai's Deceitful Heart (16:5-6)
      a. Her Untamed Tongue (16:5)
      b. Her Untamed Temper (16:6)
    3. Hagar's Defiant Will (16:6)
  B. The Truth of the Sovereignty of God (16:7-16)
    1. The Revelation to Hagar (16:7-12)
      a. The Coming of the Omnipresent One: A Revelation of Grace (16:7-8)
      b. The Command of the Omnipotent One: A Revelation of Government (16:9)
      c. The Comfort of the Omniscient One: A Revelation of Greatness (16:10-12)
        (1) Promise (16:10-11)
        (2) Prophecy (16:12)
    2. The Response by Hagar (16:13-16)
      a. Her Verbal Expression of Faith (16:13-14)
      b. Her Vital Expression of Faith (16:15-16)

VI. THE POTENTIAL OF FAITH (17:1-27)
  A. How the Covenant Was Received (17:1-16)
    1. In Absolute Subjection (17:1-3)
    2. In Absolute Silence (17:4-16)
      a. The Substance of the Promise (17:4-8)
        (1) The Principle Involved
        (2) The People Involved (17:4-6)
        (3) The Period Involved (17:7)
        (4) The Place Involved (17:8)
      b. The Seal of the Promise (17:9-14)
        (1) Its Implications (17:9-11)
        (2) Its Implementation (17:12-13)
        (3) Its Importance (17:14)
      c. The Spirit of the Promise (17:15-16)
  B. How the Covenant Was Believed (17:17-27)
    1. The Laughter of Faith (17:17)
    2. The Logic of Faith (17:18-22)
      a. The Plea for Ishmael (17:18)

- b. The Pledge for Ishmael (17:19-22)
  - (1) The Reserve Clause (17:19)
  - (2) The Royal Clause (17:20-22)
- 3. The Life of Faith (17:23-27)
  - a. A Limitless Obedience (17:23-24)
    - (1) Parental Obedience (17:23*a*)
    - (2) Patriarchal Obedience (17:23*b*)
    - (3) Positional Obedience (17:23*c*)
    - (4) Personal Obedience (17:24)
  - b. A Limited Ordinance (17:25-27)
    - (1) The State of the Rebellious Man (17:25)
    - (2) The Standing of the Righteous Man (17:26-27)

VII. THE PRAYER OF FAITH (18:1-33)
- A. The Practical Man (18:1-8)
  - 1. His Haste (18:1-2)
  - 2. His Hospitality (18:3-8)
- B. The Privileged Man (18:9-15)
  - 1. The Promise (18:9-10)
  - 2. The Problem (18:11-15)
- C. The Proved Man (18:16-22)
  - 1. Prospective Greatness (18:16-18)
  - 2. Personal Greatness (18:19)
  - 3. Positional Greatness (18:20-22)
- D. The Praying Man (18:23-33)
  - 1. Abraham's Attitude (18:23*a*)
  - 2. Abraham's Argument (18:23*b*-32)
  - 3. Abraham's Assurance (18:33)

VIII. THE POSITION OF FAITH (19:1-38)
- A. The Unholy Morality of Sodom (19:1-11)
  - 1. A Prevalent Thing (19:1-3)
  - 2. A Polluted Thing (19:4-5)
  - 3. A Persistent Thing (19:6-9*a*)
  - 4. A Pugnacious Thing (19:9*b*)
  - 5. A Punishable Thing (19:10-11)
- B. The Unholy Mentality of Sodom (19:12-38)
  - 1. Lot's Faith Corroded (19:12-26)
    - a. Lot's Worthless Witness (19:12-14)
    - b. Lot's Weak Will (19:15-23)
      - (1) His Reluctance to Start (19:15-17)
      - (2) His Readiness to Stop (19:18-23)
    - c. Lot's Wayward Wife (19:24-26)
  - 2. Lot's Family Corrupted (19:27-38)
    - a. What He Might Have Become (19:27-29)
    - b. What He Had Become (19:30-38)
      - (1) Sodom's Unbelieving Perspective (19:30-32)

(2) Sodom's Unblushing Practices (19:33-36)
(3) Sodom's Unblessed Progeny (19:37-38)

IX. THE PERILS OF FAITH (20:1-18)
  A. The Moving Pilgrim (20:1-2)
  B. The Miserable Prophet (20:3-16)
    1. Not Readily Recognizable as a Prophet (20:3-7)
      a. Abimelech's Lost Condition (20:3)
      b. Abimelech's Loud Complaint (20:4-5)
      c. Abimelech's Last Consideration (20:6-7)
        (1) Sovereignly Restrained (20:6)
        (2) Still Responsible (20:7)
    2. Not Really Regarded as a Prophet (20:8-13)
      a. His Distrustful Behavior (20:11)
      b. His Dishonest Behavior (20:12)
      c. His Disgraceful Behavior (20:13)
    3. Not Rightly Received as a Prophet (20:14-16)
      a. Abimlech Disgraced Him (20:14)
      b. Abimelech Dismissed Him (20:15)
      c. Abimelech Disdained Him (20:16)
  C. The Ministering Priest (20:17-18)
    1. The Scope of His Ministry (20:17*a*)
    2. The Success of His Ministry (20:17*b*)
    3. The Significance of His Ministry (20:18)

X. THE PRIZE OF FAITH (21:1-34)
  A. The Tremendous Miracle of Isaac (21:1-8)
    1. His Birth Forecast (21:1-2)
    2. His Birth Fulfilled (21:3-8)
      a. Dependence (21:3-4)
      b. Development (21:5-8)
  B. The Terrible Mockery of Ishmael (21:9)
  C. The Typical Message of Sarah (21:10)
  D. The Tragic Mistake of Abraham (21:11)
  E. The Tender Mercies of God (21:12-13)
    1. His Command (21:12)
    2. His Comfort (21:13)
  F. The Tearful Misery of Hagar (21:14-21)
    1. Cast Out (21:14)
    2. Crushed Down (21:15-16)
    3. Caught Up (21:17-21)
  G. The Transparent Motives of Abimelech (21:22-34)
    1. His Plea (21:22-24)
    2. His Pledge (21:25-31)
    3. His Parting (21:32-34)
      a. Abraham Working (21:33*a*)

b. Abraham Worshiping (21:33*b*)
c. Abraham Waiting (21:34)

XI. THE PROOF OF FAITH (22:1-24)
A. The Sudden Test for Which God Had Prepared Abraham (22:1-2)
B. The Simple Trust in Which God Had Perfected Abraham (22:3-12)
1. The Way of the Cross (22:3-5)
2. The Word of the Cross (22:6-8)
3. The Work of the Cross (22:9-12)
C. The Solemn Truth by Which God Had Protected Abraham (22:13-24)

XII. THE PATIENCE OF FAITH (23:1-20)
A. Abraham's Grief (23:1-6)
1. His Tears (23:1-2)
2. His Testimony (23:3-6)
a. A Stranger
b. A Sojourner
B. Sarah's Grave (23:7-18)
1. Abraham's Courtesy (23:7-8)
2. Abraham's Carefulness (23:8-18)
C. Ephron's Gift (23:19-20)

XIII. THE PRECAUTIONS OF FAITH (24:1-67)
A. The Wise Father (24:1-9)
B. The Wondrous Servant (24:10-28)
C. The Worldly Sinner (24:29-33)
D. The Willing Saint (24:34-61)
1. Rebekah Learning of Isaac
2. Rebekah Longing for Isaac
3. Rebekah Looking for Isaac
E. The Waiting Son (24:62-67)

XIV. THE PARTINGS OF FAITH (25:1-11)
A. The Fruitful Man (25:1-4)
1. Abraham's Decision (25:1)
2. Abraham's Descendants (25:2-4)
a. Zimran (25:2)
b. Jokshan (25:2-3)
c. Medan (25:2)
d. Midian (25:2, 4)
e. Ishbak (25:2)
f. Shuah (25:2)
B. The Far-sighted Man (25:5-6)
1. The Disposal of His Fortune (25:5)
2. The Dispersal of His Family (25:6)

- C. The Full Man (25:7-11)
  - 1. The Measure of Abraham's Days (25:7)
  - 2. The Manner of Abraham's Death (25:8)
  - 3. The Matter of Abraham's Desires (25:9-11)
    - a. His Paternal Desire (25:9*a*)
    - b. His Personal Desires (25:9*b*-10)
    - c. His Patriarchal Desire (25:11)
- D. The Futile Man (25:12-18)
  - 1. Ishmael's Family Ties (25:12-15)
    - a. His Notable Birth (25:12)
    - b. His Numerous Boys (25:13-15)
  - 2. Ishmael's Five Triumphs (25:16)
    - a. The Great People
    - b. The Great Places
    - c. The Great Power
    - d. The Great Princes
    - e. The Great Possessions
  - 3. Ishmael's Final Tragedy (25:17-18)
    - a. His Sorry Decease (25:17)
    - b. His Secular Desires (25:18)

CHAPTER 6—The Pilgrim: Isaac (25:19—27:46)

- I. ISAAC AND HIS BOYS (25:19-34)
  - A. The Twin Boys in the Womb (25:19-26)
    - 1. The Sterile Wife (25:19-21)
      - a. Rebekah's Pedigree (25:19-20)
      - b. Rebekah's Problem (25:21)
    - 2. The Secret War (25:22-26)
      - a. The Two Natures Experienced (25:22)
      - b. The Two Natures Explained (25:23)
      - c. The Two Natures Exposed (25:24-26)
  - B. The Twin Boys in the World (25:27-34)
    - 1. The Growing Conflict (25:27-28)
      - a. How the Boys Developed (25:27)
      - b. How the Boys Differed (25:28)
    - 2. The Great Confrontation (25:29-34)
      - a. Esau Minded Earthly Things (25:29-34)
        - (1) What He Saw (25:29)
        - (2) What He Said (25:30-32)
        - (3) What He Sold (25:33-34)
      - b. Jacob Minded Eternal Things (25:31-34)
        - (1) Family Property
        - (2) Family Priesthood
        - (3) Family Progenitorship

II. ISAAC AND HIS BEHAVIOR (26:1-35)
- A. Isaac's Walk (26:1-5)
  1. The Difficult Problem (26:1)
  2. The Divine Prohibition (26:2*a*)
  3. The Definite Promise (26:2*b*-5)
- B. Isaac's Wife (26:6-11)
  1. The Lie Was Ready (26:6-7)
  2. The Lie Was Revealed (26:8-11)
     - a. It Was Unfair (26:8-10)
     - b. It Was Unnecessary (26:11)
- C. Isaac's Wealth (26:12-16)
  1. He Was Rich (26:12-14*a*)
  2. He Was Resented (26:14*b*-16)
- D. Isaac's Wells (26:17-22)
  1. What Isaac Recovered (26:17-18)
  2. What Isaac Realized (26:19-22)
     - a. Esek: Contention (26:19-20)
     - b. Sirnah: Contempt (26:21)
     - c. Rehoboth: Carelessness (26:22)
- E. Isaac's Worship (26:23-25)
  1. The Important Revelation (26:23-24)
     - a. God's Person
     - b. God's Protection
     - c. God's Presence
     - d. God's Promise
  2. The Immediate Response (26:25)
     - a. In Spontaneous Worship
     - b. In Spoken Word
     - c. In Specific Work
- F. Isaac's Witness (26:26-33)
  1. The Approach of the Enemy (26:26-27)
  2. The Appeal of the Enemy (26:28-29)
  3. The Appeasement of the Enemy (26:30-33)
- G. Isaac's Woe (26:34-35)

III. ISAAC AND HIS BLESSING (27:1-46)
- A. The Unspiritual Father (27:1-4)
  1. Isaac's Concern (27:1-2)
  2. Isaac's Carnality (27:3-4)
     - a. Stubborn Enmity
     - b. Sensual Exercise
- B. The Unsurrendered Wife (27:5-10)
  1. Rebekah's Decision (27:5-7)
  2. Rebekah's Deceit (27:8-10)

- C. The Unscrupulous Brother (27:11-33)
  - 1. Jacob's Suspicious Behavior (27:11-27)
    - a. His Fear (27:11-13)
    - b. His Falsehood (27:14-27)
  - 2. Jacob's Stolen Blessing (27:28-33)
    - a. The Content of That Blessing (27:28-29)
    - b. The Confirmation of That Blessing (27:30-33)
- D. The Unsaved Son (27:34-46)
  - 1. Esau's Impassioned Remorse (27:34-35)
  - 2. Esau's Implacable Resentment (27:36-37)
  - 3. Esau's Importunate Request (27:38-40)
  - 4. Esau's Impulsive Resolve (27:41-46)

CHAPTER 7—The Propagator: Jacob (28:1—35:29)

- I. HOW GOD SAVED JACOB (28:1-22)
  - A. Jacob's Departure (28:1-9)
    - 1. Its Immense Importance (28:1-4)
      - a. The Word of Instruction: His Wife (28:1-2)
      - b. The Word of Inspiration: His Worship (28:3-4)
    - 2. Its Immediate Impact (28:5-9)
      - a. What Esau Heard (28:5-7)
      - b. What Esau Hoped (28:8-9)
  - B. Jacob's Dream (28:10-17)
    - 1. The Far Country (28:10-11)
    - 2. The Fresh Covenant (28:12-15)
      - a. What God Proved to Jacob (28:12)
      - b. What God Promised to Jacob (28:13-15)
    - 3. The Firm Conviction (28:16-17)
  - C. Jacob's Decision (28:18-22)
    - 1. He Acted Promptly (28:18*a*)
    - 2. He Acted Purposefully (28:18*b*-19)
    - 3. He Acted Practically (28:20-22)

- II. HOW GOD SUBDUED JACOB (29:1—30:43)
  - A. Jacob's Arrival at Padan-aram (29:1-12)
    - 1. Coming to the Well (29:1-3)
    - 2. Confidence at the Well (29:4-8)
    - 3. Conquests by the Well (29:9-12)
  - B. Jacob's Arrangements at Padan-aram (29:13—30:43)
    - 1. The Matter of His Wives (29:13—30:24)
      - a. His Fervent Love (29:13-20)
      - b. His First Lesson (29:22-31)
      - c. His Family Life (29:32—30:24)
        - (1) Reuben: The Child of Sore Distress (29:32)
        - (2) Simeon: The Child of Simple Disappointment (29:33)

- (3) Levi: The Child of Spiritual Discouragement (29:34)
- (4) Judah: The Child of Splendid Destiny (29:35)
- (5) Dan: The Child of Sustained Despair (30:1-6)
- (6) Naphtali: The Child of Supposed Deliverance (30:7-8)
- (7) Gad: The Child of Sad Defeat (30:9-11)
- (8) Asher: The Child of Sudden Delight (30:12-13)
- (9) Issachar: The Child of Snappish Dislike (30:14-18)
- (10) Zebulun: The Child of Strong Defiance (30:19-20)
- (11) Dinah: The Child of Silent Dignity (30:21)
- (12) Joseph: The Child of Sweet Devotion (30:22-24)

2. The Matter of His Wages (30:25-43)
   - a. How Jacob's Convictions Were Stirred (30:25-26)
   - b. How Jacob's Convictions Were Stifled (30:27-43)
     - (1) His Witness (30:27-30)
     - (2) His Wages (30:31-36)
     - (3) His Wiles (30:37-43)

III. HOW GOD STOPPED JACOB (31:1—32:32)

A. How Old Goals Were Challenged (31:1-16)
1. Jacob's Fundamental Concern (31:1-3)
   - a. The World Becomes Suddenly Menacing (31:1-2)
   - b. The Word Becomes Suddenly Meaningful (31:3)
2. Jacob's Family Conference (31:4-9)
   - a. Laban's Proved Dislike (31:4-5)
   - b. Laban's Persistent Dishonesty (31:6-9)
3. Jacob's Faithful Confession (31:10-13)
   - a. Regarding His Prosperity (31:10-12)
   - b. Regarding His Prospects (31:13)
4. Jacob's Final Commitment (31:14-16)

B. How Old Gods Were Challenged (31:17-35)
1. What Laban Taught (31:17-21)
   - a. Ruthless Expediency (31:17-19*a*)
   - b. Religious Error (31:19*b*-21)
2. What Laban Thought (31:22-30)
   - a. How He Met Jehovah (31:22-24)
   - b. How He Met Jacob (31:25-30)
3. What Laban Sought (31:31-35)

C. How Old Grudges Were Challenged (31:36-55)
1. Jacob's Righteous Indignation (31:36-42)
   - a. At Being So Furiously Chased by Laban (31:36)
   - b. At Being So Falsely Charged by Laban (31:37-40)
   - c. At Being So Foully Cheated by Laban (31:41-42)

- 2. Jacob's Religious Invocation (31:43-55)
  - a. The Oath: A Boundary to Laban (31:43-53)
  - b. The Offering: A Blessing to Jacob (31:54-55)
- D. How Old Guilt Was Challenged (32:1-32)
  - 1. Jacob's Confirmation from God (32:1-2)
  - 2. Jacob's Confusion About God (32:3-23)
    - a. He Could Try Negotiation (32:3-8)
      - (1) The Request (32:3-5)
      - (2) The Reply (32:6)
      - (3) The Reaction (32:7-8)
    - b. He Should Try Intercession (32:9-12)
      - (1) He Pleads the Purposes of God (32:9)
      - (2) He Pleads the Providence of God (32:10)
      - (3) He Pleads the Protection of God (32:11)
      - (4) He Pleads the Promises of God (32:12)
    - c. He Would Try Conciliation (32:13-23)
  - 3. Jacob's Confrontation With God (32:24-32)
    - a. Jacob Alone (32:24*a*)
    - b. Jacob Alive (32:24*b*-25*a*)
    - c. Jacob Altered (32:25*b*-32)

IV. HOW GOD SEPARATED JACOB (33:1—34:31)
- A. Jacob and His Brother (33:1-16)
  - 1. How Esau Found Jacob (33:1-3)
    - a. He Found a Cautious Man (33:1-2)
    - b. He Found a Courageous Man (33:3*a*)
    - c. He Found a Contrite Man (33:3*b*)
  - 2. How Esau Forgave Jacob (33:4-7)
  - 3. How Esau Favored Jacob (33:8-11)
    - a. By Generously Refusing Jacob's Offering (33:8-9)
    - b. By Generously Receiving Jacob's Offering (33:10-11
  - 4. How Esau Frightened Jacob (33:12-16)
    - a. The Offer of His Presence (33:12-14)
    - b. The Offer of His Protection (33:15-16)
- B. Jacob and His Backsliding (33:17—34:31)
  - 1. Jacob's Failure as a Pilgrim (33:17-20)
    - a. Succoth: Jacob Building (33:17)
    - b. Shalem: Jacob Buying (33:18-20)
  - 2. Jacob's Failure as a Parent (34:1-31)
    - a. The Scandal Caused by Dinah's Behavior (34:1-7)
      - (1) She Was Seen (34:1-2*a*)
      - (2) She Was Seduced (34:2*b*)
      - (3) She Was Sought (34:3-7)
        - (a) Shechem's Love (34:3)
        - (b) Shechem's Longing (34:4)

(c) Shechem's Liability (34:5-7)
b. The Scandal Caused by Dinah's Brothers (34:8-31)
(1) The Desperate Craving That Caused the Problem (34:8-12)
(a) The Worldly Plan of Hamor (34:8-10)
—He Offered Worldly Society (34:8-9)
—He Offered Worldly Security (34:10*a*)
—He Offered Worldly Success (34:10*b*)
(b) The Willing Pledge of Shechem (34:11-12)
(2) The Despicable Craftiness That Characterized the Proceedings (34:13-24)
(a) The Subtle Dishonesty of Simeon and Levi (34:13-17)
(b) The Simpler Dishonesty of Hamor (34:18-24)
—How the Proposal Was Received (34:18-19)
—How the Proposal Was Recounted (34:20-22)
—How the Proposal Was Rationalized (34:23)
—How the Proposal Was Ratified (34:24)
(3) The Dreadful Crime That Concluded the Partnership (34:25-29)
(4) The Despairing Cry That Condemned the Plot (34:30-31)

V. HOW GOD SANCTIFIED JACOB (35:1-29)
A. Jacob as a Believing Man (35:1-15)
1. Renewing Jacob's Spiritual Vitality (35:1-4)
a. The Place (35:1*a*)
b. The Purpose (35:1*b*)
c. The Preparation (35:2-4)
2. Renewing Jacob's Spiritual Victory (35:5)
3. Renewing Jacob's Spiritual Verity (35:6-15)
a. His Relationship to God Confessed Anew (35:6-8)
b. His Relationship to God Confirmed Anew (35:9-13)
c. His Relationship to God Claimed Anew (35:14-15)
B. Jacob as a Bereaved Man (35:16-29)
1. Jacob Bereaved of His Favorite (35:16-26)
a. The Loss of Rachel (35:16-21)
(1) Jacob's Strange Mistake (35:16*a*)
(2) Jacob's Sudden Misery (35:16*b*-21)
b. The Lust of Reuben (35:22-26)
(1) The Hideous Act (35:21-22*a*)
(2) The Hidden Ax (35:22*b*-26)
2. Jacob Bereaved of His Father (35:27-29)

CHAPTER 8—The Provider: Joseph (36:1—47:26)

I. JOSEPH'S BACKGROUND (36:1-43)
  A. Esau's Personal History (36:1-8)
    1. His Immediate Family (36:1-5)
    2. His Immense Fortune (36:6-7)
    3. His Impregnable Fortress (36:8)
  B. Edom's Political History (36:9-43)
    1. Esau's Progeny in Edom (36:9-19)
      a. The Descendants of the Subordinate Wives (36:9-17)
      b. The Descendants of the Special Wife (36:18-19)
    2. Esau's Predecessors in Edom (36:20-30)
    3. Esau's Preeminence in Edom (36:31-43)

II. JOSEPH'S BOYHOOD (37:1-11)
  A. Joseph's Spiritual Drive (37:1-2)
    1. Tempted to Conform
    2. Tempted to Conceal
  B. Joseph's Splendid Dress (37:3-4)
    1. The Robe of Priesthood
    2. The Robe of Progenitorship
    3. The Robe of Priority
  C. Joseph's Spectacular Dreams (37:5-11)
    1. Sheaves: Control over World Resources (37:5-8)
    2. Stars: Control over World Rulers (37:9-11)

III. JOSEPH'S BETRAYAL (37:12-36)
  A. How Joseph Was Sent to His Brethren (37:12-17)
    1. The Mission Discussed (37:12-14)
    2. The Mission Discharged (37:15-17)
  B. How Joseph Was Seen by His Brethren (37:18-27)
    1. The Conscious Wickedness of All (37:18-23)
      a. Their Combined Enmity for Joseph (37:18-19)
      b. Their Consuming Envy of Joseph (37:20, 23)
    2. The Criminal Weakness of Reuben (37:21-22, 29-30)
    3. The Calculating Worldliness of Judah (37:25-27)
  C. How Joseph Was Sold by His Brethren (37:28-36)
    1. Their Fine Bargain in Cash (37:28)
    2. Their First Bite of Conscience (37:29-36)

IV. JOSEPH'S BROTHER (38:1-30)
  A. Judah and His Sons (38:1-10)
    1. His Wayward Behavior (38:1)
    2. His Worldly Bride (38:2-5)
    3. His Wicked Boys (38:6-10)
      a. The Senior One (38:6-7)
      b. The Second One (38:8-10)

- B. Judah and His Sins (38:11-26)
    - 1. His Perverted Values (38:11-14)
        - a. His Failure to Perceive The Truth (38:11)
        - b. His Failure to Pursue the Truth (38:12)
        - c. His Failure to Practice the Truth (38:13-14)
    - 2. His Personal Vileness (38:15-23)
        - a. His Unbridled Passion (38:15-16)
        - b. His Unmistakable Pledge (38:17-18)
        - c. His Unexpected Problem (38:19-23)
    - 3. His Pretended Virtue (38:24-26)
        - a. What He Demanded (38:24)
        - b. What He Discovered (38:25)
        - c. What He Declared (38:26)
- C. Judah and His Seed (38:27-30)
    - 1. The Redeemed Child (38:28, 30)
    - 2. The Royal Child (38:29)

V. JOSEPH'S BONDAGE (39:1—40:23)

- A. The Slave Man: Completely Trusted by a Prosperous Master (39:1-6)
- B. The Successful Man: Continually Tempted by a Persistent Woman (39:7-20)
- C. The Slandered Man: Carefully Tested by a Patient God (39:21—40:23)
    - 1. Faith Demanded of Joseph (39:21-23)
    - 2. Love Displayed by Joseph (40:1-22)
    - 3. Hope Deferred for Joseph (40:23)

VI. JOSEPH'S BLESSING (41:1-44)

- A. The Providential Ways of God (41:1-8)
    - 1. The King's Dreams (41:1-7)
    - 2. The King's Distress (41:8)
- B. The Perfect Wisdom of God (41:9-13)
    - 1. His Perfect Timing (41:9)
    - 2. His Perfect Tactics (41:10-13)
- C. The Peerless Will of God (41:14-44)
    - 1. To Present Joseph to Pharaoh (41:14-37)
    - 2. To Promote Joseph Through Pharaoh (41:38-44)

VII. JOSEPH'S BRIDE (41:45-52)

- A. Her Favored Place (41:45-49)
    - 1. Highly Exalted (41:40, 45)
    - 2. Highly Extolled (41:45-49)
- B. Her Forgotten Past (41:45)
- C. Her Faithful Part (41:50-52)
    - 1. Manasseh: "Forgetting" (41:50-51)
    - 2. Ephraim: "Fruitful" (41:52)

VIII. JOSEPH'S BRETHREN (41:53—47:10)
- A. The Mystery Phase (41:53—44:34)
  - 1. How Joseph's Brethren Were Burdened (41:53—42:34)
    - a. A Predicted Famine (41:53-57)
      - (1) Its Severity (41:54-56)
      - (2) Its Significance (41:56-57)
    - b. A Perplexed Family (42:1-5)
    - c. A Pointing Finger (42:6-34)
      - (1) Simple Ignorance (42:6-9)
      - (2) Subtle Implication (42:10-17)
      - (3) Self-incrimination (42:18-23)
      - (4) Sore Intimidation (42:24-34)
  - 2. How Joseph's Brethren Were Bewildered (42:35—43:34)
    - a. Jacob's Plight (42:35-38)
    - b. Judah's Pledge (43:1-15)
      - (1) Its Sanity (43:1-8)
      - (2) Its Sincerity (43:9-10)
      - (3) Its Success (43:11-15)
    - c. Joseph's Plans (43:16-34)
  - 3. How Joseph's Brethren Were Broken (44:1-34)
    - a. The Conspiracy (44:1-3)
    - b. The Confrontation (44:4-15)
      - (1) Disaster Descending (44:4-12)
      - (2) Discernment Dawning (44:13-15)
    - c. The Confession (44:16-34)
      - (1) Judah Offering to Share the Blame (44:16-17)
      - (2) Judah Offering to Shoulder the Blame (44:18-34)
- B. The Majesty Phase (45:1-24)
  - 1. The Revelation of Joseph (45:1-16)
    - a. Of His Person (45:1-3)
      - (1) A Sudden Revelation (45:1)
      - (2) A Sobering Revelation (45:2)
      - (3) A Simple Revelation (45:3*a*)
      - (4) A Successful Revelation (45:3*b*)
    - b. Of His Purposes (45:4-16)
      - (1) His Purpose in Pardon (45:4-5)
        - (a) He Deals with Their Guilt (45:4)
        - (b) He Deals with Their Grief (45:5)
      - (2) His Purpose in Provision (45:6-12)
        - (a) Seeing Grace (45:6)
        - (b) Saving Grace (45:7)
        - (c) Sovereign Grace (45:8)
        - (d) Sanctifying Grace (45:9)
        - (e) Sufficient Grace (45:10-12)
      - (3) His Purpose in Praise (45:13)
      - (4) His Purpose in Proximity (45:14-16)

2. The Resources of Joseph (45:17-23)
   a. Their Source (45:17-20)
   b. Their Sufficiency (45:21-23)
3. The Request of Joseph (45:24)

C. The Ministry Phase (45:25–47:10)
1. Proposition (45:25–46:7)
   a. Jacob's Fears (45:25-28)
      (1) His Fears Displayed (45:25-26)
      (2) His Fears Dissolved (25:27-28)
   b. Jacob's Faith (46:1-7)
      (1) Seeking the Lord (46:1)
      (2) Seeing the Lord (46:2)
      (3) Serving the Lord (46:3-7)
2. Propagation (46:8-30)
   a. Jacob's Family (46:8-27)
   b. Jacob's Favorites (46:28-30)
3. Preparation (46:31-34)
   a. The Successful Mediator (46:31-32)
      (1) His Appearance Before Pharaoh (46:31)
      (2) His Appeal Before Pharaoh (46:32)
   b. The Successful Minister (46:33-34)
      (1) His Plain Instructions (46:33-34*a*)
      (2) His Plain Intentions (46:34*b*)
4. Presentation (47:1-10)
   a. Joseph Brought His Brethren to Pharaoh (47:1-6)
   b. Jacob Bestowed His Blessing on Pharaoh (47:7-10)

IX. JOSEPH'S BOUNTY (47:11-26)

A. Joseph's Grace (47:11-12)
1. The Position He Gave His Brethren (47:11*a*)
2. The Possession He Gave His Brethren (47:11*b*)
3. The Portion He Gave His Brethren (47:12)

B. Joseph's Government (47:13-22)
1. Purses (47:13-14)
2. Possessions (47:15-17)
3. Property (47:18-20)
4. Persons (47:21-22)

C. Joseph's Goodness (47:23-26)
1. The Principle Explained (47:23-25)
   a. Worded Very Simply (47:23-24)
   b. Welcomed Very Sincerely (47:25)
2. The Principle Established (47:26)

CHAPTER 9—Conclusion (47:27–50:26)

I. THE DEATH OF JACOB (47:27–50:21)

A. Jacob's Foreknowledge (47:27–49:27)

1. The Chosen Favorite (47:27–48:22)
   a. Jacob's Burial (47:27-31)
   b. Jacob's Bedside (48:1-6)
   c. Jacob's Bereavement (48:7)
   d. Jacob's Blindness (48:8-12)
   e. Jacob's Blessing (48:13-16)
   f. Jacob's Behavior (48:17-20)
   g. Jacob's Belief (48:21-22)
2. The Chosen Family (49:1-27)
   a. Introduction (49:1-2)
   b. Reuben (49:3-4)
      (1) His Unique Position (49:3)
      (2) His Unstable Personality (49:4*a*)
      (3) His Unscrupulous Passion (49:4*b*)
   c. Simeon and Levi (49:5-7)
      (1) Their Close Brotherhood (49:5*a*)
      (2) Their Criminal Behavior (49:5*b*-6)
      (3) Their Continuing Blame (49:7)
   d. Judah (49:8-12)
      (1) The Leader (49:8)
      (2) The Lion (49:9)
      (3) The Lord (49:10)
      (4) The Land (49:11-12)
   e. Zebulun (49:13)
      (1) His Coastal Interests
      (2) His Commercial Interests
      (3) His Continental Interests
   f. Issachar (49:14-15)
      (1) His Strength (49:14*a*)
      (2) His Satisfaction (49:14*b*-15*a*)
      (3) His Servitude (49:15*b*)
   g. Dan (49:16-18)
      (1) His Position (49:16)
      (2) His Poison (49:17)
      (3) His Pardon (49:18)
   h. Gad (49:19)
      (1) Vanquished
      (2) Victorious
   i. Asher (49:20)
      (1) Life's Routine Rewards
      (2) Life's Royal Riches
   j. Naphtali (49:21)
      (1) His Natural Wildness
      (2) His Notable Wisdom
   k. Joseph (49:22-26)
      (1) His Fruitfulness (49:22)

(2) His Foes (49:23)
(3) His Faith (49:24)
(4) His Fullness (49:25-26)
l. Benjamin (49:27)
(1) His Character
(2) His Conquests
B. Jacob's Funeral (49:28–50:21)
1. The Pledge (49:28-33)
a. Jacob's Last Words (49:28)
b. Jacob's Last Will (49:29-32)
c. Jacob's Last Witness (49:33)
2. The Preparation (50:1-3)
3. The Permission (50:4-6)
4. The Procession (50:7-14)
a. The Funeral Party (50:7-9)
b. The Formal Proceedings (50:10-13)
c. The Final Parting (50:14)
5. The Pardon (50:15-21)

II. The Death of Joseph (50:22-26)
A. Joseph's Dwelling (50:22)
B. Joseph's Descendants (50:23)
C. Joseph's Discernment (50:24)
D. Joseph's Demand (50:25)
E. Joseph's Decease (50:26)

PART ONE
The Beginnings of the Human Race
Primeval History
(1:1—11:32)

Chapter 1
THE CREATION
(1:1–2:25)

I. The Introduction (1:1)

II. The Narration (1:2-31)
   A. How Life Was Established on Earth (1:2-13)
      1. Prevailing Chaos Described (1:2)
      2. Prevailing Chaos Dispelled (1:3-13)
   B. How Law Was Established on Earth (1:14-31)
      1. The Heavenly Bodies Comanded to Rule (1:14-19)
      2. The Human Beings Created to Rule (1:20-31)

III. The Conclusion (2:1-7)
   A. God Resting (2:1-3)
      1. The Creation Complete (2:1)
      2. The Creator Content (2:2-3)
   B. God Reviewing (2:4-7)
      1. Astronomy Reviewed (2:4)
      2. Agronomy Reviewed (2:5-6)
      3. Anthropology Reviewed (2:7)

IV. The Consummation (2:8-25)
   A. Adam's Home (2:8-17)
      1. Somewhere Ideal to Dwell (2:8-14)
      2. Something Ideal to Do (2:15-17)
   B. Adam's Helpmeet (2:18-25)
      1. Adam's Desire Foreseen by God (2:18)
      2. Adam's Desire Fostered by God (2:19-20)
      3. Adam's Desire Fulfilled by God (2:21-25)

1

THE CREATION

The first chapter of Genesis is one of the most God-centered chapters in the Bible. God is mentioned by name thirty-two times in thirty-one verses. Add to that the use of personal pronouns, and He is mentioned no less than forty-three times. Thus, on the very first page of Scripture the Holy Spirit brings us into the presence of God and keeps us there. No wonder Satan hates that chapter! No wonder he has brought up his heavy artillery to discredit it in the minds of men.

Abandon Genesis 1—as unfactual and unreliable, as mere mythology, as a doctored-up copy of the Babylonian creation epic, as totally unacceptable to modern science—and Satan has won. If the Holy Spirit cannot be trusted when He tells of *creation*, how can He be trusted when He tells of *salvation?* If what He says about *earth* in Genesis 1 can be questioned, then what He says about *heaven* in Revelation 22 can be questioned. If the Holy Spirit cannot be trusted in Genesis 1, how can He be trusted in John 3:16?

The importance of Genesis 1 is emphasized by the constant use of a significant figure of speech, the *polysyndeton,* which always shows up in the King James Version by the multiple use of the word *and.* Count up the "ands" in Genesis 1—there are almost one hundred of them. In ordinary writing, of course, it is usually considered improper to have more than one conjunction in a sentence. Not so in the Bible![1] The polysyndeton is used to slow us down and draw our attention to each phrase or word thus joined together. In Genesis 1, then, the Holy Spirit would have us weigh each word and phrase, for He is writing with great precision.

I. The Introduction
(1:1)

Harold Fortescue, a budding newspaper reporter, was sent to cover a local social function. It was his first assignment. He expanded himself and submitted to his editor two dozen pages of typewritten oratory. The editor did not even glance at it, but handed it right back with the words, "Cut it in half." Crestfallen, Fortescue complied. Again the editor

1. The *polysyndeton* is one of the most common figures of speech in the Scriptures. It can be observed, for example, in Genesis 22, Luke 15, and in many other portions. Look for it and you will see it everywhere.

handed it back with the dry comment, "Cut it in half again." Grumbling under his breath the youthful reporter did as he was told. When he handed in the finished article the editor handed it back once more. "Now reduce it to a single page," he said. The horrified reporter ventured a protest. His boss cut him off. "Young man," he said, "you have evidently overlooked the fact that when the Creator of the universe gives His account of Creation He does so in *ten words*—'In the beginning God created the heaven and the earth.'"

There it stands in all its naked force; the opening statement of Scripture. No attempt is made to water it down, to apologize to a skeptical age, even to prove that God is. The Holy Spirit simply deems certain truths to be self-evident, the first and foremost, that God is. In one sublime statement He sweeps aside *atheism* by asserting His existence, *polytheism* by declaring Himself to be one, and *pantheism* by separating Himself from matter.

No statement is made as to when God created the universe, apart from the fact that He did so "in the beginning." The earth is now estimated by some scientists to be over two billion years old, with three quarters of geological time gone before geologists find the first adequate record of life in the Cambrian rocks. Picture a man walking down an avenue into the past, covering one thousand years with each step. His first step brings him to William the Conqueror, his second to the birth of Christ, his third to Helen of Troy, his fourth to Abraham. After another 130 steps he sees Heidelberg Man. Another quarter of a mile, at a thousand years a step, brings him to the oldest stone implements in Europe (according to some geologists and anthropologists, anyway). He would go on for 250 miles before he came to the earliest fossil organisms! Genesis 1 does not argue with the claim that the earth is very old. It simply states that God created it "in the beginning."

Attempts have been made to reconcile Genesis with geology. One theory is *the day-age theory*. The "days" of Genesis 1 are viewed, not as literal days of twenty-four hours, but as epochs, or ages, or vast periods of time. Elaborate charts have been drawn up to thus reconcile Genesis with geology. Certainly there is a remarkable similarity between the two.

Another theory is *the gap theory*. Genesis 1:1 records the account of the original creation. Between the first and second verses of Genesis, theorists postulate a gap of countless ages. In that gap they insert all the ages demanded by geologists, ending with the Glacial age said to be described in Genesis 1:2. The remainder of the chapter is then not an account of the original creation, but of the rehabitation of the earth as an abode fit for man.

Another theory is that the days of Genesis 1 are not days of creation but days of revelation: *the revelation theory*. The days of Genesis 1 are literal days of twenty-four hours, but they are days in the life of Moses. In six days God revealed to Moses the truths concerning creation, and on each of those days Moses recorded the revelation that was given to him. The revelation theory satisfies the Hebraist who says that the Hebrew of Genesis 1 demands literal twenty-four hour days, and it satisfies the scientist who demands long periods of time for the formation of the earth.

Certainly the first chapter of Genesis is remarkable as a statement of fact, no matter how it is viewed. Moses did not write Genesis 1 according to theories of creation current in the schools of his day, even though he was "learned in all the wisdom of the Egyptians" (Acts 7:22). Egyptian myth postulated a primeval ocean upon which appeared an egg. From the egg was born the sun god, and the sun god had four children: Geb, Shu, Tefnut, and Nut. From the rivalries of those god-born children of the sun the creation took place.[2] What a blessing Genesis 1 does not begin like that!

Instead we have a narrative that rises like the Himalayan peaks, far above all human creation epics. The Babylonian epic is the story of plot and counterplot amongst the gods, the story of banquets and rivalry and war. The Greeks pictured a mythical giant named Atlas standing at the borders of the earth upholding the wide heavens on tireless head and arms. The Hindus thought the world rested on the backs of three elephants, which in turn stood on the back of a giant tortoise, which swam around in a cosmic sea. Genesis 1 avoids all such gross ideas and gives such a remarkable statement of fact that it is the only document coming to us from antiquity that is seriously considered when the origin of the universe is discussed.

Peter Stoner, a mathematician, lists thirteen steps of creation in Genesis 1. He tabulates those as the creation of the universe (v. 1), light (v. 3), darkness dispelled from the earth (v. 4), the atmosphere established (v. 6), the seas appointed their boundaries (v. 9), the continents raised (v. 10), plant life formed, namely, grasses, herbs, and fruit trees (v. 11), the sun, moon, and stars appointed to function (v. 14), marine life created (v. 20), fowls created (v. 21), the age of the monsters decreed (v. 21), the creation of land vertebrates and "creeping things" (v. 24), and man created (v. 26). Those things are not only correctly named and listed in their proper order, but also Moses' chances of writing Genesis 1 in that way by accident would amount to one chance in 31 sextillion (31 followed by 21 zeros).

Dr. Stoner gives an illustration. He postulates a raffle with that number of tickets. To print them would call for eight million printing presses, each capable of producing two thousand tickets a minute, running day and night without stopping for five million years! One of the tickets is marked. Our chance of drawing that one ticket on the first try would be the same as Moses' chance of writing Genesis 1 by accident.[3] Because

2. See Leonard Cottrell, *Life Under the Pharaohs* (New York: Holt, Rinehart & Winston, 1960), p. 23.
3. See Peter Stoner, *Science Speaks* (Chicago: Moody, 1958), p. 11.

Moses did not write the facts recorded here by accident and because he had no means of writing Genesis 1 as a result of human reasoning (he wrote contrary to all the accepted learning of his day), he must have written it by divine revelation.

Three Hebrew words are used in Genesis 1 to describe the process. The word *bara* occurs about fifty-five times in the Old Testament and carries the idea of instantaneous, miraculous creation. Some years ago researchers announced they had been able to create artificial protein in the laboratory. Protein is the basic building block of life, so the achievement took the scientific world by storm. *Saturday Evening Post* interviewed a number of notables to get their reactions.[4] Dr. Vincent Allfrey of the Rockefeller Institute declared: "This is the biggest story of the century." A famous biochemist said: "This century will go down in history as the century when life ceased to be a mystery. Life is only chemistry." A British scientist was confident that in a few more decades one would see scientists creating life. He confidently asserted, "I no longer find it necessary to believe in God." The *Post* then interviewed some churchmen, including Monsignor George A. Kelly, spokesman for Cardinal Spellman of the Archdiocese of New York. He was unimpressed by the boasting of the scientists. "When a biochemist is able to create matter and energy *out of nothing*," he said, "then I would like to talk to him." That is what the word *bara* implies—"In the beginning God created [*bara*] the heaven and the earth."

Of the three words used of creation in the total narrative, as Wilbur M. Smith says, *bara* is the one that contains most nearly the idea of creation by miracle or divine fiat, even though the word itself does not, perhaps, contain the exclusive notion of creating *ex nihilo*. The word is reserved in Scripture for the distinctive work of God. Men can "make" things (*asah*) and "form" things (*yatsa*), but only God can create.[5]

Genesis 1 is a statement of origins, and science knows nothing of origins. Science is concerned with how things go on and has nothing to say as to how they begin. Science can measure the laws that now govern in the material universe, but those laws do not explain how the whole process was started. A man can measure the swing of a clock's pendulum and come up with an equation that will state exactly where the pendulum bob will be at any future moment. By changing certain factors

4. *Saturday Evening Post,* July 1965.
5. See Wilbur M. Smith, *Therefore Stand* (Natick, Mass.: W. A. Wilde, 1945), p. 278. Henry M. Morris has an interesting discussion of the use of those words in his *The Genesis Record* (San Diego: Creation-Life, 1976). He points out, for instance, that *bara* is used of the creation of the sea monsters on the fifth day but not of the creation of the land animals on the sixth day. He follows the *Pulpit Commentary* (22 vols. Grand Rapids: Eerdmans, 1959) in finding a reason for that in the introduction of the life (soul) principle on the fifth day. In connection with the creation of man three words are used. God determined to make (*asah*) man, and then He created (*bara*) man in His own image (1:26, 27). He also formed (*yatsa*), that is, shaped and fashioned as a potter does the clay, man's body (2:7).

in his equation he can probe into the past. For a while his answers will make sense, but there will come a point at which his equation will give him ridiculous information. If he goes back too far, the equation will tell him that the pendulum was swinging in wider and wider arcs until, at last, it was swinging in two directions at the same time! Two conclusions will emerge. First, the laws that now govern the swing of the pendulum do not explain how the pendulum first began to swing. Second, something quite different from what is now happening must have taken place in the beginning to get the pendulum started. The observer at that point is driven to mere theory because he cannot state positively when and how the pendulum first began to swing. The only way he could state with confidence, "This is how the pendulum began to swing," would be if someone who was there when it happened were to tell him.[6] In other words, that kind of information is not to be obtained by *reasoning* but by *revelation*. That, of course, is exactly how Moses derived the information for the writing of Genesis 1.

II. THE NARRATION (1:2-31)

Men today would rather believe Darwin than Moses. They forget that the science of Kepler, Copernicus, and Sir Isaac Newton is obsolete today and that the theories of today's scientists will be just as archaic in ten or twenty years. Scientists have what they call "a five year half-life." That is, in five years half of what is now "known" to be fact will be proved false and will be replaced by new theory. Our knowledge of the universe is in such a state of flux, we should challenge anyone who claims that Genesis 1 is "unscientific." Here we have God's own statement concerning origins. Humility and reverence should be our guides in exploring what that amazing chapter has to say.

The chapter divides into two major sections, one climaxing with the establishment of *life* on the earth (1:2-13) and one climaxing with the establishment of *law* on the earth (1:14-31). The parallelism between the two sections may be clearly seen.

A. HOW LIFE WAS ESTABLISHED ON EARTH (1:2-13)

1. PREVAILING CHAOS DESCRIBED (1:2)

Some believe verse 2 describes the primitive state of matter when it was first created. Others (including Franz Delitzsch, that greatest of all Hebrew scholars) believe the verse describes a later catastrophe that overtook the original creation. The word *was* can be translated "became"—"the land had become waste and void." Support for that view is seen in Isaiah 45:18 where it is stated that God did not make the earth waste and void.[7]

6. R. E. D. Clark, *Creation* (London: Tyndale, 1946), pp. 10-11.
7. The chaos of the earth was possibly one of the results of Lucifer's fall (Isaiah 14:12-17; Ezekiel 28:11-19).

Paul seems to make an interesting use of the creation story. He says, "God who commanded the light to shine out of darkness hath shined in our hearts to give the light of the knowledge of the glory of God in the face of Jesus Christ" (2 Corinthians 4:6). We can see in Genesis 1 a picture of fallen man, ruined by Satan, his intellect, emotions, and will all in a state of chaos, his conscience darkened, his body doomed to the dust. But the Spirit of God moves upon that darkness and begins a process of regeneration so that there emerges out of the chaos a new man, created in the image and likeness of the Son of God. Unquestionably many passages of Scripture have depths of meaning that can be only faintly seen on the surface.

2. PREVAILING CHAOS DISPELLED (1:3-12)

There were three stages in the process. God dealt first with the *darkness* (1:3). The statement "And God said" occurs ten times in Genesis 1. It introduces God's first set of commandments, not one of which has ever been broken. They stand in contrast with God's second set of commandments (Exodus 20), not one of which has ever been kept, except by God's incarnate Son.

The statement that dispelled the darkness is compelling. God said, "Light *be*," and light *was*. Nobody, even today, can tell us what light *is*. We know what light does, but not what light is. It is one of the most mysterious entities in the universe. In physics it has become the new absolute.[8] As such, it is at the heart of the famous equation $E = mc^2$ (energy equals mass multiplied by the speed of light squared) which, in turn, ushered in the atomic age.

And God said, Light be, and light was! In other words, God's words are not only legislative, they are executive. When God speaks, it is done. That Jesus was, indeed, God manifest in flesh is evident from His words, which had the same quality about them. When sleeping in a boat, for instance, He was awakened by the frightened disciples. The storm that had sprung up threatened to sink them all. He arose and addressed the howling wind and heaving waves. "Peace," He said, "be still!" And immediately there was a great calm (Mark 4:39). His words were not only legislative but also executive. He stood before the tomb of Lazarus, a man who had been dead four days and whose body was already de-

8. No matter how the source of light moves, or how an observer moves, the speed of light relative to the observer never changes. Imagine two space ships at rest, both brilliantly illuminated. Light travels from one to another at the constant speed of 186,273 miles per second. Now the two ships are set in motion traveling toward each other at a combined speed of a thousand miles a second. The speed with which light from each space ship reaches the other is unchanged even though the two sources of the light are coming together at the rate of a thousand miles a second. Nor would it make any difference if the space ships were traveling away from each other and the light sources getting further and further away. The speed of light from the space ships would remain constant.

composing. "He cried . . . Lazarus, come forth. And he that was dead came forth" (John 11:43-44). His words were executive. A leper came to Him, riddled through and through with that foul and fatal disease. "Lord," he said, "if thou wilt, thou canst make me clean." "I will," Jesus said, "be thou clean" (Luke 5:13). It was that same almighty word that chaos and darkness heard, and took their flight in the early dawn of time.

God dealt next with the *disorder*. He began by *raising the clouds* (1:6-8). In terms of sheer mechanical engineering, the work of the second day of creation is astounding. The amount of vapor continually suspended in the air above us is estimated at 54 trillion, 460 billion tons! Water is 773 times the weight of air, so that gives some idea of the power required to separate the waters from the waters. The annual precipitation, in the form of rain and snow, that falls upon the earth is the equivalent of 186,000 cubic miles—enough to cover the entire earth to a depth of three feet. The supply of water above the earth is maintained by evaporation—the constant lifting of water from the earth into the atmosphere by the power of the sun. We take all of that for granted!

Next He *raised the continents* (1:9-10). It would be difficult to find anywhere in print a more sublime or more simple statement of fact than what we have in verses 9 and 10. Between verses 9 and 13 there are about 126 words in our English text, and of those over one hundred are words of a single syllable! Only supernatural wisdom could compress such mighty deeds into such simple language.

Moses declared that God gathered the waters together "unto one place." The critics once declared Moses to be a simpleton for making such a statement. They said that since Moses had seen but one sea he imagined it to be the only one there was. Certainly he had never seen the mighty Atlantic and Pacific Oceans, but Moses was making no ignorant statement. We now know that, although the continents are divided, the seas occupy one bed!

So God set to the sea its bounds. A thousand years ago King Canute ruled England, Denmark, and Norway. He was so wise and able a king that his subjects wished to worship him. Canute refused the adoration of his subjects. To teach them the lesson of his own mortality he had them carry his throne to the seashore and place it below the level of the high tide mark. There he sat enthroned, watching the incoming waves. Presently they began to swirl about his feet and lap his throne. The king arose, waved his sceptre over the sea, and cried, "Stand back, stand back, ye ocean tides." But the proud waves rolled on. "We know you not, O little man," they seemed to say. "Our limits are decreed by a greater King than you."

Twice every day, since the dawn of creation's third day, the tides of the earth have owned the sovereignty of God. In the deathless words of Sir Robert Grant:

The earth with its store of wonders untold,
Almighty! Thy power hath founded of old
Hath 'stablished it fast by a changeless decree
And round it hath cast like a mantle, the sea.

Finally God dealt with the *deadness* of the planet (1:11-13). Grass, herb-yielding seed, and fruit trees rose up and covered the earth. The text employs three Hebrew words to describe that phase of creation. They are *deshe,* translated "grass," *eseb,* translated "herb," and *peri,* translated "fruit." In the first plant, the seed is not particularly noted because it is not obvious to the eye. In the second the seed is the marked feature. In the third the characteristic mark is the fruit "in which is its seed." Thus Moses catalogued the earth's vegetation by a simple, natural division, using as his guide the structure of plants and their seeds.[9]

Life appeared upon the earth; not in some struggling, fragile, lonely form, but in a variety and with a prodigality that staggers the imagination. It is estimated that there are more than one hundred thousand species of plant life on the globe, and that there are more than five thousand different forms of grass alone.

The basic command for all living things was that each reproduce "after its kind." The expression occurs ten times in Genesis 1. It is the rock upon which the whole theory of evolution perishes. God has decreed that there be no change from one kind to another kind. There may be mutation and change within any given kind, but no kind is changed into another kind. The principles of genetics have firmly established the fact that inherited life characteristics are implanted in the genes. A person who goes to Florida in the summertime may come back with tanned skin and bleached hair, but those changes are not passed on to the children. Environmental influences are not inherited, they are temporary. Only the physical changes that are due to the genes are inherited. A wide range of variations are possible so long as they lie latent in the genes, but no visible variation can occur outside the combination of existing genes within a given kind.[10]

Man, of course, has tinkered, in recent years, with the genetic structure of various organisms in the hope of producing artificial evolution. Nearly all the mutations thus produced have proved harmful, lethal, or useless to the original organism. After spending billions of dollars in research, enlisting the skills of thousands of scientists, investing count-

9. To this day botanists use a similar division dividing plants into *acotylidons,* the seedless plants, *monocotylidons,* the seed-bearing plants and *dicotylidons,* the fruit-bearing plants. That system of classification, the fruit of centuries of research, was written by Moses onto the Bible's very first page. See Smith, *Therefore Stand,* p. 319.

10. As a musician combines the notes of his instrument in a countless number of ways, to produce an infinite number of different harmonies, so nature plays on the genes. But the musician can only make those harmonies his instrument is capable of producing. In like manner, the number of variations produced in a given kind is restricted by the number of genes that kind contains. No genuinely new and inheritable characteristics ever appear within a given kind.

less hours in laborious testing, the verdict remains the same: "After its kind."

B. How Law Was Established on Earth (1:14-31)

1. The Heavenly Bodies Commanded to Rule (1:14-19)

Whole libraries have been filled with books relating to man's studies of the stars. The Bible is not a handbook of astronomy or of any other science. However, each time the Spirit of God refers to a subject that can be scientifically investigated, He does so with unerring precision.

Moses, for example, declares, "God made two great lights, the greater light to rule the day, and the lesser light to rule the night" (1:16). How did Moses know that the sun was bigger than the moon? Ordinary observation would lead to the opposite conclusion. We have all seen the giant harvest moon, seemingly eight feet in diameter, hovering over the skyline, dominating the evening sky. We have never seen the sun look as large as that. Ancient peoples thought the moon was far greater than the sun, and accounted for its lack of light and heat, as compared with the sun, by assuming it was very much farther away from the earth than the sun. Moses did not make that mistake. He said that the sun was bigger than the moon. We know, of course, that it is so much bigger that it could contain six million moons.

But Moses could have easily made the opposite mistake and said that God appointed "the *greatest* light" to rule the day. Many ancient peoples worshiped the sun as the greatest object in the heavens. But what a terrible blunder it would have been had the first page of our Bible declared the sun to be the greatest object in the sky! The star Antares, for example, is so large that it could swallow up 64 million suns the size of ours. And in the Auriga constellation the star Epsilon is so vast that its diameter is 3,000 times that of our sun and its volume some 27 billion times our sun's.

With what astonishing brevity, too, God dismisses the creation of all the stars of space. He employs just five words—"He made the stars also." What a perspective of truth. The Bible takes some fifty chapters to discuss the construction and significance of the Tabernacle. Yet it was only a very temporary sanctuary. Fifty chapters about the Tabernacle, five words about the stars. Truly the Bible looks at things from quite a different perspective from ours. The Bible is a handbook of *redemption,* that is why. It was nothing for God to create; to create He had only to speak. But to redeem, He had to suffer. That is the perspective of the Bible.

Had man written the Bible apart from the controlling inspiration of the Spirit of God, it would have been quite a different book. Chapters would have been written about the stars—the billion stars in our galaxy, the one hundred million other galaxies in known space, the postulation that known space is only one billionth of theoretical space. Sir James

Jeans tells us there are more stars in space than there are grains of sand on all the seashores of all the world. God dismisses it all as of little account. "He made the stars also." God is more interested in people than He is in planets, more interested in souls than in stars.

2. THE HUMAN BEING CREATED TO RULE (1:20-31)

a. MAN'S DOMAINS PREPARED FOR HIM (1:20-25)

Moses begins by showing how man's domains were *prepared* for him (1:20-25). The seas were filled with fish and the skies were filled with fowl—an interesting combination. Fish and fowl have much in common. Both have streamlined forms to enable them to move swiftly through their native habitats, both are covered with shinglelike layers of protective fins or feathers, both have hollow, light bones, both lay eggs, and both have migratory instincts.

Water is preeminently the seat of life. There is not a bay or creek, not a shelf or a sound on the face of the earth that does not teem with life. Even a drop of ditch water can hold 500 million microscopic creatures so small that a teaspoonful of water would be to them what the Atlantic is to us.[11] Only a God who is infinite could have worked on such a majestic scale as we see in the skies and on such a microscopic scale as we see in the seas. There is no such thing as bigness or smallness to a God who is infinite.

On the sixth day, just prior to the creation of man, God made His final preparation of the earth as man's domain. He created the vertebrates and the "creeping things." Moses gives a threefold classification. He refers to *bhemah* ("cattle"), four-footed domestic animals. He refers to *remes* ("creeping things"), creatures that move along the ground. The word means "to move" or "to swarm." He refers to *chaiyah* ("beasts"), the wild animals. Scientists have classified millions of different species of animals, including more than 800,000 different kinds of insects, 30,000 kinds of fish, 9,000 kinds of birds, 6,000 kinds of reptiles, 3,000 kinds of amphibians, and 5,000 kinds of mammals. God is truly a God of variety.

One can perhaps sympathize with the person who pictures life struggling to emerge upon the planet and, at last, succeeding as a lonely, isolated form. But where did the bewildering variety of life forms come from? The same God who with fantastic prodigality tossed out into intangible space countless stars and their satellites—and who keeps them whirling and plunging on their journeys through space at inconceivable velocities, yet with such mathematic precision that we can tell the occasion of an eclipse or the visit of a comet years in advance—the same God who did that, with equal boundless prodigality selected a single

11. Half a billion *infusoria* can live comfortably in a single drop. They appear in a thousand species, some are herbivorous, some carnivorous, some have shells, and some have none. They possess mouths, teeth, muscles, nerves, and glands. Some species have between one to two hundred sacks or stomachs, connected by an intestinal canal. The thickness of the membranes that line those stomachs have been estimated to be one fifty-millionth part of an inch!

planet and filled it with a bewildering number of forms of life. If Genesis 1 were a psalm, it would have doubtless concluded with a resounding "Selah"—There. What do you think of that!"

b. MAN'S DOMAINS PRESENTED TO HIM (1:26-31)

Having described how man's domains were prepared for him, Moses concludes the narrative section of the creation story by telling how man's domains were *presented* to him. The section begins by telling how God *created Adam* (1:26-27). The Holy Spirit does *not* say that man was created in the image and likeness of the beasts.[12] God said, "Let us make man in our image, and after our likeness." In his nature, person, and personality, in his moral and spiritual capacities, in his emotions, intellect, conscience, and will, man stands apart from the brute creation. God does not begin with man's body and relate man to the beasts. He begins with man's moral and spiritual nature, and relates man to God. Indeed, reference to the creation of man's body is relegated to a footnote at the end of the creation story (2:7).

Man is in no way related to the beasts. What animal can transmit accumulated achievements from one generation to another? What animal experiences a true sense of guilt when it does wrong or has a developed consciousness of judgment to come? What animal shows any desire to worship? What animal has hope of immortality beyond the grave? What beast can exercise abstract moral judgment or show appreciation of the beauties of nature? (When did we ever see a dog admiring a sunset or a horse standing breathless before the rugged grandeur of a mountain range?) What animal ever learned to read and write, to act with deliberate purpose, and set goals and achieve long-range objectives? What animal ever learned to cook its food, to cut cloth and make clothes, or invent elaborate tools? What animal ever enjoyed a hearty laugh? What animal has the gift for speech? Even the most primitive human tribe possesses linguistics of a subtle, complex, and eloquent nature. Man stands alone. *Physically*, he alone of all the creatures on the globe, walks upright; *mentally*, he alone has the ability to communicate in a sophisticated manner; *spiritually*, he alone has the capacity to know the mind and will of God.

Thus God created Adam. Then God *crowned Adam* (1:28-31). He crowned him in three ways; first by bestowing upon him a *posterity*—"Be fruitful and multiply" (1:28*a*). From Adam and Eve the whole human race was to spring. Adam is consistently seen in the Bible as the federal head of the human race. The doctrine of evolution, by striking at the

12. There is a resemblance between man's body and those of the beasts. But resemblance does not prove kinship. Vigorous investigations, pursued for more than a hundred years, in paleontology, taxonomy, homology, embryology, and genetics have failed to come up with any conclusive proof that man has descended from the beasts. Much of the alleged similarity between man and the lower primates is based on similarities in anatomy. But there man's supposed resemblance to the beast ends.

story of Adam and Eve, launches a critical attack upon the Word of God at a strategic point. Cut Genesis 1 from the Bible and you must also tear out Romans 5. God sums the whole human race up in Adam and traces all the sin and sorrow in the world back to him. If there were no Adam, then the Bible is false, Romans 5 is built on myth, and we have no salvation. If there were no Adam, Jesus was mistaken (Matthew 19:4-6), in which case He was not the Son of God, the Bible is based on myth, and we have no salvation. God begins with Adam and declares that the human race sprang from him.

God crowned Adam with a *position* (1:28*b*) giving him dominion over the fish of the sea, over the fowl of the air, and over every living thing. Every scientific and technological advance, every feat of engineering, every new scrap of knowledge about the nature and function of the universe is an outworking of that dominion. Despite the impairment of man's potential by the Fall, man has nevertheless been a mover of mountains, a builder of dams, a digger of mines, a conqueror of the planet. He has subdued the earth.

The writer of Hebrews had an interesting comment on that aspect of man's dominion. He said concerning man, "Thou madest him a little lower than the angels; thou crownedst him with glory and honour, and didst set him over the works of thy hands. Thou hast put all things in subjection under his feet. . . . But now we see not yet all things put under him. But we see Jesus . . ." (Hebrews 2:7-9). Adam, of course, surrendered his sovereignty to Satan. But when Jesus came, as the Last Adam, He manifested that absolute sovereignty over nature that God had intended Adam to display.[13]

Finally, God crowned Adam with a *possession* (1:29-31). He gave him paradise to enjoy. It is impossible for us to imagine what the world must have been like in the dawn of time when, pristine and unspoiled, it sprang from the hand of God. Each day must have been a day of exciting discovery for Adam. What marvelous new sounds and scents and sensations he must have experienced every day as he explored the vast, wide world that had been entrusted to him to develop and rule.

13. He had mastery over the fish of the sea, whether over a school of fish (as when, on more than one occasion, the disciples took a miraculous draught of fishes at His command, Luke 5:1-11, John 21:1-11) or over a single fish (as when Peter cast his line and took up that one fish in the lake that had a coin in its mouth, Matthew 17:24-27). He had mastery over the *cattle,* whether over the wild animals (as when they escorted Him in the wilderness at the time of His temptation, Mark 1:13) or over a domesticated animal (as when He rode an unbroken colt into Jerusalem with wildly cheering crowds waving on every side and strewing His path with palms and flowers, Matthew 21:4-11). He had mastery over the *fowl,* as when He told Peter that a cock would crow at the precise moment he finished denying his Lord for the third time (Luke 22:34, 54-62). He had dominion over *all the earth,* so that demons, disease, and death fled at His word (Matthew 8:28-34; Mark 9:14-29; Luke 4:31-36, 7:11-15; John 5:1-9, 11:17-44). He walked upon the waves (John 6:16-21), stilled the angry deep (Luke 8:22-25), multiplied loaves and fishes (Matthew 14:14-21, 15:32-39; John 6:10-14), and caused the water to blush into wine (John 2:1-11).

The narrative ends with the statement that the work of creation was "very good." The phrase is repeated again and again in the chapter. The next chapter records God's statement: "It is *not* good . . ." and goes on to describe the creation of woman as the crowning act of creation.

III. THE CONCLUSION (2:1-7)

A. GOD RESTING (2:1-3)

The opening verses of Genesis 2 seem to be a footnote to the story of creation. The rest of God is a wonderful thing—not of course that God ever grows tired! The more we understand the nature of the physical universe, the more we see that the material universe is merely an expression of the boundless energy of God. Each material object in the universe is composed of atoms, bundles of pure energy—energy passing into motion, motion passing into phenomena. Obviously the God who can create more universes than man can count, and who can lock up within the tiny breast of the atom enough energy to obliterate an island, cannot possibly grow tired.

The rest of God tells us that *the creation was complete* (2:1). "Thus the heavens and the earth were finished and all the host of them." "It is finished!" The words rang out at the close of creation as, on the cross, they rang out again at the close of redemption. There is a great satisfaction in surveying a finished work. God stood back, as it were, to cast an admiring, contented eye over the finished work of His hands.

The rest of God tells us, moreover, that *the Creator was content* (2:2-3). On the seventh day God, having ended His work, rested and then He "blessed the seventh day, and sanctified it." Thus was instituted the Sabbath. Ten times in verses 2 and 3 God is mentioned by name as though to emphasize the fact that it was *God's* Sabbath. Later on He extended it to Israel as part of His covenant with that people (Exodus 20). But, as with anything else with which man has to do, the Sabbath was distorted and destroyed. Instead of being a day of rest, the Jews, with their genius for religious minutia, encrusted the day with such enormous coverings of tradition that the day became an intolerable burden.[14]

God's Sabbath rest was soon to be broken by sin. When the Jews accused Christ of breaking the Sabbath, He replied, "My Father worketh hitherto, and I work" (John 5:17). That work took Him to the

14. By the time the Lord Jesus trod the earth, the Jews had decided that to carry a loaf of bread from one house to another broke the Sabbath; that to extinguish a lamp was work; that it was permissible to lift a child, but if the child had a stone in his hand the mother had broken the Sabbath by doing work; that it was permissible to look in a mirror, but to see a white hair and pull it out was work; that to scatter two seeds was sowing and therefore work; that to pluck a blade of grass was work; that to lift a dried fig was to lift a burden and therefore was work and a desecration of the Sabbath. It is no wonder that the Lord refused to keep the Sabbath according to Jewish traditional requirements.

cross, where it was finished to the satisfaction of God. Today we rest, not on a special day but in a Person. Ours is not a ritual rest but a real rest. We rest where God rests—in Christ and His finished work.

B. GOD REVIEWING (2:4-7)

"These," wrote Moses, "are the generations of the heavens and of the earth." The phrase "these are the generations" occurs fourteen times in Genesis. It underlines one of the basic movements of the book—generation, degeneration, regeneration. The word *generation* means "family history." In Genesis we have the family histories of Adam, Noah, the sons of Noah, Terah, Ishmael, Isaac, Esau, the sons of Esau and Jacob. But first, we have the "family history" of the heavens and the earth. That is, we have the family history of the old creation, a family history that ran on until everything was ruined by the Fall. Adam is linked, in that family history, with the creation over which he ruled. He shared the same unique pedigree. He was of the same generation.

Matthew's gospel introduces us to a new family history, a new pedigree, to "the book of the generation of Jesus Christ." We move from the old to the new, from an old family history, wrecked by sin, to a new family history from which sin is forever banished. We move from an old pedigree to a new pedigree, from creation to redemption, from "generations" in the plural to "generation" in the singular, from repeated failure to complete fulfillment. We belong to the generation of Jesus Christ. Our names are written in that book, in that family history.

1. ASTRONOMY REVIEWED (2:4)

There are three closing statements, the first of which relates to *astronomy* (2:4). "These are the generations of the heavens and of the earth when they were created, in the day that the Lord God made the earth and the heavens." In Genesis 1 it was *Elohim* who acted—a name ever linked with God as creator. It is a plural word, one that hides within its depths the fact that God is a triune God. It occurs some twenty-seven hundred times in the Bible. That plural noun is nearly always used with a singular verb or adjective, signifying the essential oneness of the Godhead.

Here, in the closing review of creation, the name Elohim is connected with the name Jehovah (LORD). Jehovah is the same God, only viewed as being in covenant relation with those He has created. The first appearance of the name Jehovah follows the creation of man, for preeminently it is God's *redemptive* name. As Elohim, He tossed the worlds into space; as Jehovah, He planned man's redemption before ever He fashioned Adam's clay. In Genesis 1 it is said that God created "the heaven and the earth"; here it is said that God made "the earth and the heavens." The earth comes first here for, as Redeemer, God's interest is centered on our little planet. The earth became the focal center of the universe, the spot where the whole mystery of iniquity was to be settled.

2. AGRONOMY REVIEWED (2:5-6)

Next comes a footnote relating to *agronomy* (2:5-6). The statement here has given rise to much speculation. What was the planet like in the distant dawn of time? Why did people live to such great ages as did the antediluvian patriarchs? What is meant by the statement that in Adam's day the earth was watered by a mist and not by rain? Probably those questions can never be satisfactorily answered. One theory is that once the earth was completely covered by a canopy of ice. Thus ensphered, it enjoyed a uniform greenhouse temperature, light was diffused, the harmful rays of the sun were screened out, energy consumption was less, and the earth was watered by a dewlike mist. According to that theory the Flood was caused by the collapse of the canopy.[15]

3. ANTHROPOLOGY REVIEWED (2:7)

The final footnote to the creation story relates to *anthropology* (2:7). "And the LORD God formed man of the dust of the ground, and breathed into his nostrils the breath of life; and man became a living soul." The Bible declares that man's body was a distinct and separate creation of God, making untenable the theory of evolution, which teaches the opposite. The word for "formed" is used of a potter's shaping clay, and implies that God became directly involved in the shaping and fashioning of man's physical frame. From beginning to end in the creation story, everything is ascribed to direct acts of God no less than forty-six times. In that footnote the creation of the human body is especially stated to be the product of God's direct activity.

Suppose we were going to make a human body. We would need fifty-eight pounds of oxygen and fifty quarts of water, two ounces of salt, three pounds of calcium, twenty-four pounds of carbon, and some chlorine, phosphorous, fat, iron, sulphur, and glycerine.[16] We bring the items home—so much dust and some water. There it is, our do-it-yourself kit for making a human body. The only problem is with the instructions. The human body is so complex an entity that no scientist can comprehend more than a fraction of its composition and functions. A mere piece of skin the size of a postage stamp requires three million cells; a yard of blood vessels, four yards of nerves; one hundred sweat glands, fifteen oil glands, and twenty-five nerve endings! Yet the evolutionist would ask us to believe that the blind forces of chance produced our

15. This theory was espoused by Theodore Schwarze, a renowned scientist and fellow of the prestigious American Association for the Advancement of Science. See Theodore Schwarze, *The Marvel of Earth's Canopies* (Westchester, Ill.: Good News, 1957).
16. Dr. Mayo of the Mayo Clinic had a humorous way of putting it. He said you would need enough potassium for one shot of a toy pistol, enough fat for seven bars of soap, enough iron for one large nail, enough sulphur to delouse a dog, enough lime to whitewash a chicken coup, enough magnesia for one dose of medicine and enough phosphorous for a few boxes of matches! The total purchase would not fill more than a couple of grocery bags.

bodies. It would be simpler to believe that *Webster's Unabridged Dictionary* resulted from an explosion in a print plant.

The Bible gives us a better explanation. It says: "The LORD God formed man of the dust of the ground, and breathed into his nostrils the breath of life; and man became a living soul." With omniscient genius God took that dust, that water, those odds and ends of things, and formed and fashioned them into a man. The human body, marvelous and intricate as it is, eloquently testifies to the wisdom and power of God. The evolutionist preys upon our gullibility. The Bible leads us to worship.

IV. THE CONSUMMATION (2:8-25)

Some years ago I was having some meetings in a large northern city. My host was a policeman. One day we were driving past some high-rise apartments that had been erected by public funds for low-income families. The buildings were new, having only been up for a couple of years. My friend said: "See those buildings? They're slums. The people have kicked holes in the walls, they have torn the fixtures out and sold them, they use the bathtubs for storing junk, they fling their garbage out the windows. It wouldn't be safe for you to go in there. It wouldn't even be safe for me." The authorities had made one simple mistake. They had changed the homes but not the hearts of slum dwellers.

It is a common error. The theory is that if we change a person's environment we will change the person. Not so. The human race began its history in the most perfect environment the planet has ever known. Adam lived in paradise. The environmental theory has already been tested under the most favorable circumstances imaginable. It is the theme of the passage before us here.

A. ADAM'S HOME (2:8-17)

1. SOMEWHERE IDEAL TO DWELL (2:8-14)

Man's first home was a garden; his final home will be a city. When Adam first opened his eyes to the light of day he looked out upon a scene of matchless beauty and tranquility. The fields were emerald green, the hedgerows ablaze with blossoms, the atmosphere laden with the fragrance of flowers, the forests ringing with joyous song. Strolling through his vast estates, Adams could pause to see a wolf play tag with a lamb, could stop to romp with a jungle lion or to inhale the perfume of the most perfect rose that ever gladdened the eyes of man. He could pause to pick a plum, to prop a burdened vine, to plant a peach tree, to gaze with awe and wonder at the tree of life—the first tree ever to become extinct upon the earth. He might wander by way of the tree of the knowledge of good and evil standing silent, mysterious, alone—the only tree forbidden to him in all his boundless domains. "Of every tree of the garden thou mayest freely eat: but of the tree of the knowledge of good and evil, thou shalt not eat of it." He would remember the divine decree.

He would continue on his way, happy that he could demonstrate his love for the living God by refraining from tampering with that tree. At last he would come to the river, for "a river went out of Eden to water the garden; and from thence it was parted, and became into four heads" (2:10). Whether Adam ever explored those rivers we do not know. Certainly he lived long enough to follow each of them to their mighty mouths. Nobody knows much about them. The first is thought to have flowed toward India, the second toward Arabia or perhaps the Caspian Sea. The third, the river Hiddekel, is the Tigris as we call it now, and the fourth is the great river Euphrates, which assumes such a large part upon the prophetic page of later-revealed truth.

What went through Adam's mind as he followed the great river of Eden to the place where it divided into four? Did he perhaps stand at the great divide and wonder about those four rivers that ran away from Eden? He could have known nothing about the later histories that would be written along the banks of those rivers.

2. Something Ideal to Do (2:15-17)

He was given a *specific task* (2:15). "And the Lord God took the man, and put him into the garden of Eden to dress it and to keep it." He was to be both a gardener and a guardian. God gave him a sense of responsibility, a congenial, challenging occupation, something meaningful and worthwhile to do. Nothing can be worse than idleness. God saw to it that Adam had work to do, but what delightful work it was! God's yoke is always easy and His burden always light.

He was given a *sacred trust* (2:16-17). "And the Lord God commanded the man, saying, Of every tree of the garden thou mayest freely eat" (the trust was stated as *pleasantly* as possible), "but of the tree of the knowledge of good and evil, thou shalt not eat of it: for in the day that thou eatest thereof thou shalt surely die" (the trust was stated as *plainly* as possible). There was superabundant prodigality on the one hand, and a single prohibition on the other hand.

Adam was given all things richly to enjoy. One thing and only one was reserved for God. A choice was placed before Adam, a necessary choice; for Adam could not have been a moral, accountable being without such power to choose. Without it he would have been a mere automaton, a puppet on a string. But God did not make a mechanical man; He made a moral man. Once the right to decide was invested in Adam, he became a moral being, but with that right there was always the possibility that his power of choice would be used amiss. So God set the alternatives before His creature, making the issues clear and plain.

B. ADAM'S HELPMEET (2:18-25)

The story of the creation of woman is full of interest. It must confront the theistic evolutionist with a serious headache. It is all very well to see God at work producing the human body by evolutionary means. A shaky alliance might be forged perhaps between the evolutionist and the biblicist when it comes to Adam. But what about Eve? The formation of the woman's body from Adam's rib must surely strike a blow at compromise. Either the Bible is true or it is false. Either Eve was taken from Adam's side and separately formed as a unique creature or she was not. If that is mere mythology, Jesus was deceived, for He certainly looked upon the incident recorded here as being historical and factual (Matthew 19:3-6).

1. ADAM'S DESIRE FORESEEN BY GOD (2:18)

"And the LORD God said, It is not good that the man should be alone; I will make him an help meet for him." Before Adam was aware of his incompleteness without a wife, God anticipated his need and planned for it. God set out to create a partner for Adam, one exactly suited to him. Adam's wife was in the mind of God long before she was ever in the arms of Adam.

Marriage is ordained of God. The whole idea originated with Him. He knows the heart's needs of every one of His children. He plans to meet those needs. Nothing can be worse than an unhappy marriage, a marriage resulting from self-will and courtship divorced from the mind and will of God. Can we not trust God to bring into our lives the one He has made just for us? C. S. Lewis puts some potent words into one of the letters Screwtape sent to Wormwood. Screwtape, of course, was a senior devil, Wormwood a junior devil being given instructions in the art of temptation. Wormwood's patient, the particular human being he was supposed to be conducting safely to hell, had become a Christian. Seeking to make the best of that deplorable situation, Screwtape, among other things, advised what he called "a desirable marriage." Admitting that marriage was God's idea, Screwtape explained to Wormwood that marriage has its uses even for the cause of Satan. He advised Wormwood to seek out some woman in the neighborhood, marriage with whom would make his patient's Christian life extremely difficult.[17]

"It is not good that the man should be alone." God's plan for us is described as "that good, and acceptable, and perfect, will of God" (Romans 12:2). Surely God knows best what kind of person we should marry.

2. ADAM'S DESIRE FOSTERED BY GOD (2:19-20)

"And out of the ground the LORD God formed every beast of the field, and every fowl of the air; and brought them to Adam to see what he

17. C. S. Lewis, *The Screwtape Letters* (New York: Macmillan, 1961), p. 101.

would call them . . . and Adam gave names to all cattle . . . but for Adam there was not found an help meet for him" (2:19-20). The Lord, it would seem, not only wanted to exercise Adam intellectually, but also wanted to energize him emotionally. As Adam named the beasts he made the simple observation that each creature had its mate. He had none. God deliberately awakened in Adam a sense of need, an awareness that he hungered for human companionship, and above all that he needed and wanted a wife.

God never awakens a desire that He cannot and will not satisfy in His own good time and way. Our problem is that we are so impatient and impulsive. We are living in a sex-inflamed world. Passions and desires are aroused and fanned into raging flames long before their time. It is difficult for a young person, in today's world, to remain pure and to be patient and wait for God to make His will plain in the matter of marriage. Our whole culture militates against the divine ideal. Happy are the man and woman, however, who will let God lead and rule in that area of life.

3. ADAM'S DESIRE FULFILLED BY GOD (2:21-25)

a. THE MAKING OF THE WOMAN FOR ADAM (2:21-22*a*)

Matthew Henry quaintly says that the woman was taken from Adam's *side*—not from his head to rule over him, not from his feet to be trampled on, but from his side to be equal with him, from under his arm to be protected, from close to his heart to be loved. It is well said. We do not see Adam running frantically all over Eden looking for a helpmeet. We do not see him sulking under a tree because his desire for a wife was not instantly gratified. On the contrary, God put Adam to sleep, took out of Adam what He needed, and quietly fashioned the ideal helpmeet for him. In other words, Adam went to sleep in the will of God so far as that whole area of life was concerned. Such a process may seem impossible to us today, but it certainly seems to be the divine ideal. While Adam quietly left matters in God's hands, the living God went to work to satisfy Adam's heart's desires.

b. THE MARRIAGE OF THE WOMAN TO ADAM (2:22*b*-25)

Adam opened his eyes at last to gaze into the face of the woman God had created especially for him (his *marriage vision*). "And Adam said, This is now bone of my bones, and flesh of my flesh: she shall be called Woman, because she was taken out of Man. Therefore shall a man leave his father and his mother, and shall cleave unto his wife: and they shall be one flesh." That was Adam's *marriage vow*. It was followed by a declaration of *marriage virtue*: "And they were both naked, the man and his wife, and were not ashamed." The thought seems to be that of chastity and moral purity. From beginning to end God has demanded purity in the relationship between the sexes. It is only within the marriage bond that sexual desires can be legitimately satisfied.

Thus the Bible describes the world's earliest wedding. It took place in paradise. It was planned by God. It embodied the highest and holiest of ideals. It set forth the absolute so far as courtship and marriage are concerned. If its ideals seem too high for us, it is surely because we have strayed so far, as a race, from Adam's garden home.

Chapter 2

THE CURSE

(3:1–4:15)

I. The Fallen Race (3:1-24)
  A. Man's Fall (3:1-8)
    1. The Subtlety of the Serpent (3:1-6)
    2. The Success of the Serpent (3:7-8)
  B. Man's Future (3:9-24)
    1. Adam Summoned (3:9)
    2. Adam Searched (3:10-13)
    3. Adam Sentenced (3:14-19)
    4. Adam Saved (3:20-24)

II. The First False Religion (4:1-15)
  A. The False Inference of Cain's Religion (4:1-7)
    1. A Purely Human Scheme (4:1-2)
    2. A Purely Human Sacrifice (4:3-4)
    3. A Purely Human Satisfaction (4:5-7)
  B. The Fierce Intolerance of Cain's Religion (4:8-15)
    1. Characterized by Force (4:8)
    2. Characterized by Falsehood (4:9)
    3. Characterized by Futility (4:10-12)
    4. Characterized by Fear (4:13-15)

2

THE CURSE

I. The Fallen Race
(3:1-24)

Contrary to the popular idea, man is not on the way up. He is a creature who has suffered from a devastating fall. His basic nature is not good but evil; all his innermost being has been disorientated by sin. The Bible confronts us with that truth at the very outset, keeps it before us throughout all its books, and ends with the direst warnings concerning the consequences of human sin. No person can properly understand human nature who fails to take into account that most basic of all the laws of human nature—the law of sin. In the chapter before us we have the beginning of it all.

A. Man's Fall (3:1-8)

Sin did not begin on earth; it began in heaven. The mystery of iniquity did not originate in the heart of a human being. It had its sad source in the breast of an angelic being of the highest order. It entered the Garden of Eden full grown, introduced there by Satan disguised as a serpent. Three chapters in from the beginning of the Bible the serpent appears for the first time; three chapters in from the end of the Bible he is seen for the last time. The results of his work are seen on every page between.

1. The Subtlety of the Serpent (3:1-6)

The word rendered "subtle" means "wise." The being with whom Eve dealt was more than a match for her except for one thing. She had the Word of God. With that Word to guide her, brief as it was in her day, she was more than a match for her foe. All the craft and cunning of the evil one would have availed him nothing had Eve simply responded to every suggestion with the simple statement: "Thus saith the Lord." Before his fall, Satan was known as Lucifer. He was "full of wisdom" (Ezekiel 28:12). Next to God he was the most brilliant being in the universe, possessed of the highest of all created intelligences. Now a fallen creature, he retains his wisdom but it is a wisdom warped, bent, and twisted by sin.

a. THE APPEAL TO EVE'S INTELLECT (3:1*b*-5)

His plan of attack in the Garden of Eden was based on subtlety. It was God's intention that headship should be invested in Adam. Eve was created second, not first. She was not made for headship; her inmost center of rule was not her head but her heart. Adam, on the other hand, was made to rule; his inmost center of rule was his intellect. Satan twisted God's order. He began the temptation with Eve, putting her in the place of headship, engaging her in an intellectual discussion concerning right and wrong. He thoroughly deceived her and plunged the race into ruin (1 Timothy 2:11-14; 1 Corinthians 11:3). So then, the temptation began with *an appeal to Eve's intellect.*

Satan opened the discussion with a *doubt*—indeed, a threefold doubt—an attack upon the Word of God, Eve's only defense. He challenged the authorship of God's Word. "Yea," he said, "hath *God* said?" "How do you know it is the Word of God? How do you know God said it? After all you weren't even there when that Word was given." It was a frontal attack upon the authorship of the Word of God. In her reply Eve misquoted God's Word, showing a carelessness that must have greatly encouraged and emboldened her foe.[1]

Having questioned the authorship of the Word of God, and hence its authority, the devil challenged its accuracy. "Yea, hath God said, Ye shall not eat of *every* tree of the garden?" "How do you know that is an accurate rendering of what was originally said? How do you know something has not been lost in transmission?"

Then he questioned the acceptability of God's Word, for the demands of God often conflict with our own desires. Satan directed Eve's gaze to the forbidden tree. He made her see how good it was for food, how pleasant it was to the eyes, how much to be desired to make one wise. He persuaded her to act in independence of God, to be "mature," to "do her own thing." Many believers, sound in the faith on the question of the authorship and the accuracy of the Bible, will yet live in disobedience to God because some truth is unacceptable to them.

Satan, then, began with a doubt. Once the doubt was entertained he followed up with a *denial.* "Ye shall not surely die," he said. It was a flat contradiction of what God had said. "Thou shalt surely die," said God. "Thou shalt not surely die," responded Satan. The whole temptation hinged on the matter of belief. Who would she believe, Satan or God? In salvation, God brings the soul back to that very point of departure and insists on belief as the great essential.

Satan followed up the doubt and the denial with a *delusion.* "Ye shall

1. She added to God's Word once, and twice she subtracted from it. God had said "Of *every* tree of the garden thou mayest *freely* eat." Eve dropped out both of those superlatives, glibly paraphrasing the Word of God and robbing it of much of its force. Later she minimized the penalty. God had said, "Thou shalt *surely* die." Eve reduced that to "Lest ye die." Then she added the statement: "Neither shall ye touch it," something God had not said. (Compare Genesis 2:16-17 with 3:2-3.)

be as gods, knowing good and evil," he said. The word "gods" is *Elohim*. Ye shall be as God Himself. He was putting into Eve's mind the same daring thought that had once entered his own and that had transformed him from the anointed cherub to the devil. Eve believed eating of that forbidden fruit would open her eyes to all kinds of wisdom. She would be able to dazzle her husband with her newfound knowledge. She threw away innocence for conscience. It was a miserable bargain indeed.

b. THE APPEAL TO ADAM'S EMOTIONS (3:6)

The temptation of Adam proceeded along quite different lines. Knowing that Adam was made to be ruled from his intellect, Satan slanted the appeal quite differently to him. He made *an appeal to Adam's emotions*. For Satan did not tempt Adam at all. He let Eve do that.

The downward path was steep. We are told of Eve that "she saw," that is, her gaze was directed fully upon the forbidden fruit. The aim was to *turn the look into a lust*. "There's no harm in looking!" we say. But often there is. Temptation often comes through the eyes. Eve saw that the tree was good for food (the lust of the flesh), that it was pleasant to the eyes (the lust of the eyes) and that it was a tree to be desired to make one wise (the pride of life). Satan was so successful with those three ingredients he has used them ever since in tempting mankind (1 John 2:16).[2]

Next we are told that Eve "took." The aim now was to *turn the desire into a decision*. God never coerces, and He will not permit Satan to do so either. Satan can persuade, but he cannot push. He could urge the Lord to cast Himself down, but he could not throw Him down. God respects our power of choice. It was a factor in the Fall, and it is a factor in salvation.

Then we read she "did eat." Satan's aim was to *turn the choice into a chain*. With that very first bite she was his. She was a sinner. "He that committeth sin is the slave of sin" (John 8:34). She had been snared by the devil and could now be taken captive at his will (2 Timothy 2:26). The choice had become a chain.

Finally we read that she "gave." The final aim was to *turn the sinner into a seducer*. That was Satan's supreme accomplishment. He fashioned the fallen woman into a tool to ensnare her husband. There is something about goodness in other people that thoroughly irritates those who are not good themselves. They feel rebuked by the lives of those who do not participate in their sins. They feel themselves consciously

2. His temptation of the Lord Jesus proceeded along the same lines. "Command these stones to be made bread" was the lust of the flesh. He showed Jesus all the kingdoms of the world in a moment of time; that was the lust of the eyes. He urged Him to do a spectacular, sensational thing by casting Himself down from the Temple crown in order to evoke the awe and wonder of the crowds below; that was the pride of life. The Lord Jesus won His victory by using the very sword that Eve so carelessly threw away. Three times He responded, "It is written" (Matthew 4:1-11).

wrong, inferior, and unhappy in the presence of those who hold aloof from their vices, and they set themselves to drag them down to their level.

Adam, however, was not deceived (1 Timothy 2:14). He sinned with his eyes wide open. It is possible that, seeing the woman he loved in all her fallen condition, knowing there was no way he could bring her back to innocence again, and loving her as he did, he deliberately stooped down to where she was to become like her. If that is the case, Adam's sin was more serious than Eve's. He deliberately followed his heart into sin.

2. THE SUCCESS OF THE SERPENT (3:7-8)

What a tremendous success it was. There must have been joy among the demons when the news came that the father of lies had triumphed so spectacularly over creatures made in the image and likeness of God. First, we note their *plight*. "And the eyes of them both were opened, and they knew they were naked." What a wretched discovery! Before the Fall, Adam and Eve were probably clothed with light, because God covers Himself with light as with a garment (Psalm 104:2) and because the Lord Jesus, in His transfiguration, was similarly arrayed (Mark 9:2-3). The moment they sinned, Adam and Eve saw the light go out. The death of the spirit within them caused the light to be extinguished and, suddenly, the physical side of their being was thrust into a prominence it had never had before. They knew they were naked. That was the knowledge for which they had sold their place in paradise, their daily fellowship with God, and their prospects of life for evermore.

Then "they sewed fig leaves together, and made themselves aprons." What a wrong decision. Those fig leaves represent man's earliest attempt to cover up his sin, to provide himself with a covering to cloak his guilt and shame. They represent every effort made by man to do something to make himself fit for the presence of God. Fig leaves would never do. They might be good enough between themselves, but they would never do to hide from the piercing eyes of God. All such human efforts wither in the presence of God.

Next we observe their *flight* (3:8). They heard the voice of the Lord God walking in the garden in the cool of the day, they fled, they hid themselves among the trees of the garden. For the first time in their lives they feared God. Before their sin the voice of God in the garden had been their joy and delight. Their daily quiet time with Him had been the best time of the day. In their folly, their minds now darkened by sin, they imagined they could hide from God. Their fall was complete.

B. MAN'S FUTURE (3:9-24)

1. ADAM SUMMONED (3:9)

Adam and Eve now learned that the wages of sin indeed is death.

God called Adam. "Where art thou?" The sobering, searching question rang through the vales of Eden. "Where art thou?" The question stabbed like a fiery sword into Adam's wretched soul. He was lost, that was where he was. The question would brook no evasion. Forth he came from the foliage to face himself at last and to face his God.

2. ADAM SEARCHED (3:10-13)

Forced to face his sin, Adam did so, but in a remarkably roundabout way. Like all of us he seems to have had great difficulty in making a clean confession of his guilt. We observe his *explanation*: "I heard thy voice in the garden, and I was afraid, because I was naked; and I hid myself" (3:10). I heard! I was afraid! I hid! The truth had to be dragged out of him. His whole being was bent. Where was the bright, honest, straightforward, upright man who once had walked the garden glades? Who was that shifty, devious, reluctant, writhing creature? Why could he not come out honestly and say: "I have sinned before heaven and in Thy sight and am no more worthy to be called Thy son"? He was a fallen man, giving the universe its first demonstration that the fallen human heart is "deceitful above all things and desperately wicked" (Jeremiah 17:9).

Next we observe his *excuse* (3:11-12). God went straight to the heart of the matter. Adam's discrimination was his incrimination. "Who told thee that thou wast naked?" Adam must be made to confess his sin. Instead of doing so, however, he came up with a despicable excuse: "The woman whom thou gavest to be with me, she gave me of the tree, and I did eat." Is there a meaner page on all the blotched record of man's life upon the earth? First he tried to blame God—"The woman Thou gavest me"; then he tried to blame his wife—"she gave me"; and finally he confessed his sin, "I did eat." God ignored the wicked inference that He, somehow, was responsible for human sin. The fact that Adam could imply such a thing and the fact that he could cowardly shift the blame to that wife over whom, a short while before, he had ecstatically exclaimed: "Bone of my bone!" demonstrates how deep were the ravages of sin.[3]

So Adam sought to shift the blame, which leads directly to his *example* (3:13). The woman tried to do the same. "The serpent beguiled

3. It is always somebody else's fault. The classic demonstration of that was at the Nuremberg Trials where the Nazi war criminals were indicted for their crimes against humanity. Josef Seuss, an administrative assistant, whimpered, "A soldier can only carry out his orders." Walter Langlesit, a battalion commander, declared: "I was just a little man. Those things were done on orders from the big shots." Colonel Hoess, commandant of the notorious Auschwitz Concentration Camp, who personally supervised the extermination of two and a half million Jews, explained: "In Germany it was understood that if something went wrong the man who gave the orders was responsible. So I didn't think I would ever have to answer for it myself." Hermann Goering, the former Reichmarschall and second-ranking man in Germany blustered: "We had a *Fuhrerstaat*. We had to obey orders." Hitler copped out by committing suicide, but no doubt he would have blamed the Treaty of Versailles.

me," she said, "and I did eat." She was much more straightforward about the matter than Adam, but still, she sought to blame the serpent. "I'm not to blame; he beguiled me. It's his fault!"

3. ADAM SENTENCED (3:14-19)

The sentence was in three parts. First came the sentence upon the serpent, then the sentence upon Eve, and finally the sentence upon Adam. The first part of the sentence involved *war*. "And the LORD God said unto the serpent, Because thou hast done this, thou art cursed above all cattle, and above every beast of the field; upon thy belly shalt thou go, and dust shalt thou eat all the days of thy life. And I will put enmity between thee and the woman, and between thy seed and her seed; it shall bruise thy head, and thou shalt bruise his heel." For the serpent, the creature that had lent its body to the evil one to be the instrument through which temptation could come, there was degradation to the dust. The silent, writhing motion of the serpent to this day forms a hieroglyphic of undulations and coils, written in the dust of the earth, written in lines full of repulsion and menace, written to remind us of the curse. Men look at the serpent with loathing, horror, and fear.

But the curse went beyond the serpent to Satan himself. God asked no questions of him. He refused to parley with him at all. He judged him then and there and declared war upon him. In that declaration of war Adam and Eve heard the gospel message for the very first time. They lifted up their heads to listen with fresh hope to the very first promise and to the very first prophecy in the Bible. It was a prophecy that embraced both comings of Christ. The second coming of Christ, to crush the serpent's head, was mentioned first, for the triumph outshines the tragedy; the bruising of Christ's heel was mentioned next, for only by means of the cross could the ultimate victory come.

In his sentence of doom Satan discovered he had been too clever, after all. He had fallen into an ambush prepared for him from the beginning. Seeking to avenge himself upon God for having cast him out of heaven, the evil one had opened the way for God to settle the mystery of iniquity once and for all. The very planet upon which Satan had sought his vengeance would become the place for the final battle. Man himself would be the instrument of his defeat and doom, for God would become a Man to accomplish that glorious end. The "seed of the woman" would put a final end both to sin and to Satan. Suddenly the earth assumed an awesome significance in the universe.[4]

4. Waterloo is a microscopic village, scarcely found on the map. Yet its name is known around the world. For it was at Waterloo in the year 1815 that the armies of the Iron Duke of Wellington met and mastered the armies of Napoleon and changed history forever. From that day Waterloo assumed an importance in men's thoughts that has nothing to do with its physical size. Similarly, the planet Earth is but a tiny speck in space. But it is on this puny planet of ours that God has decreed to resolve forever the age-old mystery of iniquity. Our planet assumes a significance in the universe out of all proportion to its size. The evil one learned that he had made the supreme blunder of his career in attacking Adam and Eve.

The second part of the sentence involved *woe.* "Unto the woman he said, I will greatly multiply thy sorrow and thy conception; in sorrow shalt thou bring forth children; and thy desire shall be to thy husband, and he shall rule over thee." There was to be sorrow—sorrow centering in the area of a woman's greatest fulfillment, in the bringing forth and in the bringing up of children. There was to be subservience. Sin would bring anguish in its train. The headship of the man, ordained of God in creation, would often be replaced by tyranny. More than ever a woman would need the protective covering provided by the headship of husband and home.

The third part of the sentence involved *work.* "And unto Adam he said, Because thou hast hearkened unto the voice of thy wife, and hast eaten of the tree, of which I commanded thee, saying, Thou shalt not eat of it: cursed is the ground for thy sake; in sorrow shalt thou eat of it all the days of thy life: thorns and thistles shall it bring forth to thee: and thou shalt eat of the herb of the field." There was to be *unrewarding toil,* hard labor on a sin-cursed earth, and, along with that, *unrelenting terror.* "In the sweat of thy face shalt thou eat bread, till thou return unto the ground: for out of it wast thou taken: for dust thou art, and unto dust shalt thou return." From that day to this the specter of death has haunted the planet. The very ground over which Adam henceforth labored reminded him daily that it was waiting to receive his remains.

Death is a horrifying thing. Men mock it. They seek to rob it of its gruesomeness by embalming the dead and surrounding their coffins with garlands of flowers. But death is still death—the king of terrors, the last enemy, the final catastrophe this side of eternity—the ultimate wages of sin.

4. ADAM SAVED (3:20-24)

This is the best part of the story. God moved in to rescue the wretched creatures who had fallen so low. He did so first in *grace* (3:20-21), for salvation is always through grace. Adam had discovered that the fig leaves of his own self-effort would not do in the presence of God. Condemned and with only time standing between himself and the final execution of his sentence, all now depended on God.

Note *Adam's confession.* He called his wife's name Eve "because she was the mother of all living." That was a confession of his faith in God. God had just pronounced the sentence of death upon the race, but had also declared that the woman's seed would bring salvation. Adam believed. He confessed his faith by calling his wife the mother of all *living,* not the mother of all dying. It was faith, pure and simple, instantly honored at the bank of heaven.

Note also *Adam's covering.* "Unto Adam also and to his wife did the LORD God make coats of skins and clothed them." There, in Eden, in paradise itself, blood was shed for the very first time. Adam and Eve must have stood there aghast as they saw the creature taken in their stead and slaughtered before their eyes—its blood shed, its covering made theirs. It was the first dramatic illustration of the ultimate cost of Calvary, of the horror and dreadfulness of sin. Sin is a radical disease, and it calls for a radical cure.

To rescue the fallen pair God acted not only in grace, but He acted also in *government* (3:22-24). He drove Adam and Eve out of the Garden of Eden. In that garden there still stood the tree of life. If Adam and Eve, in their fallen condition, had eaten of that tree, they would have lived forever in their sins. They would have become like the fallen angels, incapable of death and forever locked into the guilt and penalty of their sin. It would have been impossible to renew them to repentance. God in His government did not allow that to happen. He turned the guilty pair out of Eden and put them beyond the possibility of tampering with the tree of life. To make sure they were kept away, an armed guard was mounted at the gate of the garden. Henceforth, no doubt until the Flood came and altered the face of the earth, a cherub with a flaming sword stood at the gate of Eden to guard the way to the tree of life. A flaming sword—fitting symbol of God's wrath against sin! A flaming sword to be sheathed and slaked at last in the heart of the woman's seed.

II. THE FIRST FALSE RELIGION
4:1-15

When Cain was born his mother thought he was Christ. She thought that already the promised Seed had come, the promised one who would crush the serpent's head. "I have gotten a man, even Jehovah!"[5] As Alexander Whyte so forcefully puts it, she would have been a cold-blooded atheist had she believed anything else. Her exclamation demonstrates her saving faith in the promise of a coming redeemer.

But she was wrong. She was right in believing that the Messiah would come and that He would be of her seed. She was wrong in thinking that Cain was the one, and before long she had cause to change her mind. That first babe born into a sin-cursed world soon manifested his temper tantrums, his inborn ability to deceive and lie, his self-will and pride. Likely enough, before long, she thought that firstborn son of hers more likely to be "the seed of the serpent." By the time her second son was born she knew her mistake well, for she called the second boy Abel, "Vanity!" It was all vanity and vexation of spirit after all. The promise might indeed "be yea and amen in Christ" but it certainly was not yea and amen in Cain.

One wonders how the two boys got along on their father's farm not far from the gates of Eden. Maybe they were close in age. The use of the polysyndeton in recounting the tale might hint at it. It certainly suggests a steady progression of events. "*And* Adam knew Eve his wife:

5. So Scofield renders the exclamation in the margin of the old Scofield Bible. Some versions disagree.

and she conceived, *and* bare Cain, *and* said, I have gotten a man from the LORD. *And* she again bare his brother Abel. *And* . . ." There were no doubt the usual nursery squabbles, two unregenerate sons displaying full grown in their breasts the lawlessness Adam had introduced to the world, the natural working of the law of sin in their baby souls. No doubt there were good times too—stories around the evening fire, plots of ground for each growing boy to till, lambs and kittens and calves to feed, and perhaps picnics to the gates of the Garden to see the cherub and the flaming sword, and where they might receive instruction in the things of God. Then, as they grew, they encountered the sterner lessons of life with plenty of hard work in keeping down the weeds and fending off the wolves.

So the two boys grew to manhood, "and Abel was a keeper of sheep, but Cain was a tiller of the ground." The boys became men. Of the two, Abel chose the nobler part and became one of those great shepherds of the Old Testament, all of whom in this way or that, foreshadowed the coming Good Shepherd. Cain became a farmer, a son of the soil, a hardworking, industrious, and successful market gardener whose produce was his pride and joy.

We can picture his being up with the sun and off to his fields, his hoe in his hand, a merry whistle on his lips. Perhaps like Pearl S. Buck's Wang Lung he would revel in his soil until the soil entered into his soul. The sun would beat down upon him and his face would shine with sweat. His body would flow with a steady rhythm as he bent to his work, a perfect symmetry of movement as he turned the good earth to the sun. The earth would lie rich and dark, falling lightly apart under the edge of his hoe. The militant weeds would fall back in disarray as Cain worked steadily on.

Meanwhile Abel would be off with the flock, away up yonder on the green hills. He would sit beneath a tree, the sheep before him, his eye peeled for the coming of a cougar, his ear trained for the snarl of a lion. His mind might be busy with eternal truth as he pondered the mystery of life and death, paradise lost, the flaming sword, the way of the cross as the way back home.

They were well taught, those boys. They knew there was a God. They knew sin was an offense to Him. They knew He must be approached. It is likely they approached Him at the gate of paradise where the cherubim were. They knew that when coming to God they must bring an offering, for one does not barge into the presence of God. Thus we read that "in the process of time it came to pass, that Cain brought of the fruit of the ground an offering unto the LORD. And Abel, he also brought of the firstlings of his flock and of the fat thereof." Cain, for all his faults, was no atheist but was a conscientious, religious, exercised man—and more forward too than his brother in coming to meet God, for his approach is mentioned first. He brought of the fruit of the ground.

Then Abel came. He brought a lamb, a lamb without blemish or spot.

He built, no doubt, a small altar of stones. He cut his kindling, struck his fire, and set his logs ablaze. Then he took hold of his lamb. We can visualize the trusting, gentle, innocent thing's looking up at him with big, liquid eyes. He placed his hand upon it, and the little thing trembled at his touch. How could he do that thing? Then swift and sure he seized his knife and cut its throat and watched the red blood spurt. He watched it die. Then, with a sob in his soul, we can see him lift the silent form, place it on the flames, and offer it up to God, tears running down his cheeks. It was a dreadful way to approach God. But sin is a dreadful thing.

Cain may have looked on at all that, his sunburned face white with fury at such a hideous sacrifice. He may have looked with disgust at Abel's bloody altar and with smugness at his own. He may have clenched his fist until the massive muscles stood out in knots upon his arm as he marched in anger from the scene to stand before the altar he had reared, fresh and fragrant with the fruits of the field.

"And the LORD had respect unto Abel and to his offering, but unto Cain and to his offering he had not respect. And Cain was very wroth, and his countenance fell." It was no mere accident that Abel's offering was accepted and Cain's refused. Hebrews tells us, "*by faith* Abel offered unto God a more excellent sacrifice than Cain, by which he obtained witness that he was righteous, God testifying of his gifts" (Hebrews 11:4). Romans 10:17 says, "Faith cometh by hearing and hearing by the word of God." It is obvious, therefore, that Cain and Abel were not left to their own ideas in deciding how God was to be approached. They had been told.

Adam and Eve had told them, no doubt. Their parents had already learned that "without shedding of blood there is no forgiveness" (Hebrews 9:22, NASB). Cain and Abel had doubtless been told of fig leaves replaced by garments of skins. Abel believed; Cain did not. Abel took his place before God as a guilty, lost, helpless sinner needing an atoning sacrifice. His sins were so scarlet in God's sight that only the shedding of blood could atone. Thus, in some measure, great or small, Abel looked away to Calvary. He believed God and it was counted unto him for righteousness.

Not so Cain. He drew the tattered shreds of his own self-righteousness about him and spurned a salvation based on blood. To him such a notion was barbarous, offensive, and disgusting. He scorned a salvation like that. He came his own way, a way that seemed right enough to him and to his spiritual heirs ever since but a way categorically rejected by God. There are only two ways to approach God. He can be approached the way of the cross, or He can be approached the way of Cain. The one way leads straight to heaven, the other directly to hell.

The story of Cain, then, sets before us the world's first false religion and is therefore of consummate interest. That first false religion bears the identifying marks of all false religion ever since.

A. The False Inference of Cain's Religion (4:1-7)

1. A Purely Human Scheme (4:1-2)

True salvation revolves around three focal points—the Word of God, the work of Christ, and the witness of the Spirit. Cain's religion found a substitute for all three. Instead of orbiting around the Word of God it had its first focus in *a purely human scheme.* The Bible says: "By grace are ye saved through faith; and that not of yourselves: it is the gift of God: not of works, lest any man should boast" (Ephesians 2:8-9). It says: "The blood of Jesus Christ, his [God's] Son, cleanseth us from all sin" (1 John 1:7). God says: "When I see the blood I will pass over you" (Exodus 12:13). He says that we are "redeemed . . . with the precious blood of Christ, as of a lamb without blemish and without spot" (1 Peter 1:18-19). Cain's religion ignored all that. It was based not on divine revelation but on human reasoning. The basic philosophy behind Cain's religion was that salvation had to be earned, that it had to be merited, purchased at the cost of one's own effort and toil. Therefore Cain brought to God the fruit of that over which he had labored and toiled.

The notion that good works merit salvation is at the heart of every false religion on earth and is at the heart, also, of every false cult in Christendom. Professor Monier Williams has well said:

> In the discharge of my duties as Professor of Sanskrit, I have devoted as much time as any man living to the study of the Sacred Books of the East and I have found the one key, the one diapason, so to speak, of all these books—whether it be the Vedas of the Brahmans, the Pinanas of Siva and Vishnu, the Koran of the Mohammedans, the Zend-avesta of the Parsees, the Tripitaka of the Buddhists—the one refrain through all is salvation by works. They all say that salvation must be purchased, must be bought with a price, and that the sole price, the sole purchase money, must be our own work and deservings.[6]

Cain's religion was founded on a purely human scheme. It ran counter to the revealed mind of God. It was ascetic, impressive, and beautiful in its outward form, but it was founded on error and on willful disobedience to God's truth. It is bluntly called by God "the way of Cain" (Jude 11) and marked down as apostasy.

2. A Purely Human Sacrifice (4:3-4)

The second error in Cain's religion was as bad as the first. Instead of centering around the work of Christ it had its focus in *a purely human sacrifice.* Cain's offering was undoubtedly costly. Personally it may have been more costly than Abel's. It was the result of toil, effort, hard work, persistence, and careful thought. Upon his altar could be

6. Cited by D. M. Panton in *Gnosticism: The Coming Apostasy* (London: Thynne/Jarvis, 1925), p. 37.

seen the most beautiful flowers from his garden, probably handpicked and arranged with artistry and skill; the most fragrant herbs sought out and chosen to add the sweetest fragrance earth could afford; the biggest, ripest fruits, dug with his own hands from the stubborn soil or gathered at risk of life and limb from the topmost boughs of the trees. It was for God. It must be the best, nothing but the best.

But there was not a single drop of shed blood anywhere. Cain brought an offering but not a sacrifice; he expressed pious thoughts, but ignored Calvary; he was willing to worship, but only on his own terms. His plan of approach made good sense to him; he could not see why God should not accept it. The Bible records no sense of sin on Cain's part, no comprehension of the enormity of his guilt, and no apprehension of the atoning death of Christ. He had no sense that his offering was an offense to God, the fruit of the ground He had cursed. It was the work of his hands, the best he could do, but it was totally inadequate, an affront to God's holiness, a rejection of His Son. The millions who hurry down Cain's path perpetuate his errors. Their pious thoughts, good works, religious rituals, and social actions are valueless apart from the finished work of Christ.

3. A PURELY HUMAN SATISFACTION (4:5-7)

The third false point in Cain's system lay in the fact that it ignored the witness of the Spirit. Instead, it had as its focus *a purely human satisfaction.* Cain could stand back and survey his altar with pride, justified for all his efforts in the beautiful offering heaped up before God. "There! That should please Him. That cost me a great deal. It's beautiful! I've done my best! Even God couldn't expect more than that!" It was a purely human satisfaction. He did not have the witness from God that Abel had, that he was accepted. On the contrary although the Lord "had respect unto Abel and to his offering . . . unto Cain and to his offering he had not respect."

Cain's feeling of satisfaction and well-being did not last. It turned in a flash to resentment and rage. "And Cain was very wroth, and his countenance fell. And the LORD said unto Cain, Why art thou wroth? and why is thy countenance fallen? If thou doest well, shalt thou not be accepted? and if thou doest not well, sin [or a sin offering] lieth at the door." Cain was invited by God to come the right way, Abel's way, to bring the only kind of sin offering God can accept—Christ! The difference between Cain and Abel, between the believer and the religious person, lies not in the person himself but in the object of his trust. The one provides for himself, the other accepts what God has provided. God will accept us only in Christ. Like so many religious people today, Cain, the founder of the world's false religion, was infuriated at what he heard.

B. THE FIERCE INTOLERANCE OF CAIN'S RELIGION (4:8-15)

Cain's religion was marked by four things. It was characterized by *force* (4:8). Boiling with rage, Cain sought out his brother in the field. We wonder what they talked about. Did Abel offer Cain a lamb and the use of his altar? Perhaps so, for the Bible says, "Cain talked with Abel his brother."

From listening to Cain's spiritual heirs we can well imagine the kind of thing he would have said. "Your religion is disgusting and offensive, a religion of the shambles. Your gospel is a gospel of gore. It is repulsive to a refined, sensitive, moral human being. And what did it cost you? Nothing! Look how much effort I put into my religion. I refuse to believe my effort is worthless. Look at your disgusting altar! Look at it, red with blood, black with smoke, stinking to high heaven! Look at mine! Look how beautiful it is. Come and smell the herbs and flowers. Confess that my way is better than yours."

Then, possibly infuriated by Abel's quiet testimony, Cain, whose religion was too refined to slay a lamb, plunged his knife into his brother's heart. Thus he stamped one of the greatest of all hallmarks on false religion. It is characterized by force, by persecution, by the martyrdom of those who stand for God's truth. Before it was an hour old, Cain's religion produced the world's first martyr. Every drop of blood shed on earth ever since, in the name of religion, helps mark out the violent way of Cain.

It was marked by *falsehood* (4:9). "And the LORD said unto Cain, Where is Abel thy brother? And he said, I know not: Am I my brother's keeper?" With brash insolence Cain lied in the very face of God. That was what He thought of the holiness, righteousness, and omniscience of God! Thus it is with all false religion. It propagates, in God's name, a gigantic lie. For at the heart of all false religion are deception and fraud and, in God's name, it propagates the most atrocious untruths.

It was marked by *futility* (4:10-12), for God simply stripped away the falsehoods, exposing Cain and his religion for what they were. "What hast thou done? the voice of thy brother's blood crieth unto me from the ground . . . a fugitive and a vagabond shalt thou be in the earth." True faith made Abraham "a pilgrim and a stranger" on the earth. False religion made Cain a fugitive and a vagabond. He was a lost and cursed man who could find no rest and no peace on the earth. His life would be a wilderness, meaningless and wasted. Satisfaction would evade him, his energies would be dissipated, his life spoiled. He would spend his days wandering away from God. Such are the fruits of false religion.

It was characterized by *fear* (4:13-15). "My punishment," cried Cain, "is greater than I can bear . . . every one that findeth me shall slay me." There was no repentance in Cain's religion, no remorse, just resentment against his lot. He feared the avenging hand of man, but it concerned him little that God's hand was against him. His religion had brought him only greater guilt, deep unrest, lasting unhappiness, and pursuing fear. God cannot allow the sinner to be at peace, in his innermost soul, while enmeshed in error. The founder of the world's first false religion wandered the earth a vagabond and sank at last into a nameless grave at an unrecorded age.

He left his mark behind him in a great and thriving civilization, as many founders of false religions have done. He founded a civilization characterized by great social, secular, and scientific activity. But it was all *sinful* activity, for it ignored Christ and led directly to the Flood.

Chapter 3

THE CATASTROPHE

(4:16–9:29)

I. A World Fast Ripening for Judgment (4:16–6:22)
   A. God's Assessment of Those Times (4:16–6:7)
      1. The Ungodly (4:16-24)
      2. The Unworldly (4:25–5:32)
      3. The Unruly (6:1-7)
   B. God's Answer to Those Times (6:8-22)
      1. A Man (6:8-13)
      2. A Plan (6:14-22)

II. A World Finally Relinquished to Judgment (7:1-24)
   A. The Deliverance of the Godly (7:1-9)
      1. The Full Commitment Demanded of Noah (7:1)
      2. The Final Commission Delivered to Noah (7:2-4)
      3. The Faithful Compliance Demonstrated by Noah (7:5-9)
   B. The Destruction of the Godless (7:10-24)
      1. Its Timing (7:10-16)
      2. Its Totality (7:17-24)

III. A World Freshly Recovered from Judgment (8:1–9:29)
   A. Noah Tarrying (8:1-5)
      1. While God Remembered (8:1-2)
      2. While the Flood Receded (8:3)
      3. While the Ark Rested (8:4-5)
   B. Noah Testing (8:6-14)
      1. What Noah Sought (8:6-12)
      2. What Noah Saw (8:13-14)
   C. Noah Trusting (8:15–9:17)
      1. The Lord's Command to Noah (8:15-19)
      2. The Lord's Covenant with Noah (8:20–9:17)
   D. Noah Toiling (9:18-23)
      1. Noah the Father (9:18-19)
      2. Noah the Farmer (9:20)
      3. Noah the Failure (9:21-23)
   E. Noah Testifying (9:24-29)
      1. By Lip (9:24-27)
      2. By Life (9:28-29)

3

THE CATASTROPHE

I. A World Fast Ripening for Judgment (4:16–6:22)

A period of some fifteen hundred years lies between the Fall and the Flood. The story of those long centuries is told with a remarkable but typical economy of words. Books could be written about the period, but the Spirit of God compresses the story into one hundred forty verses, in just five and one-half brief chapters. The story unfolded thus is in three parts. One part deals with the causes of the Flood, one with the catastrophe itself, and one with the consequences.

A. God's Assessment of Those Times (4:16–6:7)

Jesus Himself commented on the period that now presents itself to us for study. He said that "as the days of Noah were" (Matthew 24:37), so would be the days prior to His return. That statement alone should invest chapters 4 through 6 with a very special interest.

1. The Ungodly (4:16-24)

Two ancestral lines are traced in Genesis 4 and 5. The line of Cain is described first, the line of the ungodly; that of Seth, the line of the godly, is reviewed next. The writer pauses with the seventh from Adam in both lines and throws a straw into the wind, to give a view of how things have been developing. He pauses with Lamech, in the line of Cain, to show the final ripening of the tares, and with Enoch, in the line of Seth, to show the ripening of the wheat. Ungodliness climaxed in the coming of the lawless one and unworldliness in the rapture to heaven of a man who walked with God.

a. Their Indifference to God (4:16-17)

The godless line began with Cain, with the founding of the world's first false religion. Cain was a restless, rebellious man, of strong character, of iron determination, an independent thinker, and a man of stubborn self-will and fierce pride. God had rejected his religion, so he would do without God altogether. At the very outset, his line manifests an *indifference* toward God (4:16-17) beginning with an indifference toward God's *person* (4:16). "And Cain went out from the presence of the Lord and dwelt in the land of Nod on the east of Eden." He turned his back upon the gates of Eden, upon the cherubim with the flaming sword, the place where men met God. Off he went into the land of Nod, the land of "wanderings." So far as we know he never came back.

In other words, Cain became an apostate. It is one thing for a man who has never known God, never had any dealings with Him, never had contact with His Word, to manifest indifference. It is inexcusable, of course, as Romans 1 makes clear, but it is understandable. But for a man to deliberately turn his back upon a God with whom he has had personal dealings—that is apostasy. And it is as an apostate that Cain is introduced by Jude.

Not content with manifesting indifference toward God's person, Cain displayed indifference to God's *paradise* (4:17). He built a city and called it after the name of Enoch his son. "Enoch" means "initiated" or "dedicated" or, as some suggest, "inauguration." Cain inaugurated something new. He built a city. His plan was to create an artificial paradise to compensate for the real one now lost. So far as Cain was concerned, God's ultimate plan for a heavenly paradise was mere "pie in the sky by-and-by." He wanted his good things *here and now,* not *there and then.* If he could not have the garden, he would make a city. He would make the world a comfortable and convenient place to live and provide his people with every luxury, every amenity his fertile brain could conceive. The land of Nod might be the land of wandering, but he would make it as permanent and as pleasant a place as ingenuity, industry, and driving energy could. And so he did. God could keep His paradise. Cain would make his own.

b. THEIR INDEPENDENCE OF GOD (4:18-24)

Man's early indifference to God soon degenerated into *independence* of God. Early antipathy became outright antagonism. Much of the history of the period is preserved in the names recorded in Genesis 4 and 5.[1]

Several of the names in Cain's line end with "el" (for *Elohim*) indicating that, for some time, the knowledge of God lingered on in the

1. Although the correct meaning of some of the names is obscure and debatable they nevertheless do give us a reasonable mirror of the times. Although the names of Scripture all have a significant meaning, the meanings are not always certain because written Hebrew does not use vowels. The context normally determines the meaning of an obscure Hebrew word. But with *names* the context does not always help. Lexicons often give alternate suggestions for the meaning of Hebrew names because the consonants can stand for different concepts depending on what vowels are supplied. So unless the context settles the question, we can only make suggestions when looking at a passage conspicuous mostly for the names it contains. Thus "Enoch" means "teacher," but it can also mean "initiated." In trying to arrive at the meanings suggested above concordances, Bible dictionaries and books that make a study of Bible names have been consulted, for instance, J. B. Jackson, *A Dictionary of the Proper Names of the Old and New Testaments* (New York: Loizeaux, 1909).

memory of Cain's race. Doubtless that was a mere formality; nobody nowadays imagines every boy named Paul was so named after the great apostle. In Cain's line even the casual and flippant use of God's name soon disappeared and God was forgotten completely.

The name *Irad* is variously rendered as "fugitive," "city of witness," or "wild ass." The idea that emerges in any case is that of an unregenerate man. The last alternative is most suggestive in view of later Mosaic instruction that the firstborn of an ass had to be redeemed by a lamb or else have its neck broken. *Mehujael* is said to mean "smitten of God" or "blot out that Jah is God." By his day men wanted nothing more to do with God. *Methusael* means "man who is of God" or "they died enquiring" suggesting, perhaps, that even among the Cainites there were some who had misgivings about the way the world was going. But their questionings seem to have produced none of the right answers, for that brief, final flickering of the candle is quickly extinguished by *Lamech.* His name means "powerful," "conqueror," "wild man." In him the conqueror came, the mighty man, the first shadow on the sacred page of the coming lawless one of the last days. Lust and lawlessness came to full flower and fruit in Lamech as they will in the Beast, the devil's messiah.

The growing independence of God in the Cainite line came to a head in Lamech's family. In him antidiluvian apathy ripened into outright defiance. A new age dawned in which science, art, philosophy, and religion took a giant step forward climaxing in active opposition to the God of heaven.

The new age was one of *moral disorder* (4:19). "And Lamech took unto him two wives: the name of the one was Adah, and the name of the other Zillah." With Lamech began an open attack on the primeval law of marriage. Lamech felt himself strong enough to defy convention and introduce a "new morality" under cover of which men could accumulate wives. Polygamy became a part of the new social order. The name of Adah, his first wife, means "ornamental." Zillah, the name of his second wife, means "shade" or "seductress." Lamech seems to have found the two of them irresistible. In Adah he embraced what the Bible calls "the lust of the eyes" and in Zillah "the lust of the flesh."

The new age was one of *marvelous discovery* (4:20-22). Three of Lamech's sons rose to prominence. Jabal was "the father of such as dwell in tents, and of such as have cattle." For centuries men had been concentrating on the cities. Jabal broke with that to initiate nomadic life adapted to cattle ranching. He was "the father" of that way of life. That is, he was its inventor, its creator, its teacher. The word for "cattle" is interesting, too, for it literally means "possession" and comes from the word "to acquire." In other words, Jabal not only fathered a new science and a new life-style, but he also dominated it—as we would say, he cornered the market. He "sewed up" the cattle business. People wanting beef had to look to him. In other words *marketing* seems to have been his specialty. He found a new and inventive way of keeping goods flowing. His very name, Jabal, according to one rendering, means "the producer."

His brother Jubal had a different specialty—*music.* His name means "the undulater" or "a joyful sound." "He was the father of all such as handle the harp and organ." Stringed instruments and wind instruments were his idea. The new world order had its entertainment media. It needed to find pleasurable ways to structure its time, ways to drown out the thought of God, so along came "the undulator" to give men a beat, a rhythm, a lively tune to help fill the void that only God could really fill.

The third of Lamech's sons was Tubal-cain, "an instructor of every artificer in brass and iron." He was the inventor of *metalurgy,* introducing an industrial revolution into the ancient world. We can imagine what the discovery of smelting and forging must have meant to that advancing civilization. Tubal-cain is called "an instructor" in all that or, as the text renders it, "Tubal-cain, the forger of every cutting instrument of brass (copper) and iron." He had a monopoly on the business. The secret of working metals would have been closely guarded, one kept in the family, for it was a secret that would have enabled his remarkably gifted family to be in a position of supremacy and power. It was the "cutting instrument" that particularly interested Tubal-cain. His clansmen, armed with those, would be a power to be reckoned with in that ancient world. His discoveries would have been as ominous and as far-reaching in his day as the discovery of atomic energy and the invention of Intercontinental Ballistic Missiles in ours.

Those three brothers dominated the godless line of Cain. Their names Jabal, Jubal, and Tubal are all derived from the same root meaning "to flow" or "to produce." They founded an age of discovery and were the innovators of prosperity, pleasure, and power. They had a sister, Naamah. Her name means "pleasant" (or "pleasure"), "lovely." Linked with the names of the two other women in the narrative she would suggest, perhaps, the pride of life that would complete the trilogy of worldliness that so marked that age (1 John 2:16).

The age was also marked by *militant defiance* (4:23-24). "And Lamech said unto his wives . . . Hear my voice, ye wives of Lamech . . . I have slain a man to my wounding [for my wound] and a young man to my hurt. If Cain shall be avenged sevenfold, truly Lamech seventy and sevenfold." The Septuagint renders that "seventy times seven," which makes Lamech's boast stand out in sharp contrast with the Lord's teaching on forgiveness. Lamech's was the first song in Scripture. It has been called "the song of the sword" because it glorified human independence, power, and vengefulness. The father of Tubal-cain, exulting in the power placed in his hands by his son's weaponry, arrogantly threatened with death anyone who might try to injure him. With boastful impiety he promised vengeance to anyone who might attack him, vengeance greater far than that promised by God to Cain. Such a song was in keeping with Lamech's character and with the spirit of the age. An age of militant defiance had come, when men flung down the gauntlet, as it were, in the very face of God Himself.

Man had everything. He was rich and increased in goods; he had an organized, urban life; he had economic matters under central control; he had all the refinements of art and culture; he had a new, free-and-easy morality; he had weapons of singular power. He had no need of God. That ancient world bore all the hallmarks that so clearly mark the age in which we live.

2. THE UNWORLDLY (4:25–5:32)

The narrative now goes back to Adam. As the world of the ungodly began to take shape right from the start, so did the world of the godly. God never leaves Himself without a witness, so from generation to generation, in step with the unfolding generations of the wicked, there kept pace a matching line of saintly men. They were unsung by the world. So far as the world was concerned they accomplished nothing, contributed nothing, invented no new earthshaking contraptions, introduced no revolutionary art forms, devised no new ways of advancing their family fortunes. They simply lived for God. All that is recorded of them is that they lived, that they brought into the world those who would carry the torch of testimony for another generation, and that they died.

They *lived*. It is recorded of most of them twice. That is not said of the Cainites. No doubt the Cainites thought they lived, that they had the world in their hands. Their social innovations, their scientific developments, their secular advancements surely marked them out as having "the good life." But God does not say that they lived at all for they were "dead in trespasses and sins." The Sethites, however, lived. Jesus said: "I am come that they might have life and that they might have it more abundantly" (John 10:10). They entered into the truth of that.

Moreover, it is recorded that the Sethites *died*. Again, the narrative is significantly silent about the death of the Cainites. Heaven had no interest in their deaths. As their lives were an empty, hollow, meaningless sham, so their deaths were an everlasting shame. But of the Sethites it is recorded over and over again, this one died, that one died. All down that amazing fifth chapter we hear the tolling of the bell—and he died . . . and he died . . . and he died"—God proving the devil a liar. "Thou shalt not surely die," Satan had said. "And he died," the Holy Spirit records. But surely that tolling of the bell would have been for the Cainites, for "the wages of *sin* is death." Not so! God took note of the death of the Sethites. The death of each saint was jubilee day in heaven, for "precious in the sight of the LORD is the death of his saints" (Psalm 116:15). Death for them was not the end, but the beginning. They had not lived for this world, but for that world. Death therefore lifted them above the sad sights and sounds of this poor world into a world where they count not time by years, and where all tears are wiped away, and where Christ sits at the right hand of God.

a. HOW THE NEW SEED COMMENCED (4:25–5:5)

The next part of the narrative begins with a new seed, to replace the terminated seed of Abel. We note how that new line was *commenced.* It commenced with *a new birth* (4:25-26). "And Adam knew his wife again; and she bare a son, and called his name Seth: For God, said she, hath appointed me another seed instead of Abel, whom Cain slew. And to Seth, to him also there was born a son; and he called his name Enos: then began men to call upon the name of the LORD." It was a brand new beginning, one of God's many new beginnings with the race. With Seth began the line that would exhaust itself in the person of Christ, the woman's promised Seed. The keynote of that new line was salvation by faith, for "men began to call upon the name of the LORD," and "whosoever shall call upon the name of the Lord shall be saved" (Romans 10:13).

With Seth's line God began not only with a new birth but also with *a new book* (5:1-5). Into the book He wrote the names, not of all of Adam's sons, but of those whose names were written in heaven. The preface to that book tells us that Seth was born in the image and likeness of Adam. Adam's children were not born in the image and likeness of God, the image that Adam once had borne, but in the image and likeness of poor, fallen Adam. No wonder Jesus said to Nicodemus: "Marvel not that I say unto thee, Ye must be born again" (John 3:7). We were born all wrong the first time—in sin, shapen in iniquity, with Adam's fallen nature, needing to be born again.

The new book records the salient features of Adam's family and then the sad fact of Adam's funeral. Adam was 930 years of age when he died (5:5). It took that long for the death sentence of Eden to catch up with him. Seth, Enos, Cainan, Mahaleel, Jared, and Enoch were all still alive at the time. Enoch was 306 years old and had been walking with God for nearly two and one-half centuries. Only one other person's death had been recorded so far—that of Abel the martyr. Thus the first two people to die went to heaven. The third person to leave the scene would be Enoch, and he did not even die. God began to populate heaven before Satan began to populate hell.

Adam lived to see the fearful fruits of the fall, to see the giddy, pleasure-mad world of the Cainites flower into a full, godless civilization. But he lived long enough to see that from generation to generation God was preserving a "seed" upon the earth.

b. HOW THE NEW SEED CONTINUED (5:6-32)

Having told how the new seed was commenced upon the earth, the

Holy Spirit describes how it was *continued.* There follows a list of names running from Seth to Noah, from the Fall to the Flood with little relief in the story. The first five names are of *patriarchs* (5:6-20). First came *Seth* ("appointed") to take the place of martyred Abel. He was Abel's substitute. *Enos* was next. His name, "mortal man," was a reminder that, for all man's vaunted "progress," man is weak and finite; no matter how long his days may be prolonged on the earth, sooner or later they must end. *Cainan* followed with a name meaning "their smith" or "a possession," as a Sethite protest against the growing militarism and materialism of the Cainite world. *Mahaleel's* name means "praising God." In a day when men were praising and congratulating themselves and flinging off all restraints, that saint poured out his life in praise of God. *Jared's* name means "descent," to remind men that although so many ages had come and gone, God's truth was marching on. He himself was in the right line of descent, another living link in a chain that would reach from the first Adam to the last.

Those then were the patriarchs. With each succeeding generation God added another voice to the testimony. And, because they did not die for centuries, each one of those worthies blended his witness with the witness of his fellows until a growing chorus could be heard. But who in those distant days cared for the concerted testimony of the godly? Their hymns were drowned out by the rowdy music, the roaring markets, and the riotous marches of the descendants of Cain. Then, as now, heaven's music was drowned out by earth's sin.

With Enoch a new note was injected into the witness, for with him began the line of the *prophets* (5:21-32). There were four of them, notable men all. The list is headed by Enoch, a prophet who towered above them all. He was the first prophet ever to appear on earth. *Enoch,* the man who walked with God, witnessed to the *presence* of God. His life story, given in very few words in Genesis with a brief added commentary in Hebrews 11 and in the little book of Jude culminated in his rapture to heaven.[2]

2. The first feature of his life was *surrounding gloom.* All about him the pace and tempo of wickedness was increasing. Indeed, he was raptured a scant seventy years before the birth of Noah. The second feature of his life was *saving grace.* Somewhere that man who, like all others born of Adam's race, "walked according to the course of this world, according to the prince of the power of the air, the spirit that now worketh in the children of disobedience" (Ephesians 2:2) had an encounter with the living God, which changed his life. Thereafter he walked with God. The third feature of his life was *simple goodness.* Hebrews 11 tells of his testimony Godward. "He had this testimony, that he pleased God." Jude tells us of his testimony manward and reminds us that Enoch proclaimed the coming of the Lord. The fourth feature of his life was *sudden glory.* God took him bodily home to heaven. He is the archetype of the rapture of the church, caught away before wickedness finally crested and before judgment finally fell. In that he stands in contrast with Noah who, representing Israel, was preserved through the terrible days of judgment and landed safely on a remade earth. Twice it is recorded of Enoch that he "walked with God." His testimony was to the presence of God, to the possibility of living a quiet, godly life in a corrupt and careless age.

Methuselah witnessed to the *patience* of God. He lived 960 years, almost a full millennium and longer than any other human being. His father, Enoch, embedded one of his prophecies in Methuselah's name: "When he dies, it shall come." Throughout all of Methuselah's long life, conditions on earth went from bad to worse; but still God held His hand, for He is of great patience, "not willing that any should perish" (2 Peter 3:9). The antediluvians took God's inaction as proof either of His nonexistence or His indifference.

Lamech witnessed to the *peace* of God. His name means "powerful," an indication, perhaps, of the awe with which even the secular, pleasure-mad Cainites regarded him. He was a power for God upon the earth. His testimony was brought into focus in the name he gave his son Noah—"rest," "comfort," "consolation." "This same," he said, "shall comfort us concerning our work and toil of our hands, because of the ground which the LORD hath cursed," or as it has been rendered, "This shall give us rest from the grievous toil and trouble." The evil deeds going on all around seem to have been in his mind when he spoke. Lamech anticipated that things could not go on as they were much longer; God would act within the lifetime of his son. In that he rested and found peace. God was not ignoring the wickedness of the planet, whatever man might think; Lamech could rest in God knowing that sooner or later He would act.

Noah witnessed to the *purposes* of God. He was "a preacher of righteousness" (2 Peter 2:5). He is the first one of the godly line of Seth to have all of his children listed. Eventually his sons, Shem, Ham, and Japheth, would become the fathers of new races of men. He built an ark "to the saving of his house" (Hebrews 11:7) and, in so doing, testified to his generation of coming judgment.

Those, then, were the unworldly, that noble line of men who lived amid vice and violence but who went forward quietly with God, living in separation from the ungodly, handing on the torch of testimony from one to another, and proving that God never leaves Himself without a witness.

3. THE UNRULY (6:1-7)

a. THEIR GREAT APOSTASY (6:1-3)

Again the Holy Spirit goes back to pick up the thread of wickedness that formed the black background on the tapestry of those times. We do not know how far back Genesis 6 goes. Some have thought it might retrace history as far back as Enoch the Sethite and Lamech the Cainite, both of whom were the seventh from Adam. In any case, the story of the growing lawlessness of Noah's day begins with a brief account of *the great apostasy of the antediluvians.* For centuries things had been coming slowly to a head. But now came *the final expression of the perversion of man* (6:1-2). "It came to pass, that when men began to multiply on the face of the earth, and daughters were born unto them, that the sons of God saw the daughters of men that they were fair; and they took them wives of all which they chose."

The first great hallmark of that age was a population explosion. Men began to multiply. The burgeoning of the world's population led to a spiritual decay, to shameless depravity, to social dilemma, and to strong delusion. Runaway population growth simply aggravated all those things and led directly to the great apostasy—the forbidden sexual liaison between women and fallen angelic beings—and to the rise of a hybrid race of "giants."

Something new and startling must have happened to bring about the fearful acceleration of wickedness evident in Genesis 6. That a new dimension of lawlessness had been injected into the lifestream of mankind seems evident from the text.[3] "It came to pass that when *men* began to multiply . . . *the sons of God* saw the daughters of *men*" (italics added). The word "men" evidently stands for the whole human race. The "sons of God" are thus carefully distinguished from the generation of Adam.[4]

Genesis 6:1-2 refers to a second and deeper apostasy in the ranks of the angels. A host of angels had already followed Lucifer in the initial rebellion against God; now some of those fallen angels fell even lower.

3. The view that the sons of God were the Sethites, and that chapter 6 shows the breakdown of separation between the ungodly Cainites and the godly Sethites, hardly seems to fit the facts. How would marriage between ungodly and godly human beings produce a race of giants? How would mere backsliding produce such enormous prodigies of wickedness as necessitated the Flood? An apostasy culminating in advanced forms of demonism does provide us with a cause commensurate with the effect. Both 2 Peter and Jude support such a view of the Flood.

4. The expression "sons of God" ("sons of Elohim") occurs only four times in other parts of the Old Testament. It occurs three times in the book of Job (1:6; 2:1) where we read of "the sons of God" presenting themselves before God, Satan being in their midst. Evidently in that context the sons of God are angelic beings. It occurs again in Job 38:7 where we read that, at the creation of the world, the morning stars sang together and that the sons of God shouted for joy. Again the sons of God are evidently suprahuman beings. The other reference is in Daniel where we are told of Nebuchadnezzar that he saw four men walking in his burning, fiery furnace. He recognized three of them as his human victims. The fourth was "like a son of God" (in that case it was God the Son in one of His preincarnate appearances), again a supernatural being.
The use of the title "sons of God" in the Old Testament, then, is confined to angelic beings and to Christ. In the Septuagint version of the Scriptures the expression "sons of God" is invariably translated "the angels of God." The term "sons of Elohim" seems to be confined to those who are directly created by God's volition rather than to beings born of their own order. It is that characteristic that, as much as anything, distinguishes between the angels and men. In the Old Testament a kindred expression is used, "sons of Jehovah," and that would have been an ideal expression to use in Genesis 6, had it been the intention in that passage simply to differentiate between Cain's descendants and Seth's. In fact, it would have been a particularly appropriate expression because Genesis 4:26 records that, since the days of Enos, men had begun to call upon "the name of Jehovah." Instead of using the expression "sons of Jehovah," however, the text uses an expression elsewhere reserved in the Old Testament as descriptive of supernatural beings.

Defying the limits set by God, they went after "strange flesh" (Jude 7). According to both Jude and 2 Peter, some fallen angels are no longer free to roam the air but are incarcerated in Tartarus, a place of imprisonment more terrible than Hades. There they are reserved in chains, awaiting their final judgment. Because of their lust, impurity, and outrage, God has locked them up. That is not so of many of the fallen angels who as "principalities and powers" hold the world in subjection under Satan their Lord. Those doubly fallen angels defied the law of their being, not merely by deceiving and consorting with members of the human race, but by the actual marriage act itself. Jude and Peter both put the sin of those fallen ones alongside the sin of Sodom and Gomorrah, the sin of going after "strange flesh."[5]

So then, Genesis 6 sets before us the great apostasy of the antediluvians, an apostasy that gave rise to a perversion of the human race. Sodomlike sins became common, sins of even greater enormity indeed because they involved the lawless intercourse of alien races with human beings. The result was the Flood. God had been patient for centuries, but those ultimate sins led to *the final exhaustion of the patience of God* (6:3). "And the LORD said, My Spirit shall not always strive with man, for that he also is flesh: yet his days shall be an hundred and twenty years." The scene shifts back to heaven and to God's decree that the end is in sight. Only one hundred and twenty more years and God would act—just time enough for Noah to build the Ark and issue one final plea and warning to his generation.

b. THEIR GODLESS ACTIVITY (6:4)

Having described the great apostasy, the narrative goes on to the *godless activity of the antediluvians.* It speaks of the giants who were in the earth in those days, then, leaping over the centuries, it makes reference to a later interruption of the *nephilim.*[6] The children brought into the world by the lawless union of "the sons of God" and the daugh-

5. It is commonly objected, on the basis of Matthew 22:30, that angels "neither marry nor are given in marriage." That is true of their natural estate in heaven. But who is to say that fallen angels cannot use their great wisdom and power to materialize in bodily form and to cohabit with human kind? We have the evidence of Scripture that angels can materialize and appear as men in bodies that can assimilate food and drink (Genesis 18:1-8; 19:13). In modern occultism demons are made to materialize. Evidence exists that demons can and do have sexual relations with human beings.

   G. H. Pember in *Earth's Earliest Ages* gives examples of that. Books on magic refer to *incubi* and *succubi,* spirits that perform those acts. The modern revival of spiritism, witchcraft, occultism, and the like is preparing the world for another invasion along similar lines in anticipation of the coming of the Beast. See the author's book *Only God Can Prophesy* (Wheaton: Shaw Publications, 1975), particularly chapter 7—"Invasion From the Pit."

6. When, centuries later, the Israelites set out to conquer Canaan they had to face the Anakim, a race of giants. There was evidently a further outbreak of the same kind of lawlessness that produced the Flood, only that time in Canaan. That helps explain Noah's curse upon his grandson, Canaan. Perhaps the second eruption was known to Moses (Deuteronomy 2:10–3:11). He notes it here, knowing Israel would have to face the problem in Canaan.

ters of men, are called "men of renown." They were probably the ancient Promethians,[7] the prodigeous creatures who gave to men the sins and secrets of the gods. The world had been a wicked place before; now it became wholly corrupt and wickedness assumed enormous proportions.

c. THEIR GROWING ANARCHY (6:5-7)

The narrative next describes *the growing anarchy of the antediluvians*; the viewpoint shifting from the earth to heaven. Mention is made of God's *discernment* (6:5). "And God saw that the wickedness of man was great in the earth, and that every imagination of the thoughts of his heart was only evil continually." The word for "imagination" is from a Hebrew root relating to pottery; it means "to fashion as a potter." Men fashioned wicked philosophies, they formed obscene artifacts, they eagerly espoused filthy causes, they made fashionable vile sins, they poured society into their mold.

The likeness to Noah's day is very evident in our age. We have our new Prometheans—our atom-smashers, our health-bringers, our food developers, our code breakers, our mind readers, our pathfinders.[8] We have our modern Epimetheans determined to exploit all new discoveries for the advancement of evil. We have our corrupters, dedicated to the spread of pornography, homosexuality, and licentiousness, deliberately trying to reshape society so that abnormality and vice is the accepted norm.

Mention is made also of God's *disappointment* (6:6). "And it repented the LORD that he had made man upon the earth, and it grieved him at his heart." While Moses uses anthropopatheia in depicting God as grieving, the fact remains that "grieve" is a love word—we do not grieve for those we do not love. The word is highly expressive, for it reveals the heartache of God over the rebellion and wickedness of men. His lovingkindness was scorned, His patience abused, His offer of salvation ignored. It stabbed Him to His heart.

Mention is made of God's *decision* (6:7). "And the LORD said, I will destroy man . . . it repenteth me that I have made them." Because God created human life He has the right to destroy it. Month after month, year after year, things had continued unchanged, with evil men and

7. The countless legends of the loves of the gods doubtless have their roots here. Hesiod tells of Prometheus, the bold explorer, who risked the wrath of the gods by bringing fire to earth for the benefit of men. He tells of Pandora from whose opened box flew out all the troubles that plague mankind. Greek mythology is full of legends that recount the loves between the gods and mortals, and that tell of strange, fearsome, trouble-laden gifts the "heroes" handed on to men. Probably those heroes are the "men of renown" of Genesis 6; Greek mythology embodies the remains of primitive truth distorted in transmission.

8. See Robert S. de Ropp, *The New Prometheans* (New York: Delacorte, 1972). Prometheus was one of the Titans, a race of giant gods. He stole fire from the gods and gave it to men. His brother, Epimetheus, accepted Pandora and her box of evils which, when opened, released a host of ills upon mankind.

seducers waxing worse and worse. The die had been cast, however, and the fatal line between God's mercy and His wrath forever crossed. The race had sinned beyond recall. The machinery of the universe was set in motion that, on a given day and hour, the fountains of the great deep would burst apart and the windows of heaven break open. The Flood would come.

B. God's Answer to Those Times (6:8-22)

1. A Man (6:8-13)

It is a principle with God that the more degenerate the times, the more definite the testimony. God always has His special man—a Moses, an Elijah, a Daniel. Before the Flood He had Noah. With the world crumbling around him, that giant figure towered above his times, hewn out of granite, standing like a lonely monolith pointing to the sky. Noah was a man *energized by God* (6:8-10). From age to age God raises up those unique, specially chosen vessels of His, men endued with special power from on high.

The divine energy imparted to Noah manifested itself in three ways. First, he was *forgiven.* He "found grace in the eyes of the LORD." In the Bible, grace is unmerited favor; it is getting something we do not deserve—Noah found grace. He was not a godly man because he came from a long line of godly men, for God has no grandchildren. He was made a godly man because he discovered eternal life in the generous, overflowing grace of God. He had access to the truth (in his day Enos, the grandson of Adam, was still alive and did not die until Noah was over eighty), he was reared in a believing family, but, just the same, Noah had to find grace for himself. He had to see himself as a sinner in need of the grace of God.

Moreover, he was *faithful.* We are told that he was "a just man and perfect in his generations" and that he "walked with God." That Noah is declared "just" (that is, justified) speaks volumes. He entered fully into the salvation of God and was given the unassailable standing before God that belongs only to the justified soul. Along with his justification he received power to live a godly life. He was "perfect" (without blemish) in a morally corrupt world. He was perfect "in his generations"—the word no doubt has reference to Noah's contemporaries. However, the word has a deeper significance. The word "generations" means "to go in a circle." It suggests that Noah found a new center of gravity for his life in God. As a planet goes in circles around the sun, so Noah's life revolved around God. Without that great central attraction the natural tendency, the normal drives in his life, would have taken him off into the outer darkness of the wicked age in which he lived. But Cainite civilization failed to attract him. He found a greater attraction in God, and henceforth his life revolved around Him. Indeed he "walked with God" (walked habitually with God is the force of the text). The only other man of whom that is said is Enoch. Methuselah, Enoch's son, was Noah's grandfather. It does not take a great deal of imagination to picture Noah, as a little boy, drinking in his granddad's stories of saintly Enoch and his amazing walk with God that ended at last in the glory land.

Then, too, in the power of the energizing Spirit of God, Noah was *fruitful.* His three sons are named. Three sons. That does not look like very much fruit, but from those three sons every man, woman, and child on the planet has descended.

Energized as he was by God, Noah was also *enlightened by God* (6:11-13). First, however, God is seen *reviewing the earth* (6:11-12). "The earth also was corrupt before God, and the earth was filled with violence. And God looked upon the earth, and, behold, it was corrupt; for all flesh had corrupted his way upon the earth." Everywhere He looked He saw open, flagrant, public licentiousness and lawlessness. Vice and violence were the order of the day. Horrible sins were flaunted and applauded.

The same kind of thing is fast becoming accepted in the modern world. Old moral standards and religious restraints have been cast contemptuously aside. The mayor of one of our great cities officially proclaimed a "Gay Pride Week" to honor homosexuals, lesbians, perverts, and the vilest forms of immorality, with scarcely a ripple of protest. Bookstores line their shelves with obscene literature of the most explicit sort. Movie houses compete to show the most degraded and disgusting pornography as "adult" entertainment. Sexual perverts are not only promoted to high government office, but are also hailed because "a fully sublimated homosexual is worth his weight in gold," as one official expressed it. Corruption stalks everywhere with head lifted high. The sins that produced the Flood have risen again in the world and are fast reaching toward heaven.

It is no wonder that God is next seen *revealing His wrath* (6:13). "And God said unto Noah, The end of all flesh is come before me; for the earth is filled with violence through them; and, behold, I will destroy them with the earth." The end. The word comes from a root meaning "to cut off." God had reached the limit of His patience, but He revealed the fact to Noah so that a way of escape might be provided for those who would take it. Even in His wrath, God remembers His mercy.

2. A PLAN (6:14-22)

A plan of salvation was to be extended to all. That plan, as in all ages, foreshadowed *the finished work of Christ* (6:14-16). Noah was to build an ark and offer a way of escape from coming wrath to that doomed generation. He was given full instructions—the ark was to be the shape of a coffin and was to be made from gopher wood (cypress), the same wood from which ancient peoples made their coffins. Gopher wood was incorruptible wood.[9] When completed, the ark was to be covered inside and out with pitch (the word used for pitch is the same word used in the Old Testament for atonement). It was to have a window and a door—Noah was to have control of the window, God was to take charge of the door.

All of that can be used to illustrate the gospel. We see Noah toiling away, the great antediluvian carpenter, producing a judgment-proof vehicle of salvation for a lost world. It all points to the Carpenter of Nazareth who provided a judgment-proof righteousness and perfect salvation for men. Atonement was assured. All who shelter in Him will never face the storm. He comes between them and the outpoured wrath of God.

The plan of salvation in Noah's day rested on *the faithful word of God* (6:17-22). "And, behold I, even I, do bring a flood of waters upon the earth . . . but with thee will I establish my covenant; and thou shalt come into the ark." God pledged Himself to save all those who believed His word. The plan of salvation for that ancient world was the same as for today. There must be a response to God's word and a deliberate turning to Christ. He is our ark, for salvation is available only in Him. The ark provided shelter from the storm, but it also provided sustenance for all who were inside (6:21). Every need was anticipated and met. Just so today; Christ not only saves—He satisfies and meets every spiritual need of those who trust in Him.

II. A WORLD FINALLY RELINQUISHED TO JUDGMENT (7:1-24)

Noah's ark was never intended to be a ship. It was a vast, enclosed chest designed solely for the purpose of housing and preserving a large number of living creatures.[10] No craft was ever expected to endure such storms. The bolts of heaven fell avalanches of water came down, the ocean deeps were rent asunder and heaved up boiling maelstroms of destruction. The hungry floods scoured the very mountain tops, searching out the sinner's hiding place. Only those in the ark were safe.

A. THE DELIVERANCE OF THE GODLY (7:1-9)

The ark was ready. The last tree had been felled, the last timber secured in its place, the last nail driven home, the last pail of pitch applied. Salvation, full and free, was now ready for all. One step of faith

9. The gates of St. Peter's at Rome were made of gopher wood. They lasted over a thousand years from the time of Constantine to the time of Eugene IV without signs of decay.
10. The ark measured 450′ × 150′ × 45′. It had a capacity of more than 3 million cubic feet, making it comparable to modern ocean-going vessels. In 1609 the Dutch Mennonite, Peter Jansen, built a ship at Hoorn, Holland, to the same proportions, only one-third the size. His vessel moved heavily in the water, but could carry one-third more cargo than an ordinary ship of the same cubic space. See Erich Sauer, *The Dawn of World Redemption* (London: Paternoster, 1951), p. 67.

was all it took to put a person in the ark, safe from the wrath of God. We see the *full commitment demanded of Noah.* "And the LORD said unto Noah, Come thou and all thy house into the ark; for thee have I seen righteous before me in this generation" (7:1). God was already in the ark. Salvation was simply the shutting in of all the saved with Him. What it meant for Noah to be "in the ark" in his day is what it means for us to be "in Christ" today. Between the saved and the storm were the judgment-proof timbers of the ark. Between the believer and God's wrath is Christ. He bore the storm for all those who now find their safety in Him.

Noah and his family had to take one step of faith. They had to make a total commitment of themselves to the salvation that had been procured for them at such immeasurable cost. Apart from that act, salvation would have been provided in vain. The gospel invitation was given to Noah in that glorious word "Come!" That gracious word rings out repeatedly in the Scripture until, at last, when God comes to close the Book forever, He sounds it out again and again. Come! Noah responded, "Just as I am, I come."

That full commitment demanded of Noah was followed by a *final commission delivered to Noah* (7:2-4). He was to take seven of each kind of "clean" beast into the ark. He had already been told (6:19) that the animals were to be taken into the ark by pairs. Those, he had been told, would come unto him. The extra, clean animals were in anticipation of the new rule, after the Flood, that man should henceforth eat meat. One of each seven, was no doubt intended for sacrifice. As the animals had once been marshaled before Adam for naming, so now they were impelled by the same divine compulsion to stand before the second head of the race for salvation. The God who commissioned ravens to feed Elijah directed the creatures of the earth to make their way to Noah. The ark was to be the serpent's lair, the lion's den. But "the saved" are changed (2 Corinthians 5:17) so perhaps the natures of the beasts were changed so long as they were in the ark.

The presence of the creatures in the ark, together with the Noahic covenant (Genesis 9:10), hints at God's ultimate purpose in redeeming the animal creation (Romans 8:19-22). The ark was a miniature new creation passing through the judgment storms unscathed to a new earth.

The record next tells of the *faithful compliance demonstrated by Noah* (7:5-9). "And Noah did according unto all that the LORD commanded him." We have to "trust and obey." What a testimony it must have been to that godless generation to see the beasts of the earth filing up the narrow gangplank in a ceaseless line, embarking for another world. The ark was soon to sail, never to return. Only those inside would be safe. Yet that unbelieving world remained obdurate and hardened in its wickedness.

It is a principle with God that He witnesses in two ways to an age about to be relinquished to judgment—by faithful preaching and by fulfilled prophecy; by sermons and by signs. In that far-off world, Noah was a "preacher of righteousness" and, as history has demonstrated so often, his witness was in vain. There was fulfilled prophecy, too. Methuselah died. His name was a prophecy: "When he dies, it shall come." The death of Methuselah was an ominous sign to that generation. There were others, also. What a strange and disturbing sight it must have been for those antediluvians to see the aimals beating a path to Noah's door to seek refuge in the ark. No doubt the rationalists had an explanation for that. In any case, the sign was ignored.

So the animals went into the ark, Noah went in, his family went in, and the rest of mankind yawned in the face of God. Only eight persons were saved. The vast and costly work of salvation was all in vain so far as the majority went. Most people simply did not believe that God intended to judge the world. Noah and his family alone took God at His word and dared all on the salvation provided for the race.

B. THE DESTRUCTION OF THE GODLESS (7:10-24)

1. ITS TIMING (7:10-16)

Probably no other biblical event is so comprehensively dated by God as is the Flood. There are repeated references to days and months and years, some eighteen time notations in all. It is as though Noah kept a diary in which he noted, day by day and month by month, the passing events of that monumental catastrophe through which he passed.

We note the *further delay* in the judgment (7:10). Noah and his family went into the ark and, for a full week, nothing happened, no doubt to the great merriment of the ungodly. Little did the careless antediluvians think they were frittering away the last, lingering remnant of God's patience, that they were abusing His grace, His longsuffering, and His kindness for the very last time. That extra week of grace was intended to bring them to repentance. Instead, they used it to treasure up for themselves the inescapable wrath (Romans 2:4-5).

Note, too, the *final dawning* of the judgment (7:11-16). The exact date is given—"the six hundredth year of Noah's life, in the second month, the seventeenth day of the month." On that day all the fountains of the great deep were broken up and the windows of heaven were opened. "And the rain was upon the earth forty days and forty nights." Did that day dawn as bright and as sunny as any that had gone before? Or did the people start from their beds awakened by an appalling thunderclap and a sudden, terrifying downpour of rain, rain which kept on coming and coming as the rivers burst their banks and the angry tides ripped in from the sea? Or was there just a slight drizzle at first and an overcast sky? We are not told. All we know is that a mysterious hour struck in the eternal counsels of God, and then all creation, above and below, arose to do the bidding of God and scour a planet rendered vile by filthy men.

2. ITS TOTALITY (7:17-24)

First the waters increased and bore up the ark, then the waters prevailed and were increased greatly upon the earth and finally they prevailed exceedingly so that "all the high hills, that were under the whole heaven, were covered." Scholars disagree as to the universality of the Flood. The language of the narrative certainly embraces the idea of a total inundation of the planet. Certainly, so far as Noah could see, the whole world was submerged beneath the judgment waters. We do not know to what extent the antediluvian population had overspread the planet, but the Flood had to have been universal.[11]

The waters of the Flood came hurrying after a fleeing race, driving men to ever higher ground until even the mountain peaks were submerged to a depth of fifteen cubits. Then the planet spun on through space awash from sea to sea with only eight people left alive, tossed here and there upon the rolling deep. "And the waters prevailed upon the earth an hundred and fifty days" (7:24). For five full months the waters covered the sea while Noah and his family thanked God for a salvation that kept them secure through it all.

III. A WORLD FRESHLY RECOVERED FROM JUDGMENT (8:1–9:29)

Mount Ararat towers 16,254 feet into the sky. Maybe it was the last resort of earth's fleeing multitudes, hurrying, panic-stricken up its slopes pursued by the relentless rising tides. The great peak on which the ark came finally to rest stands midway between Gibraltar and the Caspian Sea and midway between the Cape of Good Hope and the Bering Strait. It was a new pivot from which the races of mankind were to radiate to repopulate the globe.

11. What caused the Flood? There are numerous theories. We summarize here an interesting theory developed by the renowned Dr. C. Theodore Schwarze, Fellow of the American Association for the Advancement of Science (one of the highest honors that can be bestowed on a scientist) whose name was listed in at least five different *Who's Who* publications. Dr. Schwarze devoted thirty years to intensive research into the scientific accuracy of the Bible.

According to Dr. Schwarze, the planet was at one time completely ensphered in an ice canopy. He gives reasons for believing that and suggestions as to how it was formed. Incidental hints in the early chapters of Genesis lend credence to his theory. It would explain, for example, the remarkable longevity of the antediluvians and also why, before the Flood, the earth was watered, not by rain, but by a mist. It would also explain why the rainbow would be a sign to Noah after the Flood when rainfall became a frequent phenomenon.

Dr. Schwarze contended that an explosion tore the canopy apart so that in a literal sense "the windows of heaven were opened." The rushing ice and water descending from the sky would carry into the depths of the ocean all evidence of antediluvian civilization, scouring the planet. The intense cold accompanying the catastrophe would explain why in Siberia and Alaska whole animals have been found in a remarkable state of preservation having, apparently, been deep-frozen instantly.

The theory would also explain climatic changes on the planet and other changes affecting life here.

See Theodore Schwarze, *The Marvel of Earth's Canopies* (condensed from an original manuscript), (Westchester, Ill.: Good News, 1957).

Over Ararat the ark floated, gently tossed to and fro now that the storms had spent themselves and the upheavals in the mighty deep had given place to calm. All around was a dead and silent world shrouded from north to south, from east to west, as far as eye could see, by a watery waste. Behind, a drowned world; before, a world washed clean; the only visible object a lonely ark rocked in the cradle of the deep. Thus opens the third and final section of the story of the Flood.

A. NOAH TARRYING (8:1-5)

Immured in the ark, Noah possessed his soul in patience, waiting while *God remembered* (8:1-2). "And God remembered Noah," we read. The figure of speech used is anthropopatheia, whereby human feelings and experiences are ascribed to God. As though God could ever forget! It is a touching and lovely way to bring before us God's loving and tender care for His servant. Indeed, God's compassionate concern extended to all the creatures that were in the ark. How interminable the days and weeks and months must have seemed after the silence descended and the waters lapped ceaselessly around the ark. Had God forgotten? Was the experience to go on forever? No. God remembered.

Noah waited while God remembered and while the *flood receded* (8:3). For one hundred fifty days the judgment waters slowly ebbed away, five whole months. It took just forty days for them to cover the earth, but before Noah and his charges could finally emerge a whole year passed. God is never in a hurry. It was His will that the earth be fully ready for the redeemed and that all traces of His wrath be erased before they be permitted to come out of the ark. So Noah waited.

He waited while the *ark rested* (8:4-5). The exact date is given when the great vessel finally touched down on solid ground. It was "in the seventh month on the seventeenth day of the month." Perhaps Noah jotted down the momentous date in his diary. The Spirit of God notes that the ark "rested" on the seventeenth day. It is no coincidence, surely, that the Lord Jesus rose from the dead on the very same day of the very same month.[12] Having passed through the waters of judgment He stood in resurrection upon the earth. Thus we find our rest in Him, not in a Jewish Sabbath.

B. NOAH TESTING (8:6-14)

Three times Noah sought to find out how things were progressing on the earth. First, after patiently waiting another forty days after the ark came to rest, he opened the window and loosed two birds, a raven and a dove. The raven, being a carrion bird, found plenty with which

12. In Exodus 12:2 the seventh month was changed to the first month (known to the Jews as Abib, or Nisan). On the tenth day of that month they secured their Passover lamb. They killed it on the fourteenth day. The Lord Jesus rose from the dead on the seventeenth day.

to satisfy itself and was quite content to remain without the ark. The dove, of a different nature, could as yet find no lasting rest upon the earth and so returned to Noah. A week later he tried again and that time the dove brought back an olive leaf. What a thrill that must have been to the eight people in the ark. With what delight they must have passed that living token from hand to hand. One more week of waiting and patient Noah tried again. That time the dove came back no more. The repeated Sabbaths connected with that part of the story suggest that Noah was acting out of a spirit of deep religious exercise, not capriciously or arbitrarily. Such spiritual exercise surely augered well for the new beginning about to be made on a new earth. In many ways the whole incident anticipated the coming of the millennial age.

At length Noah removed "the covering" from the ark and looked out. Again, the exact date is given. It was the first day of the first month of his six hundred and first year (8:13). Now, as far as eye could see, the earth was dry. Surely now they could come out of the ark. But no. For another fifty-six days the door remained firmly shut, another eight weeks. But Noah could afford to wait. God was with him in that ark. It was not a question of making the best of it, but of making the most of it. To be shut in with God—how the flesh would fret and strain at such a situation, but how the spiritual man must have rejoiced. It was not too long, not a moment too long.

C. NOAH TRUSTING (8:15–9:17)

1. THE LORD'S COMMAND TO NOAH (8:15-19)

At last the great day came when the door of the ark was to be flung open. The new experience began with the Lord's command to Noah. "And God spake unto Noah, saying: Go forth of the ark, thou, and thy wife, and thy sons, and thy sons' wives with thee." As God was the first to enter the ark, so He was the last to leave. In the first year of his *seventh* century, Noah emerged to a new earth in the Sabbath rest of a finished work. Nor were the animals forgotten. God's gracious command included them along with the primeval command, "Be fruitful and multiply."

The first thing Noah did was to build an altar and to sanctify the new earth by offering up one of every clean beast and fowl in a great burnt offering. It was not a sin offering. The sin offering would come later. That offering was all for God. It was the overflow of a full heart, which wished to express appreciation for a salvation so full and free. It was typically bringing before God the highest and holiest aspects of the death of His Son. Seldom, it must be supposed, has there ever been given to God a more liberal offering in proportion to the means at the disposal of the worshiper. It became the ground of the Lord's covenant with Noah. An unbeliever looking at Noah's first act would have been aghast. What waste! What an atrocity! What a fiendish way to begin life on a new earth. God, knowing full well the nature of the human heart (8:21), was well pleased with Noah's act of devotion and faith.

2. THE LORD'S COVENANT WITH NOAH (8:20–9:17)

First of all *God spoke secretly,* to Himself as it were, in response to Noah's sacrifice (8:20-22). The fragrance of Noah's offering ascended to Him, and He said in His heart, "I will not again curse the ground any more for man's sake; for the imagination of man's heart is evil from his youth; neither will I again smite any more every thing living, as I have done." In His heart He pledged too that henceforth the seasons would come and go without interference from on high.

Then *God spoke sovereignly,* setting before Noah the terms of the new agreement now to cover life on the renewed earth (9:1-17). There were, first, certain *general provisions* to the covenant (9:1-7). A new day had dawned. One of the contributing factors that led up to the Flood was the unbridled license that men had to sin, there had been no law and order, no human restraint for crime. All that was now to be changed. Moreover, before the Flood, men had been restricted to a vegetarian diet, that too was to be changed. There were good reasons for both alterations in man's tenure of the globe. Neither the dietary nor the disciplinary stipulations of the Noahic covenant have been repealed for the simple reason that the conditions they are intended to restrain remain on the earth. "Every moving thing that liveth shall be meat for you."

> Our body appears to be not a prison, but a fortress and devised for the very purpose of sheltering us in some degree from the corrupting influence of demons. In its normal condition it effectually repels their more open and violent assaults: but if we once suffer the fence to be broken down, we are no longer able to restore it, and are henceforth exposed to the attacks of malignant enemies.
>
> It is seldom, for instance, that a person can be mesmerized for the first time without his own consent; and when such cases do occur they are probably to be referred to some special weakness, which may not infrequently be traced to a special sin. But if submission be once yielded, it is hard to withdraw it: and every fresh exercise of the power upon the same patient increases its influence.
>
> So, in the case of fellowship with demons, there are few who can become mediums without perseverance, but when a communication has been once established, the spirits are lothe to relinquish it, and are wont to persecute those who, having become conscious of their sin, are determined by the grace of God to transgress no more.[13]

Some believe that one of the means God has given to protect us against demon forces is a meat diet. Before the Flood men ate no

13. G. H. Pember, *Earth's Earliest Ages and Their Connection With Modern Spiritualism and Theosophy,* 14th ed. (London: Alfred Holness, n.d.), p. 256.

meat. One great factor in precipitating the Flood was the intercourse between "the sons of God" and the daughters of men that resulted in a demon progeny of extraordinary influence. Perhaps to create a barrier against such a thing happening again, God commanded a dietary change of revolutionary character. He commanded the eating of meat. G. H. Pember believed "it is not impossible that the permission to eat flesh, given as it was immediately after the angel-transgression, may have been intended to render man less capable of conscious and intelligent intercourse with supernatural beings, and consequently less exposed to their wiles. And if so, the desire on the part of demons to withdraw it is easily understood."[14] One of the marks of latter day apostasy is that "some shall depart from the faith, giving heed to seducing spirits, and doctrines of devils . . . forbidding to marry, and commanding to abstain from meats, which God hath created to be received with thanksgiving" (1 Timothy 4:1-3). Vegetarianism has no scriptural warrant. The Lord Jesus Himself ate flesh, even in His resurrection body (Luke 24:41-43).

The general provisions of the Noahic covenant not only dealt with diet but also with discipline. The command was given that the murderer should be executed (9:6), nor has that law been rescinded. It is evident from Romans 13:4 that the state's right to execute the criminal is God-ordained still. The sacredness of human life is based on the fact that man was made by God in His own image and for that reason the murderer must be executed by society.

Along with the general provisions of the covenant there was a *great provision,* namely that never again would God inundate the world in a universal flood (9:8-17). As token of that pledge God drew Noah's attention to the rainbow. "And it shall come to pass, when I bring a cloud over the earth, that the bow shall be seen in the cloud: and I will remember my covenant . . . the everlasting covenant between God and every living creature of all flesh that is upon the earth." What a beautiful symbol the rainbow is. Its arch is bent like a bow toward heaven, but it is a bow without an arrow; the arrow has already been spent.

D. NOAH TOILING (9:18-23)

Eight people were saved from the destruction of that antediluvian world; eight people alighted from the ark under the umbrella of a new

14. *Ibid.,* p. 372. Pember gives illustrations of the advanced forms of demonism being practiced even in his day. He mentions at least one case of a woman being "palpably embraced" by a spirit, the woman asking for the experience to be repeated (pp. 389-90). He gives several examples of spirits materializing so that they could be physically clasped (pp. 327-31). He concludes his thoroughly enlightening section on spiritism with the question: "Had Pope Innocent the Eighth a real insight of the truth when he fulminated his decretal against intercourse with incubi and succubae!" (p. 390). See R. H. Robbins, *The Encyclopedia of Witchcraft and Demonology* (New York: Crown, 1959) under "Incubus" and "Succubus" for a modern, secular treatment of the same subject.

covenant. Mention is now made of Noah as a *father* (9:18-19), for Noah and his sons were the new heads of the human race. Noah became a second Adam to mankind. The names of his three sons are again given and, as almost always, the names are given as Shem, Ham, and Japheth—in that order. In actual fact Japheth was the eldest (10:21) and Shem the youngest, but Shem takes precedence over the other two. The Lord came to earth through the line of Shem and, for that reason, the younger assumes priority.

The names of Noah's three sons are interesting. The name of the head of each of the three races of mankind is thought to be derived from the language of the race he represents. Thus "Shem," in Hebrew, means "glory," or "renown," or "the name." "Ham" is the equivalent of the word by which the Egyptians named their country, *Kem,* which means "black." "Japheth" is derived from a word that in the Aryan language means "chief of the race."[15]

The significant thing about Ham is that he was "the father of Canaan," which, of course, prepares us for what follows. The fact that Ham was the father of the Canaanites was of prime interest to Israel since it was that accursed race that opposed their entry into the promised land. It is implied that Canaan was Ham's youngest son (10:6), from which it may be concluded that the incident that follows took place some years after the Flood.

Noah is now depicted as a *farmer* (9:20). He was a husbandman (the word means "man of the ground,"[16] that is he was a man giving himself to tillage), especially, he was the cultivator of a vineyard. Armenia is still thought to be the home of the vine.

Mention is then made of Noah as a *failure* (9:21-23). He drank of the wine and became drunk, and in his stupor exposed his nakedness in a shameful way,[17] much to the amusement of Ham.

The full extent of Ham's perfidy is not known. He was, however, so lacking in common decency that, seeing his father naked and shamed, out he went to broadcast the news to his brothers rather than covering him up. His behavior subsequently brought down upon his head his father's silent disapproval and upon his son's head a resounding curse. When Shem and Japheth heard of their father's disgrace, they covered him, seeking to spare their father's feelings as best they could by walking in backward so as not to look upon his shame. From that incident stemmed one of the most remarkable prophecies in the Bible.

15. Marcus Dods, *The Book of Genesis* (Edinburgh: T. & T. Clark, n.d.), p. 43.
16. Compare "man of war" (a soldier), Joshua 5:4; "man of blood" (a murderer), 2 Samuel 16:7; "man of cattle" (a shepherd), Genesis 46:32; "a man of words" (eloquent), Exodus 4:10.
17. In defense of Noah it might well be urged that Noah did not realize the potency of fermented grape juice, the new climactic conditions after the Flood possibly being different from those that had prevailed before. Just the same, wine, mentioned here for the first time in Scripture, is in ill repute. It produced drunkenness and shame and brought to the surface the vile passions that surged in the soul of Ham.

E. NOAH TESTIFYING (9:24-29)

Noah awoke from his drunken sleep and discovered what had happened. With prophetic insight he saw, in a flash, the far-reaching significance of his sons' behavior and the spirit of prophecy descended upon him. He testified *by life* and *by lip* (9:25-27). "And he said, Cursed be Canaan; a servant of servants shall he be unto his brethren. And he said, Blessed be the LORD God of Shem; and Canaan shall be his servant. God shall enlarge Japheth, and he shall dwell in the tents of Shem, and Canaan shall be his servant."

Why was Canaan selected for a special curse? Noah passed over Ham's sin in absolute silence, for in that great prophetic utterance regarding the nations he had nothing to say about the Hamitic peoples at all.[18] He ignored all of Ham's other sons too and focused on the youngest, and him he roundly cursed, not with passion and invective, but with the long view of the seer able to see the end from the beginning. It may be that Ham, having been blessed by God (9:1) could not now be cursed by Noah. It may be that the father was punished in the son according to the outworking of divine law (Exodus 20:5). It may be that Canaan, in some way not recorded, was a partaker in his father's evil delight in Noah's shame. Most likely Noah, under the inspiration of the prophetic vision, could see all the coarseness and shamelessness of Ham being worked out fully in the vileness and filthiness of the Canaanite tribes of a future day. In any case, he cursed Canaan.

The Hamites were simply passed over by Noah and thus lacked a blessing. After an initial burst of brilliant prosperity, notably under Nimrod and in the Egyptian civilization, the Hamites have, throughout most of their history, been singularly lacking in greatness. The Negro peoples, particularly, have had to groan under the yoke of oppression and exploitation.

The Semites were blessed by Noah, the height of the blessing being that Jehovah was to be the God of Shem. The Semitic peoples would be those through whom God would channel to men both His revelations and His redemption. The promise of spiritual salvation was concentrated in the descendants of Shem.

Japheth was to be the empire builder and was, at length, to come in a special way into Shem's spiritual blessings. Japheth was the father of the Greeks (Javan), of the Romans, the Persians, the Indo-Teutonic races. The great Aryan races are Japhetic in origin. They are the peoples who, for millennia, have held the destiny of men in their hands.

But, for centuries, the ancient skeptics must have had a field day with that prophecy for, as history began to unfold, it seemed as though the reverse were taking place. It was not the Japhetic peoples but the Hamitic and the Semitic peoples who seized the reigns of human des-

18. This should destroy the notion that God has, in some way, especially cursed the Negro peoples. He cursed Canaan, not Ham.

tiny. It was the Hamitic Nimrod who became the first empire builder. It was Egypt and Babylon and Assyria that flourished. Even Carthage, the ancient rival of Rome, was not Japhetic but Hamitic, for it was a colony of Tyre, and the Phoenicians were a Canaanite people.

For two thousand years the Japhetic peoples remained in the background, but at last their hour struck. "Under Cyrus the Persian, the Japhetic race entered the arena with victorious strength. Semitic Babylon fell, and the Japhethites became the lords of the Orient. Since then no Semitic or Hamitic race has succeeded in breaking the world supremacy of the Japhethites."[19] "That night was Belshazzar the king of the Chaldeans slain" (Daniel 5:30) is more than a datemark. It marks the decisive collapse of Hamitic-Semitic world rule and the coming of Japheth into his own.

Thus ends the story of the Flood. Thus begins the story of the tower of Babel.

19. See Erich Sauer, *The Dawn Of World Redemption* (London: Paternoster, 1951), p. 77.

Chapter 4

THE COALITION

(10:1–11:32)

I. Divine Government (10:1–11:9)
   A. The Completeness of Man's Dispersal (10:1-32)
      1. The Japhetic Races (10:1-5)
      2. The Hamitic Races (10:6-20)
      3. The Semitic Races (10:21-32)
   B. The Cause of Man's Dispersal (11:1-9)
      1. Their Materials (11:1-3)
      2. Their Method (11:4*a*)
      3. Their Motive (11:4*b*)
      4. Their Mistake (11:5-9)

II. Divine Grace (11:10-32)
   A. Abram's Family Tree (11:10-26)
   B. Abram's Family Ties (11:27-32)
      1. Abram the Person (11:27-30)
      2. Abram the Pilgrim (11:31-32)

4

THE COALITION

I. Divine Government
(10:1–11:9)

The story of Babel precedes chronologically the ethnological table given in Genesis 10. The ethnic table sets before us the completeness of the dispersion of the various families of mankind; the story of the tower of Babel relates the cause of that dispersion.

The table of nations is the oldest attempt to explain, in tabulated form, the geographic distribution of the human race. It is ethnologically sound. It divides mankind into three basic races, Semitic, Aryan, and Turanean. Moses allocates the Indo-European family to the sons of Japheth, taking in thus the principal races of Europe and the great Asiatic Aryan races. In the Semitic family he includes the Assyrians, the Hebrews, and the Joktanite Arabs. In the Hamitic family he includes the Egyptians, Ethiopians, Southern Arabs, and early Babylonians.

The table of nations begins with the *Japhetic* tribes, not only because Japheth was the oldest of Noah's sons but also because those were the nations furthest removed from the geopolitical center of Palestine, which country is always placed at the heart of Bible geography. The table deals in greater detail with the *Hamitic* nations, with the Egyptians, Canaanites, and Arabs, and especially with the exploits of Nimrod, the shadowy figure behind the building of Babel. It notes the separation of the *Semitic* peoples from the other descendants of Noah and pays special attention to the Messianic line, which led to Abram. In His sovereignty, as manifested in chapter 10, God moved the Japhetic peoples to the north from whence they spread westward into Europe and eastward into India. He moved the Hamitic nations south. And He gave the central area to Shem, crowning it all at a later date by giving Israel the most central land of all. The three great continents of Africa, Asia, and Europe all come to a common fulcrum on the strategic territory pledged to Abraham between the Euphrates and the Nile.

A. The Completeness of Man's Dispersal (10:1-32)

1. The Japhetic Races (10:1-5)

In His governmental dealings with mankind, God saw to it that the races were dispersed over the globe. The confounding of human speech at Babel was intended to force the nations apart and hasten their distribution over the face of the planet. The table of nations begins with *the Japhetic races.* In all, fourteen Japhetic families are listed, thirty Hamitic families and twenty-six Semitic families, making a total of seventy families altogether.

First the *founders* of the Japhetic nations are listed, beginning with *Gomer.* Gomer's descendants are often identified with the Cimmerians who first settled on the shores of the Caspian and Black Seas and who later spread into Europe as far as the Atlantic, leaving marks of their presence in Germany and Wales.[1] *Magog* comes next. His were a fierce and warlike people ruled over by princes who bore the royal appellation "Gog" (comparable to "Pharaoh" or "Caesar"). Their descendants are thought to be the Scythians and their territory to be in the Caucasus. We would identify them today with the Russians. *Madai* is the third founding father listed. His descendants are thought to be the Medes, and their territory is linked with the southwest shore of the Caspian sea. *Javan* became the father of the Greek peoples. *Tubal* and *Meschech* found their home in northern Armenia and, again, would today be identified with the Russians. *Tiras* is thought to have been the ancestor of the Thracians or of certain tribes who found their home around the Taurus.

Having listed seven founding fathers, the narrative goes on to describe seven founding *families* beginning with the sons of Gomer. The first named is *Ashkenaz.* Jewish commentators believe that his descendants founded Germany. To this day Jews from Germany and central Europe are referred to as Ashkenazis. *Riphath* gave his name to the Riphaean mountains on the north of the Caspian. The descendants of *Togarmah* are generally identified with the Phrygians, the Cappadoceans, the Armenians, and the Taurians inhabiting the Crimea. It is significant that a number of those peoples are identified by Ezekiel with the hostile, antisemitic nation that bursts out of the "uttermost parts of the north" in the last days to descend in battle array upon Israel (Ezekiel 38-39). Magog, Meschech, Tubal, Gomer, Togarmah are all to be members of that anti-God alliance of the last days.

The sons of Javan come next into prominence beginning with *Elishah,* thought by some to be Elis in the Peloponnesus, but in any case a maritime people of Grecian stock. *Tarshish* is frequently identified with the southwest coast of Spain. It became famous in Bible times as a wealthy and important seaport. Prophetically, it stands for "the uttermost parts of the west," the western world. *Kittim* is identified with Cyprus, but also with the shores of Italy and Greece. The identification of *Dodanim* is obscure. It is interesting that many of the sons of Javan are depicted by Ezekiel as opposing the invasion of Israel by Russia in a coming day.

1. Positive identification of some of the peoples and territories cannot be made. Scholars differ on the matter.

The statement concerning the Japhetic nations closes with a summary (10:5) of the geographical, philological, tribal, and national divisions of the "Gentiles" (*goyim*). Those are the nations that came to power after the fall of Babylon and that have controlled the world ever since.

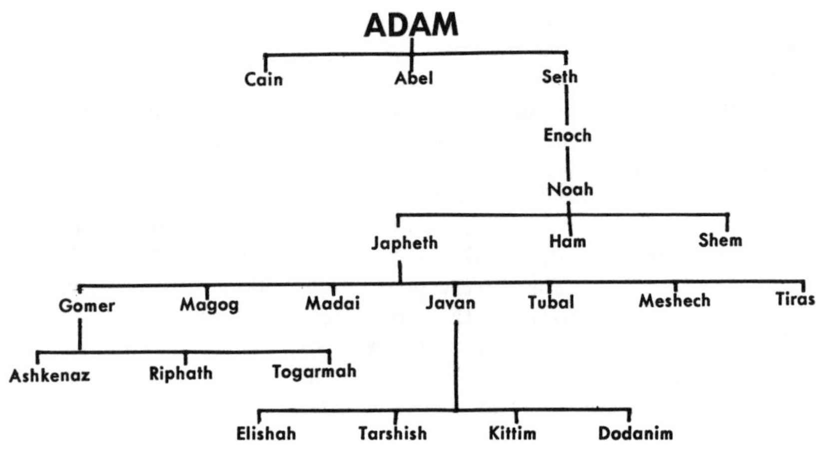

2. THE HAMITIC RACES (10:6-20)

The table next turns to *the Hamitic races.* In the early dawn of human history they were the vigorous, aggressive peoples, the early empire builders, the controllers of human destiny. It must have seemed to the old world skeptics that God's prophetic word through Noah regarding the enlargement of Japheth was singularly at fault. Not so. God's prophecies are frequently long-range and take time to mature. With those ancient skeptics it was their perspective that was at fault, not prophecy.

The Hamitic list begins with *notable names* (10:6-7), the first of which is *Cush.* The original settlements of Cush might have been on the upper Nile, and he is most generally identified with Ethiopia, although some of his descendants are thought to have migrated to Arabia, Babylonia, and India. The Bible depicts the Cushites as being black (Jeremiah 13:23) and tall (Isaiah 45:14).

Mizraim founded Egypt. The word is a dual word and would thus embrace both Egypts, upper and lower, sprawling along the length of the Nile. The original name for Egypt was Kem, thought by some to be a reference to Ham. *Phut* founded the nation of Libya on the African coast. *Canaan* occupied the territory that afterward bore his name and that, for a period, was a province of Egypt. A number of the sons of Cush are listed, most of whom settled the country between the Arabian Sea and the Persian Gulf or else Ethiopia. *Seba's* descendants seem to have occupied Nubia in northern Ethiopia. The sons of *Havilah* are identified with what was essentially Semitic territory between the Arabian Sea and Persian Gulf. That vast territory was large enough to accommodate peoples from both major races. The sons of *Sabtah* are linked both with Ethiopia and Arabia. Both *Raamah*'s and *Sabtechah*'s descendants are linked with the Persian Gulf. Two of Raamah's sons are listed. *Sheba*'s name has been linked with the great city of that name in Arabia and *Dedan*'s name is associated with the Persian Gulf.

Having listed some of the notable names in the Hamitic line, the narrative now centers on *notorious Nimrod.* He is a shadowy but evidently a most powerful figure. His name is derived from *Marad,* "to rebel." He seems to have been the prime mover behind the building of Babel. Nimrod took the sword of the magistrate, entrusted to Noah and his descendants, and converted it into the sword of the conqueror. He became the world's first imperialist and empire builder. From the amount of space devoted to him in the Hamitic line, it is likely that he was one of the giants of the postdiluvian world. His wife's name is not given in Scripture, but from secular sources we gather that she was the infamous Semiramis, the woman who first introduced idolatry on the earth and who made Babylon the eternal home of the "mysteries." The vast system

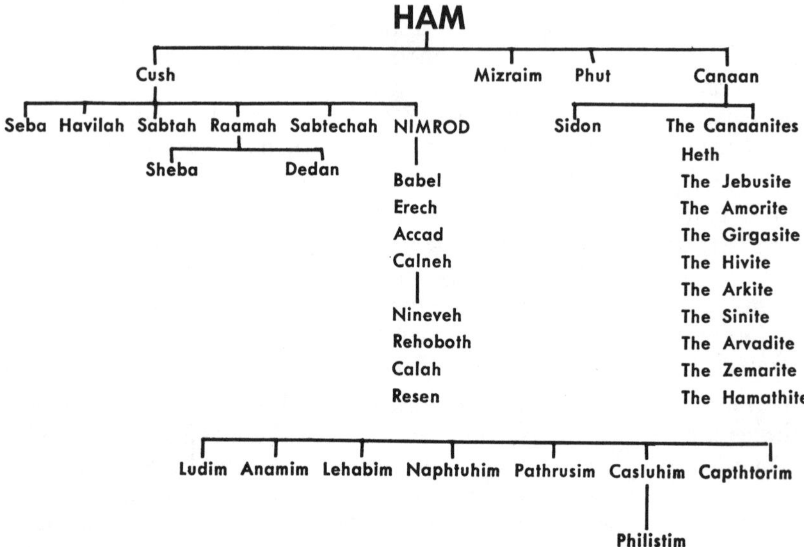
HAM
Cush
Mizraim
Phut
Canaan
Seba
Havilah
Sabtah
Raamah
Sabtechah
NIMROD
Sidon
The Canaanites
Sheba
Dedan
Heth
Babel
The Jebusite
Erech
The Amorite
Accad
The Girgasite
Calneh
The Hivite
The Arkite
Nineveh
The Sinite
Rehoboth
The Arvadite
Calah
The Zemarite
Resen
The Hamathite
Ludim
Anamim
Lehabim
Naphtuhim
Pathrusim
Casluhim
Capthtorim
Philistim

of pagan religion, which thereafter swiftly inundated the globe, stemmed from Babylon.[2]

Nimrod "began to be a mighty one in the earth" (10:8), that is, he became a hero. He enabled men to break away from the shackles of true religion, which bound them to God. He was "a mighty hunter before the Lord" (10:9). The word translated "before" is rendered "against" in some versions. He campaigned in a spirit of defiance and with evident success. Nimrod was a Hamite. No doubt the people of his day looked upon him as a champion, one who would rid them of the restrictive religious notions kept alive by Shem, the godly founder of the Semitic race.

Nimrod's empire was founded at Babel (Babylon)—the word is Semitic and means "the gate of the god." After the dispersion of the nations, Babylon became a great city ruling over the destinies of men. Wherever men went they took with them the Babylonian pagan mystery religious system. By the time of Nebuchadnezzar the city covered an area of 225 square miles. God sent the apostate, idolatrous Jews back to Babylon in exile so that there, in the homeland of idolatry, they might be forever cured of idolatry.

Linked with Nimrod's conquests are Erech, Accad, and Calneh, three cities in the area, one south of Babylon, one north of Babylon, and one northeast of Babylon. Those cities and Babylon enabled Nimrod to control what the text calls "the land of Shinar" (10:10), that is, Babylonia as distinct from Assyria.

The city of Nineveh now appears upon the sacred page. The King James Version implies that it was Asshur the son of Shem who founded that great city, but other renderings tie the founding of Nineveh to Nimrod. In the light of the context this would seem to be a better reading: "He (Nimrod) went forth into Asshur and builded Nineveh" (10:11). According to that rendering Nimrod invaded Asshur (Assyria) and left his mark there as he did in Babylonia. In time Nineveh became the rival of Babylon and, in later years, was the dreaded capital of the formidable Assyrian Empire.

Associated with Nineveh in the text are three other names; Rehoboth, Calah, and Resen. Rehoboth is unknown. The word means "the city of boulevards" and is thought to be a descriptive name for Nineveh. Both Calah and Resen are difficult to place. Some think that both cities refer to Asshur, the ancient capital of Assyria; others think they refer to suburbs of Nineveh. In any case Nineveh is described as "a great city" (10:12), a description that still applied to it in Jonah's day.

So, by every worldly mark, Nimrod was a great man in his day, and the sacred text gives him his due, such as it was. The text then returns to its description of the nations that sprang from Ham and concentrates on *near neighbors*, for the whole table of nations is written from the stand-

2. For a full discussion of this see Alexander Hislop, *The Two Babylons* (New York: Loizeaux, 1948).

point of Israel. First *Mizraim*'s descendants are listed. They are all peoples associated with Egypt. The writer gives the added note that the Philistines originally sprang from Egyptian stock. The word "Philistim" is said to be derived from an Ethiopic root meaning "to emigrate."

The descendants of *Canaan* are listed last. The first and foremost of those was *Sidon* (10:15) who founded the oldest Canaanite city which, together with its sister city, Tyre, became a famous commercial and maritime center. Phoenician explorers and colonists set forth from those cities. Carthage, the ancient rival of Rome on the African coast, was a colony of Tyre. *Heth* founded the Hittite nation. The *Jebusites* held Jerusalem until David's mighty men wrested it from them. The *Amorites* entrenched themselves on both sides of the Jordan and in the mountains that afterward belonged to Judah. Little or nothing is known of the *Girgashites.* The *Hivites* were villagers or "settlers in cities." The Arkites and the Sinites, the Arvadites and the Zemarites together with the Hamathites complete the list of Canaanite tribes. Those were the peoples whose culture and religion were so vile that God later commanded their complete extermination.

3. THE SEMITIC RACES (10:21-32)

Having dealt with the other peoples, Moses concentrates on *the Semitic races.* The list is carried down to Peleg and Joktan, in whose day the great sundering of mankind took place, doubtless a reference to the confusion of tongues at Babel. The first of Shem's sons was *Elam,* who settled the mountainous district east of Babylonia. *Asshur* comes next; he founded the nation of Assyria. *Arphaxad's* territory is said to be north of Assyria. The descendants of *Lud* were the Lydians of Asia Minor, having migrated there from countries more closely identified with Shem. The descendants of *Aram* settled in Damascus and Mesopotamia. In particular, four of Aram's descendants are named. The land of Uz was settled by his firstborn. Uz was a tract of territory southeast of Palestine in the Arabian desert, famous as the place where Job lived. His other sons, Hul, Gether, and Mash, are thought to have settled in Armenia.

Shem's third son, Arphaxad, is the most important in the entire list of nations because it was through him *the royal line* led to Abram and thence to Christ. Nothing is known of *Salah,* Shem's grandson, except that his name means "extension," implying, perhaps, that he was an early colonist. His importance lies in the fact that his son was *Eber,* the father of the Hebrew people. The name "Eber" means "emigrants." His descendants came from "the other side of the flood" (that is, the Euphrates) to Canaan (Joshua 24:2-3, 14-15). Eber's two sons both rank high in the list. *Peleg's* name means "division," appropriately enough. The division of mankind into nations and the curse of tongues at Babel are commemorated in his name. At that point Moses leaves the royal line

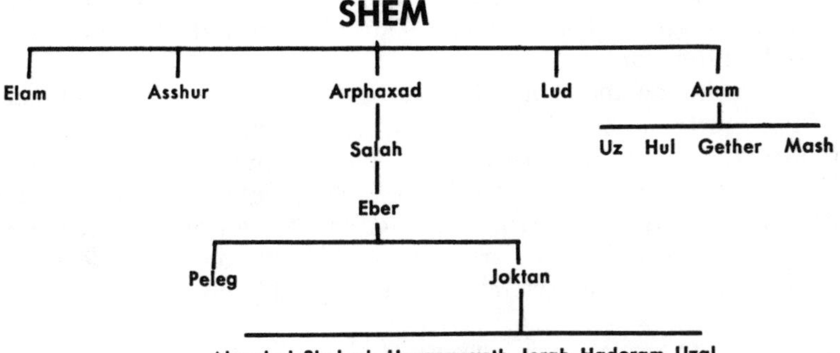
SHEM
Elam
Asshur
Arphaxad
Lud
Aram
Uz Hul Gether Mash
Salah
Eber
Peleg
Joktan
Almodad Sheleph Hazarmaveth Jerah Hadoram Uzal
Diklah Obal Abimael Sheba Ophir Havilah Jobab

for a while and ends the table of nations with a brief summary of *the related line* that ran through Joktan.

Joktan is thought to be the father of the Arabians. His thirteen sons are listed. *Almodad* is thought to have founded Yemen, *Ophir* is probably Oman on the Persian Gulf. The other sons are all more or less linked with Arabia.

In concluding the table of nations, Moses gives a brief summary. "These are the families of the sons of Noah, after their generations, in their nations: and by these were the nations divided [the word means 'disrupted,' emphasizing man's disruption in judgment] in the earth after the flood" (10:32). The whole chapter emphasizes the completeness of man's dispersal and the picture it gives, although some of its details may be uncertain today, is certainly one of worldwide dispersal.

B. THE CAUSE OF MAN'S DISPERSAL (11:1-9)

The root cause for the dispersal of the nations was the building of the tower of Babel, a project which, seemingly, was under the sponsorship of Nimrod. The building of Babel was intended to signify and promote the unity of the race. There was to be "one world." The world's first federation of nations, it epitomized the last, for human history begins and ends at Babel (Revelation 17-18). As there was a great rebel standing behind the first Babel, so there will be a great rebel behind the last one. As the first united nations organization centered everything in a cultural, political, and religious unity, so will the last. Here in Genesis is man's first attempt to build a society from which God was to be excluded. But God refuses to be ruled out of human affairs so, consequently, He came down in judgment upon the scene.

1. THEIR MATERIALS (11:1-3)

The narrative first indicates with what *materials* the world organization was to be built. Four times in the story the words "let us" occur. Three times men used the word and once God used it. The four references tell the story. First they said: "Let us make us brick and burn them thoroughly" (11:3).

God builds with stone (1 Peter 2:4-8). The coming world empire of Christ is depicted as one of stone (Daniel 2:34-35, 44-45). But man uses brick. "They had brick for stone and slime had they for mortar" (11:43). Brick is simply hardened clay, a fitting symbol for humankind. That ancient world empire, in other words, was humanistic. Nothing really lasting can be made out of hardened clay and slime. All human things are bound to be faulty and frail. The slime used by those old world builders was bitumen, a tenaciously adhesive substance. What a contrast between the precious stones of the heavenly city (Revelation 21:19) and the clay and slime of Babel! The slime is just as symbolic as the clay. It reminds us that the adhesive the coming Beast will use to bond together the last Gentile world empire will be equally tenacious and similarly vile. Not for nothing is he called "the man of sin." He will unite men in wickedness and bind them together in a godless union in which vice is glorified and enthroned.

Yet it was not all slime. Those postdiluvian builders were "of one language, and of one speech" (11:1). In other words, they had a cultural unity, they thought alike, they expressed themselves in identical terms, and they were anxious to keep it that way. Their sameness of thought and speech, their regimentation of expression is of one piece with all the rest. It points forward to the coming empire of the Beast. Already we can see how mass communication media regiment the thinking of men. Brainwashing techniques have been so perfected that China, with eight hundred million people, was able to produce in a very short space of time a uniform Maoman, with everyone shouting the same slogans, all reading the same little red book. The Beast will perfect the process and brainwash the world.

2. THEIR METHOD (11:4*a*)

The narrative tells of the *method* those first world federalists used to achieve their goal. "And they said, Go to, let us build us a city and a tower, whose top may reach unto heaven" (11:4). They were to have a political unity, symbolized by the city, and they were to have a religious unity, symbolized by the tower. The expression "whose top may reach unto heaven" contains an ellipsis. The idea can perhaps be better stated: "Let us build . . . a tower and its top with the heavens." The idea was not to build a tower so tall it would reach to heaven, but to build a tower topped by the heavens, that is, by the signs of the zodiac. Astronomical and astrological data were to be associated with that tower. God was not in their thoughts at all. Stargazing and occultism were to be the features of their religious system. Again, the whole thing looks ahead to the last world empire, which will bear the same hallmarks. The Beast will make great use of religion, but it will be religion based on occultism and the worship of himself. Likewise he will have a world-embracing political system that will lock mankind into submission to his will.

3. THEIR MOTIVE (11:4*b*)

The *motive* of those ancient world empire builders is also stated. "Let us make us a name, lest we be scattered abroad upon the face of the whole earth" (11:4). The whole idea was to glorify humanity and to bind men together in a permanent union, and that in defiance of God's will.

4. THEIR MISTAKE (11:5-9)

They reckoned without God. Moses tells of the Lord's *appearing*.

"And the LORD came down to see the city and the tower, which the children of men builded" (11:5). The appearing was followed by the Lord's *advent*. "Go to, let us go down, and there confound their language." The Lord descended in judgment upon the scene. That was their *mistake*. They had ruled God out of their thinking and thereby imagined they had rid themselves of Him, only to find at last that His answer to such folly is swift and lasting judgment. God has never permitted men to realize a lasting social order from which He is excluded, nor will He do so to the end.

II. DIVINE GRACE (11:10-32)

A. ABRAM'S FAMILY TREE (11:10-26)

Moses now came back to the tables of ancestry that had occupied him at such length in the whole section. He was now interested in drawing up Abram's family tree.[3] He went back to Shem and Arphaxad and set forth again the line as far as Peleg and then continued on until he reached Terah. There he paused, for the three sons of that man (Abram, Nahor, and Haran) are men of significance in what follows. He thus traced Abraham's descent from Noah through Seth. It was in Seth's line that God found, at last, the man upon whose daring faith the rest of the Bible is made to hinge.

B. ABRAM'S FAMILY TIES (11:27-32)

Arriving at Terah, Moses paused to look at Abram's family ties. He had two brothers, a niece, and a nephew. His brother Haran's three children were Milcah, Iscah, and Lot. Thus Lot is introduced into the story, a man who stands out, in so many ways, in contrast with Abram. Abram's second brother, Nahor, married their niece Milcah, a common-enough kind of arrangement in those days. Indeed, although the immediate narrative does not say so, when Abram himself married Sarai (11:29) he was actually marrying a half-sister (20:12). The marriage of Abram's brother Nahor is mentioned by Moses because he became the grandfather of Laban and Rebekah, both of whom would figure largely in the history of Abram's grandson Jacob. Thus Moses looks at Abram the *person* and prepares his readers for much that follows by noting some of his hero's immediate family ties. His final note along that line records the fact that Sarai was barren and had no children.

Last of all, as an introduction to the entire story of Abraham (a story so significant in the counsels of God that the Spirit of God devotes 25 percent of the book of Genesis to its details), Moses records Abram's initial venture as a *pilgrim*. Again, the immediate narrative does not record how or when the true and living God revealed Himself to Abram,

3. For the sake of convenience, the family tree of Abraham is carried on here past Abraham to show his connection with other key personages in the book of Genesis.

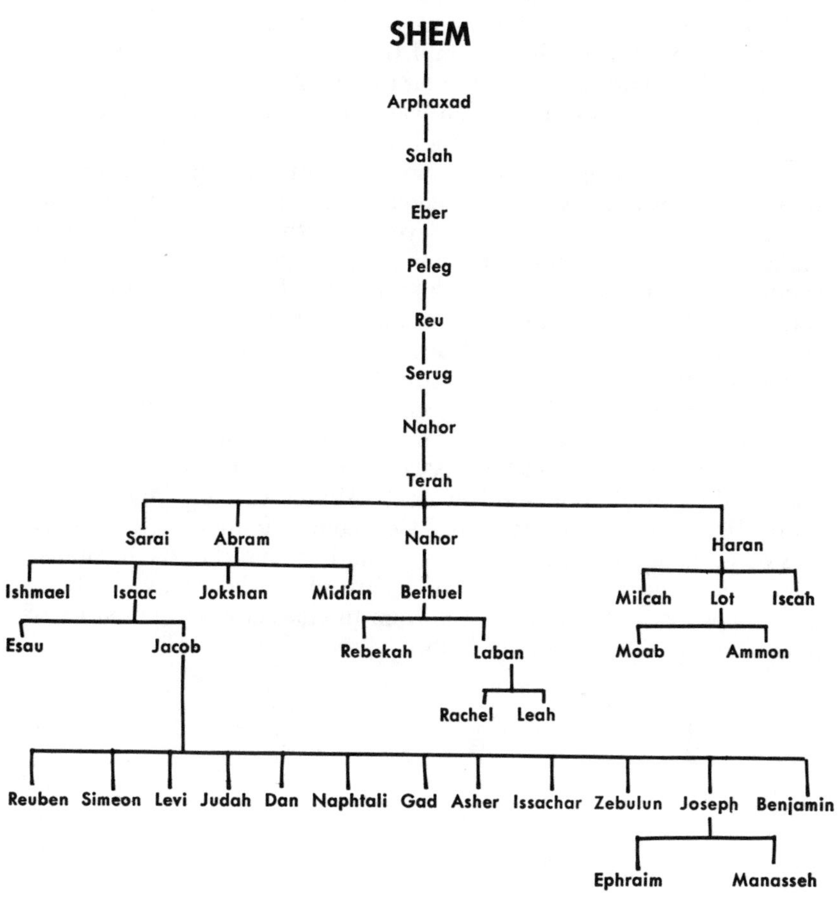
SHEM
Arphaxad
Salah
Eber
Peleg
Reu
Serug
Nahor
Terah
Sarai
Abram
Nahor
Haran
Ishmael
Isaac
Jokshan
Midian
Bethuel
Milcah
Lot
Iscah
Esau
Jacob
Rebekah
Laban
Moab
Ammon
Rachel
Leah
Reuben
Simeon
Levi
Judah
Dan
Naphtali
Gad
Asher
Issachar
Zebulun
Joseph
Benjamin
Ephraim
Manasseh

the pagan idolator of Ur. But evidently He did, because in response to that revelation not only Abram but also Terah his father, Sarai his wife, and Lot his nephew all took the *first step*. Together they left Ur of the Chaldees migrating northward until they came to Haran. Evidently, too, God's initial revelation of Himself to Abram was of such a powerful and convincing nature that Terah was not only persuaded to join the pilgrimage but actually took the lead.

Ur of the Chaldees where Abram lived was an important city of Babylonia. It was a city of luxury and attainment, and a center of moon worship. The pilgrim family journeyed until they came to the city of Haran, and there the sojourners made their *first stop*. Haran was a frontier town of the Babylonian Empire and, like Ur of the Chaldees, was devoted to the worship of the moon god. There the whole pilgrimage bogged down and, it would seem, remained inert and inactive for about twenty-five years until the death of Terah. After all, the old nature, as represented by Terah, can make only token responses to divine things. Abram greatly erred in not fully obeying God (12:1) and in allowing the world and the flesh to insert themselves between him and the divine call. But God is patient. Abram was very young in the faith. He had much to learn, and God could afford to wait. So the wasted years slipped by until, at last, upon the removal of the hindrance to further progress by the death of Terah, Abram began to take those giant steps forward that lifted him from the darkness and obscurity of paganism into the spotlight of faith.

PART TWO

The Beginnings of the Hebrew Race

Patriarchal History

(12:1–50:26)

Chapter 5

THE PROGENITOR: ABRAHAM

(12:1–25:18)

I. The Path of Faith (12:1-20)
   A. Abram Believing (12:1-9)
      1. Finding the Path of Faith (12:1-4)
      2. Following the Path of Faith (12:5-8)
      3. Forsaking the Path of Faith (12:9)
   B. Abram Backsliding (12:10-20)
      1. Famine (12:10)
      2. Foreboding (12:11-12)
      3. Falsehood (12:13)
      4. Frustration (12:14-15)
      5. Flattery (12:16)
      6. Failure (12:17-20)

II. The Price of Faith (13:1-18)
   A. The Marks of a Spiritual Man (13:1-4)
      1. Separation (13:1)
      2. Sanctification (13:2-3)
      3. Sacrifice (13:4)
   B. The Mind of a Spiritual Man (13:5-9)
      1. Worrying Circumstances (13:5-6)
      2. Wicked Neighbors (13:7)
      3. Weaker Brethren (13:8-9)
   C. The Moves of a Spiritual Man (13:10-18)
      1. Restrained by God (13:10-13)
      2. Reassured by God (13:14-16)
      3. Regulated by God (13:17-18)

III. THE POWER OF FAITH (14:1-24)
 A. The Desperate Battle (14:1-11)
  1. The Coalitions (14:1-2)
  2. The Conflict (14:3-9)
  3. The Collapse (14:10-11)
 B. The Deluded Brother (14:12)
 C. The Dynamic Believer (14:13-24)
  1. The Weakness of the Flesh (14:13)
  2. The Wisdom of the World (14:14-16)
  3. The Wiles of the Devil (14:17-24)

IV. THE PLEDGE OF FAITH (15:1-21)
 A. The Building of Abram's Family (15:1-7)
  1. The Word of God's Power (15:1-4)
  2. The Witness to God's Power (15:5-6)
  3. The Working of God's Power (15:7)
 B. The Basis of Abram's Faith (15:8-12)
  1. Calvary Shadowed: He Apprehends Its Mystery (15:8-10)
  2. Calvary Shared: He Apprehends Its Misery (15:11-12)
 C. The Brightness of Abram's Future (15:13-21)
  1. The Specific Time Involved (15:13-16)
  2. The Specific Territory Involved (15:17-21)

V. THE PAWNING OF FAITH (16:1-16)
 A. The Test of the Silence of God (16:1-6)
  1. Abram's Double Mind (16:1-4)
  2. Sarai's Deceitful Heart (16:5-6)
  3. Hagar's Defiant Will (16:6)
 B. The Truth of the Sovereignty of God (16:7-16)
  1. The Revelation to Hagar (16:7-12)
  2. The Response by Hagar (16:13-16)

VI. THE POTENTIAL OF FAITH (17:1-27)
 A. How the Covenant Was Received (17:1-16)
  1. In Absolute Subjection (17:1-3)
  2. In Absolute Silence (17:4-16)
 B. How the Covenant Was Believed (17:17-27)
  1. The Laughter of Faith (17:17)
  2. The Logic of Faith (17:18-22)
  3. The Life of Faith (17:23-27)

VII. THE PRAYER OF FAITH (18:1-33)
 A. The Practical Man (18:1-8)
  1. His Haste (18:1-2)
  2. His Hospitality (18:3-8)
 B. The Privileged Man (18:9-15)
  1. The Promise (18:9-10)
  2. The Problem (18:11-15)

- C. The Proved Man (18:16-22)
  1. Prospective Greatness (18:16-18)
  2. Personal Greatness (18:19)
  3. Positional Greatness (18:20-22)
- D. The Praying Man (18:23-33)
  1. Abraham's Attitude (18:23*a*)
  2. Abraham's Argument (18:23*b*-32)
  3. Abraham's Assurance (18:33)

VIII. THE POSITION OF FAITH (19:1-38)
- A. The Unholy Morality of Sodom (19:1-11)
  1. A Prevalent Thing (19:1-3)
  2. A Polluted Thing (19:4-5)
  3. A Persistent Thing (19:6-9*a*)
  4. A Pugnacious Thing (19:9*b*)
  5. A Punishable Thing (19:10-11)
- B. The Unholy Mentality of Sodom (19:12-38)
  1. Lot's Faith Corroded (19:12-26)
  2. Lot's Family Corrupted (19:27-38)

IX. THE PERILS OF FAITH (20:1-18)
- A. The Moving Pilgrim (20:1-2)
- B. The Miserable Prophet (20:3-16)
  1. Not Readily Recognizable as a Prophet (20:3-7)
  2. Not Really Regarded as a Prophet (20:8-13)
  3. Not Rightly Received as a Prophet (20:14-16)
- C. The Ministering Priest (20:17-18)
  1. The Scope of His Ministry (20:17*a*)
  2. The Success of His Ministry (20:17*b*)
  3. The Significance of His Ministry (20:18)

X. THE PRIZE OF FAITH (21:1-34)
- A. The Tremendous Miracle of Isaac (21:1-8)
  1. His Birth Forecast (21:1-2)
  2. His Birth Fulfilled (21:3-8)
- B. The Terrible Mockery of Ishmael (21:9)
- C. The Typical Message of Sarah (21:10)
- D. The Tragic Mistake of Abraham (21:11)
- E. The Tender Mercies of God (21:12-13)
  1. His Command (21:12)
  2. His Comfort (21:13)
- F. The Tearful Misery of Hagar (21:14-21)
  1. Cast Out (21:14)
  2. Crushed Down (21:15-16)
  3. Caught Up (21:17-21)

G. The Transparent Motives of Abimelech (21:22-34)
   1. His Plea (21:22-24)
   2. His Pledge (21:25-31)
   3. His Parting (21:32-34)

XI. THE PROOF OF FAITH (22:1-24)
   A. The Sudden Test for Which God Had Prepared Abraham (22:1-2)
   B. The Simple Trust in Which God Had Perfected Abraham (22:3-12)
      1. The Way of the Cross (22:3-5)
      2. The Word of the Cross (22:6-8)
      3. The Work of the Cross (22:9-12)
   C. The Solemn Truth by Which God Had Protected Abraham (22:13-24)

XII. THE PATIENCE OF FAITH (23:1-20)
   A. Abraham's Grief (23:1-6)
      1. His Tears (23:1-2)
      2. His Testimony (23:3-6)
   B. Sarah's Grave (23:7-18)
      1. Abraham's Courtesy (23:7-8)
      2. Abraham's Carefulness (23:8-18)
   C. Ephron's Gift (23:19-20)

XIII. THE PRECAUTIONS OF FAITH (24:1-67)
   A. The Wise Sojourner (24:1-9)
   B. The Wondrous Servant (24:10-28)
   C. The Worldly Sinner (24:29-33)
   D. The Willing Saint (24:34-61)
      1. Rebekah Learning of Isaac
      2. Rebekah Longing for Isaac
      3. Rebekah Looking for Isaac
   E. The Waiting Son (24:62-67)

XIV. THE PARTINGS OF FAITH (25:1-11)
   A. The Fruitful Man (25:1-4)
      1. Abraham's Decision (25:1)
      2. Abraham's Descendants (25:2-4)
   B. The Far-Sighted Man (25:5-6)
      1. The Disposal of His Fortune (25:5)
      2. The Dispersal of His Family (25:6)
   C. The Full Man (25:7-11)
      1. The Measure of Abraham's Days (25:7)
      2. The Manner of Abraham's Death (25:8)
      3. The Matter of Abraham's Desires (25:9-11)

D. The Futile Man (25:12-18)
   1. Ishmael's Family Ties (25:12-15)
   2. Ishmael's Five Triumphs (25:16)
   3. Ishmael's Final Tragedy (25:17-18)

5

THE PROGENITOR: ABRAHAM

I. The Path of Faith (12:1-20)

Abram was seventy-five years of age and had another full century to live. When one thinks of all that has developed for mankind as a result of the hundred-year period that now opened in Abram's life, it has to be marked down as one of the most significant centuries in all history.

He had already done very well for himself. He was successful in business, happily married to an outstandingly good-looking woman, well established in the affections of his domestics and servants, and with a lineage and pedigree that could be traced right back to Adam. But rich as he was, respected and religious as he was, when the story of Abram opens, he was a poor lost sinner hurrying on to a lost eternity. The real record of Abram's life begins with the story of his personal encounter with the living God, hinted at in Genesis 11, but now chronicled in full. So important were the results of that encounter that twelve chapters of Genesis are devoted to the development of Abraham's spiritual pilgrimage.

A. Abram Believing (12:1-9)

The story of Abram's believing begins, of course, with God. The initiative was all His. Unregenerate man is so wedded to his idols that the initiative must begin with God; even an unregenerate man like Abram, with a magnificent pedigree numbering in its names ancestors of great spiritual renown—a Seth, an Enoch, a Noah, a Shem. Most people collect the articles of their faith the same way they collect the articles of their furniture—a few items here, an item or two there; suited to their likes, designed to make them as comfortable as possible in this world of sin. The Word of God must come in power to break the hold of unregenerate belief.

1. Finding the Path of Faith (12:1-4)

There were two movements in Abram's enlightenment. There was a revelation and a response, a statement of faith and a step of faith. It began with *a statement of faith* (12:1-3). "Now the Lord had said unto Abram, Get thee out of thy country, and from thy kindred, and from thy father's house, unto a land that I will shew thee." The Word of God broke through into the darkness and deadness of Abram's soul as God spoke to him about a new place and a new people. Abram must begin a pilgrimage to another land. Of course, in the immediate context of history, that new land was Canaan, but Abram's enlightenment went far beyond an earthly country. Hebrews 11 tells us that he went out looking for a city that hath foundations, whose builder and architect is God. Abram's eyes were lifted heavenward from the very start. He would indeed find his place in the earthly country that formed the material focus of his vision, but his ultimate faith and hope came to rest in heaven itself. The spiritual was the reality behind the material.

Thus Abram's pilgrimage began where ours begins, with a vision of another country, a better country, a home forever blessed as the dwelling place of God. God speaks, we believe, faith dawns, life begins.

The statement of faith was followed by *a step of faith* (12:4). "So Abram departed, as the LORD had spoken unto him; and Lot went with him: and Abram was seventy and five years old when he departed out of Haran." The original vision resulted in Abram, his father, and his family leaving Ur. But it was only partial obedience, for Abram was told to give up both natural and national ties. There was to be a complete break with the past. Partial obedience resulted in the loss of further progress, for the whole venture ground to a halt before it had progressed very far. It was not until the death of Terah that the true pilgrimage began; but at least a step had been taken, a faltering step perhaps, but a step. Abram had found the path of faith. With many a stumble and fall, with moments of triumph, with moments of defeat, with mountaintop experiences and with dark times in the valley, with stops and starts, one moment filled with confidence, the next covered with confusion, Abraham set out to live life in a new dimension. No longer sight, but faith!

2. FOLLOWING THE PATH OF FAITH (12:5-8)

We see *Abram witnessing* (12:5). "And Abram took Sarai his wife, and Lot his brother's son, and all their substance that they had gathered, and the souls that they had gotten in Haran; and they went forth to go into the land of Canaan; and into the land of Canaan they came." Abram's decision to make a bold move for God had an immediate impact upon his family. No doubt there were the usual skeptics among his acquaintances, who assured him he was a fool to give up his brilliant prospects in Chaldea to go looking for myths. But Abram had counted the cost.

Years ago an English gentleman decided he would like to have a more bold and positive witness for Christ. He was a traveling man and spent much of his time on trains and in railway stations. He took one of his suitcases and painted on it in bold letters: "A fool for Christ's sake." He would stand the suitcase down beside him wherever he was. Invariably he attracted a curious or critical crowd. Once he had his audience, he would turn his suitcase around. On the other side he had lettered the words: "Whose fool are you?" Abram was quite willing to be a fool for Christ's sake.

His family, his servants, those who knew him best, those who knew him to be no fool, immediately threw in their lot with him. He had made his impact for a new life of faith. He had won some souls. There was a ring of unquestionable genuineness about the gold coin of Abram's faith. Others decided to bank where Abram banked. They dared their all on God as well.

Next we see *Abram walking* (12:6*a*). "And Abram passed through the land unto the place of Sichem, unto the plain of Moreh." He was still in the lowlands of faith, but he was making progress. People saw him moving forward in his new life. He was taking one step at a time. He was beginning where every believer begins; walking in the light he had and waiting for new light to be given. There is no other way to grow in grace and to increase in the knowledge of God.

Then we see *Abram waiting* (12:6*b*-7). "And the Canaanite was then in the land. And the LORD appeared unto Abram, and said, Unto thy seed will I give this land: and there builded he an altar unto the LORD, who appeared unto him." The Canaanite was a race corrupt beyond description, and cursed and condemned by God. We can picture Abram looking around the land into which he had come, seeing all the choice places in the grip of the ungodly, and saying to himself, "Well! I didn't expect this." But he did not rely on his own reasoning or his own resources as he faced the situation. He did not say, as Solomon said, "The best thing to do is make marital alliances with these Canaanites." He did not say, "I think I'll start buying up property here and gradually purchase the land."[1] He waited for God to speak and when He did, he worshiped, content to leave all details in higher hands.

Many a young believer finds disappointment awaiting him at the outset of his new life in Christ. Somebody lets him down, persecution arises. He discovers the old nature is very much alive in his experience or that other Christians have faults. God allows disappointment to occur on the threshold of the new life so that we can learn the principles of the life of faith and emerge stronger for the experience.

Next we see *Abram worshiping* (12:8). "And he removed from thence unto a mountain on the east of Bethel, and pitched his tent, having Bethel on the west, and Hai on the east: and there he builded an altar unto the LORD, and called upon the name of the LORD." He had now reached one of the high plateaus of his spiritual experience, he had planted his feet on higher ground, he was dwelling in what Paul would

1. Thus too Lord Rothschild. When asked why, as an ardent Zionist, he did not use his vast wealth to purchase Palestine for the Jews he replied, "Why should I? We already have the title deeds."

call "the heavenlies" and, above all, he was worshiping. His spiritual pilgrimage did not end on that high note, but whose does? Having reached a high point in his pilgrimage, Abraham found it impossible to stay there. He came down from the mount and began to move away from those highlands of faith.

3. FORSAKING THE PATH OF FAITH (12:9)

"And Abram journeyed, going on still toward the south." He had been encamped between Bethel and Hai—a most significant place. Bethel means "the house of God"; Hai means "a heap of ruins." As someone has quaintly said, God offers His house to those who have lost their own. With the house of God for his dwelling and a heap of ruins nearby, to remind him what the world was really like, Abram nevertheless drifted away. The tug and the lure of Egypt drew him away from Bethel, the house of God.

B. ABRAM BACKSLIDING (12:10-20)

Forsaking the path of faith, for whatever reason, always brings its own complications. A whole series of events now followed in Abram's experience, each one of which stemmed from his lack of trust in God. First there was a *famine* (12:10). There were two things in Canaan that Abram surely did not expect to find there—the Canaanite and the famine. Both were there to test him. The famine took hold of the land or, at least, came home to Abram personally after his abandonment of Bethel. Moving away from God's house will always produce a famine in the soul's experience.

Next came *foreboding* (12:10-12). Aware of the famine and out of touch with God since leaving Bethel, Abram decided upon an expedient. Egypt looked like a good solution to his problems.[2]

But as soon as Egypt came into the picture, foreboding began to fill his soul. His wife, Sarai, was a most attractive woman. Reasoning like an unsaved man, Abram said, "I know that thou art a fair woman to look upon: therefore it shall come to pass, when the Egyptians shall see thee, that they shall say, This is his wife: and they will kill me, but they will save thee alive." The dark shadow had fallen upon his soul. He was facing in the wrong direction and all before him was dark.

During the dark days of World War II, King George VI would sometimes speak to the British people over the BBC. He did so after Dunkirk. The Allied forces were in complete disarray. Winston Churchill

2. This is the first mention of Egypt in the Bible. It is referred to some six hundred times and, where typology applies, it is always a type of the world. Its significance is given in Revelation 11—it is "the place where our Lord was crucified." Egypt represents all that the world is in its attractiveness to the separated believer. Its wealth, its wisdom, its wickedness, its worship, are all alluring. What *Egypt* was to Abram, the *world* is to us. It is the devil's lair for sinners and his lure for saints. Egypt looked very attractive to Abram as a place where his needs could be supplied. He had forgotten God.

had sought to rally the nation, had organized the Home Guard (a pitiful force made up of the unfit, the aged, and men unable to serve in the regular army), and he had hurled his defiance across the channel. But the Home Guard was a paper army that paraded with broomsticks. The future seemed very dark. Then the king came on the radio and sought to touch the nation's spiritual chords, for George VI of England was a truly saved and godly man. Just behind was Dunkirk, just ahead the Battle of Britain.

Most of what George VI said that day had been forgotten, but one poem he quoted has lived on:

> And I said to the man who stood at the gate of the year:
> "Give me a light, that I may tread safely into the unknown!"
> And he replied: "Go out into the darkness and put your hand into the hand of God.
> That shall be to you better than light and safer than a known way."
> So I went forth, and finding the hand of God, trod gladly into the night.
> And he led me toward the hills and the breaking of day in the lone East.
>
> M. LOUISE HASKINS

That is exactly what God wanted Abram to do, but Abram had taken his hand out of the hand of God. His back was toward the breaking of the day and his face was toward Egypt. No wonder foreboding filled his heart.

Then there was *falsehood* (12:13). "Say, I pray thee, thou art my sister: that it may be well with me for thy sake; and my soul shall live because of thee." What a selfish, despicable request! It's a wonder Sarai ever spoke to him again. There is no knowing how low a saint will sink once he gets out of touch with God. Of course, Abram could justify the statement, because Sarai was his half sister (20:12), but a half truth is a whole lie, and using such sophistry only led him deeper into the morass. All heaven must have wrung its hands as the news of Abram's lie was made known. Yet how often we have sought refuge in similar subterfuge and pretense, if not in outright lies.

Next came *frustration* (12:14-15). The very thing Abram wanted to avoid burst upon him like a storm. Sarai was appropriated for the Pharaoh's harem. Although she was sixty-five years old, she was still a stunning woman to look upon. Poor Abram! He had said to Sarai, "Now look here, Sarai. You carry your years well. You are so good-looking I fear for both of us in Egypt. The fact that we're married will make no difference. Wives can soon be made widows where we're going. Then you'll be abducted into Pharaoh's harem or into the harem of some other lord. Let's make a deal—" How much better it would have been if he had gone into Egypt trusting in the Lord. How much better still it would have been if he had not gone to Egypt at all.

Then came *flattery* (12:16). Pharaoh, we read, "entreated Abram well for her sake: and he had sheep, and oxen, and he asses, and menservants, and maidservants, and she asses, and camels." That sudden accession of wealth might have delighted Lot. "I say, Uncle Abram, here comes another flock of sheep. And, wow! You should see the herd of milk-white cattle. And come and look at these gorgeous women slaves!" But with each such exclamation poor Abram would simply groan afresh. He had lost Sarai, he had denied the relationship, he had played the fool. He had lost Sarai. Riches acquired at such a price bore a very high price tag indeed. Yet there is many a child of God willing to get rich on such terms—at the price of denying the Lord, at the price of spiritual bankruptcy and ruin. Such gain is loss. Wealth acquired on such terms is tainted at its source.

Last of all there was *failure* (12:17-20). God intended Abram to be a blessing—"In thee shall all families of the earth be blessed," He had said. Here was Abram's first contact with a world power and a great ruler, but instead of being a blessing he was a curse. "And the LORD plagued Pharaoh and his house with great plagues because of Sarai, Abram's wife."

It could not last. Before long Abram was arrested, hauled before Pharaoh, and the shameful truth dragged out. "What is this thou hast done unto me? Why didst thou not tell me that she was thy wife? Why saidst thou, She is my sister?" To all of his searing questions Abram could answer nothing. He stood there tongue-tied and embarrassed in the presence of the indignant king. What a tremendous opportunity for personal witness to the living God he had lost because he had compromised the truth.

Then came Pharaoh's final word, his curt, contemptuous dismissal of Abram as he handed Sarai back to her husband. "Take her, and go thy way." In all, Pharaoh the pagan cut a finer figure than Abram the believer. Indeed, one can almost hear Pharaoh turn to his courtiers as Abram and Sarai slunk away down the audience chamber, "Well! If that's an example of a believer, may I never meet another!"

How important it is that we guard our testimony well, that we never by word or deed or implication so behave that we misrepresent our Lord to the world.

II. THE PRICE OF FAITH (13:1-18)

The Egyptian episode was over and Abram, a sadder and a wiser man, crossed into the promised land for the second time. No doubt he promised himself he would never again step out of the will of God. A saved man when he drifted into Egypt, he now emerged a spiritual man.

A. THE MARKS OF A SPIRITUAL MAN (13:1-4)

Three things characterized the spiritual man; the first was *separation.*

"And Abram went up out of Egypt, he, and his wife, and all that he had, and Lot went with him, into the south" (13:1). The biblical truth of separation from the world has fallen on hard times, perhaps as a reaction against isolationism. True biblical separation is not isolation, but insulation. It is living *in* the world as a believer without being *of* the world. Like a live wire, insulated against all that would short-circuit its effectiveness, the believer makes contact at one end with the source of power and at the other end with the evident need.

This world is the enemy of God. It has shown its hatred in the murder of His Son. Archimedes said he could move the world, were he given a long enough lever and a point far enough out in space for a fulcrum. Just so, the believer can lift the world, but only if he remains separate from it. A man cannot lift a barrel by standing inside it. The first mark, then, of true spirituality is biblical separation from the world.[3]

The second mark of a spiritual man is *sanctification.* Having referred to Abram's worldly wealth, the record continues: "He went on his journeys from the south even to Bethel, unto the place where his tent had been at the beginning, between Bethel and Hai" (13:2-3). Separation and sanctification are two sides of the same coin. Sanctification is not so much "separation *from*" as it is "separation *to*." It is being set apart for God. Abram, having fallen so badly in Egypt, now puts as much distance as possible between himself and the world.

Years ago a woman wanted a new coachman. She advertised and before long had three applicants, to each of whom she put the same question. "You know that steep hill just outside town and that narrow spot where the road drops away to a gully? How close could you drive my coach to the edge without losing your nerve?" The first man said, "Madam, if the wheels of the coach came within six inches of the edge I would feel quite safe." The second coachman said, "Madam, I reckon even if one of the wheels went clean over the edge I could hold those horses and recover the coach without harm." It was the third coachman who secured the job. "Madam," he said, "I would keep that coach as far away from that gully as I possibly could." That is what sanctification is all about. It is not trying to get as close to the world as possible without losing one's testimony, it is keeping as far away from it as we can by keeping close to Christ.

Abram had skirted the world once. Now he put distance between himself and Egypt by getting back to Bethel, the house of God, and re-

3. The old monks had the mistaken idea that separation from the world meant retiring into a monastery. Paul expressed the true concept of separation when he told the Colossian believers they were "in Christ at Colossae." The believer lives in two locations. He lives in a heavenly sphere (he is "in Christ"), and he lives in an earthly sphere (he is "at Colossae"). The two must be kept in balance. We can be so taken up with being "in Christ" that we forget we are in a desperately needy world. Or we can be so taken up with being "at Colossae" we forget our need for a daily walk with God. True separation from the world involves keeping the "in Christ" dimension in perfect balance with the "at Colossae" dimension.

establishing his pilgrim character. He pitched his tent at Bethel and restored fellowship with God.

The third mark of a spiritual man is *sacrifice*. Abram came "unto the place of the altar, which he had made there at the first: and there Abram called on the name of the LORD" (13:4). The tent symbolized Abram's attitude toward *this* world. He was a pilgrim and a stranger, he would not put his roots down here, he would be ready to move at a moment's notice in the will and at the leading of God. His altar symbolized his attitude toward the *next* world. He was ready for any sacrifice; he would offer up anything demanded of him by God. So he called on the name of the Lord, making up his mind that henceforth the lines of communication heavenward would be kept open.

With a wife and three teenagers and one telephone in the house, more often than not I used to get a busy signal when calling home. We all know what it is like to try and try to get through, and every time to get the busy tone. How often God gets the busy signal in our lives. Abram determined that henceforth he would keep the lines open so that he could hear God's voice. His family altar was a signal to the Lord that he was willing to hear and do what the Lord had to say.

These, then, are the marks of a spiritual man—separation, sanctification, and sacrifice. They are the things that marked Abram in the testing time ahead.

B. THE MIND OF A SPIRITUAL MAN (13:5-9)

How does a spiritual man think? What is his attitude toward life's problems and perplexities? The spiritual man's approach to life is quite different from that of the carnal man. Lot the carnal man and Abram the spiritual man stand in stark contrast with one another in the events recorded next.

1. WORRYING CIRCUMSTANCES (13:5-6)

Lot and Abram each had great flocks and herds, so many that there was not enough available pastureland for both. It would have been natural for Abram to say to Lot, "Now look here, Lot, this land belongs to me. God has promised it to me, not to you. You'll simply have to move on." But what did Abram do? He did *nothing*. That was his first reaction to worrying circumstances. He had learned all too well what happens when a child of God takes matters into his own hands.

Some number of years ago my father was greatly exercised about selling his business and going into full-time service for the Lord. There were some worrying circumstances connected with the proposed change. He asked Stephen Olford for advice. Having listened to the story and weighed the issues, Stephen said: "Len, my advice is simply this—if you don't know what to do, don't do it!"

Abram, confronted with worrying circumstances, circumstances that seemed to be clamoring for immediate action, simply waited. He was assured that God would soon make his way clear. So, he did nothing.

2. WICKED NEIGHBORS (13:7)

The situation became worse. To the problem of worrying circumstances was added the problem of wicked neighbors. "And there was strife between the herdsmen of Abram's cattle and the herdsmen of Lot's cattle: and the Canaanite and the Perizzite dwelled then in the land." It was bad enough for brethren to disagree, but to fall out, especially over material things, in the presence of the ungodly was worse. Nothing will hinder the testimony more quickly, which is why Paul warns, "Do all things without murmurings and disputings: that ye may be blameless and harmless, the sons of God, without rebuke, in the midst of a crooked and perverse nation" (Philippians 2:14).

3. WEAKER BRETHREN (13:8-9)

Added to Abram's problems was the presence of a weaker brother, for Lot simply did not have Abram's spiritual stature. It was the spiritual man who made the first move. With the memory of his altar in mind, Abram did the spiritual and sacrificial thing; he surrendered his personal rights.

He dealt with Lot with *spiritual directness*. "Let there be no strife, I pray thee, between me and thee." What condescension. He named himself first as though he were the cause of all the trouble. He came directly to the point with no beating about the bush and named the problem for what it was—strife. "Lot, this squabbling in front of unsaved neighbors over temporal, earthly things has to stop. And I'm prepared to take any steps necessary to stop it." That is the way a spiritual man thinks.

He dealt with Lot with *spiritual discernment*. "Let there be no strife . . . for we be brethren." "Look here, Lot," he said. "The things that unite us are far more important than the things that divide us." Two Christian ladies had to share the same office. One always wanted the window open; the other wanted it closed. "I feel I am going to suffocate in here!" said the one. "I'm going to catch my death of cold!" retorted the other. Someone came up with a suggestion. "Why don't you keep the window closed until one of you dies of suffocation and then keep it open until the other dies of pneumonia," he said. "Then we'll have some peace around here!" We smile at the story, but how true it is to life. How paltry are most of the things that divide us. Those two Christians were bitterly divided over a window. Yet, all the time, they were united in Christ. Said spiritually-minded Abram, "We be *brethren*." Let us never lose sight of that.

He then treated Lot with *spiritual dignity* (13:9). "My dear young brother, you choose," he said. "I'll take what you leave." With that spirit of sacrifice, Abram put aside his rights. Socially he was Lot's senior and had the prior claim, sovereignly he was by far the stronger of the two characters, spiritually he was the sole heir and beneficiary of the divine promise. But he had been to the altar, he had learned how to sacrifice. Spurgeon said: "It takes more grace than I can tell, to play the second fiddle well." That is exactly what Abram did here. The world might label him a fool for surrendering his rights and his strong position, but God blessed him for it.

C. The Moves of a Spiritual Man (13:10-18)

1. Restrained by God (13:10-13)

Before we enter into the significance of God's restraint, we must digress to see how Lot acted when he was given his opportunity. For if Abram acted with divine restraint, Lot acted with carnal resolve. There were three things that marked Lot's choice.

In the first place, Lot was *weak in his devotions.* He had "flocks and herds and tents," we are told, just like Abram, but Abram had something Lot did not have. Abram had an altar. There is no hint that Lot had any such thing or that he paused to say: "Lord, in this matter of such great importance to me and my family, what would You have me do?" Lot had no quiet time, no devotions, no period of waiting on God. He had no altar. He was weak in his devotions.

He was consequently *worldly in his desires* (13:10). He did not ask: "Is this a good place to raise children?" He asked: "Is this a good place to raise cattle?" He had two reasons for choosing Sodom and the well-watered Jordan valley, a "religious" reason and a real reason. The Jordan valley was "even as the garden of the Lord"—that was his religious reason. It was "like the land of Egypt"—that was his real reason. Lot had enjoyed Egypt. He had not profited at all from the spiritual exercise of Abram as a result of their sojourn in that land.

A man who is weak in his devotions and worldly in his desires will inevitably be *wrong in his decisions* (13:11-13). Lot chose all the plain of Jordan and separated himself from his godly uncle. Before long he had his tent pitched toward Sodom, and the Holy Spirit adds the significant note: "But the men of Sodom were wicked and sinners before the LORD exceedingly." Lot had made the wrong choice. The first question that comes to a soul is, "heaven or hell?" The second question is, "heaven or earth?" Lot had answered the first question when he left Mesopotamia; he answered the second question when he chose Sodom.

But now come back to Abram, the man restrained of God. Saintly old George Mueller used to say that the *stops* as well as the steps of a good man are ordered of the Lord. Abram was wonderfully restrained by God from choosing the Jordan valley. God was about to destroy the cities of the plain in fire and brimstone in one dreadful night of fear and flame. We say, "But Lot did not know that!" That is the very point, for neither did Abram. But God did, and because Abram kept in touch with God he was divinely restrained from making the wrong choice.

2. REASSURED BY GOD (13:14-16)

Abram was not only restrained by God, but he was also reassured by God, first in regard to *his possessions* (13:14-15). We read that "Lot journeyed east." Now we read that the Lord said to Abram: "Lift up now thine eyes, and look from the place where thou art northward, and southward, and eastward, and westward." And eastward. Yes, Abram, down there where the well-watered plains gleam like emeralds in the sun, down there where Lot's flocks and herds and tents can still be seen as specks on the horizon, down there along the reaches of Jordan, down there, toward Sodom—it's yours. "For all the land which thou seest, to thee will I give it, and to thy seed for ever."

Abram had not lost a thing. Those rolling grasslands greedily seized by Lot were still his, every stick and stone. The promises of God were not to be thwarted by the unselfishness of Abram and the materialism of Lot. God's arithmetic is not like ours. According to us if we subtract one from one we have nothing. But, according to God, if we subtract one from one we still have everything. "And everyone that hath forsaken houses, or brethren, or sisters, or father, or mother, or wife, or children, or lands, for my name's sake, shall receive an hundredfold, and shall inherit everlasting life" (Matthew 19:29). That is God's arithmetic.

Then Abram was reassured by God as to *his posterity*. "And I will make thy seed as the dust of the earth." Abram's posterity was centered in one son, only one, but in that son resided the whole Hebrew race. The moves of a spiritual man will always lead to ultimate fruitfulness. That does not necessarily mean that the spiritual man will lead thousands to Christ. He may lead only one, but that one might be a Spurgeon or a D. L. Moody.

Reading the book of Romans changed the life of Martin Luther. Reading Luther's preface to his commentary on Romans transformed the life of John Wesley. Attending a chapel of the Primitive Methodists, one of the groups following the teachings of John Wesley, led to the conversion of C. H. Spurgeon. Spurgeon touched the life of young Henry Morehouse, who in turn transformed the ministry of D. L. Moody. Attending one of Moody's meetings transformed the life of C. T. Studd and six others who became known as the Cambridge Seven. They in turn swept across the universities of England and Scotland, stirring students everywhere to lives of devotion and service for God overseas. That is spiritual posterity. That is the kind of spiritual chain reaction that results when God blesses a man.

3. REGULATED BY GOD (13:17-18)

Finally, Abram was regulated by God. "Arise, walk through the land . . . for I will give it unto thee. Then Abram removed his tent, and came and dwelt in the plain of Mamre, which is in Hebron, and built there an altar unto the LORD." Thus Abram's moves were ordered of the Lord and he moved on in obedience to the known and revealed will of God for his life—a truly spiritual man.

III. THE POWER OF FAITH (14:1-24)

There are ten kings in chapter 14, and only one of them is a king of righteousness. He does not appear until the very end. The chapter is a cameo of all of history with its kings and its conflicts and at last, at the end of it all, the coming of God's true and righteous King.

It records the first battle in the Bible, indeed in all of recorded history. It is an important chapter because it mentions for the first time the priest, the king, war, the bread and wine, and tithes. The first mention of the priest, for instance, brings into sharp focus God's thinking about priesthood. God's ideal priest is not a ritual priest after the order of Aaron, but a royal priest after the order of Melchizedek. Similarly the first mention of a king shows that God's ideal king is not a warrior king like Chedorlaomar, nor a wicked king like Bera, king of Sodom, nor yet a wise king like Amraphel of Shinar. God's ideal king is a worshiping king like Melchizedek.

This much-neglected portion of Scripture is freighted down with items of consummate interest to the child of God. Take its reference to war. Since it is the first mention of war in the Bible, we might well expect it to say something regarding the believer's attitude toward it. Abram was a separated believer, but he was not a secluded believer. He lived neither in a monastery nor an ivory tower. He was no spiritual recluse, hiding his face in the sand so as not to confront reality. He was a practical, dynamic believer in daily touch both with the living God and the facts of life. His separation from the world did not lead him into isolationism. Whereas he detested Sodom and all it stood for, and whereas he stayed aloof from Sodom's pleasures, politics, principles, prosperity, and even its people, he did not for one moment pretend that Sodom did not exist. It existed, and his dear, weak, stumbling, backsliding nephew Lot was down there. For Lot's sake, Abram was willing to get involved. But only at the right time and in the right way. That is the controlling thought behind the chapter.

In the church in which I was raised there was a brother who, during the Second World War, took his stand as a conscientious objector. He was brought before the tribunal and asked by the judge whether he would do anything at all to help the war effort. He refused and when asked his reason replied, "My kingdom is not of this world." The judge looked at him with a jaundiced eye. He had heard that one before. "Very well, young man," said the judge. *"You won't need a ration card!"* The young brother's "separation" was really isolation, and the shrewd judge saw through in a flash. Abram was not like that.

A. THE DESPERATE BATTLE (14:1-11)

The news kept filtering through to Abram. It was of prime importance to him, for he had vast holdings in liquid assets, the kind of assets an invading army likes to plunder. He was rich in cattle and silver and gold. Abram paid careful attention to the news.

First there was an insurrection in the valley. The five cities of the plain announced their intention of no longer paying tribute to the Elamites. Then came news of a great coalition of the kings of the east, followed soon after by further news that a great army was on the march westward. Next came tidings that the cities of the plain had formed a mutual assistance pact; they were fortifying their outposts, mobilizing their reserves, and turning their factories over to arms production. There were tidings out of the east and out of the north. There were wars and rumors of war. But Abram was where God wanted him to be. He was in the plain of Mamre, dwelling at Hebron, the very name of which means "fellowship." His heart was at rest. There was no more running down to Egypt. He was going to stand still and see the salvation of God.

We need to bring the battle into focus. First the narrative describes *the coalitions* (14:1-2). The battle is generally referred to as the battle of four kings against five. The participants are all carefully named. There were four kings of the east and five kings of the plain.

In ancient times there was a well-used highway that ran down from Damascus through Gilead and Bashan along the east side of the Jordan as far as Sodom and Gomorrah. At that point it was intersected by a main caravan route running east from the Mediterranean to Mesopotamia. The conjunction of those two important highways was no doubt what gave Sodom its strategic importance. Together with its sister cities, Sodom controlled the valley and lines of communication north and south, east and west.

The eastern coalition seems to have been a powerful one. No doubt the news that it was now moving westward caused quite a stir in Sodom, and the five kings of the plain joined together in an unholy alliance. It all seems so remarkably up-to-date. There was no thought of God, no repentance, no prayer, no spiritual awakening, just the formation of alliances and the outfitting of armies. The great expansionist move of the eastern powers was met by sudden solidarity in the west. And, in the background of it all, were two believers, one a backslidden believer down there in Sodom worrying himself sick over his family and his fortune; the other a separated believer watching and praying and wondering when and where and why that international upheaval would finally affect him.

The narrative next describes *the conflict* (14:3-9). "Twelve years," we read, "they served Chedorlaomar and in the thirteenth year they rebelled." Here again the law of first mention underlines an item of interest, for that is the first time those two numbers occur in Scripture.

Significantly, the number twelve is said to stand for government in the Bible and the number thirteen for rebellion and apostasy. There follows a list of the victories gained by the invading army from the east. It is an impressive list. Nation after nation went down like corn before the scythe. Some of those nations were peopled by giants, but down they went. The Horites, for example, lived in the inaccessible, virtually impregnable fortresses and rock cities of Mount Seir, but down they went. All the way down the eastern reaches of the Jordan they came, those conquering kings and then, says the Scripture, "they returned."

Excitement must have been high in the cities of the plain. They doubtless rang the bells over the sudden and unexpected withdrawal of the foe. Back they went to their southernmost base on the edge of the wilderness of El-paran. Hope ran high; perhaps they were satisfied with their spoils and would now return, laden with their plunder, to the east.

Such hopes were vain. Soon the invading armies were on the march again, coming down the west bank of the Jordan, and the hour of judgment was approaching fast. Those invaders were God's scourge, the whip in His hand with which to chastise the filthy cities of the plain, in the hope that perhaps they would repent and thus be spared their ultimate doom. But Sodom and Gomorrah had no thought for repentance. Their only thought was to look to their alliance.

Thus the narrative hurries on to tell of *the collapse* (14:10-11). The five kings of Jordan thought they had a chance. We can picture them in the war office, gathered around a map of the Fertile Crescent. It marked the flow of the Tigris and Euphrates rivers, the chief trade routes into Canaan, the Sea of Galilee, the Jordan, the Dead Sea, the coastline of the Mediterranean, the elevations and depressions, and locations of friendly, hostile, and neutral tribes. Another map showed details of the Vale of Siddim, the five cities, the bitumen pits, the trenches, and the deployment of the troops. The five kings stared at the maps. "My lords," the king of Sodom might have said, "What do you think? Do we stand a chance?"

One of the generals would have spoken. "Your majesties, I believe we do. There are six things in our favor. First, there is logistics. The enemy's supply lines are extended all the way from here to the Euphrates. Moreover, their troops are heavy with plunder, and that makes for unstable and double-minded troops. Then there are five of us and only four of them so we have the advantage of numbers. Fourth, we are fighting from fortified positions and their troops will be exposed. In addition our men are fighting for family, for home, for dear life. That alone should put backbone into them. Last of all, we know the terrain and the enemy doesn't. We can make the slime pits fight for us; with luck we'll get their infantry and cavalry bogged down there. I don't see how we can lose."

So, for one reason or another, the battle was joined. But contrary to all expectations, the defenses collapsed and the kings of the plain and those lucky enough to escape the disaster were soon in full flight. "And the vale of Siddim was full of slime pits; and the kings of Sodom and Gomorrah fled, and fell there; and they that remained fled to the mountain." There seems to be a poetic justice in it all. Sodom and Gomorrah were vile and filthy beyond words. Their sin was a stench in the nostrils of God. It was fitting that their kings should be hauled off to captivity all besmirched and bedaubed with slime. Filthy they were within, filthy they were without, a spectacle to men and angels, mute evidence that God is not mocked.

B. The Deluded Brother (14:12)

The record is brief and unvarnished. "And they took Lot, Abram's brother's son, who dwelt in Sodom, and his goods, and departed." The last time we saw Lot he was dwelling in the cities of the plain and pitching his tent toward Sodom. Now he dwelt in Sodom. One step leads to another. For a while he kept up the pretense of being a pilgrim, but soon the attractions of the capital proved too great for him and he made his home in the filthiest city on the face of the earth. He looked toward Sodom—he pitched his tent toward Sodom—he dwelt in Sodom. Sodom, a treacherous quicksand for the soul, soon sucked Lot in. Nor could all of Abram's noble efforts free him from the fatal fascination of that vile place. For though Abram later did all a fellow believer could to rescue his brother, Lot went right back into the mire. Perhaps he was driven there by the nagging of his wife. Perhaps it was the worldly needs of his children that snared him. Perhaps it was simply the desire to make more money. Perhaps the poor fellow still thought he could be an influence for God. We are not told. All we know is the deluded man went back.

C. The Dynamic Believer (14:13-24)

After a brief and passing look at Lot, the narrative returns to Abram. We see him winning a threefold victory.

1. The Weakness of the Flesh (14:13)

"And there came one that had escaped, and told Abram the Hebrew; for he dwelt in the plain of Mamre." Abram could easily have shrugged his shoulders and said, "Well, it serves Lot right! He should have kept clear of Sodom. He should never have moved out of the fellowship of the Lord's people. Besides, what is all this to do with me? There's nothing I can do about it. I am a Hebrew; I'm not supposed to become entangled in the affairs of this world. I am to be separated from the world. Even with the best of intentions, what can I do for Lot now? If the five kings of the plain with all their armaments and troop concentrations could not conquer the kings of the east, it's for sure I can't. Besides, I'm a farmer, not a fighter. God has not called me to be a soldier but a saint. I don't know anything about war." The weakness of the flesh could have suggested a thousand reasons why Abram should not become involved. But he was a dynamic believer, and he won his battle with the weakness of the flesh.

The reasons Abram might have invented we can concoct as well. Faced with a dying world, with teeming millions who have never so much as heard John 3:16, what are we willing to do? Faced with the need of weaker brothers and sisters in Christ being carried away by many hurtful and hateful lusts, what should we do? We have our own families and our business to attend to. We have responsibilities at home.

2. The Wisdom of the World (14:14-16)

The wisdom of the world would have dictated caution, would have suggested he open negotiations with the victorious kings, would have suggested sending Eliezer of Damascus on a swift camel with a letter for Amraphel and Arioch and Chedorlaomar and Tidal, king of nations. "My lords: You have amongst your captives a prisoner by the name of Lot. It is doubtless your intention to sell him and his family into slavery in Mesopotamia. May I suggest a ransom?" The world would have whispered to Abram, "Money talks. You only need to speak the language."

But Abram would have nothing to do with compromise. He refused to hide behind either platitudes or pacifism when the time came to get involved. The time for debate was over, he must act, act in the will of God and act at once. And so he did—swiftly, sensibly, and successfully. First he mobilized his own people, those "born in his house," all 318 of them. They were people brought up in the family of God and able and willing to respond in an hour of need. They were ready for instant action. They were skilled in the use of the sword. Within the hour they were marching posthaste northward. Then, as one born to battle, Abram divided his small company, took advantage of the cover of night, drove in the enemy's sentries, smote with all his might, and then pursued the shaken and fleeing foe. That incredible victory can be explained only in terms of God. God was with him all the way. Lot and his family were rescued with many other captives and a vast amount of spoil.

3. The Wiles of the Devil (14:17-24)

The concluding verses of the chapter are full of items of the greatest interest to the believer. First we have Abram's *significant meeting with the king of Salem* (14:17-20). In a few minutes a particularly seductive form of temptation was to be put before Abram. In His care and concern for Abram's soul, God saw to it that Abram was prepared. Before the king of Sodom came, the king of Salem came.

The king of Salem was Melchizedek, a priest-king and one of the great types of the Lord Jesus in the Old Testament. Some have suggested he was the Lord Jesus in actual fact. Others have speculated that he was Shem, who was possibly still alive at that time. We are not told who he was in person. His introduction into the narrative is completely historical, but it is also highly typical. Melchizedek set before Abram the bread and the wine—symbols indeed of the body and blood of the Lord Jesus one day to be offered on Calvary's cross. Thus, in type and shadow and in significant symbol Abram anticipated Calvary. Just as we look back to the cross in those emblems, so Abram looked forward to it.

His response was immediate and spiritual. He gave tithes to Melchizedek, the priest-king before whom he stood. Giving is an act of worship, a rightful response to a contemplation of Calvary. Then Abram was refreshed in his relationship with God, just as we frequently are when we take our place in worship at the Lord's table. In an attitude of worship and humble thanksgiving, Abram received a blessing from the priest-king and learned a new name for God: "the most high God, the possessor of heaven and earth." Thus Abram was fortified for the temptation now to spring upon him in all its subtle strength.

Having had his significant meeting with the king of Salem, Abram now had a *sinister meeting with the king of Sodom* (14:21-24). If the king of Salem typified Christ, the king of Sodom typified Satan. The morrow after a great victory is always a time of spiritual peril for a believer. Satan will lose no time in mounting his counterattack. Immediately after His baptism the Lord Jesus was driven into the wilderness for His temptation at the hands of Satan.

The temptation of Abram was subtle. "The king of Sodom said unto Abram, Give me the persons, and take the goods to thyself." The king of Sodom wanted the *souls,* Abram could have the spoils! The sheer audacity of the fellow takes one's breath away. Abram had redeemed both people and property, a fact that the king of Sodom ignored in a high-handed way. How clever Satan is at getting us to trade souls for spoils. There is many a man in business today, trapped and deluded by the evil one, whom God intended for the mission field.

The testimony of Abram was very simple. "I have lift up mine hand unto the LORD, the most high God, the possessor of heaven and earth, that I will not take from a thread to a shoe latchet, and that I will not take any thing that is thine, lest thou shouldest say, I have made Abram rich." Abram wanted nothing from Sodom or from Sodom's king, and no part in anything tainted with Sodom's name. He had just received a fresh revelation concerning God, and in that revelation he stood firm. He had learned in Egypt what happens when the world enriches a man. He wanted to possess nothing that came from the filthy hands of Sodom's king. What a tremendous stand to take.

There was the dynamic believer, absolutely victorious over the world, the flesh, and the devil, exulting in the remembrance of the Lord and in a new dimension of spiritual enlightenment. And there went Lot—back down to Sodom to be enriched by Sodom's king, to take what Abram refused, no doubt to be promoted and advanced to a seat in Sodom's gate and there to well nigh lose his soul.

IV. THE PLEDGE OF FAITH (15:1-21)

Toward the end of the thirteenth century, Edward I of England commissioned a colony of artists from Italy to coin currency for the English mint. The Florentine artists took sheet gold and silver, divided it up with shears, and hammered the pieces into the proper shapes. But, for all their skill, the workmen could not give each piece an absolutely equal weight. For one thing, the hammered coins had no carved rims around their edges. So it was not long before thieves discovered it was easier for them to clip a sliver or two off the rim of a shilling than it was for them to do an honest day's work. Coin clipping became a profitable enterprise of crime.

Queen Elizabeth tried to improve the nation's coinage, and new methods of minting money were introduced. But that made matters worse, for side by side with the pure, full-value coinage, there circulated the old, clipped, debased, underweight coins. The result was chaos. Every monetary transaction ended up in a squabble over the coins tendered in payment.

The Judiciary cracked down on coin clippers, and at Old Bailey terrible examples were made of convicted coin mutilators. Month after month they were dragged up Holborn Hill and executed publicly. Before public confidence could be restored, however, armies of statesmen and financiers and king's counselors and Parliamentarians were driven to distraction.

The coin of the kingdom of God is the promises of God. John Bunyan saw that. In his famous allegory *The Holy War* he tells how Mansoul, having long been under the power of Diabolus, was at last emancipated by Prince Emmanuel. One of the first acts of the king was to arrest Clip-Promise, the traitor. He was a notorious villain, says Bunyan, "for by his doings much of the king's coin was abused, therefore he was made a public example." Alexander Whyte, in commenting on that phase of the story, said:

> The grace of God is like a bullion mass of purest gold. Moses and David and Isaiah and Hosea and Paul and Peter and John are the inspired artists who have commissioned to take that bullion and out of it to cut and beat and smelt and shape and stamp and superscribe the promises and then to issue the promises as currency in the market of salvation. It is these royal coins, imaged and superscribed in the Royal likeness, that Clip-Promise so mutilated, debased and abused.[4]

Once already God had made Abram a very great promise. That prom-

4. Alexander Whyte, *Bunyan's Characters, Third Series* (London: Oliphant, Anderson, and Ferrier, 1895), pp. 95-105.

ise Abram had believed to the full—no Clip-Promise he! By believing that original great promise, he became a pilgrim and a stranger with his feet firmly set on the straight and narrow way. God was now about to amplify the promise, and once again Abram believed, and became, indeed, "the father of all them that believe." Abram had a wonderful capacity to take God at His Word. Never once did he mutilate, abuse, or debase the promises of God.

A. THE BUILDING OF ABRAM'S FAMILY (15:1-7)

Lot had just departed on his merry way to Sodom, leaving Abram shaking his head and wondering whether all his efforts to rescue and restore his backsliding brother had not been totally in vain. The king of Sodom had left, rubbing his hands over the recovery of all his goods, at no cost to himself and, no doubt, discussing with the secretary of his treasury what particular form of insanity possessed Abram so that he refused his share of the spoil. Melchizedek had gone, leaving Abram with only a memory and a new appreciation of God. Aner and Eschol and Mamre had gone, congratulating one another on their prowess in war and gloating over the rich profits they had reaped. And Abram was left alone, somewhat depressed and a little fearful perhaps lest his unexpected display of military power might not stir the Canaanites into a league against him. Moreover he had probably been listening to the excited chatter of Lot's children, which reminded him—he had no child of his own. It was at that point that God, in His love and care, came to talk with Abram about the building of his family.

1. THE WORD OF GOD'S POWER (15:1-4)

The building of Abram's family was to be by spiritual power, not by the energy of the flesh, and spiritual power is inherent in the Word of God.

First there was *the pledge* (15:1). "Fear not Abram: I am thy shield, and thy exceeding great reward." "Never mind, Abram," God said, "you still have Me!" He had proved that already by sending Melchizedek to shield Abram from the snare of Sodom's king. "I am thy shield," He said. "Abram, are you worrying about the military situation? Remember, Melchizedek is a king and I am thy shield. Are you worrying about the monetary situation? the spoils of war you have nobly refused? Remember, Melchizedek is a priest and I am your reward. You cannot lose, Abram. You have a king to protect you and a priest to pray for you, and above all you have Me."

The pledge was followed by *the plea* (15:2-3). Abram already had more than he needed of this world's goods. "Lord GOD, what wilt thou give me, seeing I go childless, and the steward of my house is this Eliezer of Damascus?" What was the point of accumulating more money when, as it seemed, a total outsider would inherit it all? "I go childless!" he said. Abram had yet to learn that fruit for God cannot be produced by natural means. At the same time, that godly man pointed to himself as the source of the problem. He did not blame God, or Sarai. He did not say, "Sarai is barren." He said, "I go childless." How easy it is to shift the blame for lack of spiritual fruit.

Next, God revealed to Abram *the plan* (15:4). "This shall not be thine heir; but he that shall come forth out of thine own bowels shall be thine heir." As David Livingstone used to say, "It is the word of a Gentleman of the strictest and most sacred honour, and that's an end of it!"

2. THE WITNESS TO GOD'S POWER (15:5-6)

"And he brought him forth abroad, and said, Look now toward heaven, and tell [count] the stars, if thou be able to number them: and he said unto him, So shall thy seed be." Men used to think they could count the stars. We now know they are innumerable. Sir James Jeans has said that there are more stars in space than there are grains of sand on all the seashores of all the world. God's promise to Abram was one to stagger the imagination. Yet it was not impossible. A God who can create galaxies and nebulae and countless worlds can certainly give Abram a countless seed. So we read "he believed in the LORD; and he counted it unto him for righteousness." Abram received a bigger bonus than ever he had dared to think. He became the heir of eternal salvation. We should note that Abram was counted righteous, not when he believed the promise that took him out of Ur of the Chaldees, but when he believed the promise regarding the Seed. For, in all ages, salvation ultimately comes to rest in the person of Christ. He is the Seed. It is not mere faith that saves—but *faith in Christ.*

3. THE WORKING OF GOD'S POWER (15:7)

"I am the LORD that brought thee out of Ur of the Chaldees, to give thee this land to inherit it," said God. In mechanics there is a law that relates to inertia, the property of all matter that makes bodies resist any change in their motion, resist any force that puts them in motion, or that speeds up or slows or stops them once they are in motion. Because of inertia, some outside force must always be applied to produce motion. That physical law can illustrate a spiritual law. Abram was in motion in Ur of the Chaldees, but he was in motion in the wrong direction. He was heading to a lost eternity. With every passing hour he gathered momentum. Then suddenly he was stopped, turned around, and set in motion toward Canaan and toward heaven. God says, "I am the LORD that brought thee out of Ur of the Chaldees to give thee this land." *That* was the working of His power. The building of Abram's family, then, was also to be the work of God. The same power that flung the stars into space and set them in motion (only now expressed in spiritual terms rather than physical) was at work to secure Abram not only a seed, but a Seed.

B. THE BASIS OF ABRAM'S FAITH (15:8-12)

Calvary was now brought to bear upon Abram's life. The Lord had been speaking to Abram about a possession and a posterity, and Abram had believed to the saving of his soul. Now he must be shown that a valid faith must ultimately come to rest on the finished work of Christ at Calvary.

First, *Calvary was shadowed* before Abram, he must come to apprehend *the mystery* of it (15:8-10). "Take an heifer of three years old, and a she goat of three years old, and a ram of three years old, and a turtle dove, and a young pigeon." Why that particular selection of creatures for sacrifice? It remains a mystery. In some deep, marvelous, complete, and mysterious way they depict various aspects of Calvary. The full and exact significance of it all eludes us. Thus it was with Abram. The mystery of Calvary was brought home to his heart, the stark tragedy of the cross, the rending, the tearing, the blood, the pain, the woe. Abram saw it, saw the dark shadows of Golgotha falling across the ages and felt them chilling his soul. He could not understand Calvary in its heights and depths but, in some measure, he did apprehend the mystery of Christ's death. That was the basis of his faith.

Then, in some small measure, *Calvary was shared* by Abram; he came to apprehend *the misery* of it (15:11-12). "And when the fowls came down upon the carcases, Abram drove them away. And when the sun was going down, a deep sleep fell upon Abram; and lo, an horror of great darkness fell upon him." It was exactly just such a horror that enveloped Christ as He hung on the tree. Birds are frequently used in Scripture to symbolize the powers of the air, the evil spirits that prey upon men's souls. The carrion birds, the deep sleep, the darkness, the horror–those things all brought home to Abram the fearful cost of the covenant into which God was bringing him. In some small measure the horror of the cross was brought home to his heart.

C. THE BRIGHTNESS OF ABRAM'S FUTURE (15:13-21)

The voice of God broke through. The unborn ages were summoned from the womb of time and made to parade before the sleeping man. He must learn that there is a *time* involved and that there is a *territory* involved in the unfolding plan of God.

1. THE SPECIFIC TIME INVOLVED (15:13-16)

Three areas of God's will were involved as that will related to Abram. There was, first of all, the *permissive* will of God (15:13-14). "Know of a surety that thy seed shall be a stranger in a land that is not theirs, and shall serve them; and they shall afflict them four hundred years; and also that nation, whom they shall serve, will I judge: and afterward shall they come out with great substance." The permissive will of God allowed the Hebrew people ultimately to be enslaved by the Egyptians. The permissive will of God is often what confronts believer and unbeliever alike with some of the thorniest problems connected with faith.

Daniel Defoe tells us how Robinson Crusoe tried to explain divine things to Man Friday, the benighted cannibal he had rescued. After teaching the savage the rudiments of English, the castaway taught his companion about the one true God, the great Maker of all things, infinite in power. Then he introduced the subject of Satan and described the evil one's attempts to destroy the race.

"Well!" said Man Friday, "but you say God is so strong, so great. If God much stronger than the devil, *why God no kill the devil?*" Robinson Crusoe pretended not to hear and found work for Friday to do at the other side of the island.

In His sovereignty God permitted the Israelites to be downtrodden in Egypt, even arranging circumstances to bring them into Egypt. The natural reaction is to ask, *Why?* God does not always tell us why. He did, however, in Abram's case. He drew aside the veil to give His servant a glimpse of the coming tragedy and a promise of an ultimate triumph for his seed.

Then there was the *personal* will of God. "And thou shalt go to thy fathers in peace; thou shalt be buried in a good old age" (15:15). It was God's will that Abram should one day die, but he would die in peace. We look upon death as the worst possible disaster that could overtake us. God's view of death, at least for the believer, is quite different. Death is not something to be feared, but welcomed, when it comes, as God's good and acceptable and perfect will.

In addition there was the *preordaining* will of God. Returning to the future of Abram's seed, God said, "But in the fourth generation they shall come hither again: for the iniquity of the Amorites is not yet full" (15:16). God's view of human affairs is so different from ours. Man tells us of the coming into Egypt of the Hyksos kings, of the building of the mighty temples at Karnak on the Nile, of the rise of a race of empire-building pharaohs who lifted Egypt from foreign domination and made her arms feared from Ethiopia to the Euphrates. History rings with the names of those kings and their exploits—kings who knew not Joseph. God ignores them all. "In the fourth generation," He says, "they shall come hither again." The only hint He gives as to the long delay has to do with the iniquity of the Amorites.

Thus it was that in the fourth generation Israel's sojourn in Egypt came to an end—Levi, Kohath, Amram, Moses, and with Moses the long, silent centuries of suffering came to an abrupt and final end. As those long, agonizing years rolled by, God watched the rise of Egyptian influence, the rise of Amorite iniquity, the ebb and flow of international affairs, all the while making the wrath of man to praise Him and, in the end, having the final say in human affairs.

2. THE SPECIFIC TERRITORY INVOLVED (15:17-21)

First, mention is made of the *guarantee* of the land promised to Abram (15:17). "It came to pass, that, when the sun went down, and it was dark, behold a smoking furnace, and a burning lamp that passed between those pieces." Abram had divided the carcasses of the animals in proper ritual form and the pieces had been spread out in the prescribed way. In his day two contracting parties ratified an agreement by walking up and down between the parts of a sacrificed animal. It is significant that Abram fell into a deep sleep and that God walked up and down alone. The contract that guaranteed the land to Abram depended solely upon God. Abram was a passive recipient of it all. In no way did fulfillment of the promise depend on him.

Then God spoke of the *greatness* of the land promised to Abram (15:18). "In the same day the LORD made a covenant with Abram, saying, Unto thy seed have I given this land, from the river of Egypt unto the great river, the river Euphrates." From the Nile to the Euphrates it would stretch in a broad sweep, taking in some three hundred thousand square miles of territory and embracing much of the land now claimed by the Arabs. Up to that point God had said: "I will give." Now He says, "I have given."

"I will not take from thread even to a shoelatchet," Abram had said to the king of Sodom. "Abram! Not just the well-watered plains of Jordan, not just the land of Canaan, but Sinai and Canaan and the Fertile Crescent and Arabia, it's all yours right across to the Euphrates river," God responded. An old farmer was once asked how he had been so prosperous. "Well," he said, "I made an agreement with God that I'd give Him His share. I would shovel into His bin and He would shovel into mine. Only He has a bigger shovel!" Abram awoke from his sleep with a fresh realization of how very big indeed God's shovel really is.

V. THE PAWNING OF FAITH (16:1-16)

Chapter 16 looks into Abram's home, and records the first biblical instance of domestic strife. There are three people in the story—Abram, Sarai, and, to make up the eternal triangle, Hagar, the other woman. If there is one thing to be gleaned from that sad part in Abram's history it is that Bible people were real people, men and women subject to passions similar to ours. Picture Abram in a business suit, Sarai in a stylish dress, and Hagar as their nice-looking maid, and the situation is as modern as today's news.

The situation was highly explosive. It took the course it did because, for all their spirituality and godly convictions, Abram and Sarai were ordinary people with hopes and fears and desires and wants just like those of anyone else. Abram wanted a son and heir more than anything in the world. Sarai was frustrated beyond words at her inability to give him one. Added to that witch's brew were an attractive slave girl, a legal loophole, some worldly reasoning, and a carnal resolve. The result was an entanglement so snarled and so twisted that four thousand years have not unraveled it.

A. THE TEST OF THE SILENCE OF GOD (16:1-6)

It is not unusual for God to be silent. Indeed, He has been silent far more than He has spoken. His silences are as eloquent as His sayings. He usually does what He did here with Abram. He gave him a revelation of His mind and will concerning a son and heir, then He waited for faith to operate. Unfortunately with Abram, as so often with us, instead of faith triumphing, the flesh triumphed instead.

1. ABRAM'S DOUBLE MIND (16:1-4)

Double-mindedness is always a serious threat to spiritual growth. We note first *the problem.* "Now Sarai Abram's wife bare him no children: and she had an handmaid, an Egyptian, whose name was Hagar"(16:1). The problem, simply stated, was a lack of fruit. The solution proposed was an activity of the flesh, one that pointed to Hagar, not to God. It was an Egyptian solution. Hagar, in all probability, was one of the legacies from Abram's disastrous expedition to Egypt. It was far easier for God to get Abram out of Egypt than it was for Him to get Egypt out of Abram. That is the great problem with worldliness; it tends to taint our decisions. Faced with the problem of Sarai's evident barrenness, Abram cast about in his mind whether perhaps there might be some other solution to his childlessness. Did it *have* to be Sarai who gave him a son? Had God actually said that his family would spring from her? Thus Abram began to reason, for "the carnal mind is enmity against God: for it is not subject to the law of God, neither indeed can be" (Romans 8:7).

No sooner was the problem introduced than there came *the proposal* (16:2-3). It came from Abram's wife. No doubt Abram had often received excellent advice from his wife, but that time her counsel was extreme folly. It might have gone like this: "My dear, I have discovered that the code of Hammurabi, the most civilized, progressive, and decent legislative code so far proposed for civilized men, is honored here in Canaan. Well, according to the code, it would be in order for you to marry Hagar, my slave. Then, when a son is born to her, I can legally make it *my* son. In this way we can get around the problem of my inability to have children. I can have them by proxy so to speak." It did not take Abram long to fall in with his wife's suggestion. So "Sarai, Abram's wife, took Hagar her maid the Egyptian, after Abram had dwelt ten years in the land of Canaan, and gave her to her husband Abram to be his wife."

We see a similar kind of thing done all the time. A church or a child of God is barren. There is seemingly no blessing, no fruit. Instead of waiting for God, Hagar is brought in, some worldly expedient is adopted. It gets results, of course—but of the wrong kind.

Before long, Abram and Sarai had to pay *the price* (16:4). As soon as Hagar saw she was about to become the mother of Abram's first child, "her mistress was despised in her eyes." The blessing and harmony of Abram's home was gone, not to be restored for some sixteen or seventeen years, and then only at the price of a painful separation. Such is the fruit of impatience in the things of God.

2. SARAI'S DECEITFUL HEART (16:5-6)

It was not long before Sarai learned something about her own deceitful heart. One of the most difficult things to sustain is a sacrifice made in the energy of the flesh. That which starts out as noble, generous, and spontaneous soon becomes a drudgery, especially when month after month the inevitable bills must be paid. When Sarai made her magnanimous offer of Hagar to Abram she doubtless thought she was being unselfish and self-sacrificing. Faced with the daily price tag, in terms of Hagar's haughty looks and sneers, she soon regretted her pledge. Her heart rose in rebellion.

Her rebellion vented itself in two ways, first, in an *untamed tongue.* "And Sarai said unto Abram, My wrong be upon thee: I have given my maid into thy bosom; and when she saw that she had conceived, I was despised in her eyes: the LORD judge between me and thee" (16:5). "It's all your fault!" she said. The tangled logic of that statement is not easy to explain. It is like the note a young fellow received from his girl friend. "Dear John, I hope you are not still angry. I want to explain that I was really joking when I told you I didn't mean what I said about reconsidering my decision not to change my mind. Please believe I really mean this. Love, Jean." Abram's face must have been a study when confronted with Sarai's logic! Sarai, of course, was thinking with her heart, and her tongue simply gave expression to her deep inner resentment at the turn events had taken. Somebody had to be blamed, so Abram received the tongue-lashing.

Sarai's rebellion then manifested itself in an *untamed temper* (16:6). She vented her spite on Hagar, "dealt hardly with her" is the way the Bible puts it. We can hardly believe it is Sarai! Is that the woman held up to us in the New Testament as the model wife who had so schooled herself in her domestic duties that she actually called her husband "lord"? Is that resentful, mean, spiteful, and tyrannical Sarai the modest, loving, faithful, and submissive wife we have come to know? How deceitful is the human heart. How it betrays itself—and in what little things. Had Abram threatened to leave her? No. Had someone stolen all her jewelry? No. Had her favorite camel sickened and died? No. What was it then? Her maid was putting on airs and graces and looking down her nose at her, that was all. And Sarai was upset and spoiled the picture being painted of a model wife.

When we get upset, it is what is inside that comes out. If we upset a bottle of honey, it is honey that comes out; if we upset a bottle of vinegar, it is vinegar that comes out. Upsetting the bottle does not determine what is inside the bottle; it only reveals it. When we get upset and say bitter, unkind things, it is because that is what is inside us. The human heart is very deceitful. Sarai's deceitful heart was revealed in a very little thing. Our hearts are just the same.

3. Hagar's Defiant Will (16:6)

"And when Sarai dealt hardly with her, Hagar fled." That was very natural. But that seems to be the whole point of the silence of God. Every member of that little household was doing the *natural* thing. Abram acted naturally in marrying Hagar, Sarai in resenting her maid, and Hagar in running away. The tests of life and the divine silences that come to the child of God are to give him opportunity to act spiritually instead of naturally. Hagar's running away from Sarai's constant nagging is understandable enough, for Hagar, after all, was only an unsaved Egyptian. But there was something especially sad about Abram's attitude. He surrendered his headship to Sarai and allowed her to nag the unfortunate Hagar into total frustration. There may have been some excuse for Sarai too, for so far her faith seems to have been a secondhand faith—a faith that leaned on Abram's. But there was no excuse for Abram. He failed as the head of his home.

Have you noticed the difference between the villains in the parables of Jesus and the villains in all other literature? In the typical novel the villain is the man who does what he ought *not* to do. He murders someone, he robs a bank, he lies or cheats or steals; but in the parables of Jesus the villain is the man who simply leaves undone the thing that he ought to have done. It is the priest, the Levite passing by on the other side, leaving the robbed and beaten traveler to his fate; it is the rich man allowing Lazarus to die at his gate, full of sores; it is the servant hiding his talent in a napkin. Those are the villains about whom Jesus told. When we see Abram simply neglecting his responsibilities as head of his home, we need to take heed to our ways as persons, partners, and parents.

The test of the silence of God, then, brings into focus a Hagar who has failed as a *maid*, a Sarai who has failed as a *mistress*, and an Abram who has failed as a *man*. As a result, Hagar the Egyptian fled. What a sad commentary that is on that patriarchal home. There she goes! She was brought up in the pagan superstitions of Egypt. Through circumstances about which we know nothing she was brought under the shelter of Abram's roof. What an opportunity for Abram and Sarai to tell her about the true and living God, to lead her in the way everlasting. But what happened? She was treated worse than a piece of furniture. She was used, then abused so that she fled from that home, her mind filled with bitter thoughts about the treatment she had received and with a totally false impression in her mind about Abram's God.

B. THE TRUTH OF THE SOVEREIGNTY OF GOD (16:7-16)

It is a blessing that God's witness to Himself is not confined to the poor and shoddy testimony we ourselves so often bear. For if Abram and Sarai have so sorely misrepresented God to Hagar, then God will step in and reveal Himself to her.

1. THE REVELATION TO HAGAR (16:7-12)

The tents of Abram were far behind. The weary fugitive with the tear-stained face had traveled fast, had crossed Sinai, and had arrived at the wilderness of Shur on the frontiers of Egypt. She was going back, back to Egypt, back into the world, back to the house of an even greater bondage than anything known in Sarai's tents. She was going back into eternal darkness, back to that gilded land of death, back to her pagan people and her pagan gods. Then, before it was forever too late, before the gates of Egypt closed behind her forever, God in His sovereignty stepped in.

Our attention is drawn to *the coming of the Omnipresent One* (16:7-8). "And the angel of the LORD found her by a fountain of water in the wilderness by the fountain in the way to Shur. And He said, Hagar, Sarai's maid, whence camest thou? and wither wilt thou go? And she said, I flee from the face of my mistress Sarai." Little did Hagar know it, but God, in His infinite grace, had been hard on her heels every step of the way.

In the coming of the Omnipresent One to Hagar we see the *grace* of God wrapped up in His sovereignty. It is the first time in Scripture that reference is made to the angel of the Lord. It is remarkable, to say the least, that the first occurrence of the Jehovah angel (probably none other than the Lord Jesus Himself in one of His preincarnate angelic appearances) should be not to Abram but to Hagar; not to the heir of all the promises, but to an Egyptian fugitive; not to a man but to a woman; not to a saint but to a sinner; not to a person of high rank, but to a slave; not to one seeking God, but to one fleeing toward Egypt. The Friend of the friendless, the loving second Person of the Godhead, met that forlorn woman beside a fountain as centuries later, clothed in living, human flesh, He met another woman at a wayside well (John 4). It was a revelation of the grace of God. He loved Hagar just as much as He loved Abram. He sought her and found her on the frontiers of Egypt as He had sought and found Abram in far-off Ur.

And, with loving tenderness, He called her by her name. He called her "Sarai's maid" not "Abram's wife." Simply being the wife of Abram gave her no special claim upon His grace. Being related by ties however binding and close to a child of God does not make one a child of God nor confer any special privilege—special responsibility perhaps, but not special privilege. Thus the Lord met her and forced her to face her lost condition. "Where have you come from? Where are you going?" He wrung from her lips the sad confession, "I flee," so that He might turn her around and set her feet on the straight and narrow way that leads to life. Before her, to be entered on the morrow, was the wide gate, the broad way into Egyptian night. Behind her was the straight gate, the narrow way, the pilgrim path, the highway of faith. In sovereign grace God found her in the very nick of time.

Then came *the command of the Omnipotent One.* "And the angel of the LORD said unto her, Return to thy mistress, and submit thyself under her hands." That is exactly why many people do not wish to be saved. Hagar was saved by putting her faith in the second Person of the Godhead who revealed Himself to her or, as we would say today, she was saved by trusting in the Lord Jesus Christ. Nothing could be easier or simpler than that. But the immediate consequence of that response to the Lord was to be a conversion, a turning around, a going back, a making of herself humble before Sarai, a willing obedience to God. Nothing could be harder, perhaps, than that. It was a revelation of the *government* of God wrapped up in His sovereignty.[5]

Finally we see *the comfort of the Omniscient One* (16:10-12). To use a vernacular expression, God does not expect us to "go it alone." To help Hagar give evidence of true conversion, God gave her a promise and a prophecy. The *promise* was that she would be fruitful. "And the angel of the LORD said unto her, Behold thou art with child, and shalt bear a son, and shall call his name Ishmael" (16:11). The name means "God shall hear." Her life would not be lived in vain, nor would she have to struggle through the difficult years ahead in her own strength. God would be looking after her and listening to her.

The *prophecy* centered in Ishmael. "And he will be a wild man; his

5. Millions of people delude themselves with what might well be called "a cheap gospel." "Only believe!" they are told, "just have faith." It is true that salvation comes to rest in the finished work of Christ and that there is nothing we can do to merit or buy it. It is true that salvation is all of grace, that it is made ours on the principle of faith, that it is "not of works lest any man should boast." At the same time faith in Christ involves commitment. To the liberated demoniac came the word of Christ: "Go home and tell." The first word of the enlightened and converted Saul of Tarsus was "Lord, what wilt thou have me to do?" Runaway Onesimus, won to Christ in far-off Rome by the great apostle, was sent right back to his master in Colossae. True conversion recognizes the claims of others as well as the claims of Christ. It involves repentance, rebirth, and restoration. It involves putting right, as far as is humanly possible, in the power of the indwelling Holy Spirit, the wrongs we have done to other people. The whole point of the book of James is that we must have a belief that behaves.

hand will be against every man, and every man's hand against him; and he shall dwell in the presence of all his brethren" (16:12). From Ishmael the Arab tribes have sprung to fulfill the role of destiny upon the stage of time so accurately predicted of them here. They remain in the background of the Bible, joining hands with Israel's foes. They found for themselves a prophet and hurled themselves like wild men against the ramparts of the world, building up a brilliant empire and spreading their creed with the sword. Christian explorers, blazing gospel trails into Africa, found that the sons of Ishmael had gone before and had set the continent ablaze in their savage hunt for slaves. Today they sit astride the oil reserves of the world and threaten the peace of the world. Their rage against Israel keeps the world in turmoil, ever on the brink of global war. It was all foreseen and wrapped up in that embryonic prophecy spoken to Hagar long ago. What a revelation of the *greatness* of God wrapped up in His sovereignty!

2. THE RESPONSE BY HAGAR (16:13-16)

Her response was twofold. First she gave *verbal expression* to her faith. "And she called the name of the LORD that spake unto her, Thou God seest me. . . . Wherefore the well was called Beer-lahai-roi" ("the well of Him that liveth and seeth me"). One translator renders that "the well of the vision of life." It was the place where Hagar passed from death to life. From henceforth the true and living God would no longer be One about whom Abram and Sarai spoke, He would be her God too. She confessed it with her mouth.

Finally Hagar gave *vital expression* to her faith (16:15-16). She returned to Abram's camp and submitted herself to Sarai. And, in due course, the promised son was born.

VI. THE POTENTIAL OF FAITH (17:1-27)

Abram's trouble was that he could not wait. God had promised him a son and a seed. In his anxiety to see that promise fulfilled, Abram decided to help God out and to hurry things up by marrying Hagar.

A naturalist once took a cocoon of an emperor moth and kept it in his study for months, hoping to witness its emergence in due time. The cocoon was flask-shaped with a narrow opening at the neck through which the moth would emerge. The great difference between the narrow opening and the size of the moth made the naturalist wonder how ever the insect would get out of its prison. At last the day came and all morning the man watched the struggles of the insect. It never seemed to get beyond a certain point. The struggle to emerge is what forces the fluids of the moth's body into the wings and makes it possible for it to fly. The naturalist did not know that and, his patience exhausted, he decided to help things along. With the point of his scissors he carefully snipped the confining threads to make the exit just a little easier. At once the moth crawled out with perfect ease. But the naturalist watched in vain to see the gorgeous wings expand and fill. They never did. His impatience and false kindness had ruined the moth. It never became anything but a stunted abortion, crawling painfully through the brief life it should have spent flying through the air on rainbow wings.

It is always a mistake to try to hasten the work of God. He has His own reasons for His seeming delays. But Abram could not wait. As a result of his impatience there followed a solemn silence in which, for thirteen long years, he received no further word from God. He was eighty-six when Ishmael was born and ninety-nine when God at last broke the silence. There were thirteen years during which Abram made no further progress in the things of God, in which he saw no fruit, and during which nothing worthy of note happened in his life.

When God did speak at last it was to gather up the various threads of promise He had already made and to weave them into one great, comprehensive covenant. It is known as the Abrahamic covenant, and is one of the most important utterances in human language. It left its mark on all of subsequent history, it rules the future with an iron hand, and it is the basis for all the blessings God has for mankind. What is happening in the Middle East today is, in part, an outworking of some of the clauses of the covenant so that things happening now in the twentieth century of the Christian era can really be understood only in the light of what was said back in the twentieth century before the Christian era.

A. How the Covenant was Received (17:1-16)

1. In Absolute Subjection (17:1-3)

The time had come for Isaac to be born. But before that could happen, faith had to be exercised, so God made a new revelation to Abram to give faith its opportunity. That new revelation was received by Abram in absolute subjection.

There are three names for God in verses 1-3. The LORD (Jehovah) appeared unto Abram; He spoke as "the Almighty God" (El Shaddai); and God (Elohim, v. 3) talked with Abram. The *Jehovah* of the Old Testament is the Jesus of the New Testament, *El Shaddai* is the Satisfier—He who pours Himself into believers' lives to make them fruitful, *Elohim* is God in the ultimate and absolute sense. Thus we gather that God the Son, God the Holy Spirit, and God the Father all joined in conveying the covenant.

Abram "fell on his face," and there he stayed throughout the entire revelation. He received the promise in a state of absolute subjection. Nothing was required of him, all was of grace. He simply had to listen, for the Abrahamic covenant was unconditional and in no way dependent upon the cooperation of Abram or even of his seed.

2. IN ABSOLUTE SILENCE (17:4-16)

The voice of God spoke on and on, and Abram lay prostrate in the dust listening as promise after promise was given. Every word spoken between verses 4 and 16 was spoken by God. The paragraph is a majestic monologue by the God whose words, when spoken in creation, brought the worlds into being. His words were spoken not to create but to confirm, to spell out a one-sided contract in which all the benefits accrue to Abram and all the responsibilities reside in Himself.

a. THE SUBSTANCE OF THE PROMISE (17:4-8)

We note that there was a *principle* involved. Count up the continuing use of the words "I will" and "ye shall," with the imperative "must" of verse 13—"I will make thee fruitful . . . I will make nations of thee . . . kings shall come out of thee." There are at least twenty-four such statements in the chapter. It is an absolute, unconditional, binding, irrevocable agreement, in which all the initiative, all the intent, and all the insistence are God's. No failure on Abram's part, no flaws, no forgetfulness on the part of his posterity, can annul the decree. God has pledged Himself to see that every single line, every jot and tittle will be fulfilled. All the factors and forces that might be harnessed to hinder or halt the agreement would be swept aside at last. As God is God, so the covenant must stand.

In keeping with that, God changed Abram's name to Abraham—that is, He added the fifth letter of the Hebrew alphabet to Abram's name. Five, in Scripture, is a number associated with grace.

Then there is a *people* involved (17:4-6). "As for me, behold, my covenant is with thee, and thou shalt be a father of many nations." The person is Abraham, the people is his seed. Like any other contract that great agreement is careful to specify exactly who is to benefit from its clauses. Abraham and the Jewish people are the beneficiaries.

There is a *period* involved (17:7). "And I will establish my covenant between me and thee and thy seed after thee in their great generations for an everlasting covenant, to be a God unto thee, and to thy seed after thee." The contract is eternal. Later on God added other covenants—the Mosaic covenant, the Palestinian covenant, the Davidic covenant; but none of the provisions of those covenants changed or altered the one with Abraham. Some of the provisions under the Palestinian covenant, for example, imposed conditions whereby Israel could continue occupancy of the promised land, but those provisions did not alter the provisions of the Abrahamic agreement. All such additions were of a temporary nature and could not annul the awesome pledge of God to ultimately make good on every single phase of His everlasting promise to Abram. Moreover, the agreement focused on a nation, not a church. The day will assuredly come when Israel will be established before all men in full covenant relationship before God as promised to Abraham here.

There is a *place* involved. "And I will give unto thee, and to thy seed after thee, the land wherein thou art a stranger, all the land of Canaan, for an everlasting possession; and I will be their God." The land of Israel does not belong to the Arabs, for all their clamor. It was not deeded to Ishmael, but to Isaac.[6]

So then the substance of the promise emerged. God pledged Himself to give a special territorial holding to the Jewish people and to be their God.[7]

b. THE SEAL OF THE PROMISE (17:9-14)

The seal of the promise was the rite of circumcision. The knife had to be taken to the flesh but in no way was the promise itself to be fulfilled by carnal means. Three things are recorded about the covenant seal. First, we note its *implications*. It was to be a supporting sign: "This is my covenant, which ye shall keep, between me and you and thy seed after thee; Every man child among you shall be circumcised . . . and it shall be a token of the covenant betwixt me and you." When a legal contract is executed, a seal is often affixed even today to show that the terms of the agreement are legally in force. In like manner the seal of circumcision was to be the visual reminder that the terms of that covenant were in force. Circumcision as a religious rite is meaningless to those not included in the terms of the agreement.

It was not only a supporting sign, but was also a spiritual symbol, intended to teach Abraham a vital spiritual lesson. Think back over the experiences through which that great believer had already come. He had become a pilgrim, he had believed God and it had been counted unto him for righteousness, he had backslidden and been restored, he had met God face to face, had learned to give way to a weaker brother,

6. The Arabs are investing vast sums in petro-dollars to launch sophisticated, Madison-Avenue promotion campaigns to erode world support for the reborn State of Israel. The image is being created of a ravished Palestinian state and of a Palestinian nation that has been displaced by the Jews. The audience is the Arab American community, pro-Arab organizations in the United States, the oil companies, liberal church people, intellectuals, the entire radical left, segments of the political far right, and the traditional anti-Jewish hate fringe. But there never was an Arab state. The last time an *independent* state existed in that area, it was a Jewish state, destroyed by the Romans in A.D. 70 and renamed "Palestine" after the Jews' inveterate enemy the Philistines as added gall to the bitter cup of defeat. The last people to lord it over the land were the British, and they deeded it to the Jews under the terms of the Balfour Declaration, a document later ratified by the League of Nations.
7. In an earlier preliminary to that covenant, God had already declared that boundaries of the land would be the Nile on the west and the Euphrates on the east. The Jews have never occupied more than a tithe of their inheritance. But in a coming day they will. Every nation that has campaigned against the Jew has eventually been tossed onto the rubbish heap. The rebirth of the state of Israel in modern times, after centuries of nonexistence, is a significant sign that God is about to take up and fulfill His promises to Abraham and his seed.

to do battle also for another man's soul. He had met Melchizedek and established a family altar. He had, however, failed to bear fruit and had resorted to carnal means to bring about some semblance of a seed. The result had been Ishmael. So, although Abraham was an excellent believer, he was wholly unable to bring forth fruit for God. He realized that now. In deep abasement before God, after thirteen silent years, He listened as God gave the solution to his problem. It was circumcision—the sentence of death in his flesh. It was a symbol of the cross of Christ cutting right across all that he was by natural birth. It was a sharp, unforgettable, painful admission that he was unable to produce, by carnal means, the kind of life that God expects. It was an agonizing realization that only through Christ can a person bear real fruit for God.

Next we note its *implementation.* "And he that is eight days old shall be circumcised among you, every man child in your generations." The number *eight* is significant; it is the number of resurrection, the number of a new beginning. In music the eighth note is the same as the first note, only an octave higher. In Israel a child was born, lived a full week and then, on the eighth day of a new beginning, the first day of the week as it were, he was circumcised. It was a symbolic way of bringing the child under the Abrahamic covenant. It did not automatically make him a child of God, as Paul proved in Romans 2 and 4. Still less is circumcision in any way connected with baptism. It was not intended to be an expression of *saving* faith on the part of the child, but of *submissive* faith on the part of the parent.

Then comes its *importance.* "And the uncircumcised man child . . . shall be cut off from his people; he hath broken my covenant" (17:14). If a parent neglected to have a child circumcised, it was the child's responsibility to get circumcised when he reached the age of knowledge and accountability. Failure to do so was a serious matter, it amounted to contempt of the covenant. As a result, the uncircumcised Hebrew became an alien to the comonwealth of Israel and a stranger to the covenants of promise. He manifested gross, willful, and criminal unbelief.

c. THE SPIRIT OF THE PROMISE (17:15-16)

"And God said unto Abraham, As for Sarai thy wife, thou shalt not call her name Sarai, but Sarah shall her name be. And I will bless her, and give thee a son also of her: yea, I will bless her, and she shall be a mother of nations; kings of people shall be of her." In other words, no more Hagars, Abraham! God had just changed Abram's name to Abraham; now He changed Sarai's name as well and in the same way, by adding the fifth letter of the alphabet to the existing name. From "high father," Abram's name had been changed to "father of many nations." Every time his name, Abraham, was pronounced he was reminded of that; he was the father of many nations. Now royal dignity was bestowed on Sarai too.

"Sarai" means "my princess," and evidently it was a name of endearment as well as a personal name, for lovely Sarai was firmly enthroned in Abraham's heart. Now God took that sweet name and gave it a whole new significance. Instead of "my princess" she was going to be "a princess"—the personal name became the positional name. That is what the grace of God does for a person. It ennobles.[8]

B. HOW THE COVENANT WAS BELIEVED (17:17-27)

1. THE LAUGHTER OF FAITH (17:17)

There are various kinds of laughter. There is the genuinely humorous laugh—the hearty, side-splitting roar that, when kept within bounds, is as medicine to the soul. How wonderful of God to bless men with the ability to laugh. He wants His people to be a happy, singing, laughing people. Then there is the hideous laugh, the foolish cackle of a man who laughs at sin, who makes merry over the misfortunes and mistakes and misdeeds of others. God calls such a man a fool. Chapter 17 introduces another kind of laugh, *the laughter of faith* (17:17). "Then Abraham fell upon his face, and laughed, and said in his heart, Shall a child be born unto him that is an hundred years old? and shall Sarah, that is ninety years old, bear?"

Abraham laughed out of sheer joy. The glorious impossibility of it! Why, when God had first spoken to him about a son twenty-five years earlier, then it was bordering on the impossible, but now! Now he was an old, old man and Sarah (in faith he immediately employed her new name), was an old, old woman. And he laughed the laughter of faith as Romans 4 makes perfectly clear. "Being not weak in faith, he considered not his own body now dead, when he was about an hundred years old, neither yet the deadness of Sarah's womb: he staggered not at the promise of God through unbelief; but was strong in faith, giving glory to God" (Romans 4:19-20).

It did Abraham's soul good. For thirteen years he had not heard from God. For thirteen years he lived with the fruits of his own impatience. Would God forgive and forget? Would God speak again? And when He did, the dear old man could not contain himself for joy.

John Bunyan was a man who knew how to transform gloom into gladness. In his own Puritan way he tells of the long days when he lay under terrible conviction of sin. "I lay long at Sinai," he said, "and saw the fire

8. When a person becomes a Christian he becomes a member of the royal family of heaven. His life should reflect that. On one occasion salty old Lord Palmerstone, Prime Minister of England, had the nerve to tell Queen Victoria a dirty joke. She looked at him with all the ice she could muster. "We are not amused," she said. It was an answer worthy of such a queen. Can we, who are sons and daughters of the living God, live on a lower plane than that? Surely not.

and the cloud and the darkness."[9] He meant, of course, that he was long under the burden of the law, long under conviction of sin, long troubled by his utter inability to produce anything pleasing to God. Then came deliverance, when his soul was set free and the vision of Sinai was replaced by the vision of Zion. Says Bunyan, "And withal, the twelfth chapter of Hebrews was set before my eyes. That was a good night for me. I had few better. I could scarce lie in my bed for joy and peace and triumph." He was like Abraham when the full import of what God had in store for him first burst in upon his soul. "Then Abraham fell upon his face and laughed."

2. THE LOGIC OF FAITH (17:18-22)

Faith says: "If God can bless me like that, He can bless other people too." Faith is never selfish, never exclusive, never thoughtless of others in need. Faith wants the flood tides of joy to sweep over others as well.

a. THE PLEA FOR ISHMAEL (17:18)

"And Abraham said unto God, O that Ishmael might live before thee!" It was not the cry of unbelief, but the expression of a godly desire that Ishmael, now on the verge of early manhood, might also be brought into the sphere of the blessing of God. Ishmael, growing up in the patriarch's home and with his mother's testimony to supplement Abraham's, was still a stranger to grace, for being born in a godly home does not guarantee that a child will also believe. God has no grandchildren. All of Abraham's faith and obedience and righteousness could not make a believing, obedient, righteous man out of his son. But, at least he could pray.

b. THE PLEDGE FOR ISHMAEL (17:19-22)

In response, God gave Abraham a twofold pledge for Ishmael. His promise was based upon His knowledge of Ishmael's heart, for God knew that mockery at divine things lurked in the depths of that young man's soul. The pledge for Ishmael had within it, first and foremost, a *reserve clause*. "And God said, Sarah thy wife shall bear thee a son indeed; and thou shalt call his name Isaac: and I will establish my covenant with him for an everlasting covenant, and with his seed after him." He was saying: "Abraham, in this matter of the covenant make no mistake, the line runs through Isaac, not Ishmael. Isaac will be the believing man." But, having given the reserve clause, God gave the *royal clause*. "And as for Ishmael, I have heard thee: Behold, I have blessed him, and will make him fruitful, and will multiply him exceedingly;

9. Like little Jess when she stood before the Kirk Session at Drumtochty aspiring to be numbered among those accepted into the fellowship of the church: "How lang haf ye been at Sinai?" demanded dour old Lachlan Cambell. Old Lachlan stood for inflexible justice. "Ye will tell the Session what has been your law-work, and how lang ye haf been at Sinai." Jess broke down completely. "I dinna ken what yir asking," she said. "I was never out o' Drumtochty."

twelve princes shall he beget, and I will make him a great nation. But my covenant will I establish with Isaac." God has kept His word. The Arab world stretches from the seaboard of the Atlantic to the Persian Gulf, and embraces some seventeen of the most strategically placed and economically wealthy countries of the world. But, as God foresaw, they do not know Him. They are gripped fast in one of the most deadly, tenacious, and militant errors the world has ever known.

3. THE LIFE OF FAITH (17:23-27)

The life of faith is a life that in essence is a life of obedience to the known will of God. God had just revealed to Abraham the need for circumcision. Abraham at once set about putting that seal to the covenant.

a. A LIMITLESS OBEDIENCE (17:23-24)

In four steps, Abraham carried out explicitly the command of God. No protests were accepted, no fears were allowed to hinder, no possible resentments were permitted to obstruct.

In the first place there was complete *parental obedience.* "And Abraham took Ishmael his son" (17:23). Ishmael was about thirteen years of age which, in the East, meant he was almost a grown man. "You first, Ishmael." We do not know whether Ishmael protested or not at the painful, humiliating, and merely religious rite that was now to be administered to him, but if he did protest his complaints were cut short. Abraham was a tribal chief and knew how to rule. It would be a rash young man indeed who would defy the will of such a commanding man as Abraham with his regal bearing, authoritarian manner, piercing eyes, and right to rule those who broke his bread.

Parental obedience was followed by *patriarchal obedience.* "And Abraham took . . . all that were born in his house." As a chieftain, Abraham's authority extended to all those who were born within his clan. He was their provider and protector, so as long as they remained with him they bowed to his authority and respected his will. Abraham therefore extended the umbrella of the covenant to those who owned him as their patriarch.

Mark Twain told how the widow Douglas took the poor waif, Huckleberry Finn, whose father was a drunken sot, into her home.

> Huck Finn's wealth and the fact that he was now under the protection of the widow Douglas introduced him into society—no, dragged him into it, hurled him into it—and his sufferings were almost more than he could bear. The widow's servants kept him clean and neat, combed and brushed, and they bedded him nightly in unsympathetic sheets that had not one little spot or stain which he could press to his heart and know for a friend. He had to eat with knife and fork; he had to use a napkin, cup and plate; he had to learn his book, he had to go to

> church; he had to talk so properly that speech was become insipid in his mouth; withersoever he turned, the bars and shackles of civilization shut him in and bound him hand and foot.

Well, he endured all that for three weeks and then took off. Back he went to the old empty hogsheds that once had been his home, back to stolen odds and ends for food and to the comfort of his pipe, back to "the same old ruin of rags that had made him picturesque in the days when he was free and happy." His friend Tom Sawyer routed him out and persuaded him to return.

Huck Finn had a choice. He could benefit from all the widow Douglas had to offer him, or he could turn his back upon it all and live a wild, untamed life of his own. He could not have it both ways. He could stay in her home, but only on her terms.

Thus it was in the patriarchal society of Abraham's day. There were great advantages to being in his clan, to being "born in his house." But responsibility went with the privilege. Abraham stood in the place of God to those who bowed to his rule. They could stay and enjoy all that he had to offer, but only on his terms. It was the same kind of patriarchal obedience that Abraham now expected from his clansmen in the matter of circumcision. All who belonged to him were to be circumcised, those who did not wish to bow to those terms had the right to leave.

Then there was *positional obedience*. "And Abraham took . . . all that were bought with his money." Abraham, in the kindness of his heart, allowed no social barriers to stand between him and his desire to bring all within the sphere of his influence under the blessing of the covenant.

Look there in the kitchen! There is a lad whose job it is to rake out the fire and remove the ashes and lift the hot and sooty pans. He is grubby and sweaty, pushed and shoved around, the lowest of the low, a slave of slaves. Here comes the great master himself. He puts his hand on the boy's shoulder, and the little fellow is scared half out of his wits. "Come, son," says Abraham, "never mind these pots and pans. I've something to tell you. I want to tell you about the living God and the exceeding greatness of His promise. I want to share with you the spiritual blessings that have come to me." So "Abraham took . . . all that were bought with his money, every male among the men of Abraham's house: and circumcised them in the selfsame day, as God had said unto him."

Of course we do not have that kind of dictatorial authority today. But we do have an obligation to those who work for us or work with us to tell them about the good things God has done for our souls. Abraham's obedience was positional obedience. He ministered spiritually to those who served him. He used his position to tell others what God had done for him. And so can we.

Moreover, there was *personal obedience*. "And Abraham was ninety years old and nine, when he was circumcised" (17:24). How many excuses he might have made! "I'm an old man, the shock would be too much for my system. I'll find some other way to express my acceptance of the covenant. I'll offer a hundred head of cattle, I'll donate a sack of gold to relieve poverty in these parts." No, Abraham was obedient. He took the knife to himself. His obedience was limitless obedience.

b. A LIMITED ORDINANCE (17:25-27)

The ordinance was given by God and was therefore of great significance but, as with any such ordinance, it is possible to go to one of two extremes. We can overestimate its value, or we can underestimate its value. We can say, "There's really no importance about this ordinance at all. I can be saved and ignore it altogether. It is not essential to salvation." Maybe not, but it is certainly the basis of further growth in spiritual things. The other extreme would be to say, "If I submit to this ordinance then I shall be saved. It is the ground of salvation, without it I can have no hope of heaven." Both extremes are wrong.

Thus chapter 17 closes with a reference to circumcision as a limited ordinance. It did nothing to change *the state of the rebellious man* (17:25). "And Ishmael his son was thirteen years old, when he was circumcised." That is a significant statement. The number thirteen in Scripture is associated with rebellion. By natural birth Ishmael was a rebel, and he remained a rebel to the end of his days. He had no heart and no mind for the things of God. On the contrary he scoffed at them. Circumcision did nothing to change the heart of a rebel.

It did nothing to change *the standing of the righteous man* (17:26-27). "In the selfsame day was Abraham circumcised, and Ishmael his son, and all the men of his house." Abraham was a righteous man long before he was circumcised. His circumcision simply manifested his inner obedience of heart.

VII. THE PRAYER OF FAITH (18:1-33)

Lot was very fond of Sodom, but Abraham had no liking for the place at all. Lot seemed to think Sodom to be a great place for raising a family; it had so many social, educational, and business advantages. Abraham kept well clear of the place; it was a sink of iniquity. Sodom and Gomorrah and the other townships of the valley were disgusting centers of pornographic filth. He marveled that God did not simply wipe them off the map. Sodom itself was so debased that it gave its name to the vilest form of perversion known to man.

The time comes in the history of all places like Sodom when God decides to act. Before proceeding against Sodom, however, God took Abraham into His confidence and revealed to His servant a new line of truth—apocalyptic truth, truth concerning the impending overthrow of an utterly vile civilization.

The revelation of that truth was an interesting test of Abraham's growth in grace and of his increase in the knowledge of God. How does a faithful, maturing, obedient child of God react to the truth that a holocaust of judgment is about to engulf a world of vile and godless men? Jonah, faced with apocalyptic truth, was glad. He pondered the impending doom of Nineveh with glee, determined to do nothing to stay its fall, careless of the thousands of little children who lived within its walls. Jesus, faced with apocalyptic truth, was moved to tears. His prophetic eye envisioned Jerusalem as it would be within a generation, the surrounding hills black with crosses and on every cross a Jew. And He wept, wept for the city whose sins called for vengeance so thorough and so complete. Faced with apocalyptic truth, Abraham prayed.

A. THE PRACTICAL MAN (18:1-8)

It was high noon, the time of day in eastern lands when all sensible people took their afternoon siestas. Abraham was sitting in the doorway of his tent enjoying whatever breeze might be blowing across the plain when he saw three men approaching. The abrupt way in which they are introduced in the narrative suggests that one moment there was nothing there, the next moment, there they were. Abraham rubbed his eyes. Whatever would men be doing out in the burning heat of the noonday sun? Then the truth dawned upon him. Those were more than mere men.

1. HIS HASTE (18:1-2)

"And when he saw them, he ran to meet them from the tent door." Now Abraham was a very old man, nearly a hundred years of age. His wife might have called after him, "Abraham! Act your age. Take care of your heart!" But Abraham knew better than that. Some deep spiritual insight taught Him that one of those men was the Lord of glory Himself. And when the Lord deigns to visit, the proper thing to do is make haste and put oneself in a position to hear. Thus Abraham ran and bowed himself to the ground. He prostrated himself before the Lord. It was an instinctive reflex and a sound and sensible thing to do, for in the presence of God nothing but the deepest reverence will do. There can be no flippancy, no hand-in-pocket casualness, no offhand frivolity.

How often we come into our meetings with idle chatter and light gossip and careless indifference. Yet has not the Lord declared, "Where two or three are gathered together in my name, there am I in the midst of them" (Matthew 18:20)? We may not always recognize His presence. Indeed, when Abraham first saw the people approaching he thought them to be "three men." But the Lord will be present Himself in the midst of His gathered saints. How important it is that we put ourselves into an attitude of humble, eager, excited expectancy. The Lord has come. No gathering of the Lord's people is to be regarded as a routine, ordinary event. Yet we saunter in and chit-chat with this one and that. We discuss the weather, the ball game. We yawn and look around, taking note of this item of trivia or the other. After all it is just another meeting. *But the Lord is there.* What haste there should be to recognize that. What a sense of reverence and awe and expectancy. How deplorable it is that professing Christians should allow themselves a familiarity with holy things that breeds contempt. How dare we address Him as "Jesus" when He demands that we address Him as "Lord." So we read that that aged man, well versed in the things of God, "ran . . . and bowed himself to the ground." Abraham's haste and humility teach us the much-neglected lesson of reverence in the presence of God. It was not a matter of forced or artificial posturing. It was a question of spiritual intuition, an overwhelming sense of the presence of God.

2. HIS HOSPITALITY (18:3-8)

"And Abraham hastened into the tent unto Sarah and said, Make ready quickly three measures of fine meal, knead it, and make cakes upon the hearth. And Abraham ran unto the herd, and fetched a calf." What an unwonted burst of activity to desecrate the hour sacred to the siesta. But the Lord had come!

Imagine a man phoning his wife from the office at five minutes to five. "Hello, dear, I'm just leaving. I'm bringing the boss home for supper and the chairman of the board, also the president of the corporation. We should be there in about fifteen minutes. By the way, get busy and bake some bread. I want to treat these important guests properly—no store-bought bread, now, but some of your own, fresh from the oven. And we'll have T-bone steaks. I'll pick some up at the store. "Bye." What a panic that would cause in most homes, what rising wrath! "What? Bake bread in this heat, on five minutes' notice? And how can I cook steaks? I don't even know where he keeps the charcoal."

In Abraham's home it was not like that. His wife did exactly what he said, did it without a murmur, without the slightest hint of criticism, panic, or complaint. But then, look how Abraham acted. Having seen to the comfort of his guests, he excused himself and dashed off to supervise the cutting and the cooking of the steaks. Then he himself, with his own hands, set the table. We read, "And he took butter and milk and the calf which he had dressed and set it before them, and he stood by them under the tree, and they did eat." Is it any wonder Sarah found it so easy to do what Abraham wanted when he was so thoughtful and considerate of her?

So then, the first glimpse we get of Abraham in a new situation is that of a practical man. In the presence of God he at once put himself in a position that told the Lord, "I'm ready to hear whatever you have to say." Laying an extra burden on his wife, he at once took responsibility for most of the chores and was not above excusing himself from the presence of the Lord of heaven in order to do so. It is no wonder Abraham had such a happy and harmonious home.

B. THE PRIVILEGED MAN (18:9-15)

There are not many people, even in the Bible, to whom the Lord appeared in visible manifestation in order to chat with them about family and foreign affairs. But He did so appear to Abraham.

1. THE PROMISE (18:9-10)

The hastily cooked meal was over and the dishes had been carried away. What a delightful revelation we have of God in chapter 18. Who could have imagined such a thing—the Lord, the creator of the universe, and two of His angels, actually sitting down with an ordinary man like you and me to enjoy a meal of homemade bread and fresh-cut steak spiced up with butter sauce and all washed down with bowls of milk. How careful the Lord was to set Abraham completely at ease. There was really no reason why the mighty Jehovah, creator of suns and stars and galaxies, should condescend to eat a human meal. He could have easily said, "Thank you, Abraham, but we need nothing to eat." But He did not. Instead, He deliberately sat down, took the food that was offered to Him, and tucked into a hearty meal. By that time, Abraham had a good idea who his visitors were, so he must have watched with astonishment as the living God cut off a piece of steak and popped it into His mouth and said, "Abraham, if you don't mind, I think I'll have another piece of that bread." Or, perhaps, "Gabriel, please be so kind as to pass the salt."

The meal was over and the dishes carried away, and the Lord glanced at Abraham. "Where is Sarah, thy wife?" He said. As if He did not know! She had her ears glued to the tent flap. "I will certainly return unto thee according to the time of life; and, lo, Sarah thy wife shall have a son." And, of course, Sarah overheard it, as God knew she would and probably intended she should. The promise had already been given to Abraham, now the sum and substance of it was poured into her eager, eavesdropping ear as well.

2. THE PROBLEM (18:11-15)

That of course, brought up the problem. "Now Abraham and Sarah were old and well stricken in age; and it ceased to be with Sarah after the manner of women. Therefore Sarah laughed within herself." When Abraham laughed in the preceding chapter, it was the laughter of faith. But Sarah's was the laughter of total disbelief. The facts of life were all against any such eventuality. Even though God had entered into covenant relationship with Abraham and Sarah, nothing, seemingly, had changed. So Sarah laughed. "Here, I've been married for something like seventy years," she thought to herself. "I'm old enough to be a great-grandmother now and somebody out there is telling Abraham that, of all women, I am about to have a baby!" It was too funny for words.

Perhaps she took a peek to get another look at the stranger who was saying such amusing things. She may have listened harder than ever to learn what He would say next, but at His next statement her hair stood straight up on end. "Wherefore did Sarah laugh?" Scared out of all caution, Sarah blurted out, "I didn't laugh," to which the Lord of glory calmly, simply, understandingly, gently replied (not to Abraham but to Sarah behind the tent wall), "Nay, but thou didst laugh." It was another proof of His sympathy and love. Sarah had lied to the living God—had *lied* to the Holy One of Israel. Yet with infinite kindness He simply passed over the outrageous offense as though it had never happened. What an illustration of Psalm 130. "If thou, LORD, shouldest mark iniquities, O Lord, who shall stand? But there is forgiveness with thee, that thou mayest be feared."

So Abraham was the privileged man, so privileged that the eternal God Himself would come down and talk with him, man to man, and tell him, in an after-dinner chat, that Sarah indeed would have a son. For God took as much interest in that son as Abraham did, or Sarah. He took more interest in it, in fact. All His purposes of grace for a lost and ruined world hinged, for the time being, on the birth of that son, who, in turn, would stand in the direct line to the coming into the world of the Son of God Himself.

C. THE PROVED MAN (18:16-22)

1. PROSPECTIVE GREATNESS (18:16-18)

Supper being over and the little family chat finished, the three visitors rose to their feet. They looked meaningfully toward Sodom, and in that look Abraham read Sodom's doom. For a moment the Lord hesitated as the other two, the angels, walked slowly away toward the cursed city. As though taking inward counsel with Himself, the Lord perhaps looked at Sodom and then at Abraham. "Shall I hide from Abraham that thing which I do," He mused, "seeing that Abraham shall surely become a great and mighty nation, and all the nations of the earth shall be blessed in Him?" Looking at His aging servant, perhaps the Lord's mind ran on down the centuries, seeing the Hebrew race in all their checkered career. Perhaps He saw the Christ Himself, coming into the world by way of that people as yet unborn. And it all began with Abraham. That one elderly man held the whole of history in his hand. He was, in prospect, a very great man.

2. PERSONAL GREATNESS (18:19)

"For I know him, that he will command his children and his household after him, and they shall keep the way of the LORD" (18:19). It had already been displayed in Abraham's haste to circumcise even Ishmael. One of the marks of greatness in Abraham was in the control he had over those who owed their allegiance to him.

3. POSITIONAL GREATNESS (18:20-22)

Having taken counsel with Himself, the Lord disclosed to Abraham what He was about to do with regard to Sodom. Its hideous sins were so offensive—their stench had reached heaven itself—that God actually came down in person to investigate on the spot the nature and extent of its filth. God shared those things with Abraham as the angels disappeared over the brow of the hill. Then we read, "Abraham stood yet before the LORD." He took up his position, his thoughts full of Lot, down there in Sodom. He stood, as it were, between the living and the dead, taking up his stand on redemption ground, prepared to plead and plead for Sodom because of Lot. It was holy boldness in the highest degree. Abraham had now become more Christlike than ever; he had become a mediator between God and man. As the Lord looked at Abraham what thoughts must have filled His heart. For He, Himself, the second Person of the Godhead, could see His own future ministry mirrored in the action of this proved and triumphant man. We can visualize Abraham standing there, his arms outstretched as though to bar the way to Sodom. So the Lord one day would stand, two arms outstretched to save, to bar the road to hell.

D. THE PRAYING MAN (18:23-33)

It was studying Genesis 18 that taught saintly George Mueller of Bristol, that modern giant of faith, one of the most important secrets of prayer. It taught him to use argument in pleading his case before God. He would remind the Lord that the orphan boys and girls entrusted to his care were not his orphans, they were God's. Had he not declared Himself to be the Father of the fatherless? It was God's work, not Mueller's. He was but the instrument. If it were God's work, was not God bound to take care of it? Could God suffer His glory to be diminished? Was not a half-believing church looking on and a wholly unbelieving world? Must not God silence the jibing tongue? Must He not silence the scoffer and the skeptic? Thus George Mueller prayed and thus he received truly astonishing answers from God. And thus Abraham prayed, besieging his heavenly visitor with plea after plea.

1. ABRAHAM'S ATTITUDE (18:23*a*)

First, he fell on his face, then he stood before the Lord, then he "drew near." Abraham anticipated present-day privilege and entered, as it were, with boldness into the holiest of all. The bars and bolts of the Law had not yet been fixed in place. On the simple ground of a future Calvary, Abraham "drew near" in an attitude of holy daring mixed with reverential awe.

2. ABRAHAM'S ARGUMENT (18:23*b*-32)

Like a true oriental, Abraham actually bargained with God. Anyone who has been in an eastern market knows how it goes:

"How much do you want for this silk scarf?"

"Fifty piasters."

"Fifty piasters! I'll give you five."

At that point the merchant seems about to break a blood vessel. He calls all his ancestors to witness the insult that has been heaped upon him. Finally he says, "Forty-five."

"Nonsense," says the buyer, "I can get one next door without being robbed." He returns the scarf to the seller. But mention of the competition evokes a further reduction in price. "As Allah is my witness I'll be ruined. Thirty piasters!" And the merchant throws down the scarf in disgust.

The purchaser walks out of the shop and heads next door, but before a dozen steps can be taken the shopkeeper comes hurrying out too, wringing his hands and calling on his god. "Come back! Come back! You can have it for twenty."

The purchaser returns to the shop, picks up the merchandise and looks at it with critical disdain. The merchant is ready. He picks a gaudy silk handkerchief. "Twenty piasters–and I'll throw in this matchless handkerchief of finest Damascus silk. May Allah witness I am being ruined; what can I do? I have a large family. Twenty piasters and this silk handkerchief free."

The purchaser takes out his wallet and places ten piasters on the counter. He picks up the scarf. "Ten piasters, Abdullah, and that's my final offer. Ten piasters and you can keep your handkerchief."

That is how it went between Abraham and God. He bargained with God as he would bargain in the *suk*. He haggled, as it were, over the price. What would God take? How many souls would be needed to save Sodom? It was done with great daring but also with very great dignity and awe. "Lord, suppose there are fifty righteous? Suppose it lacks five of the fifty? What about forty-five? Forty? Twenty? Ten?" And each time the living God, with infinite condescension, came down until at last Abraham stopped at ten.

3. ABRAHAM'S ASSURANCE (18:33)

He stopped at ten. Up until then he had complete assurance that God would hear and respond, but at the figure ten all such assurance stopped. He had arrived at the divinely set limit, and so well attuned was Abraham to the mind and will of God that he instinctively knew that he must go no lower than ten.

But why was ten the number? Suppose Abraham had gone on to five. He could still not have saved Sodom, for there were not five righteous souls in that place. There were only four who responded in the crucial hour. There were five cities in the plain. In Scripture *two* is the number of adequate witness, so it required *ten* righteous people to be in the valley, else there would not be even the minimum witness for God. Then, too, Abraham probably believed that there would be ten righteous souls in Sodom. There were Lot and his wife and his two unmarried daughters who lived in his house—that made four. There were his sons-in-law (the text uses the plural, not the dual, implying that there would be at least three of them) who, together with their wives, would make another six, thus making ten in all. So for one reason or another Abraham lost all liberty to pray further when he arrived at the number ten.

God had His way and, wonderfully enough, Abraham had his way too. Abraham's chief burden was for Lot and his family. The evil Sodomites were destroyed, but believing Lot and those who believed with him were saved. The righteous were saved after all, and God's character was vindicated to the full.

To the people of Sodom there must always have seemed something odd and fanatical about Abraham with his rigid standards of separation. They respected him, but they probably ridiculed him too. People who live for God are always looked at askance by the world. Yet, like the men of Sodom, the world will never know what it owes to the presence of godly men on the earth. When Abraham could no longer pray, judgment fell.

VIII. THE POSITION OF FAITH (19:1-38)

In our degenerate culture people who indulge in the vile passions of Sodom are termed "gay." They demand their rights. They parade and demonstrate. They broadcast their shame on radio and television talk shows. They crusade for the elimination of all legislation that interferes with their supposed right to practice their abominations. The mayor of one great American city even went so far as to proclaim "Gay Pride Week" to honor them and give them public recognition. An anemic, brain-washed culture, that has completely lost its way morally, bows to the pressure and accedes to the demands. If people are "gay," let them be "gay" in the attitude. Truly "if God does not punish America and the world, He will have to apologize to Sodom and Gomorrah."

Sodom is named six times in the Old Testament and four times in the New. Its name is synonymous with sexual perversion. It stands in the Bible as the outstanding example of an overthrow without remedy. When Jonah stalked through the streets of Nineveh, the judgment he proclaimed was canceled when repentance and revival came. The judgment of the Flood will never be repeated—God has pledged Himself to that by the rainbow in the sky. But the sins of Sodom know no remedy. As Paul teaches in Romans 1, their toleration by society indicates that the culture indulging such vices is a totally abandoned culture. More than any other catastrophe in the history of the world, the overthrow of Sodom is held up to us as the supreme example of the coming judgment of the world. Jesus said: "As it was in the days of Lot . . . thus shall it be in the day when the Son of man is revealed" (Luke 17:28-30).

The overthrow of Sodom provides us with a studied parallel based on changeless principles. Given the same set of circumstances, God acts in the same way He did before. Thus the doom of Sodom and the hair-breadth escape of Lot illustrate the impending doom of the world and the nick-of-time escape of the church.

A. THE UNHOLY MORALITY OF SODOM (19:1-11)

God sets a limit to human wickedness beyond which judgment is inevitable, unsuspected by the majority, and final in its character. "The men of Sodom were wicked and sinners before the LORD exceedingly" is the verdict already passed on the city and its culture by the Holy Spirit (13:13). The unholy morality of Sodom was, first of all, a *prevalent thing*. It was not that one or two shamefaced individuals sneaked through the night to perform their obscenities in private, behind locked doors. It was an accepted way of life.

In the previous chapter, Abraham was seen sitting in the door of his tent; in chapter 19 Lot is found sitting in the gate of Sodom. He had risen in the world. He probably had become one of Sodom's high officials, a member of its legislature no less, charged with upholding its principles and protecting the filthy privileges of its people. What a place for a professing believer! Lot was pledged to help keep the laws on the books that enabled perverts and deviates to practice their sins without fear of reproof. That was how far the morality of Sodom had tainted the values, the judgment, the sense of right and wrong of the backslidden child of God.

There Lot sat, resplendent in his official robes, surrounded by filthy-minded men, accepted by them because he now spoke their language and condoned their practices and, above all, because he had the right connections. After all, his uncle Abraham was a powerful man whose prowess in war was only too well remembered in Sodom. So there Lot sat, smiling, laughing, agreeing outwardly while inwardly eating out his soul because of the abominable customs and practices he was bound to uphold as one of Sodom's lords. Suddenly he was startled at the appearance of two angels. They had appeared to Abraham as *men*, to Lot they appeared as angels. The changed appearance typified distance; they were not nearly so close or so cordial with Lot as they had been with Abraham. He saw them in their angelic form although to his unsaved cronies they appeared to be men. The sight of an angel would have been too much for them.

Lot excused himself and hastened to meet the visitors and offered them the hospitality of his home. "Behold now, my lords, turn in, I pray you, into your servant's house, and tarry all night" (incidentally, the first mention of a house in Scripture). Abraham had a tent; Lot had a house. Abraham was a pilgrim; Lot was a citizen. Abraham was living for the celestial city; Lot was living for Sodom. When the angels visited Abraham they gladly accepted his hospitality. With Lot they were curt. "Nay," they said, "but we will abide in the street all night" (again, here is the first mention of a street). At once the prevalence of the unholy morality of Sodom leaps to view. The streets of Sodom were unsafe, especially at night. Nobody knew better than Lot the kinds of things that went on at night in the streets of that vile place, so he "pressed them," we are told. He was urgent, insistent. As a member of the city administration he knew only too well what crime and corruption stalked Sodom at night, what licentious bands of perverts prowled the streets—men worse than wild beasts, with passions fired by hell.

The unholy morality of Sodom was, indeed, not only a prevalent thing but also a *polluted* thing (19:4-5). With manifest reluctance the angelic visitors accepted Lot's hospitality. He set before them what is politely called "a feast," but the Spirit of God does not linger over it lovingly as He does over Abraham's meal. Indeed, the only thing mentioned is unleavened bread—flat, insipid, tasteless stuff. There were no fresh oven-baked rolls on Lot's table, for what has a carnal-minded man to offer a visitor from heaven? All heaven would take from him was unleavened bread. Symbolically it may have been a token gesture that sin must be put away from his life.

Supper was hardly over when there was an uproar at Lot's door. He blanched, because he knew full well what those hideous howlings meant. The young hoodlums of Sodom, with their dragon lusts, were out there demanding their dues. Now they were hammering on the door: "Where are the men? Bring out the men!" Their civil rights were affronted by Lot's barred and bolted door. They had the right to impose their horrid lusts on strangers who dared stay the night in Sodom.

The uproar increased and Lot, looking out, probably saw that the crowd at his front door was growing by leaps and bounds. Every filthy hound of Sodom had come, young pups and old dogs alike, panting and baying and growling—worse than dogs, worse than swine, all heated to the point of riot with their dreadful, hellish passions aflame. "Where are the men? Where are the men?" It was the vilest, most degraded, unholiest demand that can possibly issue from the lips of men.

The unholy morality of Sodom was a *persistent* thing (19:6-9*a*). "And Lot went out at the door unto them, and shut the door after him. And said, I pray you, brethren, do not so wickedly. Behold now, I have two daughters—" It was a brave thing to do, to put himself between the mob and his guests. But imagine a believer—a friend of Abraham the friend of God, a man who had been a pilgrim, a man who had once had a tent and who had once confessed Abraham's faith—imagine such a man calling the scum of Sodom "brethren"! That is how far the unholy morality of Sodom had warped Lot's sense of values.

He was desperate. Perhaps he thought his position as city magistrate might overawe the mob. He stood there with his back to the door, facing the mob and somehow he made himself heard. But, oh, the shame of it! He offered them his daughters. He proposed to sacrifice his own girls to their lusts if only they would go away. But ordinary passion was tame as a worm compared with the fire-breathing dragon-lust that consumed them. He urged upon them the sacred laws of eastern hospitality, but he might have saved his breath. What cared the men of Sodom, when their perverted appetites were inflamed, for the laws of hospitality and the ordinary decencies of men? They spurned him. "You don't even belong here," they roared. "Out of the way, fellow, or we'll do worse to you than we intend to do to the men behind that door." The unholy morality of Sodom was a persistent thing. If there is one thing that marks perversion, it is its deep-seated character. As a cancerous cell in a healthy body grows and spreads until it destroys the health of the whole body, so perverted lust entrenches itself and takes over the life.

But more, the unholy morality of Sodom was a *pugnacious* thing (19:9*b*). "They pressed sore upon the man, even Lot, and came near to break the door." The riot had burst all bounds. Far from dissuading the evil men, Lot had only succeeded in goading them, and in a matter of moments he would be trampled to pulp, the door of his house beaten in, and his family and guests exposed to horrors worse than the sack of a city.

The unholy lusts of those men were pugnacious. No longer did the perverts practice their abominations in secret, ostracized by the rest of the community. No longer were their shameful sins tolerated by a permissive society as something people had a right to practice if they pleased. It had gone far beyond that. Now the people were an open, aggressive, insistent force in the city with which none dared interfere. For their behavior was not looked upon by the Sodomites as criminal but as *constitutional.* They had the constitutional right to indulge their passions when and where they wished and any attempt to thwart them could be expected to lead to open riot in the city.

But if the unholy morality of Sodom was a prevalent, polluted, persistent, and pugnacious thing, it was also a *punishable* thing—not by the laws of Sodom, perhaps, but certainly by the laws of God. If society will not punish that form of behavior, then God most certainly will. In Lot's case the angels acted. "But the men [the angelic visitors] put forth their hand, and pulled Lot into the house to them, and shut the door. And they smote the men that were at the door of the house with blindness, both small and great: so that they wearied themselves to find the door." That was judicial blindness. "Whom the gods would destroy, they first make mad," said one of the ancient philosophers. Not so! Whom God would destroy, He first makes blind. There comes a point in the rising tide of human wickedness, where God acts. In preparation he blinds. The process takes various forms; in Pharaoh's case, God hardened his heart; in a coming day He will send men strong delusion so that they will believe "the lie." It is a dangerous thing to transgress with arrogance and persistence the laws of God.

B. THE UNHOLY MENTALITY OF SODOM (19:12-38)

From now on the spotlight swings from the filthiness of Sodom to the situation that existed in Lot's own family. It shows what the philosophy of Sodom had done to the thinking of a believing man. Truly we cannot keep on imbibing the world's ideologies without becoming tainted ourselves.

1. LOT'S FAITH CORRODED (19:12-26)

Outside, the fierce blasphemies of the ungodly could be heard as the mob pushed and scrambled and cursed the black darkness that had descended upon them, yet still insisting on their right to quench their perverted lusts. Inside, Lot and his wife and his two daughters collapsed upon the cushions, badly shaken. Lot turned perhaps, to his guests, with fulsome words of apology on his lips, only to be cut short.

"We have no time for that. Where's the rest of your family? You have married children? Fetch them at once, for we will destroy this place."

Whatever may have been Lot's faults, lack of courage was not one of them. A moment ago he had almost lost his life on his front doorstep. Now he must go back out, traverse the city streets, and visit the houses of his children in various parts of the town. What a scene that would be for an artist's brush–Lot hurrying through the darkened streets, dodging the grovelling hands of the blinded, fierce, human wolves that still ravaged his door, urging upon his children the imminence of coming doom. But mark well *Lot's worthless witness* (19:12-14). He ran from house to house, he awoke up his children, gathered the family of this one and that around him in the living room. He told what had happened. He urged upon them the imminent doom of Sodom. He waxed apocalyptic and described the coming judgment in words urgent but few. "Hurry! Hurry!" he cried. "But he seemed as one that mocked unto his sons in law" (19:14). "The old man's crazy!" they said.

So there he went, with tear-blinded eyes, stumbling back the way he had come, pausing now to cower behind a hedge, now in a store doorway, as howling bands of libertines blundered past. His testimony had fallen on deaf ears. His daughters, married to men of Sodom, had the mentality of Sodom. They were unable to receive spiritual truth. And Lot, with years of backsliding behind him, had no spiritual power. He was unable to carry conviction with his words.

The sudden spurt of spiritual force was spent, and Lot staggered in through the door exhausted. He then showed how greatly he had been sapped by living in Sodom. Attention is drawn to *Lot's weak will* (19:15-23). A dynamic spiritual life cannot be nourished on worldliness. How *reluctant he was to start.* At the first hint of dawn the angels began to hasten Lot. "Arise, take thy wife, and thy two daughters, which are here; lest thou be consumed in the iniquity of the city. And while he lingered, the men laid hold upon his hand, and upon the hand of his wife, and upon the hand of his two daughters." We can picture the scene—Lot being dragged out of Sodom, the whole family dillying, dallying, and dawdling on the way—the wife wanting to sort out her jewelry, the daughters wanting to get suitably dressed, Lot wanting to find his bankbook and his list of accounts receivable. It is incredible how dull a backslidden person becomes to spiritual truth.

How *ready he was to stop*. The angels had hardly dragged him clear of Sodom when Lot began to protest the rigors of the way. "Oh, not so, my Lord . . . I cannot escape to the mountain, lest some evil take me, and I die." Why, the mountain was a veritable fortress compared with the flimsy cities of the plain, over which already hung the drawn sword of doom. The wild beasts of the passes were tame kittens compared with the vile, two-legged beasts of Sodom. Besides, God had not saved him from Sodom simply to cast him away forgotten on the mountain. But the mentality of Sodom cannot comprehend a truth like that.

Then there was *Lot's wayward wife* (19:24-26). Under the constant urging of the angels, Lot and his family finally moved out of the danger zone. Instantly the judgment fell. Fire and brimstone came hurtling down from on high, hell rained down from heaven, and the wail of a lost city arose to the sky. And Lot's wife looked back.

"Look not behind thee," cried the angels, "neither stay thou in all the plain." The family, saved so as by fire, must now forget those things that are behind. The world must be divorced, even at this late hour, from their very hearts. But Lot's wife looked back. Alford says that it was a steadfast, earnest look, a wistful look, a lingering, hankering look. Perhaps she was thinking of all the trinkets and gadgets she had left behind. Perhaps she was thinking of her children. In any case, she disobeyed and looked back and was turned into a monument to a divided heart. She was turned into a pillar of salt as the fringes of the holocaust overwhelmed her where she stood. The erosions of time and weather have obliterated that mournful statue now, but the Lord Jesus has embalmed her in the Bible as a warning to us all. "Remember Lot's wife," He said (Luke 17:32).

2. LOT'S FAMILY CORRUPTED (19:27-38)

As though sickened by Sodom's sins and Sodom's shame, the Holy Spirit pauses in telling the story to talk for a moment about Abraham. The mention of Abraham shows us *what Lot might have become* (19:27-29). "And Abraham gat up early in the morning to the place where he stood before the LORD: And he looked toward Sodom and Gomorrah, and toward all the land of the plain, and beheld, and, lo, the smoke of the country went up as the smoke of a furnace." Abraham had lost nothing. He had not even lost a night's sleep. He stood there on hallowed ground, far above the smoking ruins of the world below, conscious that, on that very spot yesterday he had met face to face, not a mere angel, but God Himself. Into his heart there stole the quiet assurance that though judgment had overtaken Sodom, his prayers for Lot had not been all in vain. Lot might have stood where Abraham stood; instead he was now a fugitive, a refugee, a vagabond on the earth, beggared and all but alone.

We are told next *what Lot had become* (19:30-38). Those sad verses tell a story of the mentality of Sodom, so thoroughly absorbed by Lot's daughters, that they found it impossible to reason aright. They show us Lot drunk and dishonored, and his daughters behaving in a way that would have won the applause of any dirty-minded man in Sodom.

The older girl made the proposal to her sister, a proposal so unblushingly shameful that it betrays at once the kind of teaching she received in Sodom's schools. There was no thought of God, no knowledge of His Word, no concern for His will, no concept of His care. There was no prayer, no thought that what she proposed was morally wrong. She and her sister were completely amoral. They were spiritually dead. They reasoned like a couple of pagans, which is really what they were.

All the two young women could think of was their isolation from the world and the thought that, for all they knew, they would never again have contact with their kind. They were obsessed with the thought that they might thus die childless. They determined that they would make their father drunk and then, first the one and then the other, they would seduce the old man and at least have some chance of bearing a child.

And so they did. There was no shame, no sorrow, no compunction, no sense of sin, no concept of the holiness of God, just downright wickedness as though their behavior was perfectly normal, which, of course, it was—for Sodom. But then, Sodom was all they knew.

As a result Moab and Ammon were born, and from Moab and Ammon sprang two nations who became the bitter and persistent enemies of the people of God. The Moabites settled down and became entrenched, hostile neighbors of Israel; and the Ammonites, restless, nomadic wanderers for the most part, ever sought opportunity to side with Israel's foes.

It would be difficult to decide whether or not Lot was a truly saved man by reading his story in the Old Testament. He made no positive contribution to the life of faith. He chose the lower, the carnal, the worldly path. He left the fellowship of the faith at the earliest possible moment and was never restored to that fellowship. He made no mark for God. His family ended in disaster. The last we see of him in the narrative he is drunk and dishonored. Indeed, were it not for a brief but remarkable statement of Peter written thousands of years later (2 Peter 2:7-8) we would be justified in concluding that the root of the matter had never been in him at all. Such is the life of a backslider. May God deliver us from a life like that. Indeed, may we "remember Lot's wife."

IX. THE PERILS OF FAITH (20:1-18)

The tragedy is, of course, that Abraham had done that very thing once before. On his way into Egypt he and Sarah had agreed she would pose as his sister rather than be known as his wife. The disastrous experiences in Egypt, it might be thought, would have taught Abraham a lesson. Not so. He repeated the same grievous mistake all over again. Truly, the Holy Spirit does not gloss over the sins and shortcomings of even the greatest saints. Abraham, after all, was a man of like passions as we are. He stumbled and fell like we do. All too often, we, like Abraham, have been mercifully delivered from a wrong course of action by the grace and intervention of God only to go back to a similar thing at a later date. The sight of Lot going back to Sodom is scarcely less deplorable than the sight of Abraham going back over the same ground of failure as before.

"Now look here, Sarah, my dear—you know how it is in these parts. The chieftains around here are a wild and willful crowd, and these Philistine chiefs are powerful and unrestrained. Now don't forget. We're going into Abimelech's country as *brother and sister,* not husband and wife, right?" That was the background of the sorry incident. It seems incredible that the man who had won so many victories, who had received such unique manifestations of God's presence, could stumble so badly so soon. Behind the whole incident, of course, was Satan, making one last-ditch attempt to prevent the birth of Isaac and, hence, ultimately the birth of Christ.

A. THE MOVING PILGRIM (20:1-2)

We are not told why Abraham was on the move. He had been living in fellowship with God on the plains of Mamre. The last glimpse we had of him he was standing on the spot where he had interceded with God for Sodom, looking down toward the smoldering valley of the Jordan. Perhaps Abraham had wept over those poor ruins, wondering how and where Lot had escaped. It may be that the sight of those melancholy ruins upset him so much he decided to move away. In any case, he rounded up his flocks and herds, struck camp and moved southward along the very road that had once taken him into Egypt. From the silence of God in connection with the move it seems possible that Abraham was acting on his own accord without any direct leading from the Lord. That is always a dangerous thing to do.

The southern highway took the pilgrim and his family into the country of the Philistines, where he repeated his former sin. "And Abraham said of Sarah his wife, She is my sister: And Abimelech king of Gerar sent, and took Sarah." The astonishing fact is, of course, that Sarah was now ninety years of age and, as she herself had confessed, very old. Now hot-blooded kings, with large and delectable harems, do not choose old women to number among their wives. The inference is very strong therefore that the Lord had performed a miracle and that He had renewed Sarah's youth in readiness for her forthcoming role as a mother.

Some years ago an aging preacher was taken to see the mummified remains of the famous preacher George Whitefield. The sight was not too inspiring, for time had placed its hand upon the embalmer's work. The old preacher looked at the mortal remains of the great revivalist and, being greatly moved at the sight, he addressed them thus: "Well, George," he said, "You're not looking so good. I don't expect to be back this way, my friend. But you'll be looking much better when I see you again—in the air!"

It would seem that the Lord did not wait until the rapture to do a cosmetic job on Sarah's worn out old body. Down there in Gerar, at the age of ninety, she could compete with any nineteen-year-old in the land.

Abraham is first seen in chapter 20 as a moving pilgrim. But he had made a wrong move and was about to be checkmated by God, just as God so often checkmates us.

B. The Miserable Prophet (20:3-16)

Here is the first place in Scripture that someone is actually called a prophet. Yet what a miserable impression Abraham makes on us! There is something about a prophet acting in the flesh that rubs against the grain. We have an instinctive feeling that any person who represents God should be beyond reproach in his personal and public life. His integrity should be beyond question. Abraham had already compromised his by telling a barefaced lie.

1. Not Readily Recognizable as a Prophet (20:3-7)

Certainly, Abimelech did not say to himself, as Abraham appeared before him, "This man is a prophet of God!" The narrative focuses first on Abimelech and gives us a glimpse of *Abimelech's lost condition* (20:3). "God came to Abimelech in a dream by night, and said to him, Behold, thou art but a dead man, for the woman which thou hast taken; for she is a man's wife." God's standards on the matter of marital purity are high and unchanging whether in the patriarchal age, under the Law, or in a day of grace. To take another man's wife is a sin worthy of death in God's moral code.

For some reason Abimelech had not yet tampered with Sarah. He had appropriated her for his harem, but had not proceeded further. He went to bed that night anticipating the future with complacency, but he woke with his hair standing on end. He had just had a horrifying dream. He had dreamed himself dead and face to face with an outraged God, and all because of that new harem girl—what was her name—Sarah? Yes, Sarah, sister of the sheikh Abraham. And, perhaps, for the first time in his life, that king, who had many noble qualities about him, had been confronted with the horror of his lost condition. There is nothing quite like fear of personal and imminent death to bring one face to face with ultimate realities. So Abimelech was forced to face the fact that he was a sinner and that the wages of sin is death and that after death is the judgment.

Next we hear *Abimelech's loud complaint* (20:4-5). At once, he shifted the blame. "Said he not unto me, She is my sister? and she, even she herself said, He is my brother: in the integrity of my heart and innocency of hands have I done this." It is perfectly true that both Abraham and Sarah had acted in an inexcusable way, but that was no excuse for Abimelech's own promiscuous ways. Abimelech's moral principles were far, far below those demanded by God. In Abimelech's book it was quite all right for him to appropriate to his own use any woman he desired. Her will in the matter was not even to be considered. In his view it was perfectly proper for him to exploit his position and power and to exercise his prerogatives. He could gratify his lusts to his heart's content, especially when he threw the cloak of legality over his passions. So his protest, his loud complaint, was not very impressive after all. Possibly, in that instance, Abraham was more guilty than he was, but Abraham's poor behavior did not in any way excuse his. His loud complaint conveniently ignored the fact that, regardless of the attending circumstances, he had acted in a high-handed way and on carnal, sensual, fleshly, worldly principles. God was not impressed with his protests.

After all, human laws can be very accommodating. Had Abimelech broken the law? No. And why? For the simple reason the law was so written that his lusts could be accommodated. The same spirit is evident today. There was a time when adultery was a crime; not any more. We have rewritten the laws. There was a time when homosexuality was a crime; not any more. We have written new laws to accommodate the deviates. Man's way of handling awkward cases is to frame laws that make concession to human lusts. It is not God's way.

That brings us to *Abimelech's last consideration* (20:6-7). The last thing that entered Abimelech's mind was that he had been *sovereignly restrained*. He had every intention of forcing his lust on Sarah. God had intervened and kept him back from crossing that fatal line. "And God said unto him . . . I also withheld thee from sinning against me: therefore I suffered thee not to touch her." In a single word, God demolished all of Abimelech's pious claims. We shall never know, this side of heaven, how often God has held us back by some strange set of circumstances, from committing serious sins. But the thought that God had actually prevented his continuing on a judgment-ending path never occurred to Abimelech at all.

His last consideration was that he was *still responsible*. "Now therefore restore the man his wife; for he is a prophet, and he shall pray for thee, . . . and if thou restore her not, know thou that thou shalt surely die, thou and all that are thine." Abimelech had made no offer to put things right, proof indeed, that all his protests of personal integrity were insincere. God could read the man's heart. He could see that, had he not been frightened out of his wits, he would certainly have proceeded with his intentions of submitting Sarah to his lusts whether or not she were Abraham's wife. He acted, in the end, not because he loved righteousness, but because he feared retribution. It was to Abraham's discredit that, in his encounter with Abimelech, the pagan king did not recognize in him a prophet of God. But Abimelech was told that, all appearances to the contrary notwithstanding, Abraham *was* a prophet, and that he had better treat him accordingly.

2. NOT REALLY REGARDED AS A PROPHET (20:8-13)

Abimelech was up at dawn. The horrors of the night still haunted him. He summoned his servants and recounted to them the nightmare he had suffered, and the fear of God fell upon his servants too. Then, dressed and ready and in a towering rage, tempered by a wholesome fear of God, the Philistine king summoned Abraham to give him a piece of his mind.

It is no part of God's usual dealings with us to shield us from the embarrassments we bring upon ourselves by our sins. Having vented his wrath on Abraham, the irate king demanded an explanation. What a wretched, rambling lame-duck explanation it was when it came. Godward, Abraham confessed himself *distrustful;* manward, he confessed himself *dishonest;* selfward, he confessed himself *disgraced.*

"I did it," mumbled the red-faced patriarch, "because I thought, Surely the fear of God is not in this place; and they will slay me for my wife's sake." How *distrustful!* Why, the fear of God was so overwhelming that Abimelech, even though furious, could scarcely keep himself from trembling with fright even as he sat on his throne. And all around him his courtiers were in an equal panic with their king.

"And yet indeed she is my sister; she is the daughter of my father, but not the daughter of my mother," continued the humbled Abraham. How *dishonest!* There are few things the unsaved man despises in the believer more than dishonesty. And, of all the forms of dishonesty, none is worse than one that draws its strength from a half-truth. That a saint of God should stoop to such a trick was almost unbelievable. That Abraham should have stooped to that identical form of dishonesty twice was almost unforgivable—except that God forgives us not once, or twice, or even seven times, but seventy times seven times.

"And it came to pass, when God caused me to wander from my father's house, that I said unto her, This is thy kindness which thou shalt shew unto me; at every place whither we shall come, say of me, He is my brother." It was the presence of lawless and lustful kings like Abimelech, entrenched everywhere along the great trade routes, that so filled Abraham's heart with fear. But, how *disgraceful!* What a cowardly thing to do. But then, when we take our eyes off the Lord there is no end to the follies we can commit.

Cowardice is a terrible thing. It led Peter to deny his Lord, it led Abraham to deny his wife, it can lead us into many sad compromises. Whoever would have believed that such a great and noble man as Abraham, the friend of God, could have been so ignoble and so base. It is no wonder that Abimelech, looking at Abraham and listening to his words, did not really regard him as a prophet.

3. NOT RIGHTLY RECEIVED AS A PROPHET (20:14-16)

There is not the slightest hint that Abimelech ever asked Abraham to pray for him, even though God Himself had told him his salvation lay in that. Certainly Abimelech never asked Abraham to tell him more about the true and living God who had so greatly frightened him in the watches of the night. Nor did he ask Abraham anything about the salvation of God. He was frightened, but he certainly did not want to know God. On the contrary, he did three things calculated to make Abraham squirm yet the more.

In the first place, he deliberately *disgraced* him. "And Abimelech took sheep, and oxen, and menservants, and womenservants, and gave them unto Abraham, and restored him Sarah his wife" (20:14). Abimelech had no respect for Abraham and had no intention of availing himself of Abraham's knowledge of God. Nevertheless he had a healthy fear of the God who had shaken him so. *If this despicable fellow is a prophet then he had best be propitiated,* thought Abimelech. *Every man has his price.* So Abimelech disgraced Abraham by treating him, along worldly lines, in a far more handsome way than Abraham had treated him. *Now perhaps the fellow will overlook the fact that I appropriated his wife!* he thought. "Is that enough, sir, to make you forget your grievances?"

Then he *dismissed* him. "And Abimelech said, Behold my land is before thee: dwell where it pleaseth thee." What a rebuke it is when an unsaved man has to teach a believer common honesty and decency. In dismissing Abraham thus, Abimelech heaped coals of fire upon his head. In effect he said to Abraham, "Let me show you how a believer ought to act. He should be generous and honest and open-handed and trustworthy."

And all along he *disdained* him. "And unto Sarah he said, Behold, I have given thy brother a thousand pieces of silver." One can almost see Abimelech rise up from his throne as he said it, his voice edged with sarcasm and with a sneer on his face and a bow to Abraham. "A thousand pieces of silver, my dear, for your *brother.* What do you think of that? It is too bad, princess, that you do not have a husband, or I would have given it to him." And with that parting thrust Abraham was made to know just exactly how low an estimate Abimelech had formed of him—a prophet, indeed!

C. THE MINISTERING PRIEST (20:17-18)

As he gathered up his things and took his leave of Abimelech's court, Abraham must have felt very small. He was wounded to the quick by the polished and barely disguised sarcasms of Abimelech, yet it was at that point that Abraham's true spiritual greatness was shown. Instead of harboring resentment against Abimelech he inwardly acknowledged he had nobody to blame but himself for the whole sad episode. Abimelech had refused his services as a prophet; that could be understood. But if he had lost all opportunity ever to preach to Abimelech he could at least pray for him. And so he did.

The narrative sets before us then *the scope* of Abraham's priestly ministry. "So Abraham prayed unto God: and God healed Abimelech, and his wife, and his maidservants" (20:17*a*). What a pity it is that, of all the recorded prayers in the Bible, we have no record of what Abraham actually said when he prayed for Abimelech. Perhaps it was, "Lord, I have brought disgrace upon my testimony again. My evil heart of unbelief is as pagan as when You first met me in far-off Ur. Dear Lord, have mercy on Abimelech and all his house. I have failed to show him what You are really like. Do You show him, Lord."

Then there was *the success* of Abraham's priestly ministry. "And God healed Abimelech, and his wife, and his maidservants; and they bare children." Truly, the fervent, effectual prayer of a righteous man availeth much. Abimelech may have despised Abraham, but there was not a physician in all the world able to do what Abraham did. The cause of Abimelech's trouble was sin, and no physician could deal with that—only the Great Physician.

Finally we are told of *the significance* of Abraham's priestly ministry. "For the Lord had fast closed up all the wombs of the house of Abimelech, because of Sarah Abraham's wife" (20:18). The motive is obvious, surely. The promised Seed was to come through Sarah. The whole preceding incident was designed by the evil one either to prevent the birth of Isaac or else to so discredit that birth that nobody would ever be able to brush off the insinuation that Isaac was *Abimelech's* son, not Abraham's. Even though Abimelech had never touched Sarah, the subtle insinuations might still have remained. So to safeguard Sarah, to silence any such suspicions, God acted as He did. He frustrated and foiled the devil by rendering sterile and barren every woman in Abimelech's household. And the curse of sterility remained until such time as Abraham prayed for its removal. Abraham's priestly ministry on behalf of Abimelech and his house, exercised when he was well clear of the palace and all grounds for suspicion removed, signified that the danger was over. Satan had been foiled again.

X. THE PRIZE OF FAITH
(21:1-34)

It was a red-letter day in Abraham's life. It was a chapter in his experience to be written in bold capitals, underlined and framed, and hung forever in the gallery of faith. There had been other notable days, but never a day like that. For on that day, Isaac was born. Up in heaven the angels must have smiled to see Abraham skipping and hopping around his compound like a five-year-old. We are reminded of old Ebenezer Scrooge when he woke up after his three soul-shaking hauntings to find out it was still Christmas Day. He was so transported with joy he could hardly put his clothes on. "I don't know what to do," cried Scrooge, laughing and crying at the same time. "I am as light as a feather, I am as happy as an angel, I am as merry as a schoolboy, I am as giddy as a drunken man." He cavorted about his rooms. He burst into a laugh. "Really," exclaims Dickens, "Really, for a man who had been out of practice for so many years it was a splendid laugh, a most illustrious laugh, the father of a long line of laughs."

And so it must have been with staid old Abraham. A boy had been born into his home. His boy! Sarah's boy! God's boy! And, had it been possible for us to be there that day, we might have seen him popping in and out of his tent, laughing and chuckling, and beaming, and embracing everyone within reach.

The story of Isaac's birth, just the same, is almost crowded off the page. What a busy chapter it is. There are seven things recorded in it altogether. We meet Isaac and Ishmael, Sarah and Abraham, God and Hagar and, poking his nose in at the end, that two-faced old hypocrite Abimelech.

A. THE TREMENDOUS MIRACLE OF ISAAC (21:1-8)

That Isaac should be there at all was a very great miracle. What doubtings, what difficulties, what disasters had to be overcome before that little fellow could see the light of day. Two specific miracles are mentioned in connection with Isaac's birth. There was the miracle of the exact nature of *the forecast* (21:1-2). "And the LORD visited Sarah *as he had said,* and the LORD did unto Sarah *as he had spoken.* For Sarah conceived, and bare Abraham a son in his old age, at the set time *of which God had spoken* to him" (italics added). Three times in one sentence the forecast is mentioned.

Only God can prophesy. There are countless soothsayers, seers, and astrologers emerging in our day. They are interviewed, consulted on popular radio and television talk shows, and they make plenty of noise. But only God can prophesy. Outside of Holy Writ all prognostications regarding the future are riddled with ambiguity, error, and fraud, not to mention outright satanic deception. But God can rip aside the veil from the future and read tomorrow's happenings as though they had happened yesterday. Nine months before, God had told Abraham and Sarah they would have a son "at the set time." And so it was. Nine months later the child was born in defiance of natural law.

There was the miracle of the exact nature of *the fulfillment* (21:3-8). Isaac was promised; Isaac was born. Abraham was a hundred and Sarah was ninety. In the overflow of her excitement Sarah exclaimed: "I have born him [Abraham] a son in his old age!" Abraham laughed, and Sarah laughed and, as God had said, they called the little boy "Isaac." *Laughter.* All the doubts and disappointments of the past vanished like mist before the rising sun. God had kept His word; Isaac was born.

Two subsequent happenings are recorded by the Holy Spirit. One shows dependence, the other development. First, when Isaac was eight days old, Abraham circumcised him. How easy it is, in the wake of a remarkable answer to prayer, to forget our dependence on God. Not Abraham. He had his long-awaited answer to prayer. Now he would see to it that his utter dependence on God for the future spiritual welfare of that child be acknowledged in a way pleasing to God. The rite of circumcision was not a pleasant one; it was a painful one. Father and son suffered alike. The father experienced the anguish of seeing the little one suffer; the son felt the sudden, sharp stab of the knife as his blood was shed. Abraham confessed himself dependent on the grace of God for the spiritual welfare of his son.

Then, when Isaac was weaned, Abraham gave a great feast. He wanted the world to know of Isaac's development. He was no longer on milk. He was growing up; he was ready for meat. What a blessed thing it is when those who have been similarly miraculously born, "born of God," show signs of development. If anything, it is more thrilling than when they were born again.

B. The Terrible Mockery of Ishmael (21:9)

"And Sarah saw the son of Hagar the Egyptian, which she had born unto Abraham, mocking." What a tremendously revealing statement! It shows, in a flash, that *spirituality* is not hereditary, but that *carnality* is. Every child of Adam's race inherits a fallen, human nature, a sinful nature. Nobody, not even one born to the godliest parents, inherits a spiritual nature. That comes only as a result of a new birth.

Ishmael was now about fourteen years of age, and the birth of Isaac revealed his true nature. He had been circumcised himself the year before, but that had done nothing to change his rebellious heart. A mere religious rite, weighted down as it may be with full biblical meaning and authority, does not change the heart. A man who is a rebel at heart remains a rebel unless he is born again. He may be baptized and circumcised and confirmed and shriven and anything else religion might suggest. But that will not change him. Administering sacraments to unsaved people is a sheer waste of time.

Ishmael had been brought up in a godly home. He had seen his father's godly life, had heard Abraham's accounts of his encounters with God, had seen Abraham at prayer, had been in the camp when the living God Himself and two of His mighty angels had come by. He knew from his own mother that God indeed was a living God, a God who had a blessing in store for him too. All that meant nothing to Ishmael. He mocked Isaac, and his mocking revealed the state of his soul. He mocked at the promised seed and thus betrayed a heart like Herod's that, in a later day, would "set at nought" the Son of God.

Ishmael is set up as warning light to all teenagers. He was in his adolescence, at the age when terrible struggles take over a young person's life, when the father's authority is tested and the father's beliefs are challenged. Satan is ready with his false philosophies, the world is there with its many attractions, the flesh is asserting itself in new ways. Father's "old time religion" looks a lot less attractive and a lot less convincing than it did in childhood days. A new, cocky, self-assertive attitude surfaces. The choice of wrong companions can wreck a young life. At that age (older for his years, perhaps, than his peers today, but nonetheless a teenager) young Ishmael mocked at Isaac, and in mocking Isaac he mocked Christ. Resentment, jealousy, and hostility to the plan of God which centered in Isaac, all boiled like a witch's brew in Ishmael's soul. He wanted no part of anything that Isaac stood for in that family. So he mocked, and in mocking threw away all hope of salvation for his soul.

C. THE TYPICAL MESSAGE OF SARAH (21:10)

Sarah saw the whole thing, the curl of Ishmael's lip, the sneer on his face, and then his outright mockery of the child of promise. "Wherefore she said unto Abraham, Cast out this bondwoman and her son: for the son of this bondwoman shall not be heir with my son, even with Isaac." It cut Abraham to the heart. He had grown to love that tall, manly boy, Ishmael. But, from beginning to end, the relationship with Hagar had been of the flesh and Sarah was right. The flesh cannot inherit spiritual things. Her attitude seems harsh to us, but God took sides with her and declared she was right.[10]

10. In Galatians 4, Paul refers to the incident and declares that the whole set of circumstances embodied a remarkable spiritual allegory. Sarah, in insisting that the bondwoman and her son be cast out, was acting far beyond her own spiritual insights. In the light of New Testament revelation we can look back and see the underlying significance of it all. Four people are seen playing their parts—Isaac and Ishmael, Sarah and Hagar. All four stand in a special relationship to Abraham. *Isaac and Ishmael* represent the two natures in the believer, Ishmael standing for the flesh, the old nature, and Isaac for the new. Ishmael was the fruit of the flesh; Isaac was the fruit of faith. *Sarah and Hagar,* on the other hand, represent the principles of works and faith, law and grace. The birth of the new demands the expulsion of the old. But the move was up to Abraham, for he and he alone could take the decisive step. Ishmael and Hagar both had to be dealt with. Both had to be cast out no matter how painful the process. "Cast out the bondwoman and her child." It was no longer "works" or "law," but faith. That which was born of the flesh must be "cast out." There was to be no compromise, no middle ground. There must be a complete break with the old nature if the new nature is to develop and occupy all the believer's heart.

It was a hard lesson for Abraham, and it is a hard lesson for us to learn. The old nature is very tenacious. But once we come to see its inveterate hatred of the new nature, no choice remains. We must see that, just as sin has been dealt with at Calvary, so self has to be dealt with too—on the same terms as sin. God's answer to the flesh is the cross. It is not a question of a second conversion, but of a deeper consecration. It is not repeated salvation, but practical sanctification. The old nature and its works and principles, represented by Ishmael and Hagar, must be forever dethroned and dispossessed. The unpalatable truth must be faced that "in me (that is, in my flesh,) dwelleth no good thing" (Romans 7:18). There is much about the flesh that is repulsive to us, but there are also things about it we find endearing. God will not bless any of it. It must be cast out fully and forever.

Sadly Abraham faced up to the harsh truth. Ishmael, despite all a father's fond indulgence and wishful thinking, was not of God. He would have to go. After the decision was made and executed, with Abraham's characteristic promptness and thoroughness, there was a new dimension in his life for having dealt with Hagar and Ishmael, and all that they represented in his life of worldliness and carnality. He felt a new surge of spiritual power. He no longer feared Abimelech. He entered spiritually into all the possessions that were his in Canaan. The very heathen had to confess that, of a truth, God was with that man. What had he done? Had he mobilized his men and put Abimelech's hosts to the sword? No. He had simply dealt with the bondwoman and her son, and God had, in some marvelous and mysterious way, given him a new power with men—a power based not upon worldly or carnal principles but upon spiritual principles.

D. THE TRAGIC MISTAKE OF ABRAHAM (21:11)

There was nothing easy about casting out Hagar and Ishmael. "The thing was very grievous in Abraham's sight because of his son." The Bible does not promise some ecstatic experience as a panacea to the flesh. It offers a cross. Dying to the world and to the flesh and to the things they have produced is not pleasant, but painful. God's answer to our powerlessness is not an airy cloud, but a harsh cross; not rapture, but crucifixion. Abraham wept his heart out over the whole experience.

Years ago an enormously fat man was saved at a Salvationist meeting. He came back home elated to share the good news with his wife. He went back again to the meetings and enjoyed his salvation, but one day, he returned home looking sad. His wife wanted to know what was wrong. "Well," he said, "everyone at the meeting has a red jersey except me." That was no problem to his wife. She knitted him one—a great, big, enormous jersey, as big as a tent. He put it on and went happily off to the meeting, but back he came again looking as downcast as ever. Again his wife wanted to know what was wrong. "Oh," he said, "everyone at the Salvationist meeting has nice white letters on his jersey. I don't have any on mine." "Well, I can't read or write," said his wife. "Neither can you, but leave your jersey with me and I'll see what I can do." Across the street, a man was painting a sign on a store window and the wife decided she could copy the letters the painter was making, and so she did. She copied everything onto his jersey. That night the fellow went off to the meeting proudly wearing his jersey with the new letters on it. He came home, his face wreathed in smiles. "You've done it, my dear," he exclaimed, "you've done it. Everyone said I had the best jersey of them all." She had written in big white letters all across the enormous front of his jersey, *"This business is under new management."*

That's it! The old business has to be declared bankrupt; nothing can be salvaged from it at all. The life is then placed in new, capable hands. It was a tragic business from the start for Abraham to go into partnership with Hagar. It would have been even more tragic had he insisted on "business as usual" once he knew the issues involved. Instead, he did as God directed, cast out all worldly and fleshly expedients, and put the management of his life fully into the hands of God.

E. THE TENDER MERCIES OF GOD (21:12-13)

The story now moves from the allegorical and typical to the actual and historical. First, Abraham was faced with *the command* of God (21:12). "And God said unto Abraham, Let it not be grievous in thy sight because of the lad, and because of the bondwoman; in all that Sarah hath said unto thee, hearken unto her voice; for in Isaac shall thy seed be called." Sarah was absolutely right; she had learned the lesson. It was because Abraham had "hearkened unto the voice of Sarah" (16:2) that he had become involved with Hagar in the first place, but now Sarah could give him proper instruction.

Along with the command of God was *the comfort* of God. Abraham's eyes were now directed to Isaac or, as it would be with us today, to Christ. He was told to take a fresh look at the child of promise. When we cut off the flesh and its works, Christ will always be more clearly seen. All too often our view of Him is obscured because we are so taken up with some pet thing of our own that, did we but recognize it, is nothing but a carnal expedient after all.

Then, too, on the purely human and historical level, God in His tender mercy renewed His promise to Abraham. "Also of the son of the bondwoman will I make a great nation because he is thy seed." Among the many irons D. L. Moody had in the fire was the Y.M.C.A. Many of D. L. Moody's enterprises were born of the Spirit of God—one only has to think of the continuing spiritual impact of the Moody Bible Institute to realize that. But with the Y.M.C.A. it was different. Today the "Y" is an international organization, renowned for its educational, cultural, social, and athletic programs but utterly devoid of any spiritual impact. It was Moody's "Ishmael." It has developed and grown and become a mighty organization, but that is all it is. It is a worldly, carnal movement, good enough in its way and accomplishing earthly goals, but bankrupt as a spiritual force. All Moody's hopes for the continuing spiritual influence of the Y.M.C.A. were stillborn. It has prospered, possibly for Moody's sake. He loved it. He coveted for it the best spiritual gifts. But God's blessing was on the Institute, not the Association. Just so, God's blessing was on Isaac, not Ishmael.

F. THE TEARFUL MISERY OF HAGAR (21:14-21)

First, she was *cast out* (21:14). "And Abraham rose up early in the morning, and took bread, and a bottle of water, and gave it unto Hagar, putting it on her shoulder, and the child, and sent her away: and she departed and wandered in the wilderness of Beersheba." Why did Abraham not give the two exiles more abundant provisions for their journey? Why did he not give them cattle and tents? Certainly he was rich enough. Perhaps, because he knew the rapacious character of the Canaanites, Abraham decided that wealth in any form would only imperil the wanderers; it would attract brigands and thieves who would be emboldened by their weak and defenseless condition. In any case, it was not necessarily a bad thing for young Ishmael to have to face the harsh realities of life. It would make a man out of him.

The spiritual lesson behind Abraham's action is clear enough. We are to make no provision for the flesh. Only harsh measures will do. If we give it encouragement or indulge it, back it will come.

So Hagar was cast out. Soon she was *crushed down* (21:15-16). The water in her bottle was spent. Worn out with the rigors of the way and with her son exhausted and spent, she helped him to a shelter under a nearby shrub and sat down and wept. On the purely human level, what bitter thoughts must have been hers. What thoughts she must have entertained of Sarah and Abraham. How humanly impossible it must have been for her to think well of the fellowship from which she had been expelled. How careless we are, in our indulgence of our carnal desires, of the fearful damage we are doing to the lives of others or of the harsh thoughts we are planting in the souls of those we are using for our own ends.

But then Hagar was *caught up* (21:17-21). Behind the scenes, God was still at work and, in wonderful grace, He came to the desperate woman to minister personally and directly to her needs. In His own loving way He saved Hagar and Ishmael and sent them on their way to work out their destinies in the world.

Ishmael became a hunter. He made his dwelling in the wilderness and took the final step that cut him off from all spiritual potential by marrying an Egyptian. The scales of his life, already weighed toward the world, now went solidly down. Ishmael, having mocked at Isaac and thus spurned spiritual things, made the wilderness his home and took the world to his heart. Henceforth, between him and Isaac's seed there would be nothing but hostility and hate.

G. THE TRANSPARENT MOTIVES OF ABIMELECH (21:22-34)

Abimelech now seems to have had second thoughts about his cavalier treatment of Abraham. The words "he is a prophet" stuck in his mind and haunted him. He comes back into the story now with a *plea* (21:22-24). He saw to it that his path crossed that of Abraham and made sure too that he had his military adviser with him. Thus prepared, Abimelech accosted the patriarch. "God is with thee," he said, "in all that thou doest. Now therefore swear unto me here by God that thou wilt not deal falsely with me, nor with my son, nor with my son's son."

Apparently Abimelech judged everyone by himself. He was afraid of Abraham (even though Abraham meant him no harm and prayed for him), for he knew only too well how he would treat Abraham if he dared. He imagined Abraham to be waiting only a favorable moment to treat him the same way. Abraham said, "I will swear." His special relationship with God did not give him the right to trample on the rights of others. He was both a believer and a gentleman, two things that should always go hand in hand. With all his heart Abraham wished Abimelech well. His only regret was that his own shoddy behavior had so tarnished his testimony that he could not witness to him about the true character of God. Still, in a gentlemanly way, Abraham took the oath required of him that he would not trample on Abimelech's rights.

Next came Abimelech's *pledge* (21:25-31). In actual fact the shoe was on the other foot; it was Abimelech who was the potential aggressor, not Abraham, as Abraham pointed out. A while before, Abraham had dug a well, a very good well, a most desirable asset in a dry and thirsty land. Abimelech's men had violently wrested it from Abraham, and the patriarch had quietly suffered loss. It was the man, mark you, who a few years before had routed the kings of the east and at whose feet the king of Sodom had bowed. Yet he had suffered the loss quietly. Abimelech, tongue in cheek, denied all knowledge of the incident and, in the form and manner of the times, signed a contract with Abraham confirming Abraham's right to the well. Probably he had no intention of honoring the contract, but at least it looked good.

Finally the narrative records Abimelech's *parting* (21:32-34). "Thus they made a covenant at Beersheba: then Abimelech rose up, and Philcol the chief captain of his host, and they returned into the land of the Philistines." No doubt the pair of them congratulated each other on having got the best of Abraham. Their motives were very transparent. What they wanted was Abraham's *friendship;* that is, they wanted to make sure he would not launch any attack against them in the foreseeable future. The surrender, in return, of a well that did not really belong to them made an excellent bargain. But they had not the slightest interest in Abraham's *fellowship.* Indeed, there was no basis for fellowship at all. Abimelech felt as uncomfortable in Abraham's presence as Abraham did in his. Their worlds were eternities apart.

The chapter ends with a fresh glimpse of Abraham quietly getting on with the life of faith. He is seen *working* (21:33*a*). "And Abraham planted a grove in Beersheba." He was making preparation for usefulness and fruit in days to come. Abimelech wanted no fellowship with that; he did not care what Abraham did, so long as he left him alone. Then Abraham is seen *worshiping* (21:33*b*). "And [Abraham] called there on the name of the LORD." Abimelech had no interest in that. What did he care for "the everlasting God"? Finally we see Abraham *waiting* (21:34). "And Abraham sojourned in the Philistines' land many days." It was really his land, yet it is called "the Philistines' land." Abraham was content to patiently wait until God was pleased, in His own time and way, to give it to him. One day all would be his. Abimelech had no interest in that kind of thing.

XI. THE PROOF OF FAITH (22:1-24)

At 11:30 A.M. May 29, 1953, Sir Edmund Hiliary achieved fame. He hoisted the British flag atop Mount Everest and became the first human being ever to climb to the top of the world. It was the climax to many long months of planning. The right men had to be chosen to help, the proper equipment bought. Long hours had to be spent in training. There had to be rehearsals in Nepal and a period of acclimatization to the height and cold. There had to be early reconnaissance on the icefall. Then came the buildup, the stockpiling of supplies, and the initial climbs. Not till then were the climbers ready for the final assault.

Heavily burdened, they clawed their way upward through the cold. Every step was fraught with danger and discouragement. Disaster and death lurked in every crevasse. They kept on, forcing their way toward the summit. In places they hacked their way up sheer walls of ice, defying fatigue, raging elements, lack of oxygen, and bitter cold. Up and up the intrepid mountaineer went, clawing his way between cornice and rock, and then on up the ridge. Steps had to be cut in the snow. Time and strength were both running out when at last, a few more whacks and the summit was gained. Sir Edmund and his partner stood where no man before had ever stood, 29,002 feet above the level of the sea. No man on earth will ever climb higher than that.

In Genesis 24 another mountain rears its head—not Everest, but Moriah. Two men can be seen forcing their way to the top. The way was steeper far than Everest and the road tougher, costlier, harder. When at last Abraham and Isaac stood together on its brow they stood upon an eminence, a spiritual plateau, higher than ever reached by man before. Mount Moriah represented the highest possible pinnacle of *surrender* for one and the highest possible pinnacle of *sacrifice* for the other. Few men have ever climbed so high. Indeed, there is only one peak higher than Mount Moriah in all of Scripture, and that is Mount

Calvary. Nor was Moriah scaled in a day. Abraham had been fifty years preparing on the hills and slopes of God for the final triumph of his faith.

A. THE SUDDEN TEST FOR WHICH GOD HAD PREPARED ABRAHAM (22:1-2)

"And it came to pass after these things, that God did tempt [test] Abraham." God never tested Lot. There was never any need, for Lot's caliber was known. His shallow, empty, worldly, carnal life was so obvious that tests would have been superfluous. But God tested Abraham.

The test did not come out of the blue. "It came to pass after these things." What things? Why, all the things that had gone before, climaxing in the expulsion of Hagar and Ishmael. Again and again Abraham had been challenged to surrender. First it was his father, now it was his son. In between, it had been the well-watered plains of Jordan, then the gifts of Sodom's king, then Ishmael. And with each surrender he was learning how to scale the heights, gaining experience on the foothills, tackling the lower glaciers, preparing for the ultimate challenge. "Now then, Abraham," God said, "now tackle Moriah."

In that amazing chapter God shows off His man. Where, within all the covers of God's blessed Book, is there a chapter like Genesis 22 for displaying what Calvary meant to God the Father? We turn to Psalm 69, Isaiah 53, and Psalm 22 to see what Calvary meant to the Son. But it is Genesis 22 that shows us what Calvary meant to the Father. "Take now thy son, thine only son Isaac, whom thou lovest, and get thee into the land of Moriah; and offer him . . . upon one of the mountains." Over and above the demand for Isaac was the ultimate demand for Jesus. All that Moriah meant to Abraham in terms of agony and heartache and pain; that a thousandfold, ten-thousandfold, is what Calvary meant to God.

"God did test Abraham." It was examination time, and a stiff examination it was. But God had been preparing His man, coaching him patiently in the school of faith, giving him those little tests along the way. Now came the "finals." Here was the test for which God had prepared him. All the other tests were preparatory. Now on the stage of Abraham's life could be enacted, in type and shadow, the great drama of Calvary, so much so that, as we put our hand upon the beating of Abraham's heart, we can measure the pulse of the heart of God. As we watch Isaac make his way to Mount Moriah, we see Jesus wend His way up the parallel slopes of Calvary.

Moriah means "foreseen of Jehovah." God was not taken by surprise by Adam's fall or by the long, stark tragedy of human sin. It was all foreseen by the Lord. Take, for instance, a watch. Its sole function is to tell the time. It makes a very poor doorstop; it was never intended to power an automobile; it is intended to tell time. Its function is to move in harmony with heaven and record upon its face the revolution of the world upon its axis. If it is one of those watches that has a built-in calendar as well, then it must also record the movement of the earth around the sun. It is a watch. Here is a man. His function is to glorify God, to move in harmony with heaven. A watch that no longer truly records the passage of time has very little worth; a man who does not glorify God in his life negates the purpose for which he was made.

A watch, any watch, can begin to run fast or slow; it can even stop so that its hands no longer perform their function at all. Its face then records a lie. That eventuality, however, was foreseen by its designer and, when he had it on the drawing board, he made allowance for that. He built into the instrument a mechanism whereby it could be reset and rewound and brought back into harmony with time. He knew in advance what forces would work on that watch to pull it out of harmony with the universe. Therefore he made provision against the day of need and built into the mechanism a little winder so that the hands could be readjusted and the watch rewound. It was all foreseen.

Just so, man's sin was foreseen by the Lord. He built into the plan of creation a plan of redemption. Long before He put the sun in the sky He made provision for the Fall of man and the ruin of the race. The Lord Jesus was in very truth "the lamb slain from before the foundation of the world" (Revelation 13:8). The Fall was all foreseen and provided for in the councils of God in a past eternity.

"Get thee into the land of Moriah!" The demand rang through the soul of Abraham out there on those Canaanite hills. But after all, it was a mere echo of a greater demand made by God upon Himself out there on the everlasting hills, a demand one day to be met at Calvary within sight of Moriah itself.

B. THE SIMPLE TRUST IN WHICH GOD HAD PERFECTED ABRAHAM (22:3-12)

Over the years Abraham had learned to trust God. He knew that God was dependable. Again and again He had declared, "In Isaac shall thy seed be called." It was inconceivable therefore that Isaac could die before he had children. Even if he were to be slain, Abraham reasoned, God would have to raise him up from the dead. In that confidence in a God who is utterly dependable, Abraham went forth to his test. It was a test made no less severe by Abraham's magnificent faith.

First, Abraham learned *the way of the cross.* "And Abraham rose up early in the morning, and saddled his ass, and took two of his young men with him, and Isaac his son, and clave the wood for the burnt offering, and rose up, and went unto the place of which God had told him." The decision having been made, it was now a matter of moving steadily forward, with aching heart, to the place. *The place.* How that place must have haunted Abraham's dreams. It is mentioned again and again. The aged patriarch would look at the gentle, undulating plains around him or up at the craggy steeps. Always there would come dancing before his mind's eye a vision of the place. "And Abraham rose up early in the morning . . . and went to the place." "Then on the third day Abraham lifted up his eyes, and saw the place." "And they came to the place." It was an echo, sounding down the unborn ages—an echo recorded by Luke 23:33: "And when they were come to the place, which is called Calvary, there they crucified him." The one place foreshadowed the other.

Thus Abraham trod the way of the cross. He saddled his ass, he summoned his servants, he sent for Isaac, he split the wood, he set forth on the way, he saw the place. Then, at last, he and Isaac came to a point beyond which the others could not go. Abraham bade his young men sit down and wait for his return *and* (with amazing confidence in God) for the return of the lad. "Abide ye here with the ass; and I and the lad will go yonder and worship, and come again to you."

It was a dress rehearsal for Calvary. We read of the Lord Jesus that "He taketh with him Peter and James and John, and began to be sore amazed [sorrowful] and to be very heavy; and saith unto them, My soul is exceeding sorrowful unto death: tarry ye here, and watch. And he went forward a little, and fell on the ground and prayed" (Mark 14:33-35). There came a point in the life of the Lord beyond which even Peter and James and John could not go. Jesus went forward alone, alone with His Father to comune with Him on the way to the cross. What agonizing communion there was there beneath the shade of the olive trees, between the Father and the Son—a communion no one else could share.

The way of the cross gives way to *the word of the cross* (22:6-8). "And Abraham took the wood of the burnt offering, and laid it upon Isaac his son; and he took the fire in his hand, and a knife; and they went both of them together. And Isaac spake unto Abraham his father, and said, My father; and he said, Here am I, my son. And he said, Behold the fire and the wood: but where is the lamb for a burnt offering? And Abraham said, My son, God will provide himself a lamb for a burnt offering: so they went both of them together."

That was Gethsemane. We often think of what Gethsemane meant to the Lord Jesus, but what must it have meant to the Father? What must that agonizing question from Isaac's lips have done to Abraham's heart? What did the bloodlike sweat, the anguished tears in Gethsemane mean to the Father of our Lord Jesus Christ?

"They went both of them together." Moriah was not forced upon Isaac. He was not dragged in chains, struggling and resisting, to his Golgotha. They went together. Isaac, now a man full grown, with a mind and will of his own, walking the upward way side by side with his beloved father. Then he put the question, the awkward, probing question Abraham had been dreading all along.

The young men had been left behind, the ass had been tethered. The full weight of the wood was now felt by Isaac. "Abraham took the wood of the burnt offering and laid it upon Isaac his son." The wood had been there all the time, but now it came home to Isaac that *he* must bear its weight. The sudden weight of it brought home to him the part he must play in the drama looming ahead. We can see him look at his father—at that wise, old face now so drawn and strained—and in that face read something the like of which he has never seen before.

The wood was getting heavier step by step. Isaac looked again at his father, and in the old man's hands the young man saw that which spelled his doom—in the one hand was the knife; in the other hand was the fire. The sweat stood out on Isaac's brow. The weight he felt was his cross. He was carrying a load placed upon him by others. With the perspiration standing in beads on his brow he asked: "Where is the lamb? Where is the lamb for the burnt offering?"

Abraham was ready. There was no prevarication, simply astounding faith. "God will provide Himself a lamb." He did not know how or when or where God would do it, but He would. As Isaac looked afresh at his father's face he may have read something there that put an end to all questions. Now he knew. If the road ahead was terrible for him, it was a thousand times worse for his father. So "they went both of them together." The repetition of the statement after the give and take of the questions indicates that Isaac now possibly knew fully what lay ahead and that, in the glory and power of his strength, he submitted to the father's will.

Can we not feel what Abraham felt? Can we not enter into the anguish that rent his soul? Can we not understand how much he shrank from the deed ahead? Can we not see how leaden were his feet as he dragged them toward the brow of the hill? Can we not catch the secret glance he stole at his son, his only son, his beloved, his only Isaac? Can we not hear the inward groan as he sobbed in his soul—"Oh, my son, Isaac, my son, my son Isaac. Would God I could die for thee, O Isaac, my son, my son."

Can we not feel what God the Father felt in dark Gethsemane? "My Father!" "Here am I, My Son." "Behold, the cup. If it be possible let this cup pass from me; nevertheless not my will but thine be done." The only answer the Father could give was to point on to the cross. No lamb could be found for His Son. So "They went the both of Them together." Out from the stillness of the garden They went into the arms of the mob, on to the mock trials before the priests, the procurator, the Herodian prince; on to the spitting, the scourging, the scorn; on out into the morning sun, the Lord Jesus staggering beneath the weight of the wood and the even greater weight of this world's sin as His Father watched; then on up the hill, on to the place. Both of Them together.

In Abraham's experience there came finally *the work of the cross*. "And they came to the place which God had told him of; and Abraham built an altar there, and laid the wood in order, and bound Isaac his son, and laid him on the altar upon the wood. And Abraham stretched forth his hand and took the knife to slay his son." With deliberate care each separate act is set down. Building the altar, bringing the wood, binding the victim, baring the knife—each act is recorded. Only when the knife was poised in the air and was falling did God stay Abraham's hand. Who can measure what it cost Abraham to come to that last, final act, the raising of the knife to slay his son?

As he took the knife, perhaps Abraham saw in his mind a vivid picture from the past. He saw himself as a very young man. He remembered the first time he slaughtered a lamb. It may have been a lamb he had fed with his own hand; a woolly, frisky, trusting, lovable little lamb. We can imagine it coming bleating to him when he called, nuzzling against him and skipping along at his side at the end of the rope he had tied to its neck. Perhaps it had shied with fright at the smell of blood at the place where the altar had stood. It had looked up at him with trusting eyes as with unsteady hand he untied the rope. It may have been silent on the altar, its liquid eyes watching his every move, its little form quivering with fright. Perhaps he had felt like a murderer as he steeled himself to do the deed. And now he must slay his son. It was the work of the cross.

Was there ever such a dark, tragic work performed beneath the wide vault of heaven in all the ages of time or all the annals of eternity? God saw His Son led like a lamb to the slaughter, laid out upon the wood, and the spikes driven home. God watched the whole dark, dreadful business on Golgotha's hill. Then, God Himself had taken the great knife of His own fierce wrath against sin, had lifted it up as the darkness swept in, and had wreaked on His Son the eternal hell our sins deserved. *That* was the work of the cross, the work enacted in type by Abraham on that lonely mountain in the land of Moriah and enacted in fact at the place called Calvary.

C. THE SOLEMN TRUTH BY WHICH GOD HAD PROTECTED ABRAHAM (22:13-24)

But Abraham's hand was stayed, his falling knife was arrested by the sudden call of God. "Abraham! Abraham! And he said, Here am I. And he said, Lay not thine hand upon the lad, neither do thou any thing unto him: for now I know that thou fearest God, seeing thou hast not withheld thy son, thine only son from me. And Abraham lifted up his eyes, and looked, and behold behind him a ram caught in a thicket by his horns: And Abraham went and took the ram, and offered him up for a burnt offering in the stead of his son. And Abraham called the name of that place Jehovah Jireh" (22:11-14). That was the truth by which God had protected him. The knife was stayed in Abraham's hand because it would fall in the end not on Isaac, but on Jesus. God had indeed provided a Lamb for a burnt offering.

What thoughts must have surged through Isaac's soul as he stood there, released from his bonds as one brought back from the dead. What thoughts must have been his as he witnessed the death of the ram. Did he embrace that ram before it died? How the tears must have flowed down his cheeks as he watched it bleed. What similar thoughts should fill our hearts as we think of the Lamb that God provided, not just for Isaac, but for the sin of the world. There was no reprieve for God, no stay of execution for Christ.

Thus the Holy Spirit paints for us one of the very greatest pictures of Calvary in the Bible. The unforgettable experience of Abraham and Isaac at Moriah had its sequel. The voice of God rang out again, confirming all the blessings that God had already bestowed on Abraham and his seed. With that fresh confirmation ringing in their ears, the father and the son found their way back to where the young men waited. From there they journeyed back to the place of the well, to Beersheba in the south.

Almost by way of an anticlimax, the chapter ends with a reference to the children born to Abraham's brother, Nahor. The collateral genealogy is intended to introduce Rebekah into the story, so it is not an anticlimax after all. The firstfruit of Calvary was the church. We, who were not in the direct line of promise at all, are brought in by marriage to the Father's beloved Son.

XII. THE PATIENCE OF FAITH (23:1-20)

Some women are notoriously touchy about giving away their age. It is a secret more tightly guarded than the latest secret weapon in the Russian arsenal. When young Willie was four years old his mother took him downtown one day on the bus. The regulation was that little children could ride free until they were five years of age. The bus conductor asked Willie's mother, "How old is your little boy?" "He's four," she said. "Thank you, madam," replied the conductor. Little Willie looked up, evidently thinking that further information should be forthcoming. "And mother," he announced brightly, "is forty-one."

The Bible seemingly respects the average woman's reticence about her age, for Sarah is the only woman in the Bible whose age at death is recorded. She was 127 years old when she died. Nor is that the only time Sarah's age is given. Moses is not nearly so diplomatic in the matter of Sarah's age as was the young man who paused before venturing an answer when a widow asked him if he could guess her age. "You must have some idea," she insisted. "I have several ideas," said the budding diplomat. "The only trouble is that I hesitate whether to make you ten years younger on account of your looks, or ten years older on account of your intelligence." Moses makes no bones about it; Sarah was 127 and all the world can know it. It was a notable, remarkable age.

In chapter 23, we are to attend a funeral—another of those frequent funerals that confront us in the first book of our Bible. The Holy Spirit continually reminds us that the wages of sin is death. Genesis 23 records the funeral of one of the best-looking and best-loved women in the world. The story moves in three cycles, telling of Abraham's grief, Sarah's grave, and Ephron's gift. We are going to take those three movements and link them with three counterstatements in the New Testament, each of which features the little word "not."

A. ABRAHAM'S GRIEF (23:1-6)

For some sixty years now the patriarch had wandered throughout the promised land ever accompanied by his faithful and devoted Sarah. Abraham greatly loved his wife. Even his two tragic mistakes were centered around her and were dictated by what he considered her best interests. Now she was dead. He thought back over the long, wondrous years they had spent together seeking, despite all human faults and failures, to know and do the will of God. The Holy Spirit tenderly pauses to give us just a glimpse of *Abraham's tears* (23:1-2). There is nothing wrong with a believer shedding tears over the tragedies and heartaches of life. Jesus Himself wept at the tomb of Lazarus. But over against Abraham's tears we need to set our first New Testament text: "Ye sorrow *not* even as others which have no hope" (1 Thessalonians 4:13). Abraham knew that. Beyond all temporal blessings on this earth, Abraham was looking for "that city which hath foundations, whose builder and maker is God" (Hebrews 11:10). He may have looked up through his blinding tears, trying to pierce the blue vault of heaven and see that city where sorrow and tears are unknown. Sarah was there! Soon he would be there, home at last.

Sarah died at Hebron in the land of Canaan. Abraham must always have been glad of that. She died in the place of blessing, "in Canaan," and she died in the place of fellowship, for that is what "Hebron" means. She had begun her days in far-off Ur, a benighted pagan woman, a worshiper of the moon. She was born a poor, lost sinner the same as anyone else. She grew up a pretty little thing with a saucy tongue, and she met and married an energetic young man well on the way to making his fortune in Ur. Abraham had been a pagan too, but with a restless, unsatisfied soul. Well he knew in his heart that the moon, the queen of heaven, was no true god. But out there, behind all those shining orbs and stars, behind the black velvet of the night, there must be a true and living God. His secret doubts and heresies he had perhaps whispered to Sarah in the quiet security of their urban home in Ur. Then came the blinding revelation of that true and living God and the long pilgrimage with all its ups and downs. Sarah had shared it all. Now she was dead, but she had died "in fellowship." She had died at Hebron. To die in the place of fellowship is the next best thing to never dying at all.

"Abraham came to mourn for Sarah and to weep for her." What a scene it must have been, this white-haired old man with noble countenance and flowing beard, stooping over the cold clay of his beloved and letting the tears run unrestrained down his cheeks. Heaven had gained a notable saint. No longer would those dimples start out at the corners of Sarah's mouth when she smiled. No longer would her smile bring sunshine to the dawning of his day. No longer would Sarah's nimble tongue be heard hustling the servants to their tasks. No longer would they be able to sit together, hand in hand, watching the sun set in the western sky. Abraham's heart broke and tears ran freely from his eyes. Bitter tears they were, as everyone knows who has lost a loved one, but he sorrowed not as others who have no hope. Sarah was at home. She had exchanged the bedouin tent for an ivory palace.

But if the Holy Spirit tells us of Abraham's tears, He tells us also of *Abraham's testimony* (23:3-6). If there is one time when the believer's testimony should shine out strongly in a dark world of sin, it is when death visits the home. "And Abraham stood up from before his dead, and spake unto the sons of Heth, saying, I am a stranger and a sojourner with you: give me a possession of a buryingplace with you, that I may bury my dead out of my sight."

That was Abraham's testimony; "I am a stranger and a sojourner." From the very first moment he had set foot in Canaan he had maintained his pilgrim character. He was no snob, he entertained no disdain for his unsaved neighbors, he never once hinted that their land was really his land, and that by divine decree. He was wise in the testimony he held. He moved among his fellow men quietly enjoying the Lord and holding aloof from entanglement in the affairs of this world. Always helpful, ever courteous and friendly, Abraham at the same time expected nothing from unsaved people—no favors, no concessions, no special respect. The principles of his life of faith were as far removed from the principles that animated men like the king of Sodom and Abimelech as night is from day. Yet Abraham never intruded his beliefs, never insisted on his "rights," never expected anything from the unsaved. If he bought something, he paid in cash and in full. He was in the world but he was not of the world. He was a sojourner and a stranger. Lot might become impatient at Abraham's other-worldly ideas, but the patriarch himself was content to wait upon God and let God work out all things according to His good and perfect and acceptable will. It was Abraham's heavenly wisdom that enabled him to take such a detached view of earthly things. "I am a stranger, a sojourner with you" was his testimony.

A *stranger*. A stranger is a person who finds himself in a culture and society to which he does not naturally belong. He feels ill at ease in that company, alien to it, rejected by it. He knows that no matter how friendly he may be, he does not really belong. He is a stranger. His heart turns longingly toward home. That was how Abraham felt in Canaan, how Jesus felt in this world—how we should feel in a world that, indeed, is not our home.

A *sojourner*. A sojourner is a temporary resident, one who is only staying for a little while. His citizenship and home are somewhere else; he is only traveling for a while in these parts, then he is going home. That was Abraham's attitude toward Canaan, yes, *Canaan!* Every stick and stone was his. He could smile at the king of Sodom's gestures, at Abimelech's wordy posturing. Did they but know it, their houses and lands were all his. God had given the land to him. As he journeyed from north to south of the land he must have found great interest in taking note of all that was his in the undoubted will of God. But it was of more interest to him to know that heaven was his. The death of Sarah had put that into full focus at last.

When I was a boy I liked to do something most other English boys liked to do in those days. We would pay our penny and spend an hour or two on the platform of the local train station. Ours was a busy one. The main trunk lines from London and the north of England came plunging out of the long Severn tunnel to run right through our town. Branch lines snaked up into all the coal mining valleys around. The main line hurried on into Wales. Consequently, every minute or two another train would arrive with a great flourish of steam and a squealing of brakes and a banging of doors and bustling of crowds. We loved the puffing of the little, fussy, snorting engines that pulled a carriage or two up into the valleys. We loved the giant locomotives that roared their defiance at all restraint, straining to take off again with great puffings of steam and smoke. We loved the rattle and clatter of the endless lines of boxcars bumping and shoving each other as they jostled down the center track. The smells and sights and sounds live with me yet.

But one thing stands out in my mind. One day I had wandered down the far end of the platform to look with interest at a dozen wicker baskets filled with pigeons and doves. A kindly porter told me what they were for. "We're going to put them on different trains, son," he said. "Some will go north, some south, some on into Wales, and some back east. They will all go exactly the same distance. These are racing pigeons, you see, and the day after tomorrow, at twelve o'clock precisely, they will all be released. They'll climb into the air and circle around once or twice, then they'll head straight for home. The idea is to see which one gets home first."

I have often thought of that. Not by accident is the Holy Spirit likened to a *dove*. When we accept Christ as Savior, He comes to make His home in our hearts. He brings with Him a homing instinct. He teaches us that this world is not our home, that heaven is where we belong. And He yearns in us for the glory land, He sets our hearts in that direction and teaches us to walk the straight and narrow way. Abraham found it so. "I am a stranger and a sojourner with you," he said to the sons of Heth.

Their reply was most instructive. "Thou art a mighty prince among us," they said. They never said that of Lot. Abraham, the separated believer, who refused to become entangled in the affairs of the world, considered by Lot as impractical and exclusive, *that* was the man who won the respect of the unsaved. The prevalent idea is that we must become involved in the world's affairs, we must run for this office and that, become active in this club and that movement if we are going to do anything to alter the world's social inequities. That was Lot's philosophy, but it was not Abraham's. Evan Roberts, an untutored Welsh miner—with the smell of coal on his clothes, reared in an obscure Welsh village, and considered a fanatic by many—nevertheless did more to change the social climate of Great Britain in six months than did all the Parliamentarians in sixty years. For that unworldly individual knew God and was used of God to spark the Welsh Revival, which left its mark not only on Wales but also on England, Scotland, Ireland, and the United States of America both spiritually and socially for many years.

B. SARAH'S GRAVE (23:7-18)

Sarah's grave is important because her tomb was the only piece of real estate in all of Canaan that Abraham actually possessed during his lifetime. That brings us to our second New Testament text, a text that embraces not only Abraham, but Isaac and Jacob as well. "These all died in faith, *not* having received the promises, but having seen them afar off" (Hebrews 11:13, italics added). It made no difference to Abraham that one small cave and one little field represented the sum total of tangible real estate made out in his name. Had he spent all his life for *that?* No, he had spent his life getting to know God, and he now knew God so well that he had not the slightest shadow of doubt that every inch of the promised land from the Nile to the Euphrates would one day belong to his seed.

It is most instructive to see how Abraham went about securing the title to his tomb. In the first place, he was *courteous in his talk* (23:7-8). Why do so many Christians seem to have bad manners? The Lord Jesus was the most courteous of men. Politeness is not only a social asset; it is a spiritual grace, as will be evident from even the most cursory reading of the New Testament epistles. When the children of Heth offered Abraham the choice of their sepulchres Abraham at once responded in a courteous way. "And Abraham stood up, and bowed himself to the people of the land, even to the children of Heth" (23:7). It was a gracious social custom, and one that in no way compromised any conviction he might have as a believer, so Abraham employed it. He then appealed to the local chieftains, "Entreat for me to Ephron the son of Zohar." Abraham was no uncouth blunderer, he was a cultured, polite gentleman who understood the value of courtesy.

Moreover he was *careful in his transactions* (23:8-18). The tomb was offered to him as an outright gift with what looked like unstinted generosity. Abraham, however, knew the customs better than to take the offer at its face value. To this day an Arab will instantly give you anything in his home you might be incautious enough as to openly admire. Abraham knew only too well that the sons of Heth would have been astonished and outraged had he taken them at their word. He therefore opened negotiations for the purchase of the cave of Ephron. The details are typically cultural. Abraham stated the case (23:8-9), satisfied the customs (23:10-13), and secured the contract (23:14-18), and when it was all over, the tomb and the title were his for four hundred shekels of silver. Ephron knew he was asking top price for his property. For all his blandishments and protestations he knew Abraham simply had to have a burying place, and he did not hesitate to get the best of the bargain. "My lord, hearken unto me: the land is worth four hundred shekels of silver," he said and then added hastily, "what is that betwixt thee and me? bury therefore thy dead" (23:15). Abraham did not stoop to haggle. Waiving all the usual give and take of barter in an oriental market, he simply and with majestic dignity handed over the first price that was asked.

C. EPHRON'S GIFT (23:19-20)

"After this, Abraham buried Sarah his wife in the cave of the field of Machpelah before Mamre: the same is Hebron in the land of Canaan. And the field, and the cave that is therein, were made sure unto Abraham for a possession of a buryingplace by the sons of Heth." "I give it thee, I give it thee, I give it thee," cried Ephron again and again—three times in one verse (23:11). Over against that we set one more New Testament text. "My peace I give unto you: *not* as the world giveth, give I unto you" (John 14:27, italics added). The world does not give, it takes. When Jonah decided to go the way of the world he went down to Tarshish, found a ship and "paid the fare thereof"—he *paid.* But God is a generous giver.

Ephron never had any intention of giving Abraham that cave and field. He knew exactly what he was going to ask for it when the negotiations reached the crucial point, and he asked plenty. The other day I heard a man on the radio offering a large, expensive Bible to anyone who would send in for it—so long as they sent twenty-five dollars to support his work. That is worldliness—give something to me and I will give something to you. The noted psychiatrist Dr. Eric Berne, in his best-selling book *Games People Play,* points out that we do not even give so much as a handshake or ask the question "How are you?" without expecting something equivalent in return.

Abraham faced life's *tears* with natural but not inconsolable grief. He faced life's *testings* knowing that although the promises of God seem terribly slow of fulfillment, they are all settled in heaven. Not even the sight of the sons of Heth with their crafty faces and their broad grins and underhanded calculations could upset him. He faced life's *treacheries* with equanimity, knowing that man's word may or may not be sure, but God's word is.

XIII. THE PRECAUTIONS OF FAITH (24:1-67)

The Holy Spirit lingers lovingly over every detail in chapter 24, the longest chapter in Genesis, for every detail speaks of Christ and His church. That is not surprising. After all, the Holy Spirit expressly tells us that marriage is intended to mirror that higher and holier relationship (Ephesians 5:21-33). In Genesis 22 we saw Isaac going to Mount Moriah as the father's beloved son obedient unto death, even to the death of sacrifice. In Genesis 23 we had the death of Sarah, a type of the sweeping changes that took place in Israel's status once the church was introduced into human affairs. In chapter 24 Rebekah, a type of the church as the bride of Isaac, is brought into Sarah's very tent. The whole chapter, while an interesting and instructive story full of local color and warmth, is at the same time a full length study of the way in which the Father's beloved Son obtained His bride, the church.

A. THE WISE SOJOURNER (24:1-9)

"Abraham was old, and well stricken in age" (24:1). The Jews divided old age into three stages. From sixty to seventy was what they called "the commencement of old age," from seventy to eighty was what they termed "hoary-headed age," after eighty a man was said to be "well-stricken in years." Abraham was about one hundred forty years of age at that time and Isaac was about forty. The time had come to seek out a bride for his son.

The old patriarch viewed with horror what he saw all about him in Canaan. The daughters of Canaan were a worldly, wicked, wanton crowd with no knowledge at all of the true and living God. They were snared in the most frightful forms of pagan idolatry. There could be no thought of Isaac marrying one of them.

The Bible gives definite instructions about the marriage of believers. There is to be no marriage with an unbeliever. H. V. Morton, the renowned traveler, once saw a camel and a donkey harnessed to the same plough. The wretched donkey had a terrible time of it. The camel obviously did not like being so closely tied to its opposite number and was gazing about it with the supercilious, disdainful air that can be adopted only by a camel and a man. And the poor little donkey had all the weight of the yoke chafing its shoulders. Neither one nor the other could get in step. Such an unequal yoke is forbidden by God, whether it be in business, religion, or marriage. The thought that Isaac might be thus unequally yoked was a nightmare to Abraham.

But where could he find a bride for his son? His thoughts turned back to far-off Haran where his own testimony, years before, had borne fruit. He may or may not have known Rebekah personally, but he certainly knew about her (22:23). Thus Abraham took the initiative and sent his servant forth to seek out a bride for his son. It was thus, in a past eternity, that the eternal God took counsel with Himself in regard to His Son. He would have a bride for His Son, one fit for Him, one capable of sharing the lofty position that was His. He would send the Holy

Spirit into the world to find that bride—but not until Calvary had paved the way. "Blessed be the God and Father of our Lord Jesus Christ, who hath blessed us with all spiritual blessings in heavenly places in Christ: according as he hath chosen us in him before the foundation of the world, that we should be holy and without blame before him in love" (Ephesians 1:3-4).

B. THE WONDROUS SERVANT (24:10-28)

The servant is unnamed. We are told that he was Abraham's "eldest servant of his house that ruled over all that he had" (24:2). We presume that the servant was Eliezer of Damascus (15:2), but the text does not say so. The silences of God are sometimes as significant as His sayings. Frequently in the Bible an unnamed man is used as a type of the Holy Spirit, whose delight it is to draw attention to the Son rather than to Himself. Certainly the type fits here. In God's purposes the execution of the divine will in the world is entrusted to the Spirit. It was He who came at Pentecost to begin the great work of seeking out for Christ His blood-bought bride, the church. In Genesis 24 the servant always acted in accordance with the will of Abraham and with Isaac's interests in mind.

Charged with his great commission, the servant set forth on his long arduous and difficult task. "He arose, and went to Mesopotamia, unto the city of Nahor." Abraham was living near Hebron at the time, so the servant had a considerable journey before him. Northward he went up the Jordan valley and on past Damascus, then around the Fertile Crescent into "the eye of the East" until at length, crossing the Euphrates, he reached his destination. Those were no aimless wanderings, but a well-planned expedition. The servant knew what he was about.

When he arrived at his destination, the servant prayed. All must be done in fellowship with God in heaven. Then he proposed a practical test: as women came to the well he would ask for a drink, and the girl who offered to draw, not just for him but for his camels also, she would be the God-chosen one. It was no small test. A camel will drink about five gallons of water, and the servant had ten of them. To draw some fifty gallons of water from the well and empty them into the trough in the heat of that climate was a big undertaking. Such a woman would make a very good wife.

Presently Rebekah came along and, all unknown to herself, met the conditions. The servant at once rewarded her for her willing spirit with a generous gift. Then he discovered that she was the daughter of Bethuel and the granddaughter of Nahor, Abraham's brother. The rest of the story followed quickly and naturally. The servant was taken to Rebekah's home where he told about his great mission. He was abroad to find a bride for Isaac, Abraham's beloved son, and it was evident Rebekah was the chosen of God. It was all so artless, so natural and yet, at the same time, so evidently of God, the natural overlaid with the supernatural. Here was no chance meeting. Here was a meeting planned in heaven and now taking place on earth. As the servant presented the cause and claims of Isaac, Rebekah listened with all her heart and with wide open eyes.

Woven into the warp and woof of the fabric of that very human story we see the golden threads of another and far greater story. We see the coming of the Spirit of God into the world with a great mission to win and woo a heart here and a heart there to heaven's Beloved. Only occasionally does He speak of Himself. His great work is to make much of the Son and to tell of the Father and His wondrous ways. His great task is to seek out those who will become the bride of Christ. How wonderfully He takes advantage of life's ordinary circumstances using them to further His quest. He never forces, never violates the human will, never overwhelms, never uses weird and uncanny means to ravish the soul. Ordinary things happen; a visit here, a chance meeting there, an unexpected conversation, a book passed on by a friend—and all the time the Spirit of God is at work. Until, at last, the gospel is presented and the hour of decision dawns. It was the servant's way with Rebekah; it is the Spirit's way with a soul.

C. The Worldly Sinner (24:29-33)

Rebekah had a brother, and what a scheming, grasping person he was. The first thing Rebekah did when the servant's initial gifts were bestowed upon her was to run home and share the wondrous news. "And Rebekah had a brother, and his name was Laban: and Laban ran out to the man, unto the well" (24:29).

Look well at Laban. The thing that impressed him was not the wonderful story or even the accompanying signs. The thing that counted with Laban was the *gifts*. He was not particularly interested in the father, the son, or the servant. He was interested in the gifts. He longed to get his hands on the rich gifts the unnamed servant brought. "And it came to pass, *when he saw the earring and the bracelets* upon his sister's hands, and when he heard the words of Rebekah . . . that he came unto the man" (24:30, italics added). The earrings and the bracelets—those came first with Laban.

But Laban had to hear the whole story, whether he would or no. The servant's work was to speak of Isaac, but all the while that worldly man's eyes were on the gifts. Later on in Genesis Laban would appear again, and his true character was to be seen. He would be revealed for what he was, a man quite able to use a believer just so long as he could make money out of him. Laban remained an unregenerate man to the end, quite willing to pay lip service to God (24:50) but without any real interest in the spiritual dimensions of life. Rebekah was absorbed in the story; Laban was taken up with the gifts. Initial gifts were given to Laban, too, by the servant (24:53), but he thereupon set about trying to hinder the servant in his primary work (24:55-56).[11]

Laban was given something. We are not told what it was, but we do observe that it did nothing to warm his worldly heart. He manifested no interest either in the father or the son. He remained a worldly sinner to the end of his days. Subsequent exposure to the ultimate truths of God's Word did not do him the slightest good. He had the coveted gifts but, no doubt, those soon lost their power to attract and hold his heart. It is only Christ who can fill the heart, and Laban remained cold and indifferent to that which spoke of Him.

D. THE WILLING SAINT (24:34-61)

With Rebekah it was quite different. Her heart warmed at once to what she saw and heard. There was something about the story of Isaac that kindled a response in her heart. She had never seen him, had come to know of him indeed solely by the word of the servant, but already she felt that she knew him. Already she gave him her heart.

At length the great question was faced: "Wilt thou go with this man?" (24:58). In His sovereignty and grace God manipulates all the circumstances of time and space to bring a person to the place of decision, but He will never force the issue. He never pushes a person over the line, does not decide for us. The servant took every advantage of the unfolding circumstances that opened up before him, but he made no attempt at all to coerce or force a decision. He used no high-pressure appeals. He presented the simple facts of the case, told the story of Isaac and of his own mission, and invited Rebekah to give herself to the unseen man dwelling afar off with the father. Then it was up to her.

No doubt Rebekah could have invented a hundred reasons why she should say no to the invitation. She might have said, "How do I know your story is true?" or, "I do not want to give up my present life-style. I'm quite happy where I am." But there were no excuses, just as there was no coercion. She instantly gave in and gave her heart to the unseen Isaac.

Then came the long journey to meet the one to whom she had now given herself. What a journey it must have been as she, and those influenced by her, "rode upon the camels and followed the man." Here

11. Laban has many heirs and successors in Christendom. There are those whose loved ones have entered into reality in Christ and in whose hearts the Holy Spirit has done His full and amazing work. But that has only made a passing impression. It often happens that those who neglect the heart and core of the message nevertheless manifest interest in the "fringe-benefits" of the faith. Laban-like, they are fascinated with the "gifts." Laban was so occupied with the servant and his gifts he had very little interest in Isaac. His present-day counterparts are taken up with the Holy Spirit and the sign-gifts which, from the very beginning, had only a temporary significance. But those "gifts" they covet and long to possess. The sole purpose of the gifts given by the servant was to authenticate his story and to draw Rebekah's heart away to Isaac. Once their purpose had been accomplished, that was the end of it.

again the golden strands of that greater story can be seen woven into the fabric of a very human tale. The servant was there to guard and to guide. He knew the way. Rebekah was not left to stumble along as best she could. Every provision had been made to bring her safely to her new home. Just so, the Holy Spirit at once begins to guide those who commit themselves to Christ, and it is He who undertakes to see us safely home.

We think of Rebekah *learning of Isaac*. She had a hundred questions to ask. "Is he tall, dark, and handsome? How old is he? What is his occupation? Is he very rich? What is he really like? Is he a happy man? Is he kind and thoughtful? Why did he send so far for a wife?" It is astonishing how little we really know of Christ when first we give ourselves to Him. The Christian life is one long learning experience under the tutorship of the Holy Spirit, who delights to talk to us about Christ.

Imagine the delight with which the servant spoke to the eager young woman about the man she was going to meet. He would tell her about the father and his love for Isaac, how Isaac was heir to all things, how all the plans and purposes of God centered in him. He might tell her that every mile of the road they were now traveling had been given by God to Isaac. He would tell of Ishmael's mockery. And, above all, he would tell of Mount Moriah and how father and son had gone together to that dread place and how Isaac had returned, as it were, from the dead. She learned of Isaac. That was the servant's work, to speak of him.

Think too of Rebekah *longing for Isaac*. The more she learned about him, the more her heart yearned. At first he was just a name, but gradually he began to form in her mind and heart and she came to love him more and more. She loved him now, not just for the gifts he had bestowed through the servant—they were mere trinkets after all, but for himself, for who he was and for what he had done. She would dream of him at night. She would tell her companions all that she had learned of Isaac. She began to long for him.

As the journey wore on, Isaac became more and more real to her. He was less and less a shadowy person and more and more a living, real, vital, wonderful man to whom she had given her heart. As the past began to recede in her mind, so the future loomed ever bigger and more important—a future filled with Isaac.

That is what the Holy Spirit is after in our own hearts—to fill them with longing for the Lord Jesus until, like the psalmist, we cry from the depths of our heart: "As the hart panteth after the water brooks, so panteth my soul after thee, O God" (Psalm 42:1). The Spirit of God would have us think less and less about the world and its ways and more and more about Christ. Our hearts, like the hearts of those two disciples on the Emmaus road, must begin to burn within us with longing for our Lord.

Think also of Rebekah *looking for Isaac*. "And Rebekah," we read, "lifted up her eyes . . . and . . . she said unto the servant, What man is this that walketh in the field to meet us?" (24:65). She learned that Isaac would be coming for her, and that was the most precious truth of all. Isaac was as eager to meet her as she was to meet him. So she would begin looking for him as the end of the journey drew near.

E. THE WAITING SON (24:62-67)

And all the time Isaac was waiting. He had been to Moriah, his work was done. The calling of the bride was the work of another. His task now was to wait in the father's presence, until the appointed time when he could go forth to meet his bride. The time must have seemed long, but finally the great day dawned and Isaac went to meet his bride and escort her home. "And Isaac brought her into his mother Sarah's tent, and took Rebekah, and she became his wife: and he loved her."[12]

Rebekah was not Sarah, but a different person entirely. The church is not Israel. However, it has been brought into the position formerly occupied by Israel. Both Abraham and Isaac had been affected by the death of Sarah; Isaac's comfort is described in chapter 24, Abraham's in chapter 25.

The church has been brought into the place of spiritual privilege presently vacated by Israel. The Lord Jesus finds all His joy in the church, His blood-bought Bride. Israel is never regarded as the bride of Christ; she is the wife of Jehovah and, in a coming day, is to be restored to her lost position as Genesis 25 intimates. But right now the focus is on Christ and His church.

Today, the Lord Jesus is waiting at God's right hand. His work is done and there He sits, in communion with the Father, His thoughts filled with the work the Holy Spirit is doing in the world. One of these days the time of waiting will be over and He will arise and go forth to meet His bride. Then the cry will ring out, "Behold, the Bridegroom cometh!" (Matthew 25:6). What a day it will be!

XIV. THE PARTINGS OF FAITH (25:1-11)

We have come to the last chapter in Abraham's life, and a wonderful chapter it is. It is a great thing to see a man stepping out boldly for God at the age of seventy-five, to see him cutting family ties, pulling up his roots already sunk deep into Mesopotamian culture, starting out on the pilgrim way. It is even more impressive to see him, a full century later, going on as strong for God as on the day when he first pulled out of Ur. It is a great thing to start well; it is even better to finish well. That is what Abraham did.

12. Note the first and second mentions of love in the Bible. In Genesis 22 the first mention is the love of the father for the son. Here we have the second mention of love—the love of the son for the bride. Bible typology is consistent.

A. THE FRUITFUL MAN (25:1-4)

Sarah had been dead now for twenty years or more. According to some chronologers Shem died the same year at the truly phenomenal age of some six hundred years. He had been the last living soul to remember the Flood.[13] With the death of Shem, Abraham began to feel his loneliness and isolation as a pilgrim patriarch, wandering, a homeless stranger in a land pledged to him but not yet possessed. Perhaps that great sense of loneliness or perhaps the clear, guiding voice of God led Abraham to make his decision. He would get married again.

1. ABRAHAM'S DECISION (25:1)

Abraham's decision was an important one, for half a dozen sons were now born to him including Midian whose descendants, the Midianites, became notable enemies of Israel. His new wife's name was *Keturah,* and a lovely name it is. It means "incense" or "she who makes incense to burn." If she lived up to her name her very presence must have been a benediction. She was a woman who added a fragrance all her own to every task and every circumstance of life. Where she went, the incense burned. She was an Old Testament Mary whose box of ointment, when broken and outpoured, filled her home with perfume. Keturah, we would like to believe, was the kind of woman whose life evokes worship in others. She would lift heavenward, like ascending incense, the thoughts of those around. We cannot wonder that Abraham, in his loneliness, was attracted to a woman like that.

There is, of course, a deeper significance. As in the story of Isaac and Rebekah, the golden threads of a higher and loftier theme are woven into the coarser fabric of the marriage of a mere man, even so notable and godly a man as Abraham. We have New Testament warrant for seeing typology here (Hebrews 9:13), Sarah having "waxed old and vanished away" as the writer of Hebrews puts it. Isaac and Rebekah fill the picture. Now comes Keturah. The Jewish covenant of works and exclusive salvation having passed away, Christ and His church fill the scene. But the church is only a parenthesis in God's dealings with Israel, as Romans 11 makes clear. God has not yet finished with Israel as a nation and intends to restore her to a place of fruitfulness and blessing in the millennial reign.

Keturah typifies Israel in a future day when the nation will once more become a channel of blessing to all mankind. The sons of Keturah

13. Very little is known about Shem, where he lived, what he did, the size of his family, the convictions that he had. Abraham was a distant descendant of Shem (his great-great-great-great-great-great-great-grandson if the chronologies are complete), and Abraham lived an utter pagan in thriving Ur of the Chaldees. One supposition is that Shem and Melchizedek were one and the same person, though there is little proof to substantiate that. But, if it were so, if the famous Melchizedek of Salem were indeed the long-lived Shem, then Abraham must have doubly felt his loss.

represent those nations that will have roles and play during the Millennium.

2. ABRAHAM'S DESCENDANTS (25:2-4)

Abraham had six sons by Keturah, seven grandsons, and three great-grandsons, all of whose names are recorded here by the Spirit of God. Those names have to be significant since they have found a place in the sacred text. We know very little about the fortunes of the descendants of Abraham. The Midianites became active enemies of Israel, and Sheba and Dedan are seen taking sides with Israel against Gog and Magog in a coming day. Apart from that we know little or nothing about the nineteen individuals whose names are written here.

Bible names, however, are always significant. We must always tread lightly, of course, when trying to fix their meanings, but we can at least suggest a line of truth hinted at by them. Proceeding with caution, then, we come first to *Zimran.* His name means "song" or "singer." The inference would be that he was a happy fellow with something of his mother's rising disposition about him. He had a soul filled with song.

Next comes *Jokshan* and his name is said to mean "difficult," "scandalous." That would lead to the justifiable inference that he must have been a difficult young man to handle, a completely different type from his older brother. If the connotation "scandalous" means anything, then he must have rebelled completely against parental authority and plunged into a lawless way of life. The names *Medan* and *Midian* mean much the same. Both are said to carry the connotation of judgment. Perhaps both of those boys were rebellious too.

The name *Ishbak* is given various meanings—"forsaken," "empty," "abandoned." Here again there seems to be a hint of failure and disappointment. That is most extraordinary in Abraham's family. It would hardly seem that Abraham has lost the ability to "command his children and his household." Indeed the context makes it clear that he was still able to enforce his will (25:6). There must be another and deeper significance in the names. The last of the boys was *Shuah,* and his name is given as meaning "pit," "crying," "humiliation."

How are we to account for the characters the names imply? In the first place, just because a man is godly does not guarantee that his children will be godly. Abraham undoubtedly insisted on obedience in his household, but there was no way he could legislate holiness. Abraham was a man of lofty spirituality, sound common sense, and parental responsibility. Keturah exerted a happy, worshipful influence. Yet here are half a dozen boys, only one of whom appears to manifest any mark of spirituality at all. One of them fathered a race always marked in the Old Testament by implacable hatred for God's people, and another fathered Bildad, one of Job's most caustic critics.

Yet God loved those boys as He loves all people, and He wrote their names down in His Word, for Abraham's sake. There they are, names without faces, staring at us out of the past with dumb, lifeless lips trying to speak to us. There they are, names calling to us across the void of centuries, especially to those of us born into the homes of believing parents.

But one cannot help but feel there is a deeper significance to the names. When we remember that, typically, Keturah symbolizes the restoration of Israel to the place of privilege after the church interlude is over, then the names of her sons assume typical significance. They point forward to the Millennium and, taken in the order in which they appear, they suggest the history of the Gentile nations, in their relationship to Israel and Israel's Messiah, during the Millennial age.[14]

B. THE FAR-SIGHTED MAN (25:5-6)

With the years of his life drawing to a close, Abraham wisely decided to ensure the succession of the covenant and the safety of Isaac. He did two very important things to achieve those ends.

The first thing recorded is *the disposal of his fortune*. "And Abraham gave all that he had unto Isaac" (25:5). Isaac was constituted his heir and became coregent of all his vast possessions. There was no room for questions or quarrels. Isaac was the heir.

Just so we read of Christ that God hath appointed Him "heir of all

14. *Zimran* means "singer" or "song." That is how the millennial age will begin. It will begin with songs of praise to the Lord for all that He has done for the earth. Isaac Watts' hymn will come into its own: "Joy to the world, the Lord is come, Let earth receive her King!" From pole to pole the redeemed nations will sing the praises of the Lamb.

Jokshan means "hard," "difficult," "scandalous." As time goes on, more and more children will be born onto the millennial earth. They will have never known the world as we know it, misruled, ravaged by disease, death, war, economic inequity. They will only have known the prodigal bounty of the millennial earth, the peace and the prosperity of the Savior's reign. But those children will be as much children of Adam as any born today. As those born into Christian homes today sometimes grow up to be *gospel* hardened, so they will grow up to be *glory* hardened. There will be some whose behavior will bring scandals even in that age.

Medan and *Midian* alike signify judgment. The Lord will reign throughout the Golden Age with a rod of iron. Those who challenge His authority will be instantly, fairly, but unsparingly judged. Death will be the exception rather than the rule during the Millennium and, for the most part, when it comes it will be the result of judgment.

Ishbak means "empty," forsaken," "abandoned." As the millennial age draws toward its close, disaffection will increase. The secret rebels will tend to congregate further and further from Jerusalem, the center of the millennial earth. The unleashing of Satan from the abyss will give those abandoned ones a rallying point for their smoldering rebellion. The name "Ishbak," with its suggested connotations, seems to suggest the spiritual condition of those who will flock to Satan's standards once they are raised.

Last of all comes *Shuah* meaning "pit," "cry," "humiliation." For is not Satan released from the bottomless pit? Will there not be tumultuous crying as the unregenerate multitudes find at last a champion who will lead them against their hated King? And will not the result be humiliation as their armies are swept away in the explosion of the planet and the instant summons to the Great White Throne?

things" (Hebrews 1:2). Jesus prayed, "All mine are thine and thine are mine" (John 17:10). He is the Father's heir, coregent with God of all things in the universe. There is not a blade of grass, a speck of cosmic dust, a drop of ditch water that does not belong to Him. He owns it all.

We next read concerning Abraham of *the dispersal of his family.* "But unto the sons of the concubines, which Abraham had, Abraham gave gifts, and sent them away from Isaac his son, while he yet lived, eastward, unto the east country" (25:6). It was a prudent move, for it ensured that nobody would be able to contest Isaac's claims in the future.

In like manner, the Father has ensured that the future belongs to Christ. There will be contesting of His claims to be God's heir. In this life, no doubt, there are many who would challenge Christ, but the future is all His. The Father has taken care of that (Philippians 2:9-11).

Abraham, the far-sighted man, took care of the future for Isaac his son. His sovereign and determining will was thus brought fully to bear on future issues.

C. THE FULL MAN (25:7-11)

The Spirit of God seems almost reluctant to leave the story of a man who became "the friend of God." He lingers over the closing scene. God had acknowledged worshipers long before the time of Abraham. But where, in all the sin-cursed earth before, did God ever have a *friend?* So the Spirit tarries over Abraham's death bed and touches again and again upon the things that happened as Abraham prepared to go home to his Friend.

1. THE MEASURE OF ABRAHAM'S DAYS (25:7)

"And these are the days of the years of Abraham's life which he lived, an hundred threescore and fifteen years" (25:7). At that time Isaac was seventy-five, Jacob was fifteen, Esau was fifteen, Eber, the grandson of Shem, was four hundred sixty. Abraham had been born only two years after the death of Noah. He had outlived his beloved Sarah by nearly half a century. He had been called to the pilgrim pathway when he was seventy-five, and had walked the straight and narrow way for a hundred years.

"These," says God, "are the *days* of the years of Abraham's life." A life, after all, is made up of days. In His wisdom God has punctuated time in that way. He gives us strength for the day. We need to learn that fact of divine arithmetic. Abraham lived some sixty-three thousand days, and some thirty-six thousand of them he lived as a believing man. Walking with God is a matter of taking life a day at a time and keeping short accounts with God every day. We must begin the day with Him, seeking His blessing, and close the day with Him, seeking His benediction. So God counted up the days of Abraham's life, the measure of his days.

2. The Manner of Abraham's Death (25:8)

"Then Abraham gave up the ghost, and died in a good old age, an old man, and full of years; and was gathered to his people" (25:8). There are not many people who die in a *good* old age. A preacher friend of mine once heard it said that the devil has no happy old men. He decided to put the theory to the test and asked every old man he saw if he was happy. He failed to find one. He helped one old man carry a heavy suitcase up a hill. When he parted from him he asked his perennial question, "Sir, are you a happy old man?" and was cursed to his face. He did find one happy old man—an old blind man he helped across a street. He was not surprised to discover that that happy old man was a Christian. The devil has no happy old men. This world is a great thief. It robs men not only of their youth and health, it robs them of peace and joy and innocence and everything else.

When my own grandfather was dying, my father asked him how it was with him. He said, "Len, there's nothing to dying—it's the living that counts! If you live right you'll die right." Balaam wished to die the death of the righteous, but he had no desire to live the life of the righteous. Of course, he did not die the death for which he wished. A good old age begins with a good youth and a good manhood.

Moreover, he died full. The King James Version says that he died "full of years," but the text really says that he died full. He died satisfied, or better still, satiated. He had lived life to the full. He was replete. He had all that he could take, not just of life's richest blessings, but of life itself. He was ready to die. A person sits down to his Christmas dinner and at last he pushes away from the table—full! He cannot eat another thing, not so much as a crumb. Abraham was full, full of living, satisfied and more than satisfied. Then the Lord took His dear friend on home. It was as though He said, "Now, my friend, come on up here. I have a new dimension of living to set before you and it will last for ever, for all eternity."

3. The Matter of Abraham's Desires (25:9-11)

In wondrous grace God was now about to gratify what must have been the three greatest desires of Abraham's heart.

There was the matter of Abraham's *paternal* desires (25:9). "And his sons Isaac and Ishmael buried him." What more could a good, full, old man want than that? Here was Ishmael, the son of the bondwoman, the dear lad he had been obliged to send away so many years ago, come home to bury his old dad. Moreover, whatever dislike he might once have had for Isaac was all buried now. The two of them appear to have acted in perfect harmony at the graveside of the patriarch.

There was the matter of Abraham's *personal* desire (25:9-10). They "buried him in the cave of Machpelah, in the field of Ephron the son of Zohar the Hittite, which is before Mamre; the field which Abraham purchased of the sons of Heth: there was Abraham buried, and Sarah his wife." If Abraham had one personal desire in death it was that he might lie for the rest of time alongside his beloved Sarah. And God granted that desire, too.

Finally, there was the matter of Abraham's *patriarchal* desire (25:11). "And it came to pass after the death of Abraham, that God blessed his son Isaac; And Isaac dwelt by the well of Lahai-roi." Abraham's desire as a patriarch, that the covenant blessing be confirmed to Isaac, was fulfilled. Thus God, in grace, fulfilled the dying wishes of His friend.

D. THE FUTILE MAN (25:12-18)

In keeping with his normal historical perspective, Moses kept his eye on the Messianic line in chapter 25. When dealing with the genealogies of Genesis, he invariably cleared up collateral lines and got them out of the way before pursuing his major line of interest. That is what he has done here. He rounds out the story of Ishmael and gets him out of the way before concentrating on the story of Isaac. Ishmael did not actually die at this point in the story, but his death and manner of life were recorded here so that the ground could be cleared for Moses to proceed with his major theme.

The Lord had promised Abraham that the son of the bondwoman should not go unblessed. Since Ishmael had spurned spiritual things in mocking at Isaac, God could not bless him with spiritual blessings. But He did bestow temporal blessings upon him.

Here was a man who was rich and increased with goods, who felt his need of nothing. Here was a man who was destitute of spiritual wealth, poor, wretched, miserable, blind, and naked in the things that mattered most. Like his half nephew, Jacob, Ishmael founded twelve tribes. From those tribes sprang the Arab peoples who have contributed much, perhaps more than most, to the world's culture and the world's cruelty. The atrocious African slave trade was largely the work of the Arabs. The abysmal spiritual darkness of Islam is yet another Arab contribution to the woes of the world. And persistently, to this day, Israel's bitterest foes have been of Ishmaelite stock.

ISHMAEL'S FAMILY TIES (25:12-15)

Ishmael's pedigree and progeny are both recorded here. The Holy Spirit begins by recording Ishmael's *notable birth.* "Now these are the generations of Ishmael, Abraham's son, whom Hagar the Egyptian, Sarah's handmaid, bare unto Abraham" (25:12). Sarah, Hagar, and Abraham—and the latter named twice! The emphasis seems clearly to be on the fact that Ishmael was without excuse for his rejection of God.

He had been born into a family of high and rare privilege. Of all the countless thousands of families on the earth in those days, wrapped in pagan darkness and superstition, it was Ishmael's remarkable privilege to have been born into a home where the truth of God was known and obeyed. He was born of a man who became known in Scripture as "the friend of God."

Nobody will pretend, of course, that there were no frictions in that home. There were lamentable snarls and tangles, petty spites and squabbles, especially where the two women were concerned. But there can be no doubt that godly old Abraham loved that boy and that he did all a father could to secure for him those spiritual blessings only God can bestow. But Ishmael was rebellious. He resented the birth of Isaac and all that his birth meant for the future. He could see nothing in Isaac at all except that Isaac had seemingly taken the place in his father's affections that once had belonged exclusively to him. Of the eternal purposes of God centered in Isaac, and hence through him to Christ, Ishmael could see nothing. He was blind, with the total blindness of the natural man, to spiritual truth. Growing up in that patriarchal home, Ishmael majored on the negatives, the faults and the failings and the imperfections of others. He grew up to be a rebellious teenager, "turned off" as we would say, to spiritual things. He wanted no part of any blessing that had to come through Isaac.

Yet the Lord loved Ishmael as much as He loved Isaac and His heart yearned over the rebellious young man. Again and again He picks up his name, writes it into His Book, then, seemingly sadly, puts it back down again. Ishmael, in spite of all the advantages of his birth and training, wanted no part of any Messiah the coming of whom would mean that he must acknowledge Isaac. He mocked at Isaac, and was as obdurate in his stubbornness as his descendants have been to this day to the salvation that is "of the Jews."

But there was more. Ishmael not only had Abraham for his father, he had Hagar for his mother, and Hagar knew God. Both Abraham and Hagar had begun life as pagans. Abraham had met God in the booming cities of far-off Babylon; Hagar had met Him in the wilderness on the borders of Egypt. Hagar was as much a believer as Abraham after her encounter with the living God. Her belief changed her behavior and sent her back to dwell, as long as she may, within the shelter of Abraham's fold. Ishmael was altogether without excuse. Although he might well have resented Sarah and been bitter toward Abraham, he had not the slightest reason in the world for rejecting the testimony of his mother.

Ishmael, blessed with a notable birth, grew up to reject all that Abraham stood for in purely spiritual terms. There is no hint anywhere that Ishmael ever bowed to the eternal purposes of God in Christ or that he ever came to know God for himself. He could not help but know about God, the circumstances of his birth and upbringing took care of that, but he never came to know God for Himself.

The Bible speaks next of Ishmael's *numerous boys*. "These are the names of the sons of Ishmael, by their names, according to their generations . . ." (25:13-15). Then follows a list of all twelve of them. Now why does the Holy Spirit take time and space to record those names? Why, for instance, does He not simply say that Ishmael had twelve sons and leave it at that? For the most part the actual histories of those sons have long since become blurred where they have not been forgotten altogether. Scholars, it is true, make some attempt to locate the areas of the Middle East where the sons of Ishmael eventually located, but the results are meager, uncertain, and vague.

We have before seen that the names in the Bible are often significant, even prophetic. In some notable instances (Methuselah, for example, Jacob, and Maher-shalal-hash-baz) a whole future history was wrapped up in a name and often, not just the future of the individual but of the race. The names of Ishmael's sons are introduced in a special order; presumably the order of their birth, but not necessarily so. They are linked together in a peculiar way. The first seven names are linked by a polysyndeton, a literary device always used for special emphasis by the Holy Spirit. Then that device is dropped only to be picked up again to link the next two names together. Finally the list concludes with three names not linked at all by the polysyndeton device. There has to be a reason for that structural form.

One cannot help but be fascinated by the way the Holy Spirit writes so many names into the Bible. Surely, if we believe in the plenary, verbal inspiration of the Scriptures, those names are there for a reason. Every single word is God-breathed and profitable. We cannot lightly dismiss those names or write them off as necessary links in a chain. For where do those particular links lead? It would be an unwarranted digression to pursue it further here, but a case can be made for the prophetic significance of the names of Ishmael's twelve sons.

Ishmael has become outstanding in the affairs of men for one supreme reason—Islam. The Islamic religion is just such a religion as one would expect to surface amongst a people descended from the monotheistic Abraham through a related people impervious to Jewish and Christian testimony alike. Scornful of Christ, why not invent a Messiah of one's own? That is exactly what one would expect from Ishmael's descendants. The God who cared for Ishmael as much as He cared for Isaac seems to have written a veiled warning against Islam into His Word by writing down in order and by arrangement the names of Ishmael's sons. Just as the names of Keturah's sons were significant, so are the names of Ishmael's sons. They form a species of prophecy and, taken together, they spell out the story of Islam—its great spiritual tragedy, its great social triumphs, and its great secular tenacity.

2. ISHMAEL'S FIVE TRIUMPHS (25:16)

Names! Towns! Powers! Princes! Nations! Ishmael made his mark on the world. Attention is drawn first to Ishmael's *people.* He, his sons, and their descendants made a name for themselves. The names of those men were evidently names to be reckoned with in that ancient world. Arab names were names to be reckoned with when Mohammed burst out of the desert solitudes of Arabia with his hordes of fanatical troops to break the power of the West, sweep across North Africa, and hammer at the very heart of Spain. Arab names, the names of Arab scholars, became renowned in the world when Europe wallowed in the cultural and scientific night of the Dark Ages. Arab names are names to be reckoned with even today.

Attention is drawn to Ishmaelite *places.* As the Muslim hordes overran the civilized world, Islamic capitals became the great power centers of earth and remained so for centuries. Cairo. Damascus. Baghdad. Those were the places where policy was made and where art and science flourished.

Attention is drawn to Ishmaelite *power.* The Arabs were the ones who first stabbed into black Africa to exploit the human resources of the continent. It is the Arabs who hold the world to ransom today. The great industrial nations of Europe, Japan, and even the mighty United States all have to tread softly because of the virtual Arab monopoly of the oil resources of the world. Arab petro-dollars have catapulted the Arabs to a position of enormous economic power so that small Arab states can blackmail great industrial powers (Japan for instance) and demand a pro-Arab stance in world affairs as a prelude to the sale of oil. Arab oil embargoes and price hikes threaten every industrial nation and the world itself with runaway inflation. Arab petrodollars are bankrolling deep Islamic penetration into black Africa. The church in Africa is facing the greatest challenge to its existence it has faced since first the Muslim hordes obliterated Christianity in the Middle East, Turkey, and North Africa. Fifty years ago nobody would have suspected such a resurgence of Arab power.

Attention is drawn to Ishmaelite *princes.* In the heyday of the Arab conquests, the sheikhs and caliphs of the Arab world dominated human international affairs. They bottled up Christianity in Europe and stood astride all roads to expansion by the Western powers. Today few nations dare make moves of any significance without first considering how the leaders of the Arab world might react. Suddenly the presidents and sheikhs of tiny Arab countries have become international tycoons, their voices heeded and conferences monitored in all the capitals of the world.

Attention is drawn to Ishmaelite *possessions,* especially to the nations controlled by the Arab peoples. They control the most vital, sensitive, and wealthy countries of the globe. The British and French empires maintained themselves so long because of their control of Arab lands. British and French influence in the world has waned in almost exact proportion to their loss of influence in the Arab world. Britain has gone from Egypt, from Palestine, from Jordan, from Iraq, from Aden, from the sheikhdoms of the Arabian Gulf, and consequently Britain is finished as a world power. Russia knows the strategic importance of those Arab countries and covets them as the key to world dominion. Russia's one great asset in the Middle East is the mutual Arab-Russian hatred of the Jew. To indulge that hate the descendants of Ishmael are prepared to pay almost any price and dare almost any risk.

Those, then, are the five triumphs of Ishmael. They are all carnal, worldly triumphs. History shows how Ishmael has enjoyed in full measure all that God pledged to him. The Spirit of God, however, jots down Ishmael's triumphs in the barest fashion possible. He spends no time on them, does not elaborate on them at all. We are not to be particularly impressed by them. He will devote chapter after chapter to telling of the wanderings of Jacob and twenty-five percent of Genesis to tell about Joseph but all of Ishmael's triumphs can be disposed of in a dozen names and about as many words. It is as though God would say, "So much for Ishmael. He has had his good things. In the light of eternity they are not worth another thought."

3. ISHMAEL'S FINAL TRAGEDY (25:17-18)

In concluding what He has to say about Ishmael, the Spirit of God draws attention to the *sorry* nature of Ishmael's *decease*. "And these are the years of the life of Ishmael, and hundred and thirty and seven years: and he gave up the ghost and died; and was gathered unto his people" (25:17). There it is, just the bare record of his death and burial, stark, unembellished, final. There is no lingering over his "days"; the mention of the years will suffice. The death and burial of Ishmael is in deliberate contrast with the death and burial of Israel. Jacob on his deathbed (Genesis 49) gathered his twelve sons around him too, and then poured out his heart to them along spiritual lines. For each one he had some word from God before he died. But not Ishmael. The Bible records nothing said to his sons at all. He died as he lived, a spiritual bankrupt, leaving nothing of eternal value to his children. Such was the sorry nature of his decease.

Finally attention is drawn to the *secular* nature of his *desires*. "And they dwelt from Havilah unto Shur, that is before Egypt, as thou goest unto Assyria: and he died in the presence of all his brethren" (25:18). Egypt. Assyria. Those were the two great world powers of antiquity. Both stand for the world—Egypt for the world in its cleverness and Assyria for the world in its cruelty. Ishmael lived neither in Egypt nor Assyria, but his desires were toward both. He lived as close to them as he could and molded his life upon their patterns. That is God's epitaph on his life.

"And he died!" The word means "to fall down." It signifies that "his lot was cast" in the presence of his brethren. At last the world he loved and for which he lived and that he so greatly desired slipped away from his grasp. He went out into a world for which he was totally unprepared and toward which his desires had never been.

Chapter 6

THE PILGRIM: ISAAC

(25:19—27:46)

I. Isaac and His Boys (25:19-34)
   A. The Twin Boys in the Womb (25:19-26)
      1. The Sterile Wife (25:19-21)
      2. The Secret War (25:22-26)
   B. The Twin Boys in the World (25:27-34)
      1. The Growing Conflict (25:27-28)
      2. The Great Confrontation (25:29-34)

II. Isaac and His Behavior (26:1-35)
   A. Isaac's Walk (26:1-5)
      1. The Difficult Problem (26:1)
      2. The Divine Prohibition (26:2*a*)
      3. The Definite Promise (26:2*b*-5)
   B. Isaac's Wife (26:6-11)
      1. The Lie Was Ready (26:6-7)
      2. The Lie Was Revealed (26:8-11)
   C. Isaac's Wealth (26:12-16)
      1. He Was Rich (26:12-14*a*)
      2. He Was Resented (26:14*b*-16)
   D. Isaac's Wells (26:17-22)
      1. What Isaac Recovered (26:17-18)
      2. What Isaac Realized (26:19-22)
   E. Isaac's Worship (26:23-25)
      1. The Important Revelation (26:23-24)
      2. The Immediate Response (26:25)
   F. Isaac's Witness (26:26-33)
      1. The Approach of the Enemy (26:26-27)
      2. The Appeal of the Enemy (26:28-29)
      3. The Appeasement of the Enemy (26:30-33)
   G. Isaac's Woe (26:34-35)

III. Isaac and His Blessing (27:1-46)
   A. The Unspiritual Father (27:1-4)
      1. Isaac's Concern (27:1-2)
      2. Isaac's Carnality (27:3-4)

- B. The Unsurrendered Wife (27:5-10)
  1. Rebekah's Decision (27:5-7)
  2. Rebekah's Deceit (27:8-10)
- C. The Unscrupulous Brother (27:11-33)
  1. Jacob's Suspicious Behavior (27:11-27)
  2. Jacob's Stolen Blessing (27:28-33)
- D. The Unsaved Son (27:34-46)
  1. Esau's Impassioned Remorse (27:34-35)
  2. Esau's Implacable Resentment (27:36-37)
  3. Esau's Importunate Request (27:38-40)
  4. Esau's Impulsive Resolve (27:41-46)

6

THE PILGRIM: ISAAC

I. Isaac and His Boys
(25:19-34)

The story of Isaac is attached one way or another to the story of either Abraham, Ishmael, or Jacob. There is only one chapter in Genesis devoted solely to Isaac and his own individual experience. For the overall view we might divide Isaac's story as follows—(1) Isaac and his brother (25:12-18); (2) Isaac and his boys (25:19-34); (3) Isaac and his behavior (26:1-35); and (4) Isaac and his blessing (27:1-46).

There is no break in the narrative leading on from Ishmael's affairs to those of Isaac. The significant polysyndeton continues right on with its rhythmic "and," "and," "and." "*And* these are the years of the life of Ishmael . . . *and* he gave up the ghost *and* died *and* was gathered unto his people. *And* they dwelt in Havilah . . . *and* he died in the presence of all his brethren. *And* these are the generations of Isaac . . . *and* Isaac was forty years old when he took Rebekah to wife" (italics added). Before we know it, we have passed out of one life into another. Ishmael and all his affairs are forever dismissed as the Spirit of God returns to the mainstream of divine revelation, to the story of Abraham and Isaac and Jacob, to the story that leads to Bethlehem and Calvary and the land beyond the sky.

Yet, although there is no break in the rhythm of the story, although the same steady, unhurried pace continues without a pause, one senses an inaudible sigh of relief. So much for Ishmael! Now let us look at Isaac! Let us look afresh at the man who went to Moriah to offer himself as a living sacrifice to God.

The section of the story that opens up before us tells of the birth of Isaac's boys. Here we have the first record in the Bible of the birth of twins. There was nothing identical about those twins, either about their looks or their likings. Indeed, it would be difficult to find a greater contrast than that which existed between Esau and Jacob. Here were two boys, born at the same time, born in the same place, of the same parents, to the same advantages and opportunities. Yet from the outset one of them set out in his own stumbling, erring way to please God; the other set out to please himself. One was ruled by the heavenly vision, the other by worldly and carnal things. "Not of blood, nor of the will of the flesh, nor of the will of man"—it is written all over Esau. "But of God!"—it is written all over Jacob (John 1:13).

In chapter 25 we see the two boys first in the womb and then in the world. The competition between them was fierce; so much so that we instinctively feel there is more to the story than the mere record of the birth of twins and of intense domestic rivalry. We sense that the Holy Spirit has a deeper truth to teach than that. We find what we are looking for in Paul's word to the Galatians: "The flesh lusteth against the Spirit, and the Spirit lusteth against the flesh: and these are contrary the one to the other: so that ye cannot do the things that ye would" (Galatians 5:17). In the struggle between Esau and Jacob we see mirrored the struggle between the flesh and the Spirit.

A. THE TWIN BOYS IN THE WOMB (25:19-26)

1. THE STERILE WIFE (25:19-21)

The struggle goes back beyond the birth of the boys to Rebekah herself. It begins with the problem of the sterile wife. "And these are the generations of Isaac, Abraham's son: Abraham begat Isaac and Isaac was forty years old when he took Rebekah to wife, the daughter of Bethuel the Syrian of Padan-aram, the sister of Laban the Syrian." Our attention is drawn at once to *Rebekah's pedigree* (25:19-20). It is set in marked contrast with that of Isaac. Isaac was the well-beloved son of Abraham; his pedigree was faultless. But Rebekah's was marred. She was not born in the same miraculous way that Isaac was, the heir of such notable privileges, the scion of such a pedigree as he. She was born of a pagan tribe. The only member of her family who rose to any degree of fame was her brother, and he was an unprincipled scoundrel. Rebekah's pedigree tells us we cannot expect much from our natural birth. Rebekah had taken the great step of faith that had united her with the father's beloved son and put her into the family of God, but so far as her natural pedigree was concerned, the Holy Spirit seems to note at once that we cannot expect anything from that. "That which is born of the flesh is flesh."

Then we observe *Rebekah's problem.* "And Isaac entreated the LORD for his wife, because she was barren: and the LORD was entreated of him, and Rebekah his wife conceived" (25:21). With what consummate skill the Holy Spirit weaves spiritual truth into the most ordinary, the most usual of natural events.

Rebekah, linked by decision and choice with the father's beloved son, and wholly committed to him, illustrates, as we have previously seen, the relationship between the believer and Christ. She was united to the beloved in the most intimate and sacred of ties. Nevertheless, she was barren. The fact that she had given herself to Isaac did not guarantee fruitfulness any more than accepting Christ as Savior guarantees spirituality and fruitfulness for God. There are many Christians, truly saved, truly linked in saving faith to the Lord Jesus, who remain spiritually barren and who never bring forth any lasting fruit for God. Rebekah's problem is their problem. They are barren.

Now the barrenness was not in Isaac; the text makes that perfectly clear. The trouble lay with Rebekah, not with Isaac. If we are to trace the problem of our spiritual barrenness to its proper source we must acknowledge that the problem lies in us and not in Christ. He is all that He should be; that fact is beyond doubt. Our failure to bring forth fruit cannot be laid at His door, it must be laid at ours. Rebekah, even in her relationship with the father's beloved son, could not bear fruit of herself. A miracle had to take place in her life before she could bring forth new life. The flesh never becomes anything except flesh. Isaac knew the problem and he initiated the solution by interceding for Rebekah. Thus we read: "And Isaac intreated the LORD for his wife, because she was barren." He did not blame Rebekah, for while the fault lay in her, it was not really her fault at all. She had inherited death in her womb. Just so, there is nothing in human nature that can bear spiritual fruit; we have inherited barrenness along that line. However, just as Isaac interceded for Rebekah, so the Lord intercedes for us. He carries on an intercessory ministry on our behalf at the right hand of God. That is the truth of John 14-17. Instructing His disciples, Jesus said, "The branch cannot bear fruit of itself . . . no more can ye . . . Herein is my Father glorified, that ye bear much fruit" (John 15:4, 8), and He went on to pray earnestly for that very thing.

2. THE SECRET WAR (25:22-26)

The narrative turns now from the sterile wife to the secret war (25:22-26). As soon as Rebekah conceived and showed evidence she was now to be fruitful, she became aware of something else—a battle was raging within. She had two natures within her, and those two natures were at war. In her barren condition there was no such struggle, but the moment fruitfulness began, the struggle began. It is a common enough spiritual experience. Those whose lives are most fruitful for God are most aware of the struggle between two opposing natures within. In the verses that follow, the existence of the two natures is first experienced, then explained, and then exposed. Step by step, Rebekah's actual physical experience is designed to teach spiritual truth. In other words, Rebekah's experience is a type of the Romans 7 experience of the believer, and should be regarded in that way.

First, then, the struggle between the two natures, the secret war, was *experienced* (25:22). "And the children struggled together within her; and she said, If it be so, why am I thus? And she went to inquire of the LORD." Faced with the perplexing fact that a battle was raging within, a battle she could not understand, Rebekah did a very sensible thing. She asked the Lord about it.

We have all experienced what Rebekah experienced. As long as we are content to live carnal, worldly lives we have no problem, but once we are determined to meet the conditions that lead to fruitfulness, the battle begins. Many a young believer has been as perplexed as Rebekah at that state of affairs. The idea persists that all we need is some ecstatic experience, some baptism of superholiness, and all problems connected with carnality will be solved. The contrary is true. The old nature is neither eradicated when we trust Christ nor is it canceled when we yield to Him for fruitfulness. It is an ever-present foe, bitterly hostile to any work of the Spirit in us, and quick to contest every Spirit-born effort toward fruitfulness for God. Far from being eradicated, the flesh seems to be stimulated into virile and murderous activity by any sign of developing holiness of life.

Next, the secret war was *explained.* "And the LORD said unto her, Two nations are in thy womb, and two manner of people shall be separated from thy bowels [being]; and the one people shall be stronger than the other people, and the elder shall serve the younger" (25:23). In its primary interpretation, the Lord's response had to do with the Israelite and Edomite races that would descend from Esau and Jacob and to their future fortunes in the world. But the narrative has a far deeper significance. It pictures the relationship between the two natures in the believer. The old nature is the elder of the two for the simple reason that it was there first; the new nature does not arrive upon the scene until the new birth. The future, however, lies with the new nature. Ultimate victory is assured for the new nature. "The elder shall serve the younger." God has pledged Himself to support the new nature in its struggle for mastery; therefore, in the end, it cannot lose. It will triumph eternally whereas the old nature in the believer has no future at all beyond the tomb and the principle of death can render its power null and void even in this life.

Finally, the two natures were *exposed.* "And when her days to be delivered were fulfilled, behold, there were twins in her womb. And the first came out red, all over like a hairy garment; and they called his name Esau. And after that came his brother out, and his hand took hold on Esau's heel: and his name was called Jacob" (25:24-26). At last the two natures stood out, visibly exposed for what they were. Esau was red, that is, he manifested the Adamic nature in all its power (the name "Adam" means "red"). Esau suggests the Adamic nature untamed. He looked more like a baby animal than anything else, all covered with hair. Hair is ever a symbol in Scripture of natural energy. The lower nature was evident in Esau's very appearance, and Rebekah, repelled by him, gave her love to Jacob.

It would seem that Esau had tried to murder Jacob in the womb. If so, it was another of those murderous Satanic assaults upon the Seed that came to a head at Calvary. But Jacob triumphed. Jacob holding on to the heel of Esau points us to Calvary, where the spiritual struggle was eventually resolved. One can picture (typically, of course), Jacob's saying: "See, I have him. I am laying hold of the splendid victory of Christ at Calvary and in that triumph, I triumph." Now, of course, Jacob never actually said that. He was just an infant, yelling as lustily as his newborn brother. But the symbolism is there just the same.

For our victory over the flesh comes directly from Calvary. "Knowing this," wrote Paul, "that our old man is crucified with him [Christ], that the body of sin might be destroyed, that henceforth we should not serve sin" (Romans 6:6). It is through the cross that we triumph over all that we are by natural birth. It is through the cross that the old nature is dealt with and put in its place, the place of death. That is the great lesson of the twin boys in the womb. The struggle within, when brought out into the open, is seen to be resolved in terms of the death of Christ.

B. THE TWIN BOYS IN THE WORLD (25:27-34)

The two boys still represent opposing principles, only now those principles are brought out into the open. The conflict and its issue is now enacted where everyone can see it, for sooner or later the inner struggle we experience will manifest itself openly in our lives. We will either adopt the princples exemplified in Esau or the principles exemplified in Jacob.

1. THE GROWING CONFLICT (25:27-28)

Time did not heal the breach between the brothers. As the years went by the rivalry between them grew. There is no discharge in the warfare between the Spirit and the flesh. In the case of Esau and Jacob the struggle went on to come to a head when Jacob brought Christ into the world and Esau brought Herod.

The Spirit of God tells us how those boys, now brought to the birth, *developed*. "And the boys grew: and Esau was a cunning hunter, a man of the field; and Jacob was a plain man, dwelling in tents" (25:27). Esau was a man of the field, Jacob a man of the fold; Esau chose the kind of life that delighted Cain, Jacob chose the kind of life that delighted Abel; Esau's passion was to kill, Jacob's was to protect. We must not get the idea that Jacob was a weakling, he was anything but that, but his instincts and interests were pastoral, protective, and productive, whereas Esau's were to kill and maim and destroy.

In other words, the natures of those boys were exactly opposite from one another, and they developed more and more with the passing of time. Truly, the things we cultivate in our lives are the things that ultimately control us. If we cultivate a taste for unsaved company, for impure literature and worldly lusts, then those are the things that will rule us in the end, but if we develop a taste for the Scriptures, for the fellowship of believers, and for soul-winning, then those things will ultimately control our lives.

We note then how the boys developed; we note also how they *differed.* "And Isaac loved Esau, because he did eat of his venison: but Rebekah loved Jacob" (25:28). Esau reigned supreme over Isaac's affections by the simple process of pandering to his appetites; Jacob reigned over Rebekah's heart simply by being himself. Esau said in effect to Isaac: "*Love me because I do what I do.* I can gratify your lusts, make you feel good, indulge your desires." "However, the kingdom of God is not meat and drink; but righteousness, and peace, and joy in the Holy Ghost" (Romans 14:17). Esau knew nothing of that. He pandered to Isaac's appetites. Jacob, on the other hand, said to Rebekah, "*Love me because I am what I am.*" Christ makes His appeal to us simply on the ground of being who He is. "Lovest thou Me? Lovest thou Me, more than *these?* Lovest thou Me?" That is how He addresses Himself to His own (John 21:15).

There is, then, a growing conflict. Two principles are at work, one pandering, low, carnal, earthly, fleshly and devilish; the other selfless and pure.

2. THE GREAT CONFRONTATION (25:29-34)

The conflict led directly to the great confrontation. Sooner or later the opposing principles had to confront each other openly, and their eternal issues had to be made clear and plain. The two boys represented different sets of values entirely: Esau minded *earthly* things and Jacob minded *eternal* things. The principles they embodied knew no middle ground.

Esau minded earthly things (25:29-34). He wanted everything here and now. His bent was revealed in one incident, a small thing it would seem, but freighted down with eternal consequences. Esau's whole way of life was to be exposed for what it was, utterly destitute of spiritual values. "For the natural man receiveth not the things of the Spirit of God: for they are foolishness unto him: neither can he know them, because they are spiritually discerned" (1 Corinthians 2:14). It all happened so suddenly. A few hasty words and the door of spiritual privilege slammed shut behind Esau forever. A few hasty words, but "out of the abundance of the heart the mouth speaketh," so those few hasty words exposed the utter darkness of Esau's soul. A few hasty words, but they showed that the root of the matter was not in him at all; he was an unregenerate, ungodly, unspiritual man, a man ruled by appetite, a man who exemplified everything that the Bible means when it speaks of "the flesh."

The scene is full of fascination. Jacob's behavior, we must admit, had little to commend it. In some ways, what he did was as bad as what Esau did. But we are not dealing with what Jacob did so much as with what Jacob desired, and there was nothing wrong with his desires—he desired that which was spiritual. What Jacob desired was what God desired, whereas Esau had no thought about God at all.

Esau had been out hunting, and even though the chase had been long and zealous, he had caught nothing. Now he was hungry and tired. Perhaps God had set the stage for the open display of Esau's true desires by withholding game from Esau's snares. He was plodding up the hill, trailing his spear and his bow, bone weary and hungry enough to cook and eat his boots. He was discouraged but getting closer to home when, like a flash, the Spirit of God tells us *what Esau saw.* "And Jacob sod pottage: and Esau came from the field, and he was faint" (25:29). He saw his brother Jacob bending over a pot from which emerged the most delicious fragrance in the world. The aroma of that stew drove every other thought out of Esau's head. The moment he saw that deliciously bubbling pot and caught the first whiff of what Jacob was cooking, Esau's eyes glistened, his mouth watered, and his appetites took over. In Esau was exemplified the full power of carnal appetite when, at last, it assumes its undisputed sway.

Then we are told *what Esau said.* "And Esau said to Jacob, Feed me, I pray thee, with that same red pottage; for I am faint: therefore was his name called Edom. And Jacob said, Sell me this day thy birthright. And Esau said, Behold I am at the point to die: and what profit shall this birthright do to me?" (25:30-32). What profit! Esau was selling the eternal, but how utterly blind he was. "I am going to die," he said. There was more profit to him in that birthright in death than there was in life, for it dealt with the future and with the eternal. But Esau cared nothing for the eternal. The flesh never does. The flesh lives for the here and now.

Finally we are told *what Esau sold* (25:33-34). It was both a deliberate and disdainful act. "And Jacob said, Swear unto me this day; and he sware unto him: and he sold his birthright unto Jacob. Then Jacob gave Esau bread and pottage of lentils, and he did eat and drink, and rose up, and went his way: thus Esau despised his birthright." The birthright (had he but had the spiritual discernment to see it) contained within it a throne. "Let nations bow down to thee" (Genesis 27:29). Esau sold it for a bowl of stew.

The New Testament gives us the Holy Spirit's evaluation of Esau's act. It calls him "a profane person." He was bluff, hearty, generous, impulsive, likeable. He was the oldest son of the only God-chosen family on the face of the earth, heir to a primacy that offered him a direct link to the Messiah and to priestly as well as princely rights. But he was profane; that is, he was unhallowed, unsanctified, defiled, polluted, common. "For one morsel of meat," is the fittingly contemptuous King James rendering; "For one morsel of meat Esau despised his birthright" (Hebrews 12:16). One morsel of meat! All earth's lustful passions are thus cataloged in a phrase. It was the bartering of eternal glory for present passion. It was evaluating God's promises as cheap and worthless. The use of the polysyndeton underlines the deliberate, disdainful, dreadful way the bargain was made—the priceless, eternal things tossed aside.

"Then Jacob gave Esau bread *and* pottage *and* drink *and* he rose up *and* went his way: thus Esau despised his birthright."

Esau minded earthly things. *Jacob minded eternal things* (25:31-34). For with all his faults and failings, and they were many, Jacob's affections were set on things above. He knew the value of that birthright. He knew it represented Christ. That birthright carried with it a right to the family *property* (the right of the firstborn to a double portion of the father's inheritance); it carried the right of family *priesthood* and, above all, it carried the right of family *progenitorship* that, in the patriarchal family, led directly to Christ. Esau could not have cared less about either the priesthood or the progenitorship. Jacob did. He passionately wanted both, for he saw beyond the temporal to the eternal.

In the great confrontation between the flesh and the Spirit, Esau, motivated by the flesh, lost out forever. Jacob, motivated by a passion for the eternal, won through. Look carefully, says the Spirit of God, "lest any man [among you] fail of the grace of God . . . lest there be any fornicator or profane person, as Esau, who for one morsel of meat sold his own birthright" (Hebrews 12:15-16).

What principle controls us? For which world are we living?

II. ISAAC AND HIS BEHAVIOR (26:1-35)

Isaac was overshadowed. He spent most of his life standing either in the shadow of his illustrious father, Abraham, or else standing in the shadow of his equally illustrious son Jacob. Genesis 26 is the only chapter devoted to Isaac alone. It marks the progress he made as a believer alone in the world. It tells of a man whose spirituality had already crested and reached its height years before when he went to Mount Moriah but who managed, with a stumble here and there, to somehow keep going for God.

A. ISAAC'S WALK (26:1-5)

The very first verse of the chapter shows us that erosion had already set in. Isaac had the stature neither of Abraham nor Jacob. He was a man easily molded by circumstances, willing to let them bend and shape him rather than seizing them and forcing them to serve him.

The chapter begins by telling of *the difficult problem* Isaac faced. "And there was a famine in the land . . . and Isaac went unto Abimelech, king of the Philistines unto Gerar" (26:1). Being a believer does not exempt a person from the ordinary disasters that overtake mankind. If a Christian builds his home on a geological fault line, the earthquake, when it comes, is just as likely to shake down his house as that of the atheist next door. God, however, often does protect His own and, even when the worst happens, causes it to work out for their good (Romans 8:28). Isaac, then, found himself overwhelmed by the same famine conditions that were plaguing his ungodly neighbors in Canaan.

As so often happens, the outside pressure created inward pressure. The famine was outside, the flesh was inside, and the two joined forces and drove him to a hasty, carnal decision. He decided to go down to Egypt until the famine was over. A hundred years before, his father had done the same thing with disastrous results. Isaac must have known about it, for the story was part of the heritage of truth he had received and that, handed on from generation to generation, finally came to rest in the Word of God. Despite the warning of Abraham's experience, Isaac set his course for Egypt. In other words, the problem was in control.

Next comes *the divine prohibition.* "And the Lord appeared unto him and said, Go not down into the land of Egypt" (26:2*a*). That was that! Isaac was not about to act in outright disobedience to the revealed Word of God. Egypt, in the Bible, stands for the world in which we live, the world that is the avowed enemy of God. The friendly, outstretched hand of the world, we must remember, is stained with Jesus' blood.

But God is an eminently practical God, so we find that the prohibition was followed by *the definite promise* (26:2*b*-5). Isaac was told to remain in the land of promise. Seven times over God asserted His sovereign will in the matter and pledged Himself to be to Isaac all that He had been to Abraham. It was a repetition, indeed, of the Abrahamic covenant only now confirmed directly with Isaac. Thus God's word came through in the crisis hour as remarkably relevant and up to date. Five times in that affirmation, Abraham's obedience was emphasized as a means of encouraging Isaac to trust and obey. Isaac's attention was thus turned away from the situation in which he found himself and regarding which he was about to make a wrong move, and it was directed instead to the word of God. How important it is, at all times and especially in times of crisis, to be occupied with God in His Word!

So much, then, for Isaac's walk. Journeying through this world, faced with problems without and pressures within, he was taught that his steps must be ordered of the Lord. He must not take things into his own hands. He must be guided by the word of God.

B. ISAAC'S WIFE (26:6-11)

We read that "Isaac dwelt in Gerar." God had told Isaac to stay in Canaan, but He had not told him to go to Gerar. Isaac should have had more sense. The very same reasons that prevented him from going to Egypt should have prevented him from going to Gerar. Now, instead of repeating Abraham's mistake in going to Egypt he was about to repeat Abraham's mistake in going to Abimelech. For Abraham stumbled twice, once by going to Egypt and once by going to Gerar, and although Isaac knew about both those mistakes, he chose to ignore what he knew. To act thus, to get as close to the world as possible without actually going right into it, was going to force Isaac to learn by bitter experience what he refused to learn from God's word. Gerar was the halfway house to Egypt. Isaac's halfhearted obedience to God landed him in some very hot water. World-bordering is almost as bad as out-and-out worldliness.

1. THE LIE WAS READY (26:6-7)

Isaac was hardly settled in Gerar before he resorted to lies. That alone should have been proof to him that he was in the wrong place. Despite God's marvelous revelation to him of His presence and protection, Isaac made lies his refuge. Most of us have been astonished at the facility with which we can concoct a lie when cornered. We are dismayed at the tenacity of the old nature, at the fact that our hearts are indeed deceitful above all things and desperately wicked. The lie was ready. "The men of the place asked him of his wife; and he said, She is my sister: for he feared to say, She is my wife." He excused himself, of course, on the ground of expediency. His wife was a beauiful woman, and he was afraid that the Philistines might kill him and seize her for themselves if he told the truth. Already he had lost sight of the covenant promise of God. A harbor of lies is no real port in a storm. God will always see to it that all such places of refuge are found out and destroyed.

2. THE LIE WAS REVEALED (26:8-11)

For a long time the lie was undetected, as God waited patiently to see whether or not Isaac would renounce it himself. But time passed and Isaac became so used to living with his lie he became careless in his behavior and acted in such a way that his deception was instantly exposed. Nothing is harder than to consistently maintain a lying position over a lengthy period of time. If a lie is to be maintained, the whole life must be reconstructed to revolve around it. One day Isaac forgot himself, was caught, and his deception pounced on by the Philistine king.

We are inveterate liars. Deception is ingrained into the very fiber of our beings.[1] The new birth implants truth in the soul, however, for Jesus is the Truth, and the Holy Spirit is called "the Spirit of truth" (John 14:17). The Bible is God's truth. The last thing the world expects from a believing man is a package of lies. The Philistine king, therefore, pounced on Isaac's lie and whipped him with it, and rightfully so. "Your lie was *unfair*," he said (26:10). "By telling us lies about

1. Mark Twain has an interesting passage on lies. He says, "I don't remember my first lie, it was too far back; but I remember my second one very well. I was nine days old at the time, and had noticed that if a pin was sticking in me and I advertised it in the usual fashion, I was lovingly petted and coddled and pitied in a most agreeable way and got a ration between meals besides. It was human nature to want to get these riches and I fell. I lied about the pin—advertising one when there wasn't any. You would have done it; George Washington did it, anyone would have done it. . . . I never knew a child that was able to rise above that temptation and keep from telling that lie . . . even George."—Mark Twain, *The Three R's* (New York: Bobbs-Merrill, 1973), p. 211.

your wife you exposed us all to temptation. Your lie might have been protection for you, but it was provocation for us." Lies always hurt other people, for they put other people in a false position, especially if they whole-heartedly believe the falsehoods they are told. Satan himself is the father of lies—the lie is the basic idiom of his language. Isaac might, perhaps, have considered his lie "a white lie," but any lie is devilish and a grief to the Holy Spirit of God.

"Your lie was unfair," said the resentful king. "Moreover it was *unnecessary*" (26:11). To prove it he charged his people: "He that toucheth this man or his wife shall surely be put to death." Isaac was content with that. What strange creatures we are. Isaac had no trouble resting on the word of a pagan king, but he found it difficult to rest on the unfailing word of God. How often we treat God with the same insulting lack of belief.

C. ISAAC'S WEALTH (26:12-16)

The narrative now turns to a pleasanter theme and tells us of Isaac that *he was rich* (26:12-14*a*). Everything he did prospered. Did he plant grain? It brought forth an hundredfold, far beyond anything that might be expected even in fertile soil. An hundredfold—ten thousand percent on his investment! Did he raise cattle? His herds multiplied. So "the man waxed great, and went forward, and grew until he became very great." Now that he had abandoned his false position, the blessing of God rested upon him in a marked and abundant way until his wealth was overwhelming.

Next we observe that *he was resented* (26:14*b*-16). "And the Philistines envied him. For all the wells which his father's servants had digged in the days of Abraham his father, the Philistines had stopped them [filled them with earth]. And Abimelech said unto Isaac, Go from us: for thou art mightier than we."

In the typology of the Old Testament, the Philistines represent unregenerate men who occupy ground that belongs to the people of God. The Philistines were of Grecian stock. They had taken possession of the land given by God to Abraham and his seed, but they had not come into the land God's way, by means of redemption through the blood, by means of believing the promises of God, by means of walking in obedience to God's Word. They had come in some other way and had settled down where they did not belong, there to remain as persistent enemies of the true people of God. They represent the unbelievers who have taken up positions in the professing church, there to remain as liberals and as unbelievers, holding on to things to which they have no right and opposing the true saints of God. The Philistines remained a problem in Canaan until the coming of David, who effectively put an end to them. Just so, false professors in the church will never be rooted out until the coming of Christ.

That brings us to the wells that the Philistines, in Isaac's day, deliberately stopped up. Those wells were a source of life and refreshment. They could represent what Christ Himself has for the human soul. Jesus said to the woman at Sychar's well, "Whosoever drinketh of this water shall thirst again: but whosoever drinketh of . . . the water that I shall give him [it] shall be in him a well of water springing up into everlasting life" (John 4:13-14). Abraham had, symbolically, ministered Christ to needy souls by digging his wells, thus making the life-giving water available to all. The Philistines stopped up those wells and did so spitefully and with deliberate evil intent. They did not want the water themselves and they did not want anyone else to have it, either. How like the liberal theologians and their followers who have crept into the church, who seize positions that belong only to God's people and who then proceed to choke the channels of blessing that come to men in the gospel through Christ.

Moved with envy, the Philistines set out to oppose and resist all that was represented in the land by Abraham and Isaac. The father and the son, in their gracious ministry of providing wells in a thirsty land, were opposed by those enemies. Finally they asked Isaac to leave the land altogether, resenting both his influence and his power.

D. ISAAC'S WELLS (26:17-22)

1. WHAT ISAAC RECOVERED (26:17-18)

Attention is now focused on the actual wells provided by Isaac himself in that dry and thirsty land. We notice, first, what Isaac *recovered.* "And Isaac digged again the wells of water, which they had digged in the days of Abraham his father; . . . and he called their names after the names by which his father had called them" (26:18). In eastern lands in Bible times, all waste lands were commonly called "God's lands," and anyone who was able to provide a means of reclaiming and irrigating them automatically became their proprietor. To give a name to a well was a recognized way of publicly advertising a property right in the area. To stop up or destroy a well once dug was a wanton act and, in a land where water was at a premium, was considered an act of war. It was a deliberate encroachment on the territorial rights of another.

The Philistines, in stopping up the wells of Abraham, gave evidence of their own bad faith. They had already entered into treaty agreements with Abraham (Genesis 21:22-34) about his rights in the land—not that any such treaties were necessary in that God had already given all the land to him. By stopping up Abraham's wells the Philistines were, in effect, tearing up their treaty with Abraham.

But, to return to Isaac, he recovered Abraham's wells, thereby asserting his own title to those so-called "God's lands." Translated into spiritual experience, Isaac's action symbolizes the rediscovery of truth concerning Christ once enjoyed by the church but buried in tradition, liberal theology, and false teaching by those who have crept into the church. Isaac must have found great joy in rediscovering the wells his father had dug, just as a believer today will rejoice in the discovery of truth concerning Christ once enjoyed by others but long since buried by false teaching or simply forgotten with the passing of time.

2. WHAT ISAAC REALIZED (26:19-22)

He realized there was more. There were more wells to be dug, not just his father's wells, but more. How wonderful! There is always more to be found in Christ. It is good to enjoy truth brought to light by others, but it is even more precious to have the Holy Spirit reveal truth directly to one's own heart. Isaac fought no great battles, built no mighty cities, erected no imposing monuments. He quietly dug wells. At that stage of his life, in other words, he left a trail of blessing behind him everywhere he went. Since the Holy Spirit lingers so lovingly over that section of the story, it must have spiritual meaning. What does it matter to us today that nearly four thousand years ago a man named Isaac dug three comparatively insignificant wells in a corner of Canaan? Why should the Spirit of God deem them of such importance as to record this and that about them and to record, for all time, their names? There has to be a spiritual significance.

Isaac's three wells are significant because of their names, and their names are significant because they embody not only spiritual truth, but because they showed Philistine response to Isaac's works. They symbolize therefore the attitude of the unsaved church member toward the efforts of the true believer.

The first well was called *Esek* and it stands for *contention*. "And Isaac's servants digged in the valley, and found there a well of springing water. And the herdmen of Gerar did strive with Isaac's herdmen, saying, The water is ours: And he called the name of the well Esek; because they strove with him" (26:19-20). Isaac was a peace-loving man who hated strife. But there are times when, like it or not, even the most peaceable believer has strife forced upon him. Indeed we are to "contend earnestly for the faith." Every cardinal truth of the church has been bitterly assailed by the "Philistines" within its ranks. "The water is ours," cried the Philistines of old. "The truth belongs to us," say the liberals, the existentialists, the ritualists, the cultists, the ecclesiastical establishment. Not so. The truth belongs to God's Isaacs, not to the worldly Philistines.

The next well was *Sitnah*. If Esek signified contention, that well stood for *contempt*. "And they digged another well, and strove for that also: and he called the name of it Sitnah" (26:21). The word means "hatred" and comes from a Hebrew root word meaning "to lie in wait as an adversary." The name Satan comes from the same root. And there we have it! The ultimate source of all opposition to divine truth, especially truth that relates to the person and work of Christ, is Satan himself. He is consumed with contempt toward the things of God and a bitter envy, hostility, and rage against anything that ministers Christ to a needy heart.

Then comes *Rehoboth.* "And he removed from thence, and digged another well; and for that they strove not: and he called the name of it Rehoboth; and he said, For now the LORD hath made room for us, and we shall be fruitful in the land" (26:22). That well's name signifies the world's basic *carelessness* toward Christ. That time the Philistines simply ignored Isaac, their attitude being one of careless indifference. "Let the fellow get on with his digging! Sooner or later we'll take the wells away from him anyway," was the attitude. Isaac had found another source of satisfaction, another well of water, and the world simply yawned in his face the way the world shrugs its shoulders at most of the activities of God's people. "So what, who cares?" is the attitude of most.

E. ISAAC'S WORSHIP (26:23-25)

1. THE IMPORTANT REVELATION (26:23-24)

Isaac's exercise in the matter of the wells led naturally to worship. Any occupation with Christ should lead to that. Two things are recorded in connection with that. First there was an important revelation to him. Isaac took his stand at Beersheba, a place linked with Abraham's dealings with the Philistines. The name means "the well of the oath," for there the Philistines had sworn to leave Abraham alone so long as he left them alone. It was there that the Philistines had been forced to confess that Abraham had something they did not have; he had God. Isaac now took his stand there and there God came to him and once again spoke to him about the covenant, speaking to him about the Lord's *person* ("I am the God of thy father Abraham"); the Lord's *protection* ("fear not"); the Lord's *presence* ("I am with thee") and the Lord's *promise* ("I will bless thee and multiply thy seed"). What more could a man want?

2. THE IMMEDIATE RESPONSE (26:25)

That important revelation to Isaac was followed by an immediate response by Isaac. "And he builded an altar there, and called upon the name of the LORD, and pitched his tent there: and there Isaac's servants digged a well" (26:25). Isaac's response was threefold. He responded in *spontaneous worship* by building an altar, that is, he gave the Lord his heart, his life, his all. He responded in *spoken word* for he "called on the name of the LORD"; he confessed with his mouth the truth that now thrilled his heart. He responded in *specific work,* for there he digged a well. True worship is never abstract daydreaming. It results in things getting done for God. Another well! Another landmark of blessing in enemy country, in a dry and barren land! They were digging now close by where Abraham had dug. In other words, they were adding to what had been discovered by that dear man of God so long since gone home to his reward.

F. ISAAC'S WITNESS (26:26-33)

Again the Philistines showed up. The Holy Spirit chronicles *their approach* (26:26-27). *Then* (right after Isaac's time with the Lord, for that is the source of all true power) the Philistines came to sing a different tune. They came in force—their king, one of his close confidants, and the army chief of staff. "And Isaac said unto them, Wherefore come ye to me, seeing ye hate me, and have sent me away from you?" It is not often the world approaches a believer in that manner, though if we lived closer to the Lord it would happen more often than it does. Isaac knew he was in a very strong position. He had always been in a strong position, had he but known it. Knowing the strength of his position, under the protection of God Himself, Isaac had no intention of yielding an inch, be it a hundred kings and a thousand military chiefs.

The approach was followed by *the appeal* (26:28-29). The visitors lost no time in coming down to issues. "We saw certainly that the LORD was with thee: and we said, Let there be now an oath betwixt us, even betwixt us and thee, and let us make a covenant with thee; that thou wilt do us no hurt, as we have not touched thee, and as we have done unto thee nothing but good, and have sent thee away in peace: thou art now the blessed of the LORD." What an extraordinary statement. The unblushing gall of those men! They had persecuted him, plundered him, pursued him, robbing and opposing him at every twist of the road, yet they blandly claimed they had done him nothing but good! Certainly the unregenerate man's appraisal of his own behavior is flattering to himself rather than true to fact. In any case, the men now wished to make peace with Isaac. And why? Because it was evident that the Lord was with him. They paid lip service to the Lord they did not know.

Then came *their appeasement* (26:30-33). Isaac feasted them and forgave them. However, he wanted no part in their fellowship so he sent them away. "And Isaac sent them away, and they departed in peace." Again we see the consistent hallmark of the believer—separation from the world. "And it came to pass *the same day* that Isaac's servants came, and told him concerning the well which they had digged, and said unto him, We have found water. And he called it Shebah: therefore the name of the city is Beer-sheba unto this day." Once the meaningless peace overtures of the ungodly had been received and the unbelievers themselves allowed to depart, and once Isaac had again taken his stand with the Lord in separation from the world—then new sources of satisfaction in Christ could be enjoyed.

Interestingly enough, the unbelievers were as glad to leave Isaac as Isaac was to see them go. They paid tribute to the fact that the Lord was with Isaac and that the Lord's blessing rested on him and on all that he did, but they had no desire to stay and seek the Lord for themselves. Isaac knew Him and they knew that Isaac knew Him, but they had no interest in knowing Him.

G. Isaac's Woe (26:34-35)

All the while Isaac had an Esau growing to manhood at home. It is a strange fact that many a man, whose life has made great impact on others, fails to make an impact on his own children. Perhaps they are too familiar with sacred things. Esau had never shown any interest in God's Word.

And now, he was forty years of age. He decided to get married, and in his choice of wives he broke the hearts of his parents. "And Esau . . . took to wife Judith the daughter of Beeri the Hittite, and Bashemath the daughter of Elon the Hittite: which were a grief of mind to Isaac and to Rebekah." More will be said about those two pagan charmers when we come to consider Esau in that full-length review God gives of his life in Genesis 36. Suffice it to say here that Esau's choice of wives showed how far down the highway to a lost eternity he had already gone.

Isaac and Rebekah were not perfect. They had made their mistakes, played at favorites, stumbled and fallen, and at times drifted from God. But, beneath it all, they both had a sincere love for the Lord and, as we have seen, Isaac's testimony in the world was impressive. One of their sons grew up to become one of the greatest of all Old Testament saints; the other grew up to break their hearts. For if Satan cannot attack a man any other way, he will attack him through his family. We have often seen that.

III. Isaac and His Blessing (27:1-46)

Esau attempted to buy back with a dish of venison what he had sold for a mess of pottage. The plan did not work. Chapter 27 is one of the saddest chapters in Genesis. Everybody is doing the wrong thing—especially Isaac. Normally we think of Isaac as one of the outstanding types of Christ in the Old Testament. And so he was in Genesis 22. But Isaac is no type of Christ in Genesis 27. If he is a type of anything here, he is a type of the backslidden, worldly, carnal Christian. It is a sad fact that while we may at one stage of our lives mirror the beauties and graces of the Lord Jesus, we may at another stage reflect the exact opposite. Such is the human heart, even the regenerate human heart.

We step across the threshold of Isaac's home needing to be reminded that it was the home of a believing man, for it will be difficult to recognize it as such. Few ungodly homes exhibit such unlovely behavior as did the family of Isaac that sad day. The chapter is a warning and rebuke to carnal though believing parents.

A. THE UNSPIRITUAL FATHER (27:1-4)

The situation displayed in Genesis 27 did not develop in a single day. It had its roots when Esau and Jacob were born and when Isaac and Rebekah each chose a favorite son. In that deadly favoritism was sown the seed now to be exhibited in full flower.

Things had been going wrong in their home for years. The secret resentments and rivalries had been more or less hidden until now, suddenly, God Himself opened the front door to invite the whole world in for a look. Their whole domestic life was dragged out into the open, written down, and published in a book; a book that would run through more editions than any other book ever printed and that would be translated into more languages than any other book on earth. Think of it! To have one day's affairs printed and read, discussed, preached, and commented on for all the rest of time. Surely each member of Isaac's family would wish, if it were possible, to relive that day—differently. But nobody can relive a day. What is written is written.

The story begins with the head of the home. Once he was a Christlike man. Where in all the Bible can we find so Christlike a man as Isaac when he became obedient unto death on Mount Moriah? Once that man had been a well-digger, leaving behind him a trail of blessing and refreshment for others. But that was a long time ago. He had now become sadly unspiritual.

The story focuses first on *Isaac's concern.* "And it came to pass, that when Isaac was old, and his eyes were dim, so that he could not see, he called Esau his eldest son, and said unto him, My son: and he said unto him, Behold, here am I. And he said, Behold now, I am old, I know not the day of my death" (27:1-2). Isaac was one hundred thirty-seven years of age. His stepbrother Ishmael had died at that age and that, perhaps, is what made Isaac think he was about to die. He was mistaken. He lived another forty-three years (35:28), dying at the ripe old age of one hundred eighty.

Still, Isaac's thoughts were full of death, and he decided to take care of his will. The greatest thing he had to bequeath was his patriarchal blessing, a blessing that involved not just a property settlement, but the right of progenitorship, the right to stand in direct line as an ancestor of the coming Christ of God. That particular blessing could not be lightly bestowed nor was its disposal left up to the patriarch. The blessing had to be bestowed in accordance with the revealed mind and will of God. Isaac, then, was right in what he wanted to do, but absolutely wrong in deciding to give the blessing to his favorite, his beloved Esau. He had long since been told "the elder shall serve the younger." Either he had forgotten it or else he chose to ignore it. The blessing was for Jacob, not Esau. God had said so.

It is an excellent thing to be exercised about spiritual things. We need to see to it, however, that we discharge our spiritual obligations in accordance with the revealed will of God. David was right in wishing to see the sacred Ark safely and permanently housed in Jerusalem; he was wrong in putting it on a cart. Moses was right in wishing to help his Jewish kinsmen; he was wrong in smiting the Egyptian. Saul was right in wishing to consult God before the fateful battle of Gilboa; he was wrong in resorting to witchcraft to get the guidance he so belatedly desired. It is possible to have a commendable spiritual exercise and have it spoiled and brought to nothing by executing it in a wrong way.

We are told next of *Isaac's carnality*. "Now therefore take, I pray thee, thy weapons, thy quiver and thy bow, and go out to the field, and take me some venison: and make me savoury meat, such as I love, and bring it to me, that I may eat; that my soul may bless thee before I die" (27: 3-4). It is Paul who gives us the best commentary on that. "For they that are after the flesh do mind the things of the flesh; but they that are after the Spirit the things of the Spirit. For to be carnally minded is death; but to be spiritually minded is life and peace. Because the carnal mind is enmity against God: for it is not subject to the law of God, neither indeed can be. So then they that are in the flesh cannot please God" (Romans 8:5-8). Let us see how that principle worked out in the life of Isaac.

We see him, first, exhibiting the *stubborn enmity* of the carnal mind. "The carnal mind is enmity against God." Isaac wanted his own way. He knew the blessing should go to Jacob, but Jacob was no favorite of his. He had God's word for it that the elder (Esau) must serve the younger (Jacob) but that meant nothing to him. The carnal mind in Isaac was not subject to the law of God. He was willing to set aside God's Word to have his own way.[2]

Next we see Isaac exhibiting the *sensual exercise* of the carnal mind. "They that are after the flesh do mind the things of the flesh." Isaac loved Esau, not because he was a holy man of God, not because he walked the pilgrim way, but because he did eat of his venison. It was carnal, sensual exercise that motivated Isaac and that now controlled him in his determination to bestow the patriarchal blessing on the wrong man. "Make me savoury meat such as I love . . . that I may eat, that my soul may bless thee." He thought spiritual blessing could be imparted in the energy of the flesh. Run your eye down the chapter. Savory meat is mentioned six times, vension seven times, and eating eight times. Here was a man controlled by carnal appetite. Over twenty times ref-

2. The same principle is to be seen at work throughout the Bible. It is seen in *Abraham's* marrying Hagar, in *Lot's* choosing Sodom, in *Joshua's* making his covenant with Gibea, in *Saul's* sparing Agag and his cattle, in *Solomon's* political marriages, in *Jonah's* fleeing to Tarshish from the presence of the Lord, in *Peter's* opposing Christ's determination to go to Calvary, in *Ananias's* and *Sapphira's* keeping back part of the price. We can see the same principle at work all too often in our own hearts and lives. The carnal mind is not subject to the law of God. How often we will wrestle with a clear biblical command simply because we do not like the way it cuts across our wants and wishes, prejudices, preconceived ideas, and pet theological notions.

erence is made to his fleshly desires. He had a carnal mind for "they that are after the flesh do mind the things of the flesh." Isaac was exercised rightly enough but it was fleshly exercise. He thought he could do a spiritual thing in a carnal way.

B. THE UNSURRENDERED WIFE (27:5-10)

Alexander Whyte has a discerning word on Rebekah. He says,

> With all her beauty, and with all her courage, and with all her ambition to be in the covenant line, Rebekah lacked the best thing in a woman, covenant line or no—womanly sensibility, tenderness, quietness, humility, and self-submission. . . . "And the wife see that she reverence her husband" says Paul with his eye on Rebekah. Yes; but what if she cannot? What if there is so little left that is to be reverenced in his husband . . . ? What if a wife wakes up to see that she has yoked herself to death to a churl, or to a boor, or to an ignoramus, or to a coxcombe, or to a lazy, idle log, or to a shape of a man whose God is his belly, or his purse, or just his own small, miserable self . . . ? Well, she will need to be both a true woman and a true saint if she is to do what is right. . . . Let her determine to be a New Testament wife to him. Let her believe that Jesus Christ said, and still says, Take up thy cross daily![3]

Rebekah was married to a man who had little left about him to love. If the Bible says, "Let the wife reverence her husband," it also says, "Husbands, love your wives as your own bodies." Once Isaac had loved Rebekah (24:67), but he had another first love now. "Make me savoury meat such as I love," he said.

Rebekah was a clear-minded, practical, strong-willed, down-to-earth woman. We detect, way back in Genesis 24, that she was a woman who combined realism, resolution, and romance in her makeup. Isaac, on the other hand, was a placid, mild, submissive kind of person, forever overshadowed by his more forceful relatives and friends. To that must be added the fact that he had grown carnal with age. The story of Rebekah is intended to teach some sobering lessons to all practical, capable, determined women who find themselves married to submissive, pliable men. The great temptation for such women is to boss and bully their husbands. As a result the woman becomes increasingly masculine, and the man becomes increasingly feminine. A truly strong woman will use her strength to minister strength to her husband, not to rob him of whatever backbone he might once have had. Rebekah's is the story of the unsurrendered wife.

It might well be argued that Isaac had forfeited all right to Rebekah's respect when he had denied her down there in Gerar. It is a great pity Rebekah never knew her mother-in-law, for Sarah could have taught her how to submit, even in the face of such a shattering ex-

3. Alexander Whyte, *Bible Characters, The Old Testament* (London: Oliphants, 1952), 1:109-10.

perience. Not once but twice Abraham, strong man that he was, had let her down in exactly the same way. Yet she could still call him "Lord" despite it all (1 Peter 3:6). Rebekah could have learned much from a woman like that. Unfortunately she never had the chance to learn from Sarah so she had to learn life's hard lessons by bitter personal experience.

The text sets before us *Rebekah's decision.* "And Rebekah heard when Isaac spake to Esau his son . . ." (27:5-7). At once she summoned Jacob, her favorite, and reported what she had just overheard. She would outsmart her husband. No doubt she assured herself that "Scripture" was on her side (it is amazing how proficient we are at finding proof texts that support our wayward desires) for God had sworn that the blessing must go to Jacob. Surely the end would justify the means. But God, who controls all the factors of time and space, has no need for our clever little schemes. He could have chased away all the deer from the forests and fields for miles around so that Esau would find no venison, just as He later gathered the fish into Peter's net. He could have spoken in so compelling a way to Isaac that he would not have dared to disobey. But, no. Rebekah must act for herself.

Next comes *Rebekah's deceit.* "'Go now," she said to Jacob. "Go now to the flock, and fetch me from thence two good kids of the goats; and I will make them savoury meat for thy father, such as he loveth. And thou shalt bring it to thy father, that he may eat, and that he may bless thee before his death" (27:8-10). A pinch of salt here, a dash of pepper there, a little sage, perhaps, a good, big clove of garlic, the juice of an onion, all braised and broiled to perfection. Then a sprig of mint and a spicy sauce, and who's to tell the difference between goat and venison? Not Isaac, anyway. All down the chapter we see Isaac being deceived by his senses. His sight had failed him; he was blind. His smell deceived him; he thought from the earthy smell of the garments that Jacob was Esau. His taste failed him; he thought goat was vension. His feeling failed him; he thought a goat's skin was Esau's hairy arm. His hearing rang true, but he could not believe what he heard.

We have the sorry spectacle of a wife deliberately setting out to deceive her husband, having first persuaded herself that it was right and proper for her to do so. She would pay for it, of course, in the end. God does not permit His people to get away with that kind of thing. Before that day was over her beloved Jacob would be fleeing for his very life to far-off Padan-aram. "For a few days," she consoled herself. The "few days" lengthened out to a year, to seven, to fourteen, to twenty years, and she never saw her beloved boy again. She died before ever he came back. Nor did she ever see her big, burly grandsons. Possibly she never heard a word about Jacob again. Truly the way of the transgressors is hard.

C. THE UNSCRUPULOUS BROTHER (27:11-33)

Jacob, in his own devious way, set his affection on things above.

Probably, at that stage of his career, he did not know the Lord personally even though he knew about Him and coveted all that God could do for a man. He wanted the blessing of God but was not overly scrupulous how he obtained it. Still, the blessing of God was his guiding star.

1. JACOB'S SUSPICIOUS BEHAVIOR (27:11-27)

First, our attention is drawn to his *fear*. He feared that he might be found out in the very act of pretending to be Esau and thus bring down a curse rather than a blessing on his head. "I am a smooth man," he said. He surely was! "I shall seem to him as a deceiver," he objected. It did not bother Jacob that he *would* be a deceiver if he did what his mother suggested. He did not want to *seem* a deceiver. He wanted to keep up appearances even while practicing deliberate fraud. He deceived himself long before he set out to deceive his father.

Attention is drawn to his *falsehood* (27:14-27). Dressed in Esau's workday coat, his hands and arms covered with rough goat's hair, and with a mouthwatering dish of spiced-up goat in his hands, Jacob set out to deceive his dad.

He was an accomplished liar. "Who art thou?" demanded the blind old man. "I am Esau [lie number one], thy firstborn [lie number two]; I have done according as thou badest me [lie number three]: arise, I pray thee, sit and eat of my venison [lie number four], that thy soul may bless me." Four lies in a single breath! "And Isaac said unto his son, How is it thou hast found it so quickly, my son? And he said, Because the LORD thy God brought it to me [lie number five]." That time he added the name of the living God to his deception to give it added acceptability.

Poor old Isaac was still not convinced. He sensed something was wrong, but he could not put his finger on it. He tried again, summoning Jacob closer so that he might feel his flesh. "The voice is Jacob's voice," he quavered, "but the hands are the hands of Esau." Thus Isaac made the final mistake of a carnal man. He went by his feelings. Convinced in spite of himself, he sat up and made a hearty meal. Then, satisfied and replete, he prepared himself to discharge his patriarchal obligations.

2. JACOB'S STOLEN BLESSING (27:28-33)

What a magnificent blessing it was. The Holy Spirit first records the *content* of that blessing (27:28-29). It bestowed on Jacob unlimited prosperity and power, the fatness of the earth, sovereignty over the nations, lordship over his brethren, divine protection—it was the blessing of the Lord that maketh rich and addeth no sorrow thereto.

Then we are told of the *confirmation* of the blessing (27:30-33). With a sigh of relief Jacob scurried away, leaving the old gentleman leaning back, well fed, complacent, satisfied in a job well done and pleased with himself for having outwitted even the Eternal in giving his blessing to Esau. He was just nodding off to sleep when the tent flap was raised again. Isaac sat bolt upright. There could be no mistaking that boisterous hail. "Let my father arise, and eat of his son's venison, that thy soul may bless me." Esau had come to collect what had never belonged to him at all.

It was a moment of rude awakening for Isaac. The King James Version says, "Isaac trembled very exceedingly." The margin of the Scofield Bible renders it, "He trembled with a great trembling, greatly." He shook like an aspen leaf. His poor old frame was shaken all to pieces, the very chair rocked beneath him. It was not just physical infirmity, it was a rude awakening from years of spiritual torpor. Isaac was a man suddenly alive to spiritual verities, horrified at what he had tried to do, at the enormity of his presumption and indulgence in seeking to discharge a holy duty in a fleshly way. He had acted in the flesh and God had simply overruled him. He was shaken to the depths of his being. Groping after Jacob's name he cried, "Who? Where is he that hath taken venison, and brought it to me, and I have blessed him?" Then, with the full, swelling tide of Holy Ghost conviction, he added, "Yea, and he shall be blessed."

D. THE UNSAVED SON (27:34-46)

Esau had an unsaved man's view of eternal verities. He thought they could be bought and sold, that they were in the market to be knocked down to the highest bidder. In some ways Esau was not altogether to blame. Of recent years his own father had betrayed little of the Spirit of God in his life.

Four things are told us about this unsaved son. First, we have *Esau's impassioned remorse* (27:34-35). "He cried with a great and exceeding bitter cry . . . Bless me, even me also, O my father." The New Testament says that Esau found no way to change his father's mind. Esau was not repentant, not for a moment. He was simply brokenhearted because he had been disappointed in his carnal expectations.

On Saturday, April 18, 1874, Britain arrayed herself in mourning. One of her heroes had died and was being buried in the national shrine. David Livingstone was on his way to interment in Westminster Abbey. His pallbearers included men whose names were to resound in history, not least of whom was the American adventurer H. M. Stanley. The Abbey was crowded. *Punch* took a page to write Livingstone's epitaph:

> Open the Abbey door and bear him in
> To sleep with king and statesman, chief and sage,
> The missionary, come of weaver kin,
> But great by work that brooks no lower wage.

Somewhere, lost in the vast assembly, there stood a tattered, down-at-heel, ill-kempt beggar. Nobody spared him a second thought. But, as the entourage went by, that piece of human flotsam, heaved up by seeming chance upon the shores of humanity that lined the funeral route, was heard to say, "We were lads together, Davie and I. We went to school together. We sat together, dour Davie and me in the school house in Shuttle Row. But Davie chose Christ and I dinna. Now all the world honors him and who cares a halfpence for me." That unknown beggar had sold his birthright for a mess of the world's pottage, and now it was too late to get it back. Esau wrung his hands in vain. His impassioned remorse could no more bring back the blessing than it could reverse the spin of the earth upon its axis or cause it to retrace its path around the sun.

We have, further, *Esau's implacable resentment* (27:36-37). "Is he not rightly named Jacob?" he cried. "He hath supplanted me these two times." His resentment was both right and wrong. It was understandable. Jacob's methods were underhanded and mean, and wholly unnecessary when God had already vowed the blessing to him. We can understand Esau's resentment. But, he had sold his birthright of his own free will. Nobody had forced his hand. Jacob had persuaded but he had not compelled. Esau had treated his birthright with utter disdain. It was rather late in the day for him to be filled with resentment, because payday for his folly had come.

We are told of *Esau's importunate request* (27:38-40). "And Esau said unto his father, Hast thou but one blessing, my father? bless me, even me also, O my father. And Esau lifted up his voice, and wept." Isaac did find a blessing for Esau, one that involved both wealth and war, but nothing of lasting, eternal worth. He would get on in the world, make a name for himself, even break off Jacob's yoke from his neck. That was all that was left. Remorse alone cannot win through to spiritual blessing; it takes repentance for that, and Esau showed no trace of repentance at all.

On the contrary we have *Esau's impulsive resolve* (27:41-46). "And Esau hated Jacob . . . and Esau said . . . The days of mourning for my father are at hand; then will I slay my brother Jacob." Perhaps he could win with murder what he could not buy with meat; if venison could not buy him the blessing, maybe violence would. If he murdered Jacob then he, Esau, would be his father's sole surviving heir. His resolve was overheard and told to Rebekah, who, in turn, went and told her favorite son. "Now therefore, my son, obey my voice," she said. It was the same formula she had used to get him to deceive his dad. Poor Rebekah still had to meddle! Perhaps the aching, empty years ahead would teach her patience in the things of God.

Chapter 7

THE PROPAGATOR: JACOB

(28:1–35:29)

I. How God Saved Jacob (28:1-22)
   A. Jacob's Departure (28:1-9)
      1. Its Immense Importance (28:1-4)
      2. Its Immediate Impact (28:5-9)
   B. Jacob's Dream (28:10-17)
      1. The Far Country (28:10-11)
      2. The Fresh Covenant (28:12-15)
      3. The Firm Conviction (28:16-17)
   C. Jacob's Decision (28:18-22)
      1. He Acted Promptly (28:18*a*)
      2. He Acted Purposefully (28:18*b*-19)
      3. He Acted Practically (28:20-22)

II. How God Subdued Jacob (29:1–30:43)
   A. Jacob's Arrival at Padan-aram (29:1-12)
      1. Coming to the Well (29:1-3)
      2. Confidence at the Well (29:4-8)
      3. Conquests by the Well (29:9-12)
   B. Jacob's Arrangements at Padan-aram (29:13–30:43)
      1. The Matter of His Wives (29:13–30:24)
      2. The Matter of His Wages (30:25-43)

III. How God Stopped Jacob (31:1–32:32)
   A. How Old Goals Were Challenged (31:1-16)
      1. Jacob's Fundamental Concern (31:1-3)
      2. Jacob's Family Conference (31:4-9)
      3. Jacob's Faithful Confession (31:10-13)
      4. Jacob's Final Commitment (31:14-16)
   B. How Old Gods Were Challenged (31:17-35)
      1. What Laban Taught (31:17-21)
      2. What Laban Thought (31:22-30)
      3. What Laban Sought (31:31-35)
   C. How Old Grudges Were Challenged (31:36-55)
      1. Jacob's Righteous Indignation (31:36-42)
      2. Jacob's Religious Invocation (31:43-55)
   D. How Old Guilt Was Challenged (32:1-32)
      1. Jacob's Confirmation from God (32:1-2)
      2. Jacob's Confusion About God (32:3-23)
      3. Jacob's Confrontation With God (32:24-32)

IV. HOW GOD SEPARATED JACOB (33:1–34:31)
   A. Jacob and His Brother (33:1-16)
      1. How Esau Found Jacob (33:1-3)
      2. How Esau Forgave Jacob (33:4-7)
      3. How Esau Favored Jacob (33:8-11)
      4. How Esau Frightened Jacob (33:12-16)
   B. Jacob and His Backsliding (33:17–34:31)
      1. Jacob's Failure as a Pilgrim (33:17-20)
      2. Jacob's Failure as a Parent (34:1-31)

V. HOW GOD SANCTIFIED JACOB (35:1-29)
   A. Jacob as a Believing Man (35:1-15)
      1. Renewing Jacob's Spiritual Vitality (35:1-4)
      2. Renewing Jacob's Spiritual Victory (35:5)
      3. Renewing Jacob's Spiritual Verity (35:6-15)
   B. Jacob as a Bereaved Man (35:16-29)
      1. Jacob Bereaved of His Favorite (35:16-26)
      2. Jacob Bereaved of His Father (35:27-29)

7

THE PROPAGATOR: JACOB

I. How God Saved Jacob
(28:1-22)

We have little trouble identifying with Jacob. He is one of the most human and understandable people in the Bible. The next eight chapters of Genesis will focus on that very great man. We shall see God *saving* Jacob (28), God *subduing* Jacob (29-32), God *separating* Jacob (33-34), and God *sanctifying* Jacob (35). The actual story is spread over twenty or thirty years of Jacob's life, for God never hurries and never skimps His work in a human soul. He is working for eternity.

A. Jacob's Departure (28:1-9)

Having deceived his blind, old father and having defrauded his brother Esau, Jacob's situation at home became untenable. "We'll bury Father, Jacob," Esau said, "and then I'll bury you!"

1. Its Immense Importance (28:1-4)

In the first place, Jacob did not sneak off into the night. He was sent off under circumstances sufficiently impressive to leave a lasting impression on his mind. Old Isaac seems to have been frightened entirely out of his carnality by the events that had just happened. With true patriarchal spirituality he summoned Jacob and gave him instructions regarding the future. He had two words for his son, one social and one spiritual; one dealing with the matter of a wife and one dealing with the matter of worship. Decisions in both areas will affect a man's life for time and for eternity. One cannot be too careful in dealing with either one of them.

First we have Jacob's word of *instruction,* which related to the choosing of a *wife* by Jacob (28:1-2). "And Isaac called Jacob, and blessed him, and charged him, and said unto him, Thou shalt not take a wife of the daughters of Canaan. Arise, go to Padan-aram." On no account was Jacob to marry a pagan. In the home of his maternal grandfather there lingered yet a knowledge of the true God, a heritage, no doubt, of Abraham's testimony in days gone by. Jacob must go there and seek a wife. The unspeakable vileness of Canaanite religion made it imperative that Jacob hold himself aloof from any entanglement with Canaanite women. Esau had already disgraced himself by marrying idolatrous heathen women; Jacob must not do the same.

Bethuel, Rebekah's father, was Abraham's nephew. That he knew something of the Lord is evident from his response when Abraham's servant had come there seeking a bride for Isaac years before. Having listened carefully to the servant's story, Bethuel had said, "The thing proceedeth from the LORD" (24:50). "You have my blessing," Isaac said, looking at his son. "You have my blessing, Jacob, but you are not to marry a pagan."

Next came the word of *inspiration*, which related to Jacob's *worship* and to the patriarchal responsibilities that would one day be his. Isaac, in giving that word, was no longer speaking as a parent, but as a patriarch, and the Spirit of illumination and inspiration was upon him. He set before Jacob *the truth of a productive life* (28:3), *the trust of the patriarchal line* (28:4*a*) and *the title of the promised land* (28:4*b*). What Isaac wanted for his toughminded, difficult, willful boy was what every spiritually-minded father wants for his child. He wanted to see Jacob married to a believer, and he wanted to see him walking in the ways of the Lord. Jacob's departure from home, then, was a matter of immense importance.

2. Its Immediate Impact (28:5-9)

Jacob packed his bags, said his farewells, girded himself for the journey, and left. The immediate impact was seen in an unexpected quarter. Esau took note of one fact. Isaac had sent Jacob away, not because he was afraid of reprisals Esau might institute, for with God's blessing resting on Jacob there was nothing Esau could do to harm him. He had sent him away because of his fear of the women of Canaan. The wheels began to turn in Esau's carnal mind. *So that's why father refused to give me the blessing*, he thought. *He's put out because I did not marry a believer.* He decided to ingratiate himself with Isaac. "Then Esau went unto Ishmael, and took unto the wives which he had Mahalath the daughter of Ishmael Abraham's son, the sister of Nebajoth, to be his wife" (28:9). There! That should fix it! Now he was as good as Jacob. Now, perhaps, he could get back into his father's good graces and get back the blessing given to Jacob. Such is the reasoning of the unsaved man. Esau may have imagined that by keeping up outward appearances he could obtain that which could only be imparted to faith. He added a little religious gloss to the outside of his otherwise carnal and worldly life. All he proved, of course, was the impossibility of the natural man ever understanding spiritual things. What made good sense to Esau was the height of folly with God.

B. Jacob's Dream (28:10-17)

It would seem that at that stage in his life Jacob was, as yet, an unsaved man. He had been brought up in a believer's home. His father and his grandfather were both men who knew the living God. Jacob himself knew the value of spiritual things and, in his heart, craved after the spiritual realities known to Isaac and Abraham. But so far he had had no personal encounter with God. There were three stages in his conversion.

1. THE FAR COUNTRY (28:10-11)

"And Jacob went out from Beersheba, and went toward Haran. And he lighted upon a certain place, and tarried there all night, because the sun was set; and he took of the stones of that place, and put them for his pillows, and lay down in that place to sleep." He had been on his way for a day or two and was tired, anxious, frustrated, and afraid. The threats of his twin brother were still ringing in his ears. There was no thought about God in Jacob's mind beyond the fact that he was going where Isaac had told him to go, no hint of repentance or remorse for what he had done. He found a suitable spot for the night, hunted up a suitable smooth stone for a pillow, looked up at the stars, yawned in the face of God, and fell off to sleep. He was the Old Testament prodigal paying the first installment on the "account rendered" for his past behavior.

2. THE FRESH COVENANT (28:12-15)

God is a God of infinite grace, and not so easily does He allow His prodigals to wander away. Jacob may pitch his tent and ignore God, but God would slip quietly and unseen into Jacob's camp and invade Jacob's dreams. We note, first, what God *proved to Jacob* that night (28:12). "And he dreamed, and behold a ladder set up on the earth, and the top of it reached to heaven."

A young fellow once said to his girl friend: "I dreamed about you last night." Naturally she was intrigued and wanted to know all about it. He said, "I dreamed I proposed to you. I wonder what that means!" She said, "That's very simple. That means you have more sense when you're asleep than you have when you're awake!"

That night Jacob had more sense when he was asleep than he had ever had before when he was awake. That night he learned that the God of Abraham his grandfather and the God of Isaac his father could become the God of even Jacob.

He learned, moreover, that there was such a place as heaven, and that heaven is not only an actual place; it is an accessible place. Centuries later, in talking to Nathanael, the Lord Jesus identified *Himself* as the ladder that Jacob saw. He is the link between earth and heaven, for as God and man He bridges the immeasurable distance between Deity and humanity, heaven and earth. We can approach God and reach heaven only through Him. That night Jacob learned a truth centered in Christ. It was a saving truth.

We note further what God *promised to Jacob* (28:13-15). In his vision, Jacob heard the voice of God speaking to him about the *Lord* and about the *land* and about his *life*. It was a reconfirmation of the original promise made to Abraham, reaffirmed to Isaac, and now coming to rest on Jacob, the unconditional promise of God. Jacob was to awake from that dream in the sure knowledge that his was the chosen line which would lead directly to Christ.

3. THE FIRM CONVICTION (28:16-17)

"And Jacob awaked out of his sleep, and he said, Surely the LORD is in this place; and I knew it not. And he was afraid, and said, How dreadful is this place! this is none other but the house of God, and this is the gate of heaven." Compelled to leave his father's house, Jacob found that God, in infinite grace, was offering him *His*. He was saved from that moment on.

C. JACOB'S DECISION (28:18-22)

The closing verses of the chapter chronicle Jacob's first steps as a changed man. Some of his acts, of course, betray his spiritual immaturity, but nevertheless they mark the new dimension of spiritual life that had arisen in his soul and they give evidence of genuine conversion.

First of all Jacob acted *promptly*. He "rose up early in the morning" (28:18*a*). A new life pulsated in his soul. He skipped out of his bed with the morning light with the joybells ringing in his soul. Heaven above was deeper blue and the earth around was sweeter green! It was not just that it was a new morning; he was a new man.

Then we read that Jacob acted *purposefully* (28:18*b*-19). He took the stone he had used for a pillow and set it up as a pillar. He poured oil upon it to sanctify it and called the place "Bethel." The Spirit of God notes that "the name of that place was called Luz at the first." The name Luz means "separation"; Bethel means "the house of God." The man who had been "afar off," separated from God by sin and wicked works, was now "brought nigh." Jacob, in setting up that memorial to his conversion was, in a sense, giving public testimony to what had happened to him. That is always a good sign.

Finally, he acted *practically* (28:20-22) acknowledging the Lord's presence, the Lord's provision, and the Lord's protection. He vowed a vow, we are told. It is the first time a vow is mentioned in the Bible; trust Jacob to make it! "And Jacob vowed a vow, saying, If God will be with me [or, better, '*since* God will be with me'; he is not using the language of uncertainty but of assurance] and will keep me in this way that I go, and will give me bread to eat, and raiment to put on, so that I come again to my father's house in peace; then shall the LORD be my God." That was Jacob's verbal confession of his inner heart conversion.

But he has not finished yet. "If God will be with me . . . then shall the LORD be my God; and this stone, which I have set for a pillar, shall be God's house: and of all that thou shalt give me" he adds, addressing God directly, "I will surely give the tenth unto thee." That was practical evidence of Jacob's conversion. Up to now the ruling passion in his heart had been greed. He always had to get. Now he wanted to give. He stood there like an Old Testament Zaccheus. Zaccheus, we recall, having taken the Lord Jesus into his heart and home, at once began to express his gratitude in terms of giving (Luke 19:1-10). "This day is salvation come to this house," was the Lord's comment. Zaccheus was not saved because he gave; he gave because he was saved. The same was true of Jacob.

Thus, Jacob, in the first flush of his conversion, promised the Lord that he would never forget two things. He would never forget God's place, and he would never forget God's portion. It was an excellent start.

II. How God Subdued Jacob (29:1–30:43)

Jacob had been saved. It is one thing, however, for a person to be saved; it is another thing for him to be subdued. The subduing process would take up the next twenty years of Jacob's life. How slow we are to learn even the basic elementary truths of the life of faith. The story of God's subduing Jacob tells of his arrival, of his arrangements, and of his arrest in Padan-aram. We are going to look first at the events that have to do with the founding of Jacob's family. At Padan-aram, Jacob took two matters into his own hands—the matter of marriage and the matter of money. Here we are going to look at the first of those.

A. Jacob's Arrival at Padan-aram (29:1-12)

The life-transforming encounter with the God of Bethel was over, and the memorial stone stood there as a tribute to Jacob's saving faith. Now Jacob had to work out his salvation with fear and trembling in a hostile world.

1. Coming to the Well (29:1-3)

"Then Jacob went on his journey" or, as it can be rendered, "Then Jacob lifted up his feet." What a graphic description of a newborn pilgrim! How his feet must have dragged after he had put those first few frantic miles between himself and Esau. What heavy thoughts burdened him, shut out from home as he was, with a blank and uncertain future ahead, a vengeful brother behind. But now he lifted up his feet. He had a new spring in his step, a new song in his heart. He marched along head held high, whistling to himself, the miles melting away beneath his joyous stride.

North and east he went, following the Fertile Crescent on its great 450-mile arc into Mesopotamia. Then, at last, he reached the fabled land about which he had heard so much from grandfather Abraham, the land from which the old pilgrim had come some 150 years before. Before him was the familiar sight of a wayside well with several flocks of sheep lying around and a group of shepherds lolling in the shade. Those were not the mild and picturesque shepherds we see on Christmas cards. They would be fierce-looking men with daggers in their belts and swarthy, bearded faces, men accustomed to roughing it in the wilds in all kinds of weather, men able to face wolves, lions, or thieves. They would have eyed the approaching stranger with a mixture of curiosity and hostility. Jacob came to the well.

2. CONFIDENCE AT THE WELL (29:4-8)

He hailed them. He was not bashful with strangers. He was a shepherd himself and as tough as any of them. Jacob was never marked by embarrassment or by a sense of inferiority. "My brethren, whence be ye?" he said. "Of Haran," was the short, uncommunicative reply as they gave him what we would call "the brush-off." They were not interested in him.

At Bethel, Jacob had learned what God is like; at Haran he was to learn what man is like. Up until now Jacob had always been the big man, the son of a wealthy and influential chief, the man with many servants at his beck and call. It was different now. Now he was the outsider, the alien, the unwanted stranger seeking to make a way for himself among men who had no use for him at all.

But Jacob was not thin-skinned. "Know ye Laban?" he asked. "We know him!" was the laconic reply. What a wealth of hidden meaning lay hidden behind that bare response. Everybody for miles around knew Laban, and before long Jacob would know him too—know him to his cost. Had Charles Dickens been asked to describe Uncle Laban, he would doubtless have used the same language he used to describe Ebenezer Scrooge. For Uncle Laban was "a squeezing, wrenching, grasping, scarping, clutching, covetous old sinner! Hard and sharp as flint, secret and self-contained as an oyster. The cold within him froze his old features, nipped his pointed nose, shrivelled his cheek, stiffened his gait." That was Scrooge and that was Laban; they were cut from the same piece of cloth. "Know ye Laban?" "We know him!"

Undaunted, Jacob tried again. "Is he well?" His persistent friendliness brought a slight thaw. "He is well, and, behold, Rachel his daughter cometh with the sheep." Probably Rachel was heavily veiled and Jacob scarcely gave her a second glance. Turning back to the shepherds he demanded why they did not water their flocks. "Lo, it is yet high day!" he said, or as it could be rendered, "The day is great yet," or "Much of the day still remains." He could not understand why men would lie around when there was work to be done. It was that burning, driving energy of his that marked him out as a man bound to succeed.

In response the shepherds almost waxed eloquent. They told Jacob they could not water the flocks until all the shepherds arrived. They gave no reason. Perhaps the arrangement protected the well from dust—better to open it once when all were gathered than keep on opening it all day. Perhaps the agreement was intended to ensure fair distribution of the precious water supply. The reason is not given, but the whole scene impresses us with Jacob's confidence.

3. Conquests by the Well (29:9-12)

Rachel had arrived and, with a courtesy unknown in those rough times among such backwoods people, Jacob moved the stone despite the glares of the others and watered his cousin's flocks. Normally, the shepherds probably shoved in first and left the women to fend for themselves when they were through. They must have stared at Jacob, but if they were tempted to intervene and put the presumptuous stranger in his place, there was something about the jut of his jaw and the solid muscles of his arm that gave them pause. They let him alone. He had conquered them.

Then he conquered Rachel. Unused to such attention and service she stood by in astonishment. Her wonder grew when he introduced himself as her cousin in the normal, emotional way in those times. "I am Rebekah's son," he said simply as he embraced her. With her soul on fire, Rachel left the well and ran home to tell her father that a stranger had come, that he was at the well, that it was his nephew! It was the romantic story of Rebekah at the well in reverse. Thus Jacob arrived at Padan-aram.

B. Jacob's Arrangements at Padan-Aram (29:13–30:43)

Throughout chapters 29 and 30 we see Jacob making his own arrangements. He had no thought of asking God His will regarding marital and monetary matters. Filled with self-confidence, he felt quite capable of handling his own affairs.

1. The Matter of His Wives (29:13–30:24)

a. His Fervent Love (29:13-20)

Whatever else may have been base alloy in Jacob's soul, the love he had for Rachel was purest gold. That love was kindled the moment he first saw her face and it never left him until his dying day.

Hearing of Jacob's arrival from Rachel, Laban hurried out to meet his nephew. He did not know, of course, that Jacob was a semifugitive. His mind was probably filled with visions of the earrings and jewels with which his sister Rebekah had been loaded when she had come home with similar news from the well years before. Laban knew that

Jacob was from a very wealthy family—so he gave him a royal welcome, rolling out the proverbial red carpet in true oriental style. Never had Jacob been so kissed and embraced and fussed over before. "Bone of my bone! Flesh of my flesh!" cried Laban. One would think he was marrying Jacob himself.

Jacob accepted his uncle's offer of hospitality and, crafty as ever, made himself at home saying not a word about his inglorious departure from Hebron. He would talk, no doubt, about his mother's continuing beauty and his father's success in business. But not a word about Esau, we can be sure. And all the time Uncle Laban was trying to size up this brash young nephew of his. They were a pair well met.

Now Jacob was too clever to hang around Laban's home idly for long. Idleness was not one of his faults. He began to make himself useful to his uncle, invaluable indeed, so much so that Laban offered him a full-time job. "Because thou art my brother, shouldest thou therefore serve me for nought? tell me, what shall thy wages be?" (29:15). Within a month Laban began to wonder how he had ever managed his farms before Jacob came. Never had he seen such industry, such business acumen, such cleverness in closing a deal, such an uncanny skill with cattle and sheep. The lad was worth a fortune to anyone shrewd enough to get his name on the dotted line.

But if Uncle Laban had been doing some figuring, so had Jacob. A month in Laban's home and he had fallen deeply in love with Rachel. Leah, no doubt, was well enough, but she had something wrong with her eyes. Perhaps she was shortsighted or had a squint. The text says she was "tender-eyed." Whatever it was, Jacob had nothing against Leah, but he had eyes for Rachel alone. Leah simply did not exist so far as he was concerned; Rachel filled his vision. Thus, when Laban opened the question of wages, Jacob was ready. "Rachel!" he said, "I want Rachel. I'll serve you seven years for Rachel." The bargain was struck and "Jacob served seven years for Rachel: and they seemed unto him but a few days, for the love he had to her" (29:20).

b. HIS FIRST LESSON (29:21-31)

The story unfolds in three parts. First came *the demand* (29:21-22). "And Jacob said unto Laban, Give me my wife, for my days are fulfilled." True to his word, Laban gave orders for the wedding. Jacob had agreed to marry Rachel according to the customs of the land. "Jacob, my son," Laban might have said, "you understand, of course, you will not be able to see your bride during the ceremony. She will be heavily veiled. The wedding will take place at night, Jacob, and right after the ceremony the bride will retire to your quarters, still heavily veiled. You will linger awhile to accept the congratulations of the guests—" And thus, along those lines, it was arranged.

Next comes *the discovery* (29:23-29). The marriage took place.

Jacob retired to his darkened quarters and consummated his marriage, only to wake up the next morning to discover he was married to the wrong woman. What a scene there must have been both in his own quarters and in Laban's living room when Jacob realized the trick that had been pulled on him. It was Jacob's first lesson. To all his infuriated accusations, however, Laban blandly replied, "My dear fellow, we have a rule in this country. *We respect the rights of the firstborn*" (29:26). It must have been like a blow in the face to Jacob.

There is a "poetic justice" in the dealings of God with men. God sees to it that in what measure we meet it is measured to us again (Matthew 7:2). Observe that law in action here. Laban callously palmed off Leah on Jacob, Jacob all the while thinking the bride he was receiving was Rachel. What cared Laban that his methods were underhanded, despicable, and mean? What cared he that he was trampling on the tenderest and most sacred feelings of Jacob's heart? He did not care. But go back seven years in Jacob's life. See him standing there before his old, blind father pretending to be Esau. Jacob had callously palmed himself off on Isaac, Isaac all the while thinking that the blessing he was bestowing was going to Esau. What had Jacob cared that his methods were underhanded, despicable, and mean? What had he cared that he was trampling on the tenderest and most sacred feelings of Isaac's heart? He had not cared. Now he had to reap just what he had sowed. The mills of God grind slowly, but they grind exceedingly fine.

Shocked and stunned, Jacob was forced to face cold facts. Like it or not, he was married to Leah according to the custom of the country and he had consummated that marriage. "Fulfill her week," Laban urged, pouring oil on the troubled waters, "then I'll let you marry Rachel too—for another seven years of service."

Next comes *the difficulty* (29:30-31). Jacob finished out his week with Leah in the letter if not in the spirit of the agreement and married Rachel. Then his domestic difficulties began. Was Leah an unwilling pawn in that dismal game or was she in love with Jacob herself and a willing accomplice? We do not know, but once married to Rachel, Jacob wasted no more time on Leah. He simply ignored the woman; his whole sun rose and set on Rachel. In her he lived and moved and had his being. Leah was pushed back on the shelf and treated as though she did not exist.

Jacob, however, reckoned without God. God loved Leah as much as He loved Rachel, no matter what Jacob might feel, and He took action, making it impossible for Rachel to bear children and evidently possible for Leah. In a culture where sons—big, strapping, healthy sons—to support their father and boost his business and bring fat dowries, were essential to a man's communal standing, it did not take long for the lesson to sink in. If Jacob wanted sons, he would have to consider Leah, for he was not going to get them from Rachel. And Jacob wanted sons.

c. HIS FAMILY LIFE (29:32–30:24).

This lengthy section records the birth of Jacob's children down to the birth of Joseph. It is a sad record, for Jacob's home became a battlefield where two embittered women fought and struggled for Jacob's affection. Jacob, torn between his devotion to Rachel and his desire for sons, was pulled this way and that.

His firstborn was *Reuben, the child of sore distress* (29:32). That came out in Leah's sad comment at the time. "Surely," she said, "the LORD hath looked upon my affliction; now therefore my husband will love me." Note how Leah acknowledged the LORD (Jehovah). Some knowledge of Him had lingered in Laban's family since Abraham's days. Jacob, during his seven long years in Laban's home, must often have spoken about Him, too. Leah, in her bitterness and loneliness, acknowledged Jehovah in the birth of her boy. She was the first one of Jacob's family to confess her faith in Him.

Next came *Simeon, the child of simple disappointment* (29:33). Leah was evidently disappointed in her hope that Reuben would win her the affection of her husband. It did nothing of the kind. Perhaps, on the strength of her new status as a mother, she had tried to assert herself. She seems to have been put in her place, either by Jacob or Rachel. When Reuben was born, Leah had said, "God hath seen." Now she said, "God hath heard." He had heard the wordy encounters in that unhappy home where the tongues of Jacob and Rachel were sharpened on Leah, and He had heard Leah's anguished cries to Him. She called her second son *Simeon* ("hearing").

Leah's third son was *Levi, the child of spiritual discouragement* (29:34). Leah said: "Now this time will my husband be joined unto me, because I have born him three sons." *Levi* means "associated" or "joined." Spiritual discouragement was evident in Leah's life. With her first two sons she acknowledged God, but not this time. She gave God no credit at all. Yet, next to Judah, there was no more illustrious son born to Jacob than Levi. Not even Leah's spiritual discouragement could prevent God from manifesting His grace.

Then came *Judah, the child of splendid destiny* (29:35). By now Leah had recovered her spiritual optimism. "Now will I praise the LORD!" she cried. God honored her for that, for Israel's kings sprang from Judah and, in the fullness of time, the Son of God Himself came into the world through Judah's line. Leah was no longer fretting because her sister had so effectively monopolized Jacob's heart. Leah had found an outlet for her love in the Lord. She no longer needed people to make her happy, her joy and praise was in God. Having reached that high note in her spiritual life Leah ceased having sons. What need had she of further assurance? The Lord was better to her than a hundred sons.

Dan was next, *the child of sustained despair* (30:1-6). With Dan the spotlight comes back to Rachel. She had been eating out her heart with jealousy. She wanted what Leah had, and Leah wanted what she had. With total unreasonableness she at last vented her temper on Jacob: "Give me children or else I die!" she said. Jacob must have looked at her in astonishment. "Do you think I am God?" he retorted.

Then came one of those unlovely little tricks that could only lead to further unhappiness. Rachel began to scheme. If Jacob could not play God, then she would. "Behold my maid Bilhah," she said to Jacob, hinting at her willingness to take advantage of a legal technicality. If Bilhah, her slave girl, were to have a child by Jacob, then, legally, the child could be regarded as hers. Thus Dan was born, and Rachel, with false assurance, declared, "God hath judged me and hath also heard my voice and hath given me a son." She called him *Dan,* meaning "judge" or "vindicator." It was all rather sad.

Rachel, however, was so pleased with the success of her scheme that she employed it again. Thus was born *Naphtali, the child of supposed deliverance* (29:7-8). "With great wrestlings have I wrestled with my sister," Rachel declared, "and I have prevailed." When Dan was born, Rachel had acknowledged God. She had acknowledged Him as Elohim, her spiritual stature being inferior to that of Leah, but when Naphtali was born, Rachel did not acknowledge God at all. She simply triumphed over Leah in the flesh. The deliverance Rachel imagined she had experienced was a delusion, however, for spiritual victories cannot be won in the flesh.

All that time Leah had been watching her sister's pathetic performance. Then she decided two could play the same game, for she herself had given birth to no more children. Sinking to the carnal level on which her sister chose to fight, she married off her maid Zilpah to Jacob. The resulting son was *Gad, the child of sad defeat* (30:9-11). "A troop cometh!" exulted Leah. It seems to be a spiteful jibe at her sister. Leah gave no acknowledgment to God in the birth of Gad, for how can God be acknowledged when the flesh is in control? It is sad to see Leah taking that lower ground. Had God changed? No. Had any of her sons died? No. She came down from the spiritual plateau of praise simply to get even with her sister.

Then came *Asher, the child of sudden delight* (30:12-13). When the maid Zilpah bore a second son, evening the score with Rachel, Leah cried, "Happy am I, for the daughters will call me blessed." The name *Asher* means "happy." The daughters to whom Leah referred would be of course, her women friends. She was happy, or so she said. Had she not evened the score with her rival? But there was no acknowledgment of God in that birth, and Leah was deceiving herself. It is a long way down the spiritual ladder from praise to mere happiness. As someone has said, "Happiness depends on what happens!" Instead of finding her joy in God, Leah was finding a fleeting happiness in winning a carnal victory.

The circumstances surrounding the birth of *Issachar, the child of snappish dislike*, were not happy (30:14-18). The family quarrel between the two sisters reached an all-time low in the circumstances that led to Issachar's birth. Evidently the birth of Asher had not brought the happiness for which Leah craved. Rachel still held complete sway over Jacob's heart.

Reuben was about four years old at the time he arrived home with the mandrakes. It was harvest time and the fields were full of reapers; fun and festivity were in the air. Little Reuben had been out in the field and had picked a bunch of flowers for his mother—much to the amusement, no doubt, of the men in the fields. He arrived home with some "love-apples"—the word "mandrake" comes from a root word meaning just that. The plant grows abundantly in Israel. It has dark leaves and a carrotlike root, white and reddish blossoms with a sweet smell, and a fruit like an apple. The root can easily be pinched into the rough figure of a man. People thought the plant could excite passion and promote fruitfulness in a barren woman. Rachel was tired of waiting for God to make her fruitful. Maybe some love-apples would help. When she saw the mandrakes she struck a bargain with her sister. "You can have Jacob for a night or two," she said, "in exchange for Reuben's mandrakes."

The charm worked backward. Far from making Rachel fruitful, it was Leah who once more began to have sons. "God hath given me my hire!" cried Leah. She acknowledged God in the birth of Issachar, evidently wanting it to be known that the mandrakes had no part in her new fruitfulness. Even so she could not refrain from giving expression to her dislike of her sister by incorporating the meaning of "hire" into the baby's name. Leah had evidently lost spiritual ground. She called God "Elohim" and never again, in the context here, rose to the height of praise or to calling God by His covenant name.

Then along came *Zebulun, the child of strong desire* (30:19-20). "And Leah conceived again and bare Jacob the sixth son. And Leah said, God hath endued me with a good dowry; now will my husband dwell with me, because I have born him six sons." The name Zebulun means "dwelling" or "habitation." But despite that loud trumpeting of victory, Leah never did persuade Jacob to come and live permanently with her. Yet God honored the longings of her hungry heart, for when His Son came into the world, He came to dwell in Nazareth in Zebulun.

Then came a change. Leah had a daughter, *Dinah, the child of silent dignity* (30:21). Perhaps Jacob had other daughters (37:35; 46:7), but Dinah alone is named. Her name means the same as that of Dan—"judge" or "vindicator." Possibly the name was meant to be another slap at poor, childless Rachel. But Leah said nothing at all about the actual birth of the girl. She took it in her stride with silent dignity. It was the last child she was to bear, the seventh. There was no more to be said.

Finally, at long last, came *Joseph, the child of sweet devotion* (30:22-24). "And God remembered Rachel . . . and she conceived, and bare a son; and said, God hath taken away my reproach: And she called his name Joseph; and said, The LORD shall add to me another son." Thus, at last, Rachel triumphed both naturally and spiritually. She acknowledged God not once, but twice, once by His name Elohim and once as Jehovah. She attained the spiritual plateau from which Leah had descended after the birth of Judah, and after her carnal squabbling in the matter of the maids and the mandrakes. But Rachel now climbed even higher, for in the birth of Joseph her faith reached out for more. "The LORD shall add to me another son," she said. And so He did.

2. THE MATTER OF HIS WAGES (30:25-43)

We have seen Jacob's arrangements in the matter of his wives; now we must see his arrangements in the matter of his wages. It is the same old story of planning and scheming in the flesh.

a. HOW JACOB'S CONVICTIONS WERE STIRRED (30:25-26)

"And it came to pass, when Rachel had born Joseph, that Jacob said unto Laban, Send me away, that I may go unto mine own place." When Joseph was born something happened to Jacob. He realized that Mesopotamia was not his home. His home was far away in the land of promise. At once he made the great decision, he would get back into the land, the place where God had put His name. His convictions were stirred.

b. HOW JACOB'S CONVICTIONS WERE STIFLED (30:27-43)

To stifle Jacob's convictions, all Laban had to do was offer Jacob a raise in pay. Many a person has been sidetracked from the Lord's service in the same way. The devil, however, is a poor paymaster as Jacob soon discovered. Laban changed Jacob's wages ten times, each time in his own favor, we can be sure. The principle of the poetic justice of God was still operating in Jacob's life.

What cared Laban that Jacob was his own kin, his nephew? What did he care he was taking advantage of a weaker man temporarily in his power? He did not care. To Laban, Jacob was a mere tool to be used and tossed aside once he had been made to minister to his own personal ambitions. But wait! Go back some fourteen years in Jacob's life. Recall how Jacob treated Esau the day Esau came in weak from the hunt and wanted some of Jacob's stew. What had Jacob cared that Esau was his own kin, his very twin? What had he cared that he was taking advantage of a weaker man temporarily in his power? He had not cared. To Jacob Esau had been a mere tool to be used and tossed aside once he had been made to minister to his own personal ambitions. Truly, "whatsoever a man soweth that shall he also reap."

Jacob was making his arrangements in the matter of his wages and being cheated again and again. But he would get his own back before he was through.

Note what is said about *Jacob's witness* (30:27-30). "And Laban said unto him, I pray thee, if I have found favour in thine eyes, tarry: for I have learned by experience that the LORD hath blessed me for thy sake." What a good testimony that was! Weak and stumbling though he was, Jacob's faith combined with his business sense had made its impact. Laban knew only too well it was not just Jacob's skill as a business man that made him such a valuable employee, it was his relationship with the Lord.

Note what is said about *Jacob's wages* (30:31-36). Jacob agreed to continue to oversee Laban's affairs, but he must be allowed to lay the foundations for his own financial future. He would go through Laban's flocks and cull out the brown sheep and the speckled and spotted goats. He would put those off by themselves. Those would be Laban's. That would leave all the solid-colored sheep and goats in a separate flock, the white sheep and the black goats. Those would be Laban's too. The entire existing flock would be Laban's.

Now then, he, Jacob, would not breed from the *existing* brown sheep and speckled and spotted goats. Laban could do what he liked with them. He could remove them to other fields, entrust them to other hands. But, all *future* brown sheep born of the white sheep and all the spotted and speckled goats born of the black goats should be Jacob's, along with any multiplication of their similarly-marked offspring. In other words, Jacob was willing to start with nothing. That would give God a chance to bless him in the proposed arrangement and would remove any suspicion of cheating from Laban's mind. But it must be agreed that any future brown sheep and spotted and speckled goats arising from the solid-colored flocks and herds must be Jacob's. That was the deal.

Laban must have looked at Jacob as though he were crazy. Everybody knew that eastern sheep were mostly solid white and rarely brown, and that eastern goats were predominantly black and rarely spotted and speckled. Yet Jacob was willing to found his future fortune on odds as long as those? It was too good a bargain for Laban to resist. He closed the deal on the spot and, before Jacob could change his mind, sent his hands to cull out and remove all the marked sheep and goats.

As he put three days' journey between Jacob and the culled-out brown sheep and spotted and speckled goats, the old Syrian farmer must have shaken his head in perplexity. He still had Jacob's testimony ringing in his ears: "So shall my righteousness answer for me in time to come . . .

every one that is not speckled and spotted among the goats, and brown among the sheep, that shall be counted stolen with me." There had to be a catch to it somewhere, but Laban, up on all the tricks of the trade and an old hand in skullduggery, could not detect it for the life of him.

But Jacob knew what he was doing. He had no intention of trying to use the brown sheep and spotted and speckled goats he had so painstakingly removed from the flocks and herds and handed over to Laban. He was going to trust God, work hard and try a trick or two of his own. Not for nothing had he served his fourteen-year apprenticeship with Laban. Not for nothing had he been born and raised in a family that had marvelous skill in raising flocks and herds.

Jacob seems to have stumbled across Mendel's Law. An experienced and observant cattle-breeder, Jacob had no doubt already experimented with selective breeding. He could not state his discoveries in scientific terms, but he had learned that animals have both dominant and recessive traits. The dominant trait in Laban's flocks produced mostly white sheep but, even starting with a pure white flock, Jacob knew he could produce brown sheep. The same held true for the goats. Starting with black goats, he knew eventually he would get spotted and speckled goats. The hidden recessive traits would produce in time a nucleus both of sheep and goats from which he could build his own flocks.

Jacob trusted too that God would be gracious and give him a better percentage than he might ordinarily expect. And, being Jacob, he would add a little bit of guile as well.

Note what is said about *Jacob's wiles* (30:37-43). Off he went into the hills with two magnificent flocks, one a flock of pure white sheep and the other a flock of jet black goats. There was not a single less-attractive, off-color animal among them. Laban had taken care of that. It was now in Jacob's interest, as well as Laban's, to make sure that the flocks multiplied rapidly. The more offspring that could be produced, the higher his chances of getting a start with his nucleus of colored sheep and spotted goats.

The first thing he did seems strange. He cut some good, stout sticks from nearby hazel, poplar, and chestnut trees (some think they were storax, almond, and plane trees). Those sticks he peeled so that naked wood appeared in strips and bands. He put these spotted, speckled, and peeled sticks in the watering troughs. Why? Did Jacob believe in prenatal influence? Possibly he did. We tend to scoff at such an idea today, but people have scoffed at things in the past that later ages have discovered to be true after all.[1]

1. Even today we do not know all the factors involved in the DNA molecular structure of a living creature, nor have we yet mastered all the influences that go together to form individual characteristics. Perhaps Jacob knew something we still do not know. We think he was foolish. Just because a pregnant woman sees an ape and is frightened at the zoo while carrying her child does not mean the child will be ugly. Jacob was nobody's fool when it came to cattle raising.

It was not long before the flocks and herds began to multiply and the kind of sheep and goats Jacob wanted began to show up in unusually large numbers. Now Jacob went after two things—quality and quantity. To ensure *quality* he used his aphrodisiac rods only when the stronger cattle were mating. Then he consistently separated the stronger animals from the weaker ones so that presently he began to develop a fine strain of virile, healthy sheep and goats. That was simply employing a sound principle of selective breeding. To ensure *quantity*, every time a brown lamb was born or a speckled or spotted kid, he separated it from the rest of the flock. Those, of course, were his. He allowed those sheep and goats to breed among themselves, thus increasing his chances of getting more of the same kind. Soon his portion of the flock began to increase greatly—not because of any tricks he had used, but, as he later told Laban, because God chose to bless him (32:10).

So we read of Jacob that he "increased exceedingly, and had much cattle and maidservants, and menservants, and camels, and asses" (30: 43). As his flocks and herds multiplied, Jacob branched out into other related lines of business. His native shrewdness helped, so did hard work and sound investment, so did simply being the best man in his field. But more than anything else, God prospered Jacob; and because God chose to bless him, he soon became a very wealthy man indeed and a power to be reckoned with in the land.

III. HOW GOD STOPPED JACOB (31:1–32:32)

At Padan-aram Jacob founded both his family and his fortunes, becoming rich in children and in material things. But his true home was not on the Euphrates but in Canaan, the promised land. All the blessings of God for his soul were in Canaan, not in Mesopotamia. God could not allow him to settle forever in the very land from which, years before, he had called Abraham. So, in His wisdom, God allowed things to turn sour on Jacob. He was about to arrest him and send him back to Canaan.

He evidently thought the peeled rods were effective, however much we may smile at his "simplicity" today.

Many a scholarly page has been written about Jacob's peeled rods. We know today, for instance, that certain chemicals can and do have a significant prenatal influence if they reach the embryo or the DNA in the germ cell at the right time. Perhaps the chemicals in the trees Jacob chose for his rods had some such effect. For Jacob, we recall, actually put the peeled rods into the troughs that contained the drinking water for the animals. One such chemical substance is known to have aphrodisiac qualities and has not only been used from ancient times to promote fertility but is still used. Some authorities claim it as a fact that white-streaked rods do act as a stimulus to cattle. Jacob evidently believed the rods would be effective in producing increased numbers of offspring.

A. How Old Goals Were Challenged (31:1-16)

Jacob was challenged again and again concerning things that had crept into his life, things needing to be dealt with and put away or put right. In chapter 31 we are going to examine the first of four great challenges Jacob now had to face, the challenge of *old goals* (31:1-16). So far Jacob had been motivated by two goals—to marry Rachel and to get rich. He had achieved both, but neither was adequate, for neither marriage nor money can fulfill the deepest needs of a person's life. The Lord therefore placed a very ugly fly in Jacob's ointment.

1. Jacob's Fundamental Concern (31:1-3)

It happened all of a sudden. *The world became suddenly menacing* (31:1-2). "And he [Jacob] heard the words of Laban's sons, saying, Jacob hath taken away all that was our father's; and of that which was our father's hath he gotten all this glory. And Jacob beheld the countenance of Laban, and, behold, it was not toward him as before." Laban's face had become a mask of scowls instead of being wreathed in smiles as before when Jacob had worked solely for him. Jacob had kept strictly to the agreement he had with Laban and had prospered legitimately, but jealousy is never reasonable. Jacob could see that lawsuits were impending against him—not orderly lawsuits in the established courts of the land, but rough and ready lawsuits of the frontier, backed by force and fueled with hate. The world had become suddenly menacing.

At the same time *the word became suddenly meaningful* (31:3). "And the Lord said unto Jacob, Return unto the land of thy fathers, and to thy kindred; and I will be with thee." It had been a long time since Jacob had heard the clear voice of God, but now, in his altered circumstances, he did and it blew away all the cobwebs. Everything came into focus; he had been arrested by God! He must get back to the promised land. What a blessing it is when the world, which looks so attractive to us, finally turns sour on us. It is then that we are willing to listen to what God has to say to our souls.

2. Jacob's Family Conference (31:4-9)

How to get away from Laban—that was the problem. Should he simply tell Laban he was leaving? Then Laban would summon his confederates and either stop him or else strip him and send him back beggared of everything, family and fortune alike. No, Jacob decided that if he must leave Padan-aram, it must be secretly. So he called a family conference, not in his home where the discussion might be overheard, but out in the fields. He did not summon his sons, they were too young to count much as yet. Nor did he summon the slave-wives; the less who knew what was going on the better. He summoned Rachel and Leah.

He shared with his wives two things about their father that troubled him. He talked of *Laban's proved dislike* (31:4-5). "I see," he said. "I see your father's countenance, that it is not toward me as before; but the God of my father hath been with me." Since Laban and his sons had made no attempt to conceal their mistrust and dislike of Jacob, he had no need to labor the point. Laban's daughters knew their father only too well.

Then he spoke of *Laban's persistent dishonesty* (31:6-9). "And ye know that with all my power I have served your father. And your father hath deceived me, and changed my wages ten times; but God suffered him not to hurt me." Poor old Jacob! "Your father hath deceived me!" he cried. He still had not seen himself in the mirror that was Laban. How vocal we are when somebody wrongs us. How blind we are to the wrongs and ills we have done to other people. "Your father deceived me!" What about all the dirty tricks he had pulled himself in his earlier years? He had forgotten them.

Robert Burns, Scotland's beloved bard, once sat behind an elegant society lady in church, a woman very conscious of her manicured appearance, her expensive clothes, her position in the community. Burns, sitting behind her, saw an insect crawling up her back, heading toward her collar. He took his pen and jotted down a little jingle—

> Oh that God the grace would gi'e us
> To see ourselves as others see us!

Jacob had not yet seen himself, but that was coming. All he could think of now was Laban's persistent dishonesty. "Ten times!" he exclaimed. "He changed my wages ten times."

3. JACOB'S FAITHFUL CONFESSION (31:10-13)

Jacob now gave his wives his testimony. It was significant, for it revealed how much backtracking Jacob had been doing in his soul during the new crisis in his life. He had come right back to God.

His first confession had to do with his *prosperity*. His prosperity, he confessed, resulted not from his own cleverness but from God's grace (31:10-12). God had shown him in a dream how to mate the cattle. Sure, he had observed genetic laws! Sure, he had used all the tricks he knew to stimulate reproduction! But his successes were far, far beyond anything that could be attributed solely to human skill. God had shown him what to do. Jacob may have known something about recessive traits in animals, but he knew nothing about genes, nor could he know which animals had the kinds of genes best suited to his goals. But God knew. And God had aided him by showing him in dreams which animals to mate with which. There it was. Jacob's confession. His prosperity resulted not from his own cleverness but from God's grace.

His second confession had to do with his *prospects,* which resided not in his own conniving but in God's guidance (31:13). "Wives," he said, "let me tell you what God has been saying to me. He has been saying, I am the God of Bethel . . . arise, get thee from this land, and return unto the land of thy kindred." He confessed there was no future for him in Padan-aram; his future lay in the place where God had placed His Name. It is a great lesson for the believer to learn. True prosperity is spiritual, not material, it does not reside here, but where God is. We have to look higher than this world for true prosperity. Thus Jacob, suddenly faced with the loss of everything, came home to the heart of God.

4. Jacob's Final Commitment (31:14-16)

It only remained for Rachel and Leah to assure him they were one with him in what he proposed to do. They readily agreed, for they too were tired of Laban's tricks. It was clear to them Laban would cheat them just as he had cheated their husband. "Now then," they said, and it is heartwarming to see the sisters united, "whatsoever God saith unto thee, do." Surely a man cannot ask for anything better than that, to have his own loved ones endorse, wholeheartedly and without reservation, his own desire to do the will of God. Thus God stopped Jacob from pursuing old goals.

B. How Old Gods Were Challenged (31:17-35)

"Thou shalt have no other gods before me!" So stated the first of the Ten Commandments when later, at Sinai, the Law was codified for the children of Israel. The commandment had not yet been engraved in the stone and handed over to Israel, but Jacob knew it well. His grandfather had abandoned idolatry and the worship of false gods in that very same land of Mesopotamia years before. Jacob knew that no believer could worship a false god, nor could a believer tolerate the presence of graven images in his home.

Jacob's wives, however, were true daughters of Laban. Laban had some knowledge of the true and living God, but he was ever a pagan at heart. His daughters, particularly Rachel, felt the pull and tug of Laban's superstitions, and Rachel kept some of Laban's household teraphim in her home. Those things now had to be brought into the open, judged, and put away. Jacob must address himself to the difficult task of getting rid of old gods. The task was to be rendered simpler by the ignominious way in which the images themselves were shown to be nothing but foolish blocks of wood or stone.

1. What Laban Taught (31:17-21)

We are given two interesting sidelights into Laban's character. We learn, for instance, what Laban taught. Laban had inculcated two principles into the minds of his children, and he is now about to see them put into practice against him.

By his own example he had taught them *ruthless expediency* (31:17-19*a*). We read, "Then Jacob rose up and set his sons and his wives upon camels; and he carried away all his goods . . . to go to Isaac his father in the land of Canaan. And Laban went to shear his sheep." (A change, we might add—he was usually shearing Jacob!) The expedient thing for Jacob to do was to slip away while his father-in-law was busy, so Jacob, with the full connivance of his wives, used Laban's own principle against him. He had come to Laban as an accomplished trickster himself, but a score of years in Laban's company had added to his wiles. Laban's own daughters did not hesitate to fall in with Jacob's scheme.

Laban had also taught his children *religious error* (31:19*b*-21). That is why Rachel stole her father's idols. She had seen them in the home from childhood days and had seen her father reverence them.[2] Laban should have known better. Abraham's testimony still lingered in the land. Jacob, whose able hand God had used to bring great material prosperity to his home, had never been impressed with his Baals. But with a kind of half-faith, Laban had paid lip service to Abraham's God and had paid due attention to his Baals. No wonder Rachel, a true daughter of Laban, carried them off. He had taught her well. Rachel, of course, also knew of Jacob's God and had been brought into a personal relationship with Him, but she still stood in awe of her father's gods. Thus, Jacob set his face westward and the broad banks of the Euphrates became a thin line on the horizon, but all unknown to him Laban's household gods were being carted along in Rachel's saddlebags.

2. What Laban Thought (31:22-30)

Laban was a man enslaved by his own inadequate thoughts of God. We note *how he met Jehovah* (31:22-24). Arriving home from the shearing, Laban discovered that Jacob was gone, Rachel and Leah were gone, his grandchildren were gone, all Jacob's vast holdings, which he had planned to seize, were gone, and his household gods were gone. Laban was beside himself with fury. He gathered together sufficient force to make short work of Jacob and lashed his mounts in pursuit of the fugitives.

Across the Euphrates he went, up around the Fertile Crescent, on down into Canaan as far as Mount Gilead in the northeast quarter of the land. The distance he covered was about three hundred miles. Jacob had taken ten days to cover it, pushing his caravan as hard as he could;

2. There would be the Baal of the oil press to ensure that his vats were filled with oil; the Baal of the vats and jugs to ensure that the oil and wine would remain sweet and good. There would be the Baal of the olive press—a marvelous little god, a god who could produce oil of olive to be eaten with bread, to be used for cooking, to be rubbed into one's aching limbs. There would be Baals of the highways and of the beehives and of the barley and wheat. Without them, Laban believed, the fertility of his fields and cattle would be gone.

Laban did the distance in a week. At last he spied Jacob's encampment and prepared for a violent onslaught next day.

But that night Laban met the living God, Jacob's God, Abraham's God, in a dream. "Take heed that thou speak not to Jacob either good or bad," he was warned. "Let him alone," God said. "He is mine."

Years ago, in days when a country's flag still stood for something, an Anglo-American was traveling abroad and had the misfortune to be seized by extremists who held him hostage under threat of death. An American and a British consul asked to see the prisoner as a prelude to negotiations. At a favorable moment the British consul stepped forward and threw the British flag over the prisoner, and the American did the same with the Stars and Stripes. "Now then," they said, "fire on those flags if you dare!" Thus God threw His banner over Jacob and warned Laban not to touch him. Laban, who all his life had heard from this one and that about the true and living God, finally met Him face to face.

Like so many others who have had such a confrontation, Laban did not like it at all, for God put His finger on Laban's sin, especially his sin of animosity toward the only believing man he had ever really known. He warned Laban of judgment to come if he persisted in his chosen path. Laban had met the Lord.

Next we are told *how he met Jacob* (31:25-30). The story emphasizes Laban's bias (31:25-28), bitterness (31:29), and blindness (31:30). He blustered away at Jacob in his usual hypocritical way—"Why did you run away? Why didn't you let me kiss my children goodbye? Why didn't you let me throw a farewell feast for you?" It was all pious cant. "It is in the power of my hand to do you hurt," he snarled, "but the God of your father spake unto me yesternight." Then, coming to the point, "Wherefore hast thou stolen my gods?"

And there we have it—the wretched nature of idolatry, the fierce, satanic grip it gets upon a soul. Just last night Laban had met the true and living God; yet he still referred to the wretched little clay idols as his *gods*. That is the first time images are mentioned in Scripture, and it is the first direct reference to heathen gods.

"My gods!" cried Laban. Behind the image there lurks the demon; the worship of the idol gives the demon a hold upon the devotee. "My gods!" cried Laban. Gods indeed! Mighty gods! Gods that could be stolen! Gods that could be packed up like old pots and pans and stuffed into a bag! Gods that could be bounced and jostled over three hundred miles without word or whimper! Gods that could influence wind and weather, it was believed, yet gods that could not even cry out to the deluded man, "Here we are, Laban, on our heads in Rachel's saddlebag!" "My gods," the deluded Laban cried with the voice of the true God yet ringing in his soul.

3. WHAT LABAN SOUGHT (31:31-35)

Jacob, of course, knew nothing about Rachel's theft of the teraphim. He might not have been so confident if he had. "Search the place!" he snapped. "Put to death the thief if thief there be." And search Laban did. He poked and pried into everything, and Jacob stood there and watched, his temper rising. At length Laban's search brought him into Rachel's tent. She looked her father in the eye. "Come on in, Father. Take a look around. You'll pardon me if I remain seated. I'm not feeling well today. You won't find your gods in here, but you're welcome to look." And look he did, in vain. And no wonder! Rachel was sitting on them. It is to be hoped that Rachel learned the lesson of those old gods of hers—useless, futile things they were. Imagine a god being sat upon! What useless idols we cherish, all too often, in our hearts. Oh, that we had the grace and sense to get rid of them.

C. HOW OLD GRUDGES WERE CHALLENGED (31:36-55)

For years Jacob had been building up resentments against his uncle. There is no record that he had ever vented those grudges before, but now, his patience exhausted, he turned on Laban in a rage. He looked at his ransacked camp, at the frightened faces of his children, at Laban's armed men, and he gave Laban a piece of his mind. Grudges he had been nursing for years came spilling out.

1. JACOB'S RIGHTEOUS INDIGNATION (31:36-42)

"And Jacob was wroth and chode with Laban." The word *wroth* means "to be burned"; the word *chode* comes from a root meaning "to seize" or "to tear." Jacob, burning with anger, was ready to tear somebody up. He was angry at being *furiously chased* by Laban (31:36). "What is my trespass? what is my sin, that thou hast so hotly pursued after me?" He was angry at being *falsely charged* by Laban (31:37-40). "I have slaved for you for twenty years. I have not eaten your food, I have provided my own. There was never a lamb or a kid, a sheep or a goat that fell foul of a wild beast but that I, personally, made good the loss. In twenty years you have never lost so much as a single lamb. I have borne the burden and heat of the day, the cold and frost of night. And you come here and treat me like a criminal and accuse me of stealing your household gods!" He was angry at being *foully cheated* by Laban (31:41-42). "You have changed my wages ten times! Ten times you have tried to cheat me! And had it not been for the fact that God, my God, the living God, stood between you and me last night even now you would do me harm." He certainly laid it on the line.

Well, Jacob lost his temper and, as usually happens in such cases, he lost his testimony along with it. Laban went back to Padan-aram, forever embittered, convinced he had been cheated, deeply resentful against the only believer he had ever known. Such is the price of a lost temper and of paying a person back in his own coin.

2. JACOB'S RELIGIOUS INVOCATION (31:43-55)

Something would have to be done. It would not do to part from Laban in that way. Laban had nothing to say to Jacob's charges. He knew only too well how much he really owed to Jacob but had no intention of owning himself in the wrong. Instead, he waved his hand toward the shocked witnesses of the furious quarrel, toward Rachel and Leah, to the children, to the nearby flocks and herds. "These are all mine!" was all he could say. Then, like the old hypocrite he was, he proposed that he and Jacob should make a covenant. Jacob responded at once, setting up a pillar and calling on all present to join in building a permanent memorial to the compact now about to be made. The incident is of particular interest because it reveals what a thoroughgoing hypocrite Laban was and what a spiritual man Jacob had become since his recent meeting with God.

Two things are connected with the pillar. First, there was *the oath* (31:47-53). The oath demonstrated that, to Laban, the pillar was a boundary, a guarantee for the future, nothing more. It meant that Jacob would not treat Rachel and Leah badly now that their father would no longer be present to protect them. It was a gratuitous insult. Laban had no grounds for any such thought. Jacob had always loved Rachel with passion and had always treated Leah with courtesy. The pillar meant too that Jacob would take no more wives—again, Jacob had never wanted more wives; the only wife he had ever desired was Rachel. That he had Leah and the others were Laban's fault, not his. To Laban, furthermore, the pillar meant that he, Laban, would not cross that boundary mark to annoy Jacob. That was the oath.

Laban called the pillar "The Heap of Witness" and "Mizpah!" Then, calling on Jacob's God, as though Jacob were the one needing to be watched, he cried, "The Lord watch between me and thee when we are absent one from another!" That was not meant as the lovely sentiment it is sometimes taken to be; it was meant as a warning to Jacob. To Laban, then, the pillar was a boundary, a guarantee for the future, a guarantee that threw all the onus and stigma of the past on Jacob.

But, connected with that pillar, was not only the oath, there was *the offering* (31:54-55). The offering demonstrated that, to Jacob, the pillar was not a boundary but a blessing; it was good-bye to the past rather than a guarantee for the future. "Then Jacob offered sacrifice upon the mount, and called his brethren to eat bread . . . and early in the morning Laban rose up, and kissed his sons and his daughters, and blessed them: and Laban departed and returned unto his place." He did not embrace Jacob but, with a sore heart for his lost daughters, he embraced them and his grandchildren, and "returned to his place." Back he went to Padan-aram, back to the darkness of paganism, back to nurse his grievances. Thus he passed out of Jacob's life and out of God's Book.

D. How Old Guilt Was Challenged (32:1-32)

Padan-aram was now in Jacob's past. Everything connected with Jacob's life there had been dealt with by God. With a sigh of relief Jacob saw Laban, his sons, and his servants disappear finally over the distant horizon. He turned over a page in his life, only to discover a dark blot from a past page that had soaked through. He now had to face the question of Esau.

Jacob now had to learn one of the most basic, far-reaching lessons a believing man can ever learn—that God does not condemn sin in the sinner and condone it in the saint. Years and years ago Jacob had dealt with Esau in an unbrotherly and unscrupulous way. He had forgotten all about that; the crowded years at Padan-aram, the rush and bustle of life, had made it easy to forget. But God had not forgotten—and neither had Esau. Jacob had to face in full the long account he had run up with his brother so many years before. It is always that way. God cannot possibly bless us with spiritual blessings until we face our trespasses and put right, where it lies within our power, the wrongs we have done. God's dealing with old guilt in Jacob's life reminds us He will deal with it also in ours.

1. Jacob's Confirmation From God (32:1-2)

Jacob had learned the great lesson of salvation at Bethel, twenty years before; now, at the Jabbok, he had to learn the equally great lesson of sanctification. What happened at Bethel took care of his beliefs; what happened at the Jabbok took care of his behavior. There was a great crisis in his life when he became a saved man; there was an equally great crisis in his life when he became, in a practical sense, a sanctified man. Positionally, of course, salvation and sanctification are inseparable acts of God in the soul's experience; practically, many of us do not enter into the truth of sanctification at the time of our conversion.

Since the time God met him at Padan-aram and told him to return to Canaan, Jacob had been obedient. He had come a long way. Notice now *what Jacob saw.* "And Jacob went on his way, and the angels of God met him" (32:1). Jacob had had his unseen angel escort all the way—well indeed it was for Laban that he did not tamper with Jacob—but now he saw the angels for the first time. He learned that his deliverance from Laban was not the result of his own cleverness and courage, but the result of active divine intervention in his affairs.

John Wesley spent fifty-two years in the saddle riding through muck and mire, fronting dangers at every turn as he preached revival to his generation. In those days highways were dangerous places for a lone man. Stage coaches traveled with armed guards, for highwaymen lurked in the hedgerows, and footpads hid behind trees waiting a chance to shoot down the unwary wayfarer. Gibbets were a common sight, set up on the highways as a grim reminder to holdup men that they would be hung if caught, and tarred and left to rot as a warning by the way.

John Wesley was riding one day along a lonely stretch of road when he noticed shadowy forms ahead, forms that vanished behind a hedge almost as his eye took them in. He could not turn back; that was not his way, yet to go on meant danger and possibly death. There was no hope of human help on that deserted road, so John Wesley prayed. Almost at once he heard hoofbeats coming up behind him, and he turned in his saddle as another traveler rode up alongside. Wesley gave the newcomer a cheery greeting than silently the two spurred on down the path, on past the place where the robbers lay concealed. Seeing two men instead of one, the robbers let them pass. Wesley then turned to say something to his companion, only to discover that there was nobody there! The mysterious rider had vanished into thin air. John Wesley had received an unusual glimpse of his angel escort along the way.

We note then what Jacob saw and also *what Jacob said.* "And when Jacob saw them he said, This is God's host: and he called the name of that place Mahanaim" (32:2). The name means "the two hosts." There was the visible host, Jacob and his sons and his servants, and there was the invisible host, the marshaled angels of God marching silently, unseen, but mightily potent side by side with him. The same angel host marches with all of God's children as they seek to walk humbly with their God. Jacob's sudden vision was a confirmation to him from God. He was in God's will.

2. JACOB'S CONFUSION ABOUT GOD (32:3-23)

Unbelief is deeply entrenched in the human heart. Even with the vision of the angel escort still dancing before his eyes, Jacob began scheming and planning again as he tried to think of ways to circumvent Esau's fiery rage. For it had dawned on him now. Before he could hope to live in peace and prosperity in the promised land, he must do something about Esau. The greater part of chapter 32 is concerned with all the expensive and unnecessary plans Jacob evolved for pacifying his brother.

First, thinking to *try negotiation* (32:3-8) he sent messengers ahead to make contact with Esau together with a flattering, fawning message. "Thy servant Jacob saith thus, I have sojourned with Laban . . . and I have oxen, and asses, flocks, and menservants, and womenservants: and I have sent to tell my lord, that I may find grace in thy sight." Bowing and scraping! My lord this and my lord that! If a soft answer can turn away wrath, Jacob was certainly going to give it every opportunity.

Back came the messengers. "We came to thy brother Esau, and also he cometh to meet thee, and four hundred men with him" (32:6). That was Esau's grim reply. Not a word of greeting for Jacob, not a word about the past, not a word about his intentions, just a pointed warning of his ability to deal with Jacob now from strength, not weakness as before. "A brother offended is harder to be won than a strong city!" Already Jacob had forgotten the unseen host that marched with him in the spirit world. "Then Jacob was greatly afraid and distressed: and he divided the people that was with him, and the flocks, and herds, and the camels, into two bands, and said, If Esau come to the one company, and smite it, then the other company which is left shall escape" (32:7-8).

Jacob was still scheming, ignoring God, who was saying, "Trust me, Jacob." Jacob was saying, "I do trust you, Lord, but—"

During the first world war a businessman had to visit a factory where munitions were made. As he approached the gate he saw a big sign that read "IADOM!" It puzzled him, but he soon forgot about it and went on about his business. But he noticed the same sign everywhere. It was pasted on walls, it appeared on doors, it was even displayed in the director's office. He searched his memory in vain for such a word and was too reticent to ask what it meant. When his business was over the director's secretary escorted him to the factory gate. "You saw our sign, of course," she said. "How could I miss it!" he exclaimed. "But what does it mean?" "Why," she said, "it's an acrostic—it means 'It All Depends On Me!' " That was Jacob! "It all depends on me" had been his motto all his life.

When negotiation broke down Jacob thought he should *try intercession* (32:9-12). The prayer he now offered to God was one of great boldness and beauty. It was the prayer of a desperate man, a man who suddenly realized that "it doesn't all depend on me" at all; it all depends on *God.*

The prayer is in four parts. First, Jacob pleaded *the purposes of God* (32:9). "O God of my father Abraham, and God of my father Isaac, the LORD which saidst unto me, Return unto thy country, and to thy kindred, and I will deal well with thee—" He said in effect, "If I had not been obedient to you, Lord, I would be hundreds of miles away from Esau right now!" It is a great thing to be able to come to God and say, "Lord, here I am in the very center of Thy will. You know the circumstances that have arisen. They are beyond me, but they are your responsibility because I am right where you want me to be, right now."

Then he pleaded *the providence of God* (32:10). "I am not worthy of the least of all the mercies, and of all the truth, which thou hast shewed unto thy servant; for with my staff I passed over this Jordan; and now I am become two bands." He was standing near the conjunction of the Jabbok and the Jordan. Twenty years before he had come that way with nothing but a staff in his hand and now, in the providence of God, he had become a wealthy man—not because he deserved it. On the contrary, God had given him both enrichment and enlightenment far beyond anything he could have thought. He was a new Jacob.

He pleaded *the protection of God* (32:11). "Deliver me, I pray thee, from the hand of my brother . . . for I fear him." Now Jacob came to the point. Esau had a reputation for cruelty. "Lest he will come and smite me, and the mother with the children," Jacob cried, using a proverb of the times. The literal rendering of his cry was "lest he smite . . . the mother upon the child." The picture is of a hunter destroying a hen, even as it spreads its wings to protect its brood; a picture of unsparing determination, of an eye that knows no pity, of a hand that will not spare. Jacob had visions of his camp turned into a carnage heap, strewn with dead. He could see Rachel dead, Leah dead, the slave-wives dead, Judah dead, Joseph dead. He pleaded the protection of God from the violence of Esau.

He pleaded *the promises of God* (32:12). "And thou saidst I will surely do thee good, and make thy seed as the sand of the sea." That is always a potent argument with God. Take Him boldly back to His promises. That is, again, what saintly George Mueller used to do. George Mueller set out to raise a monument in Bristol to the faithfulness of God. He wished to demonstrate to an unbelieving generation that God is, and that He is the rewarder of them that diligently seek Him. Time and time again, Mueller built, staffed, and maintained those great orphan houses of his, and God tested him. His biographer, A. T. Pierson, tells how Mueller would pile up arguments in prayer. He would remind the Lord that the orphan houses were *His,* that the orphans and their needs were *His* responsibility, that *He* was the pledged "Father of the fatherless." Comments Pierson, "Of course, God does not need to be convinced: no arguments can make any plainer to Him the claims of trusting souls to His intervention, claims based upon His own Word, confirmed by His oath." Then why did George Mueller use such arguments with God? Says Pierson, "We are to argue with God, we are to argue our case with God, not indeed to convince Him but to convince ourselves."[3]

But Jacob was still Jacob. Unable to leave matters in God's hands, he decided to *try conciliation* (32:13-23). He prepared 200 she-goats and 20 he-goats, 200 ewes and 20 rams, 30 camels together with their colts, 40 cows and 10 bulls, 20 she asses and 10 foals—all as a conciliatory present for Esau. It gives us some idea of his wealth, that he could classify such a magnificent tribute as a mere present.

Then, with all his native caution, Jacob separated the various classes of animals into five droves and sent them off to Esau with a respectable distance between each. He wanted to keep on bringing before Esau his sincere hope of reconciliation. The principle Jacob employed was

3. Arthur T. Pierson, *George Muller of Bristol* (New York: Fleming H. Revell, n.d., p. 149.

In Micah 7:20 we read, "Thou wilt perform the truth to Jacob, the mercy to Abraham, which thou hast sworn unto our fathers from the days of old." Note the progress of thought. What was mercy to Abraham was truth to Jacob. God was under no obligation to extend covenant blessing to Abraham, hence to Abraham it was a simple act of pure mercy. But having put Himself under voluntary obligation, Jacob could claim as truth what to Abraham had been mercy.

the same principle that lay behind the trespass offering, later to become a part of Israel's sacrificial system. The trespass offering taught that, if a man wished to get right with God, then he must necessarily get right with the person he had wronged. He must make restitution and add more than he stole.

3. JACOB'S CONFRONTATION WITH GOD (32:24-32)

We come now to the second great spiritual crisis in Jacob's life. At Bethel he saw the ladder, at the Jabbok he saw the Lord; at Bethel he became a believing man, here he became a broken man; at Bethel he became a son of God, here he became a saint of God. He came away from Bethel with a new spring in his step; he came away from the Jabbok with a lasting limp in his walk. At Bethel he died to his sin; here he died to self.

We see Jacob *very much alone* (32:24*a*). "And Jacob was left alone," we read. His wealth had already gone on before, his family, his fortune, his servants had all been sent away. And now Jacob was alone. Most of us hate to be alone. We structure our time to the full because we dare not be left with absolutely nothing to do but face God. Yet there is nothing we need more than to be left alone with God.

But if Jacob was very much alone he was also *very much alive* (32:24*b*-25*a*). "And Jacob was left alone; and there wrestled a man with him until the breaking of the day and . . . he saw that he prevailed not against him." That is, the unknown assailant was getting nowhere with Jacob. The old, carnal, stubborn, fighting, self-sufficient, unyielding Jacob was very much alive. The battle went on all night. How soon was it before Jacob realized he was really wrestling with God Himself, or that his assailant was none other than the second Person of the Godhead, who had come to confront him with his desperate need for full and unconditional surrender to God?

Then we see a Jacob who was *very much altered* (32:25*b*-32). That night was the climax of twenty years of God's patient dealing with Jacob. We are in such a hurry; God never is. We can have instant everything today—instant meals, instant entertainment, instant transportation, instant communication—but we cannot have instant holiness. God takes His time to bring us to spiritual maturity. He never crowds us or ravishes us; He always waits and woos.

We see in Jacob, now, a man *broken* by God (32:25*b*-27), no longer fighting but clinging. "When he [the angel] of the Lord saw that he prevailed not against him [Jacob], he touched the hollow of his thigh; and the hollow of Jacob's thigh was out of joint, as he wrestled with him." The hollow of the thigh is the hip socket and, of course, nobody can wrestle with the hip socket broken. All Jacob could do now was cling.

"And he [the angel of the Lord] said, Let me go, for the day breaketh.

And he [Jacob] said, I will not let thee go, except thou bless me." There is the basic difference between Esau and Jacob. With all his faults, deep down in his heart where the ultimate issues of life are decided, Jacob wanted the blessing of God; Esau never did. Thus we see a broken Jacob clinging and confessing.

"What is your name?" the heavenly visitor demanded. Did not the Lord know Jacob's name? Of course he did. But once before when Jacob was asked that question he had said, "I am Esau!" "My name is Jacob!" now cried the broken man. Jacob! Cheat! Supplanter! One who "takes you by the heel!" or, as we would say today, "one who twists your arm!" "Oh, Lord," cried Jacob, "you know me. I am Jacob. I am just a cheat, a liar." That was all God wanted. He simply wanted Jacob to be broken in His presence, seeing himself as he really was in himself, confessing all that he was by natural birth. "I am Jacob!" Now God could work.

The man thus broken by God could be *blessed* by God (32:28-30). God breaks us only so that He can make us anew. "Thy name shall be called no more Jacob, but Israel: for as a prince hast thou power with God and with men, and hast prevailed." The name "Israel" comes from a word meaning "to be chief." Thus the man who now enters Canaan, the land of blessing, is not the same man who left it twenty years before, a man who could cheat his brother, deceive a blind father and outwit an unscrupulous uncle. The man who now entered Canaan was Israel, God's prince, the man who had learned that the heart of God could be taken by storm if surrender and supplication are the means employed. The new name Jacob received that day was a token of a new nature, so long dormant but now to be triumphant in his life.

With holy boldness Jacob asked his visitor to tell him His name. He wanted to know Him better. "Tell me I pray thee, thy name," he said. In the Old Testament, God revealed Himself to men preeminently by His names. It was thus, for instance, that Abraham grew in his knowledge of God. It was not presumption therefore on Jacob's part to ask the stranger His name; it was faith. If he was Israel, then Israel he would be! "What is your name?" he asked. The Lord did not tell him, because Jacob already knew who had broken and blessed him. But, in response to Jacob's faith, the midnight wrestler added another blessing to the one already given.

"And Jacob called the name of the place Peniel ["the face of God"], for I have seen God face to face, and my life is preserved." A sense of awe and amazement swept over Jacob's soul. He had seen God! He had looked into the face of God in one of His rare preincarnate appearances in visible form. And his soul was thrilled.

The chapter ends with Jacob *branded* by God and bearing in his body henceforth the "slave-brand of Jesus Christ" (32:31-32). He halted upon his thigh. We picture him fording the Jabbok, leaning heavily on his staff and limping into the camp where his wives and children were in the morning light. "Wives! Children!" he would call, and they would come running, staring at a different Jacob. "What happened?" they would ask. "Why," he would say, "I met God last night and I shall never walk the same again."

IV. HOW GOD SEPARATED JACOB (33:1–34:31)

A. JACOB AND HIS BROTHER (33:1-16)

It was a broken Jacob who stumbled into camp after his encounter with God. He had passed another great milestone in his life. We think of Jacob as we met him first; Jacob *lying*. We remember Jacob *listening*, out there on the hillside on that first, unforgettable night away from home, the night God first appeared to him. Jacob was *learning* during the long twenty years of his exile. What a dull, slow learner he was, as are most of us. Now we see Jacob *limping*, a broken man, a blessed man, a man with a new name, and a new nature now in control. Later we shall see Jacob *leaning*, an old, old man, down there in Egypt with his boys gathered around to hear his parting words before venturing forth upon his last great journey into the unknown.

In our study of his remarkable life, we have seen God *saving* Jacob and we have seen God *subduing* Jacob. Now we will see how God *separated* Jacob (chapters 33-34). The story is in two parts. In chapter 33 we have the story of Jacob and his brother; in chapter 34 we have Jacob and his backsliding. We shall begin with Jacob and his brother (33:1-16). The story is told from the standpoint of Esau rather than from that of Jacob.

1. HOW ESAU FOUND JACOB (33:1-3)

Esau had come up from Edom with four hundred men at his back. If a renewal of hostilities with Jacob was in the making, Esau was ready. Down there in the rock cities of Seir he had already carved out a name for himself and a position of considerable power. Esau knew nothing about Jacob's angel escort and nothing of Jacob's changed heart. He only knew that if Jacob had any more tricks up his sleeve, he had better not try to pull any of them on him. He looked with grim satisfaction at his household cavalry, armed to the teeth and spoiling for a fight. So he spurred on his way to meet Jacob his twin.

He found *a cautious Jacob* awaiting him (33:1-2). "And Jacob lifted up his eyes, and looked, and, behold, Esau came, and with him four hundred men. And he divided the children unto Leah, and unto Rachel, and unto the two handmaids. And he put the handmaids and their children foremost, and Leah and her children after, and Rachel and Joseph hindermost." That is, he put the more expendable ones up front where they would be first to meet any hostile intent on the part of Esau. That would give the others, and especially his beloved Rachel and

Joseph, a chance to get away. That blatant coddling of Joseph could not have done much to defuse the hatred the other brothers were generating toward him.

Jacob fell to planning again. How deeply entrenched in the human heart, even the regenerated heart, is mistrust of God. Such is the flesh. What a good thing it is that God is not touchy.

But if Esau found a cautious Jacob he also found *a courageous Jacob* (33:3*a*). For Jacob was no coward. He "passed over before them," we read. That is, he went on ahead of them, putting himself in the van in the place of danger. In the modern Israeli army a strict code of courage is enjoined on all officers, all of whom must take commando or paratroop training. The words "Forward march!" have been expunged from the Israeli military vocabulary and have been replaced by the words "Follow me!" In the Israeli military code, unless an officer is prepared to put himself up front, in the place of danger, he simply does not qualify to command other troops. Thus Jacob put himself up front. It was the act of a courageous man, the act of an eastern shepherd. We can forgive Jacob for many of his shortcomings when we see him doing that.

Then, Esau found *a contrite Jacob* (33:3*b*). "And he passed over before them, and bowed himself to the ground seven times, until he came to his brother." He would take a few paces and bow, take a few paces more and bow again. What a scene it must have been. There was Esau, a wild, hairy man sitting on his swift Arab horse gazing down at his brother. There was Esau's escort, a band of unruly ruffians such as Jacob had not seen all his life. There was the little knot of wives and children, still arranged as Jacob had placed them, looking with scared eyes first at Esau and then at Jacob. There were Jacob's shepherds, tough customers themselves but no match for Esau's armed men. And there was Jacob, bowing and scraping, bowing and advancing and bowing again, bobbing up and down like a cork on the waves. And all about them, stretching far away into the distance to the Jabbok were Jacob's flocks and herds. Thus Esau found Jacob.

2. HOW ESAU FORGAVE JACOB (33:4-7)

Chapter 33 is a great commentary on the reconciliation of brethren. If we have offended a brother it is not the slightest use going to him in a contentious spirit or in a spirit of self-justification. The way to come is with reparations in hand and in a humble, contrite spirit. That spirit disarmed Esau on the spot, and he forgave Jacob fully, freely, and forever. (Esau's descendants, however, did not share in that spirit of forgiveness.)

"And Esau ran to meet him, and embraced him, and fell on his neck, and kissed him: and they wept." It was a typically oriental thing to do, something foreign to westerners, but something as natural as a sunrise to an easterner. The Bible does not put a great premium on emotion but, on the other hand, neither does it ignore it. There are times when a display of emotion is healthy and better than ten thousand words. There were no lengthy speeches. Jacob did not launch into a long explanation about his new-found penitence. There was no intellectual exchange at all. Instead, there was something far more powerful, something that cleared the air much more quickly and cleanly, like a torrential downpour at the end of a torrid day. There was a good, healing, emotional exchange. The tears that flowed down the cheeks of the estranged brothers washed away all the bitterness and ill-will of more than twenty years.

Once the emotional outburst was over there came the formal introductions and never again, during the lifetimes of Esau and Jacob, did the old animosities raise their heads. What a fine person Esau was in so many ways—generous, likeable, noble, yet lost. And that is what creates the problem for so many people. It did for Robert Laidlaw.

Robert Laidlaw was a successful New Zealand business man. He tells us in his little book *The Reason Why* just how that very problem troubled him once. "I know a polished, cultivated gentleman who is not a Christian," he says, "and I know a rather crude, uncultured man who is a Christian. Do you mean to tell me that God prefers the uncultured man simply because he has accepted and acknowleged Christ as his Savior?" That was his problem. Here is how he solved it. "A Christian is not different in *degree* from a non-Christian, he is different in *kind,* just as the difference between a diamond and a cabbage is not one of degree but of kind. The one is polished, the other is crude, but the one is dead while the other is alive, therefore the one has what the other has not in any degree whatsoever—life! And such is the difference God sees between a Christian and a non-Christian."

That was the essential difference between Esau and Jacob. As a man, Esau was a far more open, honest, out-going person than Jacob. He was a very fine fellow, but he was spiritually dead. Jacob was a natural-born schemer and a man with many glaring faults, but he had spiritual life. It was a difference of kind, not degree.

3. How Esau Favored Jacob (33:8-11)

Esau now turned his attention to the great quantity of expensive animals Jacob had sent him as a present. "What meanest thou by all this drove which I met?" he asked. "These are to find grace in the sight of my lord," said Jacob. He was saying, "Years ago I cheated you, Esau. I deeply regret it now. I should like to make restitution. I want you to know that my regrets go far deeper than mere words."

At once Esau *refused* the trespass offering (33:8-9). "I have enough my brother, keep that thou hast unto thyself." Such was Esau. In one gracious statement he could cancel all of Jacob's debt. But then, when he saw that his refusal of the gift troubled his brother, he just as generously *received* it. In the East, the acceptance of a present is the equivalent to a bond of friendship, and Jacob wanted to make sure that his old guilt would never be raised against him again. "Take, I pray thee, my blessing that is brought to thee; because God hath dealt graciously with me, and because I have enough," he said (33:11). Note again the essential difference between Esau and Jacob. Both men said, "I have enough," but Jacob made mention of God and Esau did not; Jacob had a testimony and Esau had nothing. The name Jacob used for God in giving his testimony was not Jehovah, His covenant name, for Esau's carnal mind could never appreciate that glorious and gracious name for God. He used the name "Elohim" hoping, perhaps, that the thought of God as the God of *creation* might strike some note in Esau's dead soul, whereas the thought of God as the God of *covenant* was far beyond Esau's power to grasp. In giving that brief word of testimony to his brother, Jacob stepped down to Esau's level and used the kindergarten language of faith. It was a sensible thing to do. Paul did the same thing when preaching to the intellectuals of Athens who, for all their vaunted philosophy, were wholly unable to comprehend spiritual truth.

4. HOW ESAU FRIGHTENED JACOB (33:12-16)

Esau now offered to accompany Jacob, offering him the courtesy of *his presence* (33:12-14). That frightened Jacob, not because he had any fears that Esau would do him harm, but because he had learned the problems of the unequal yoke. Jacob, with his vast, slow-moving flocks and herds could not be sensibly yoked to Esau with his four hundred mounted cavalry. It made no sense, and as soon as Jacob pointed that out to Esau, his brother saw it too.

The unequal yoke never makes any sense whether in business, marriage, or social entanglement. We are honor-bound to be friendly with unsaved people but we are equally responsible not to become fettered to them. Jacob used commendable tact in declining his brother's generous offer. Tact should always be used when our overtures of friendship to unsaved neighbors are followed by reciprocal offers which, however, involve an entanglement it would be best to decline.

Esau saw Jacob's point, but, if Jacob could not accept the offer of his presence, surely he could accept the offer of *his protection* (33:15-16). "And Esau said, Let me now leave with thee some of the folk that are with me." Again Jacob carefully sidestepped the involvement. "What needeth it," he said, "Let me find grace in the sight of my lord." And once again Esau, who had made the offer because he thought perhaps that Jacob, who looked so weak and unprotected, needed an escort to shield him from robbers and brigands, bowed to his brother's judgment. Thus they said their farewells and Esau went on his way back to Seir.

Throughout the conversation there is implied, on Jacob's part, a half promise to visit Esau in Seir. Whether he ever did so at a later date we are not told. Probably both Esau and Jacob knew that it would be a last goodbye. The boys had chosen divergent paths. Esau had chosen the present evil world and Jacob had chosen the world to come. The two had little or nothing in common beyond their birth into the same family and their somewhat tarnished boyhood memories. At the same time it is not impossible that Jacob might have made a trip to Edom to see his brother. One would like to think he did redeem his promise. As we can see from Genesis 36, the family records of Esau somehow fell into Moses' hands. Who knows? Perhaps Esau gave Jacob a copy of those archives down there amid the spectacular rock dwellings of Petra at some time not recorded in God's Word.

B. JACOB AND HIS BACKSLIDING (33:17–34:31)

The latter part of chapter 33, and chapter 34 deal with Jacob and his backsliding. They are very sad chapters in Jacob's life, dealing with the boiling over of the big pot of troubles that had been brewing for years in the undisciplined lives of his children. We are going to tread lightly down the section. It is easy enough to point the finger at other people's failures, and the two areas in which Jacob failed are two areas in which many of us have failed today. He failed as a pilgrim and he failed as a parent. His failures in those two areas were now going to cost him dearly.

1. JACOB'S FAILURE AS A PILGRIM (33:17-20)

The patriarchs were all wealthy men, but with Abraham and Isaac and with Jacob (up until this point) the pilgrim character was never lost. The pilgrim character was symbolized by a tent and an altar; a tent that manifested a pilgrim walk in a wicked world, and an altar that manifested pure worship amidst so much religious corruption. As pilgrims, the patriarchs were men on the move, ever willing and able to obey the call of God. It is that aspect of testimony that now broke down in Jacob's life.

We follow Jacob first to *Succoth*. There we see *Jacob building* (33:17). He built a house and made shelters for his cattle, signifying that he was going to settle down, tired of the pilgrim life, tired of being forever on the move. Everybody else had a house, why should he not have one? He could certainly afford one, a big one—a mansion, if he so desired. For the moment he had lost sight of the mansion being prepared for him in glory in order to settle for a house at Succoth on the east side of the Jordan, in the valley just south of the Jabbok. Jacob had stopped just short of the promised land after all.

The first mention of a house in the Bible is in connection with Lot. Abraham the pilgrim dwelt in a tent on the plains of Mamre; Lot the backslider dwelt in a house in Sodom. Here in Genesis 33 is the first mention of a house in connection with the patriarchs. The Holy Spirit ignores it altogether in Hebrews 11, that great faith chapter, where He says of Abraham, "By faith he sojourned in the land of promise, as in a strange country, dwelling in tents with Isaac and Jacob, the heirs with him of the same promise" (Hebrews 11:9).

Here, then, was Jacob's first mistake. He decided to settle down and take it easy even if so doing meant settling short of Canaan and meant the abandonment of his pilgrim way of life. He simply wanted to be like everybody else, at least for a while.

We move along to *Shechem*. There we see *Jacob buying* (33:18-20). We do not know how long Jacob lived at Succoth. Probably it was for a number of years and no doubt for much longer than he intended. It was long enough, anyway, for his daughter Dinah to grow up to womanhood—she was about six when he first settled down. Eventually, however, he made a move and off he went to Shalem, a city of Shechem. "And Jacob . . . pitched his tent toward the city," we read (33:18). How that statement reminds us of Lot! Jacob, it would seem, had gone back to being a pilgrim, but he was still a reluctant pilgrim. He had gone back to his tent, but wanted to get as close to the world as he could while still outwardly professing to be a migrant for God in a God-dishonoring world.

Shechem was a prominent city located on Mount Gerizim. That mountain became famous in later Hebrew history as the place from which the blessings of the Law were proclaimed. Just across the way stood Mount Ebal where the corresponding curses of the Law were heralded in the ears of Israel. Shechem was near the site where the great capital city of Samaria would one day stand. It was here that Jacob dug that famous well on which the Lord Jesus sat when He met the woman from Samaria and talked to her about the water of life.

Jacob purchased some property at that time, buying it from Hamor, the father of a young man named Shechem. It was those business dealings, no doubt, that first introduced Dinah to the young man whose influence was to be so disastrous. How much better it would have been for Jacob if he had left all such business dealings alone. Just like so many of us who try to give backsliding the aura of religious respectability, Jacob "erected an altar and called it El-Elohe-Israel ("God, the God of Israel"). It sounded very good but it was Jacob, not Israel at work, Jacob and not God. There is not the slightest hint that God instructed Jacob to purchase for cash what had been promised by faith. No doubt Jacob intended his altar to be a testimony to the pagans round about him. If so, his intentions were soon brought to nothing by the behavior of three of his children. He should have gone deeper into Canaan, as Abraham did. He should have put distance between himself and the evil Canaanite city toward which he had pitched his tent. When God insists on complete separation from the world it is because He knows best.

2. JACOB'S FAILURE AS A PARENT (34:1-31)

The noticeable lack of discipline in Jacob's family now began to come to a head. God is not once mentioned in the events that follow, and we cannot help but believe that the incidents recorded would never have happened if Jacob had remained a pilgrim and a stranger rather than trying to become like the world. Whether the story of Esau's remarkable successes in Edom had upset Jacob we are not told. Was he trying to emulate his brother by making a mark for himself? It might well be. Jacob remains silent throughout the chapter, silent, that is, until the very end when it was too late. He seems to have lost all control over the behavior of his children.

a. THE SCANDAL CAUSED BY DINAH'S BEHAVIOR (34:1-7)

We make every possible allowance for the young woman. After all, she was a child of the backwoods, so the lights of the big city were very bright for her. The nomadic life in which she had been raised did nothing to equip her for the temptations of the exciting city nearby. Such moral training as she might have received did not arm her against the flatteries of a dashing young prince like Shechem. The world can also look very attractive and alluring to children brought up in the shelter of a Christian home. Often those brought up in godless homes know by bitter experience what a shallow, shameful place the world is. Those brought up in a separated environment often find the world fascinating, that is, if they have not been taught to fear it.

We observe first how *Dinah was seen* (34:1-2*a*). "And Dinah the daughter of Leah, which she bare unto Jacob, went out to see the daughters of the land. And . . . Shechem the son of Hamor . . . saw her." That was when the trouble started. Whatever was Jacob up to, we wonder, to allow his daughter such freedom in such a place? Perhaps he just had no idea who Dinah's companions were, but if so, more's the pity. A young person's peers very quickly become the most important opinion-makers in his life, and peer pressure, once established, is very strong. So, off Dinah went to visit her unsaved friends and, of course, she was seen. Shechem saw her, recognized her, made it a point to get to know her better, and fell madly in love with her. The moral principles of Shechem, however, were not those of the spiritually-minded Jacob, and Dinah soon forgot her father's principles under the spell of that charmer from Shechem.

So, before long, *Dinah was seduced* (34:2*b*). She was no match for Shechem. Here she was, a country girl, being paid court by a prince of the realm. He swept her off her feet, persuaded her that her father's scruples were old-fashioned, persuaded her that moral standards were relative, not absolute, and that in Shechem and, indeed, in all of Canaan, "everybody did it." There was no sin in it; it was just doing what came naturally. So, throwing caution and even common sense to the winds, Dinah gave in.

We are told next how *Dinah was sought* (34:3-7). Young Shechem had now fallen hopelessly in love with Dinah, and, moved by that honest passion, he sought to make amends for the wrong he had done. He urged his father to enter into formal negotiations with Dinah's family so that he could marry the girl. In all that follows Shechem proved himself to be an honorable man.

But news of his seduction of Dinah had already leaked out at home. "Jacob held his peace," we are told (34:5-6) but not so Dinah's two closest brothers, Simeon and Levi. They were infuriated at the insult that had been heaped upon the family and could think of nothing but hot, swift, terrible vengeance to clear the family name.

b. THE SCANDAL CAUSED BY DINAH'S BROTHERS (34:8-31)

The story unfolds in four tragic steps. It begins with *the desperate craving that caused the problem* (34:8-12). At the bottom of everything was Shechem's passion for the girl he had shamed. No price would be too great for him to pay to obtain the girl to be his lawful, wedded wife. Thus marriage negotiations were begun. Old Hamor, with a strong streak of the fox in him, approached Jacob and his sons to see what arrangements could be made to smooth troubled waters.

His offer was an out-and-out worldly one. He offered them worldly *society*. "Make ye marriages with us," he said. The offer may not have been without its appeal. Jacob's sons were of marriage age and he must have given serious thought to the problem of where to find them wives. But he was a patriarch, and marriage out of the will of God was not to be considered so far as he was concerned. Then Hamor offered worldly *security*. "Dwell with us," he said. That, too, must have been a temptation. Jacob lived in a hostile, pagan world. An alliance with a powerful clan must have been bait hard to resist. Finally Hamor offered worldly *success*. "The land shall be before you," he said, "dwell and trade ye therein and get you possessions therein." Twenty years before Jacob would have jumped at the offer. It was a generous enough proposition from a worldly point of view. But that was the whole point. It was a worldly offer. While it was the best an unsaved man could offer, Hamor was tendering the wrong coin, coin minted of base alloy, coin that could not possibly tempt the man who had met God at the Jabbok. Had Jacob accepted the offer it would have wiped out the patriarchal line in a single generation.

However, before Jacob could speak, young Shechem broke in. His father had spoken with the voice of persuasion; he spoke with the voice of passion. He would do anything, anything to obtain his heart's desire. "Ask me never so much dowry," he urged, "and I will give it." But it was that desperate craving that caused the problem. Had Hamor been able to come with a simple offer of reparations the story might have been different. But Shechem wanted Dinah, no matter what the cost.

The story next tells of *the despicable craftiness that characterized the proceedings* (34:13-24). It is hard to believe that such professing believers as Simeon and Levi could act as they did. Truly, when a person is out of touch with God there are no depths to which he cannot sink. The duplicity now practiced was twofold. There was the *subtle dishonesty* of Dinah's brothers (34:13-17). They took over the negotiations. "You are offering the wrong kind of currency," they said. "We won't do business that way. We are evaluating the wrong done to us not in terms of riches but in terms of religion. You have done far more than defile our sister; you have dishonored and violated our religious convictions. We have no intention of marrying our sister to a pagan, no matter who he is. Before we can even consider a marital alliance with you people you must accept our basic religious premise. You and all your clan must be circumcised. Apart from that there can be no further discussion. However, if you will accept our terms we will accept yours." That was the subtle dishonesty of Simeon and Levi. They had not the slightest intention of allowing Shechem to marry Dinah. What they really wanted would become only too plain before long. All dishonesty is wrong, but dishonesty wrapped up in Bible texts is the very worst kind.

We next see the *simpler dishonesty* of Shechem's father (34:18-24). Hamor was a rascal, but he almost seems like a saint when compared to Simeon and Levi. Back to the city he went with his son to call the clan into council. To get the whole city to submit to the painful rite of circumcision was going to take some convincing! Hamor took the line that once the marriage contract was signed the Shechemites could proceed at leisure to totally assimilate the Israelites and could then enrich themselves with the vast liquid assets Jacob so obviously possessed. "Shall not their cattle and their substance be ours?" he urged (34:23). "All we need to do is go along with this religious scruple of theirs, then we can swamp them!" The cupidity of the city fathers was aroused and Hamor's arguments prevailed.

Next comes *the dreadful crime that concluded the partnership* (34:25-29). The agreement was signed and the rite of circumcision administered to all the men of Shechem. Two days passed to allow the full effect of the painful operation to be felt. Then, when the Shechemites were totally incapacitated, Simeon and Levi, two lone and violent men, struck the town. Up and down the streets of Shechem they went, bursting into every house, systematically massacring every man in the place. It was a deed worthy of the gestapo.

Dinah, who had been taken into Hamor's household in preparation for the promised forthcoming marriage, was seized and dragged back home. The sheep and oxen and all the portable wealth of the city was taken as spoil. The women and children of the city were treated like captives taken in war. The Holy Spirit lists each sordid detail (34:27-28), and each word falls like a lead weight of doom in the scales of the Holy One. Simeon and Levi had acted worse than Assyrian shock-troops. Moses, who tells the story in all its naked horror, still feels the outrage and the shame of the deed even after the passing of over four hundred years.

Finally we have *the despairing cry that condemned the plot* (34:30-31). Jacob stood and stared in horror at the vast amount of spoil that Levi and Simeon had hauled into his camp. He stopped his ears at the pitiful cries of the new-made widows and the orphaned children of Shechem. He looked with dismay at his sons. "You have made me both vile and vulnerable," he cried. "Ye have troubled me to make me stink among the inhabitants of the land . . . they shall gather themselves together against me, and slay me, and I shall be destroyed, I and my house." He never forgave them. He felt naked and betrayed by them. They had ruined his testimony, they had acted worse than the Canaanites and Perizzites, they had made his very name a stench to the ungodly.

But God is gracious. His next word to Jacob was, "Arise and go to Bethel and dwell there and make there an altar unto the Lord." Jacob had no doubt been foolish and soft in the way he brought up his children. No doubt some of his own poor example, at times, had contributed to his children's spirit of rebellion. But his heart was right. He had not acted criminally. What had just happened was to be laid at the door of Simeon and Levi, not at his. But, lest a worse thing happen, he had best get back to Bethel, back to the house of God, back to where he first was saved. And there he had best renew his vows. For, so far as Jacob was concerned, God's promises, protection, and purposes remained unchanged.

V. HOW GOD SANCTIFIED JACOB (35:1-29)

We have now come to the last chapter in the story of Jacob's spiritual life. We have seen how God *saved* Jacob (28), how God *subdued* Jacob (29-32) and how God *separated* Jacob (33-34). The final chapter, chapter 35, tells how God *sanctified Jacob.* From that point on the great focus of Genesis is on Joseph, not Jacob, although Jacob, of course, does appear and become prominent in the narrative once more at the time of his death.

There are three locations in the chapter—Bethel, Ephrath, and Mamre. The chapter records four burials and three funerals. God was still cutting the ties that bound Jacob to earthly things. Some of those ties were very dear. The death of Rachel, for instance, must have seemed to Jacob to be "the most unkindest cut of all."

We think instinctively of David Livingstone. The great warrior knelt, bent and broken before the lonely grave at Shupunga where he had just laid to rest the mortal remains of his loved Mary. Livingstone's wife, though the daughter of intrepid pioneer African missionaries, had never been really strong enough for the roughness of the trail. For years she had struggled on but, at length, worn out and with little children to care for, she gave up and returned home while her husband pressed on. Before Livingstone's mind there danced the three rivers, the Zambezi, the Congo, the Nile, each pouring its floods into a different sea. Whoever unlocked the secret of those rivers would unlock Africa. Ever before Livingstone's mind there danced the horrors he had seen, the unspeakable atrocities of the slave trade. Ever before him danced his mandate from on high, his commission to reach the lost souls of men. Explore! Emancipate! Evangelize! It was a three-fold cord not easily broken, so Livingstone forged on alone, and Mary tarried at home, with the little ones, to pray.

But the gossipers were at work. "Livingstone cannot stand his wife," they said. "His one desire is to be as far from her as he possibly can." Word of the talk reached him and, against his better judgment, he summoned Mary back to his side. She came, she sickened, and she died. There he knelt, his hot tears running down his sunburnt face, weeping out his heart. "Mary! Oh, Mary! I loved you when I married you and the longer I lived the more I loved you! Oh Mary, how often we have longed for a quiet, peaceful home of our own since we were cast adrift in Africa! God pity the children!" There he knelt beneath the great, spreading baobab tree feeling, for the first time in his life, it would be a good thing to die.

We come back to Jacob and a chapter of funerals, one of which left him bereaved beyond words. The Bible draws a courteous veil over Jacob's secret grief. But doubtless he did cry in agony that night, in the loneliness of his tent (a tent made desolate the more by his loss of Bilhah, Rachel's maid, by the sordid sin of Reuben).

Thus, with gentle hand but firm, God broke Jacob's earthly ties. Once the sad chapter is done, the years would come and go with scarcely a word about Jacob. Seventeen of those years will be spent in luxury in Egypt. There we shall be given one more long look at Jacob as he prepared to strike his tent, pull up stakes for the very last time, and take his journey home. We shall see a man, full of the Holy Spirit, blessing his boys, speaking with prophetic power, worshiping, leaning on his staff. After the chapter now before us we shall be able to leave Jacob and go on to other things. The sanctifying work will have been well and truly done.

A. JACOB AS A BELIEVING MAN (35:1-15)

Everything came to a head with a decisive word from God. Jacob was almost out of his mind. Dinah was sitting desolate in his camp, shamed and a widow before ever a wife, thanks to the fury of her brothers. Levi and Simeon were scowling defiantly about them, giving back the askance looks of the camp. The story of last night's dark deeds was speeding across the length and breadth of the land. If ever a man needed a decisive word from God it was Jacob the morning after the

Shechem massacre. And when the word came, there was no mistaking its power.

1. Renewing Jacob's Spiritual Vitality (35:1-4)

Three areas of Jacob's spiritual life needed to be thoroughly renewed. First he needed his spiritual vitality renewed, to have new life put into some of his basic beliefs. Beliefs, like hinges, can get rusty if not kept oiled and used. Jacob's beliefs needed to be revitalized.

The process began with the mention of a *place* (35:1*a*). "And God said unto Jacob, Arise, go up to Bethel, and dwell there: and make there an altar unto God, that appeared unto thee when thou fleddest from the face of Esau thy brother." He was to go back to Bethel, the place of sacred and fragrant memories. It was at Bethel that Abraham the pilgrim first staked his claim to Canaan and built his first altar in the land. It was back to Bethel he had come after his disastrous backsliding in Egypt. It was at Bethel that Jacob first met God, first saw the ladder, first became a truly believing man. Bethel! There are some places in life that we associate with holy memories, just as there are some places we shun because they haunt us with our sins. To come back to Bethel was to come back home.

Mention is next made of the *purpose* (35:1*b*). "Dwell there," Jacob was told. "Build an altar there." God evidently wanted Jacob to soak his bruised soul in the healing balm of sacred memories. Bethel was a mere dozen miles north of Jerusalem, the place where Melchizedek had lived, king of righteousness, priest of the Most High God, blesser of Abraham. God wanted Jacob to go to Bethel and dwell there as He would have us take our journey to Calvary, pitch our tent there awhile, and have our faith renewed, our spiritual lives revitalized.

Then came the *preparation* (35:2-4). "Put away the strange gods that are among you, and be clean, and change your garments," Jacob said to his household. "We are going up to the house of God." Here and there along the way Jacob's wives and children had picked up idols. Rachel perhaps still had Laban's household Baals. Levi and Simeon no doubt had quite a haul of local images from the sack of Shechem. Those must be put away. "And they gave unto Jacob all the strange gods which were in their hand, and all their earrings which were in their ears; and Jacob hid them under the oak which was in Shechem." That is the first burial in the chapter. It would have been better if those images had been burned, not buried. We are ready enough to put our idols away, in times of spiritual awakening, but all too prone to put them where we can go back to them later if we wish.

2. Renewing Jacob's Spiritual Victory (35:5)

"And they journeyed: and the terror of God was upon the cities that were round about them, and they did not pursue after the sons of Jacob." The surrounding communities were evidently plotting vengeance for the Shechem massacre. Had that vengeance been aimed solely at Simeon and Levi, it would have been justified, but vengeance gets out of hand. Doubtless, once the killing began, the Canaanites would have made a clean sweep of every living soul in Jacob's camp. Thus the purpose of God to bring blessing to the world through Jacob would have been foiled. So God acted. A supernatural dread, not of Jacob but of God, fell upon the land. The world had to learn that, despite their many sins, sins that God Himself would deal with in His own perfect way, Jacob and his people were on the victory side, and that to fight them was to fight against God.

3. Renewing Jacob's Spiritual Verity (35:6-15)

God was going to bring Jacob back to basic truth. He must learn that the soul must not rest on miracles, even the kind of miracle that held the Canaanites in check, but on God's own Word. Thus *Jacob's relationship to God was confessed anew* (35:6-8). He built an altar and gave it a name—El-bethel, "The Mighty God of the house of God." It was a great step forward to get beyond God's house to God Himself. The floodtide of Jacob's feelings, when he arrived back at Bethel, carried him on, as God meant it to do, to a fresh confession of his love and care for God Himself.

Then came the first funeral. Dear old Deborah died, his mother Rebekah's nurse. Jacob, of course, had known her all his life. To her he had come as a toddler with his broken toys and bleeding knees. When he had arrived back in Canaan he had discovered his mother was dead. He also learned the whereabouts of his mother's handmaid and naturally took her under his wing. Perhaps she could mother his boys as she once had mothered him. Deborah must have been very old. Some one hundred fifty years had passed since she herself had left Padan-aram to accompany Rebekah when she had come to marry Isaac. It was a great comfort to Jacob to have her back and, no doubt, a great comfort to his wives as well, for she was a link with Padan-aram. How eagerly Deborah must have asked after Laban and old friends of years gone by. Then, too, she was a link with Rebekah, a link with home, a link with Jacob's past, with boyhood days, with life's early memories. But God was gently severing all those ties and separating Jacob to Himself, so Deborah died and was tenderly buried under a notable terebinth tree, a landmark in those parts, now to be called "The oak of weeping." It was the snapping of one more tie that bound Jacob to earthly things.

Then *Jacob's relationship to God was confirmed anew* (35:9-13). "And God appeared unto Jacob." That was something new. He had spoken to Jacob about his standing in the patriarchal line, He had quickened his senses in a dream. But now He appeared unto him. He spoke to Jacob about his personal name (35:9-10), about his promised fame (35:11), and about his perpetual claim (35:12-13). Poor, stumbling Jacob was still *Israel*. The Almighty God would see to it that nations and kings sprang from his seed, and the promised land was his despite all appearances to the contrary. Here were spiritual verities upon which Jacob could bank, verities unchanged by all that had happened since last he had come that way. They rested upon God's unbreakable Word, therefore they were unchanged.

Next *Jacob's relationship to God was claimed anew* (14:15). "And God went up from him in the place where he talked with him, and Jacob set up a pillar in the place where he talked with him, even a pillar of stone: and he poured a drink offering thereon, and he poured oil thereon. And Jacob called the name of the place where God spake with him, Bethel." At that very spot the ladder had reached from earth to heaven. Now, at that spot he saw God as He "went up," up the ladder as it were, back to heaven. His family and all the world must know the significance of that place. Hence the pillar and the ceremonial outpouring of the drink offering and the oil. The stone would speak to us of Christ; the drink offering (doubtless an offering of wine) of the outpoured blood that saves;[4] the oil of the outpoured Holy Spirit. Jacob, with his quickened understanding of spiritual verities, would dimly apprehend those things perhaps. Thus he staked afresh his claim to Canaan, not basing his claim on his personal merits nor on his pedigree as a child of Abraham, but on the finished work of Christ.

B. JACOB AS A BEREAVED MAN (35:16-29)

Jacob's renewed backsliding was immediate and was instantly punished. He moved away from Bethel; God had told him to go there and dwell. Backsliding could no longer be tolerated in his life, so his disobedience was quickly punished. Jacob was now a sanctified man, and the mistakes of his kindergarten years in the school of God could no longer be condoned. Two bereavements are now recorded. They seem to be separated in point of time, but they are placed in conjunction to enable us to see the cumulative effect they must have had on the maturing pilgrim. They were part of God's plan to loosen earthly ties and make this world a dreary place and the world to come more and more real.

When a man would ascend in a balloon he must throw out ballast. The higher he would go the more ballast he must cast away. That is what was happening to Jacob. The things that weighed him down, that bound him to earth, those things were being taken from him. In the same way God would wean us from the things of time and sense and draw us to Himself.

4. It was a noteworthy act. Here we have the first instance in Scripture of the drink offering, an offering not included among the later Levitical offerings but an offering included in instructions for the land (Numbers 15:5-7). It was Jacob's expressive way of laying hold of the now confirmed promise. The drink offering, as it was later used in Israel, was always poured out, never drunk. It symbolized Christ pouring Himself out for us on the cross.

1. JACOB BEREAVED OF HIS FAVORITE (35:16-26)

a. THE LOSS OF RACHEL (35:16-21)

First we see Jacob bereaved of his favorite, a record being given of the events that led up to the tragic event. After that, Jacob would have no more interest in the world; it would be effectively crucified to him in the death of his beloved. We notice *Jacob's strange mistake* (35:16*a*). "And they journeyed from Bethel. . . ." But *why?* Who can tell why we grow so quickly tired of the place where God has met us and where He has put His name? Abraham had moved away from Bethel because of a famine, perhaps Jacob moved away because of a funeral (35:8). Material considerations moved Abraham, emotional considerations perhaps moved Jacob. Neither reason is good enough. Abraham well nigh lost Sarah as a consequence of his backsliding; Jacob lost Rachel.

The tragic move seems to have had a direct bearing on what followed. Rachel was about to have her second child, and her condition was far advanced. For that reason alone Jacob should have stayed where he was. Travel was rough in those days. For Rachel to be jostled and jolted on the back of a camel was more than her waning strength could bear. They had almost come to Ephrath (the original name for Bethlehem) when the tragedy took place.

We are told of *Jacob's sudden misery* (35:16*b*-21). Benjamin was born and Rachel lived long enough to see him, to know that she had borne Jacob a second son, and to call his name Benoni. "Call him Benoni," she whispered with her dying breath. "Call him 'son of my sorrow.'" Poor Jacob! He could never deny Rachel anything upon which she set her heart. How could he deny her now? But he did. Tenderly but firmly he substituted a name of his own, "Benjamin!" "Call him 'son of my sorrow,'" wept Rachel. "I'll call him the son of my right hand!" said Jacob.

Thus Rachel died and was buried, and her tomb remains as a landmark to this day. Rachel died and Jacob's heart died with her, along with all its worldly ambitions. It was *Jacob* who buried Rachel. It was *Israel* who moved on. He had now become a pilgrim indeed, his feet like lead, his heart torn asunder, his hopes and affections now all fixed on things above, where Christ sits at the right hand of God.

b. THE LUST OF REUBEN (35:22-26)

But the writing hand moves on. Now it must record a shameful, despicable act. We have been told of the loss of Rachel; now we must be told of the lust of Reuben. How could Reuben, Jacob's oldest son, act in such a sordid way? What he did would have been crime enough at any time, but to do it at such a time marks him as a vile and lustful man indeed. Reuben, we are told, defiled Bilhah, his father's wife. Now Bilhah had been Rachel's maid, and Rachel had given her to Jacob. If there was one person in all the camp that dark day who could have brought a measure of comfort to Jacob surely it must have been Bilhah. But Reuben was so unprincipled, so lacking in common decency, humanity, and morality, that, the sinfulness of his act aside, he could commit incest with such a person at such a time. Who knows what flirting and philandering had gone on before?

We are only told that Reuben was so lost to decency and self-control, so utterly shameless, he could liven up the funeral hours by defiling one of his father's wives. It was a hideous act in itself. But when compounded, as it was, by the period when it was done and by the place where it was done and by the person to whom it was done, the act was unforgivable.

"And Israel heard it." *Israel,* not Jacob. If the Jacob nature had been in control, Reuben would have been a dead man. But it was the Israel nature that took the blow, and because Israel ruled the broken pilgrim's heart, nothing was said. Doubtless Reuben breathed a sigh of relief. But, from that moment on, an axe was poised over his head, unseen and unsuspected by him, ever hanging there awaiting the appropriate moment to fall. For God *always* punishes sexual immorality; sooner or later the axe always falls. Moral, social, spiritual, physical, and psychological whips are all available to God with which to chastise those who transgress.

At that point in the narrative the sons of Jacob were listed (35:23-26). The purpose is to draw special attention to Reuben's position in the family and to underline the consequent responsibility that he had so lightly despised. "The sons of Leah," the record runs, "Reuben, Jacob's firstborn—" He is the only one of the twelve to have a comment attached to his name. His position as the firstborn added still further to his sin. Nothing was said, however, about his wicked act. Reuben's indictment was to be read out later, when Jacob was on his deathbed, read out publicly, formally, fearfully. His unconfessed and uncleansed sin was to dog his future days.

2. JACOB BEREAVED OF HIS FATHER (35:27-29)

There was to be one more funeral when Jacob was *bereaved of his father* (35:27-29), although Isaac did not actually die at that point in history. Jacob had left Bethel and had left a lonely marker on the way that would lead to Bethlehem. His old nurse was dead, his beloved Rachel was dead, Dinah was nursing her heartache and shame, Levi and Simeon were still in the camp having brazened out their deeds, Reuben had acted worse than a pagan. So nursing his many hurts Jacob came at last to Isaac, his blind old father.

The death of Isaac is instantly recorded as though to emphasize that Jacob must find his consolation in God and God alone. He was "old and full of years" we are told; in actual fact he was 180 when he died. Jacob and Esau buried him. There is something attractive about that.

Here they were, twins by birth but torn asunder by disposition, desire, and destiny, united now for the last time to bury their aged dad.

Thus God cut the last tie that bound Jacob to earth. He had in very truth been set apart for God, a sanctified man. There were other sorrows in store, but those are part of the story of Joseph who, within one short chapter (devoted to Esau and his portion in life) would take over and dominate the last quarter of the book of Genesis.

Chapter 8

THE PROVIDER: JOSEPH

(36:1–47:26)

I. Joseph's Background (36:1-43)
  A. Esau's Personal History (36:1-8)
    1. His Immediate Family (36:1-5)
    2. His Immense Fortune (36:6-7)
    3. His Impregnable Fortress (36:8)
  B. Edom's Political History (36:9-43)
    1. Esau's Progeny in Edom (36:9-19)
    2. Esau's Predecessors in Edom (36:20-30)
    3. Esau's Preeminence in Edom (36:31-43)

II. Joseph's Boyhood (37:1-11)
  A. Joseph's Spiritual Drive (37:1-2)
    1. Tempted to Conform
    2. Tempted to Conceal
  B. Joseph's Splendid Dress (37:3-4)
    1. The Robe of Priesthood
    2. The Robe of Progenitorship
    3. The Robe of Priority
  C. Joseph's Spectacular Dreams (37:5-11)
    1. Sheaves: Control Over World Resources (37:5-8)
    2. Stars: Control Over World Rulers (37:9-11)

III. Joseph's Betrayal (37:12-36)
  A. How Joseph Was Sent to His Brethren (37:12-17)
    1. The Mission Discussed (37:12-14)
    2. The Mission Discharged (37:15-17)
  B. How Joseph Was Seen by His Brethren (37:18-27)
    1. The Conscious Wickedness of All (37:18-23)
    2. The Criminal Weakness of Reuben (37:21-22, 29-30)
    3. The Calculating Worldliness of Judah (37:25-27)
  C. How Joseph Was Sold by His Brethren (37:28-36)
    1. Their Fine Bargain in Cash (37:28)
    2. Their First Bite of Conscience (37:29-36)

IV. JOSEPH'S BROTHER (38:1-30)
   A. Judah and His Sons (38:1-10)
      1. His Wayward Behavior (38:1)
      2. His Worldly Bride (38:2-5)
      3. His Wicked Boys (38:6-10)
   B. Judah and His Sins (38:11-26)
      1. His Perverted Values (38:11-14)
      2. His Personal Vileness (38:15-23)
      3. His Pretended Virtue (38:24-26)
   C. Judah and His Seed (38:27-30)
      1. The Redeemed Child (38:28, 30)
      2. The Royal Child (38:29)

V. JOSEPH'S BONDAGE (39:1—40:23)
   A. The Slave Man: Completely Trusted by a Prosperous Master (39:1-6)
   B. The Successful Man: Continually Tempted by a Persistent Woman (39:7-20)
   C. The Slandered Man: Carefully Tested by a Patient God (39:21—40:23)
      1. Faith Demanded of Joseph (39:21-23)
      2. Love Displayed by Joseph (40:1-22)
      3. Hope Deferred for Joseph (40:23)

VI. JOSEPH'S BLESSING (41:1-44)
   A. The Providential Ways of God (41:1-8)
      1. The King's Dreams (41:1-7)
      2. The King's Distress (41:8)
   B. The Perfect Wisdom of God (41:9-13)
      1. His Perfect Timing (41:9)
      2. His Perfect Tactics (41:10-13)
   C. The Peerless Will of God (41:14-44)
      1. To Present Joseph to Pharaoh (41:14-37)
      2. To Promote Joseph Through Pharaoh (41:38-44)

VII. JOSEPH'S BRIDE (41:45-52)
   A. Her Favored Place (41:45-49)
      1. Highly Exalted (41:40, 45)
      2. Highly Extolled (41:45-49)
   B. Her Forgotten Past (41:45)
   C. Her Faithful Part (41:50-52)
      1. Manasseh: "Forgetting" (41:50-51)
      2. Ephraim: "Fruitful" (41:52)

VIII. JOSEPH'S BRETHREN (41:53–47:10)
- A. The Mystery Phase (41:53–44:34)
  1. How Joseph's Brethren Were Burdened (41:53–42:34)
  2. How Joseph's Brethren Were Bewildered (42:35–43:34)
  3. How Joseph's Brethren Were Broken (44:1-34)
- B. The Majesty Phase (45:1-24)
  1. The Revelation of Joseph (45:1-16)
  2. The Resources of Joseph (45:17-23)
  3. The Request of Joseph (45:24)
- C. The Ministry Phase (45:25–47:10)
  1. Proposition (45:25–46:7)
  2. Propagation (46:8-30)
  3. Preparation (46:31-34)
  4. Presentation (47:1-10)

IX. JOSEPH'S BOUNTY (47:11-26)
- A. Joseph's Grace (47:11-12)
  1. The Position He Gave His Brethren (47:11*a*)
  2. The Possession He Gave His Brethren (47:11*b*)
  3. The Portion He Gave His Brethren (47:12)
- B. Joseph's Government (47:13-22)
  1. Purses (47:13-14)
  2. Possessions (47:15-17)
  3. Property (47:18-20)
  4. Persons (47:21-22)
- C. Joseph's Goodness (47:23-26)
  1. The Principle Explained (47:23-25)
  2. The Principle Established (47:26)

8

THE PROVIDER: JOSEPH

I. Joseph's Background
(36:1-43)

"All Scripture," says Paul, "is given by inspiration of God and is profitable." A chapter such as the one before us might, at first glance, give us pause. But, because Esau is an important type of the flesh in Scripture, chapter 36 evidently contains spiritual truth for us. Just the same, it is one of the more difficult chapters of the Bible, the kind of chapter we normally skip over in our reading. Quite apart from the distaste modern westerners have for genealogies, the chapter has other problems, not the least of which is the fact that Esau's wives appear with names quite different from those by which they were introduced elsewhere in Genesis.

The chapter gives us the pedigree of the flesh, and a most unpromising pedigree it is. The names inserted here clear up the important collateral line of Esau for us before plunging into the wonderful story of Joseph. Edomite history continually bisected that of the Israelites. The struggle that began in Rebekah's womb continued down the centuries until it blossomed into full-scale war between the descendants of Jacob and Esau. So, while Genesis 36 may appear at first sight to be somewhat unpromising, it is not without its rewards for those who will venture thoughtfully down its somewhat thorny path.

A. Esau's Personal History (36:1-8)

Chapter 36 begins with *Esau's immediate family* (36:1-5). At once it confronts us with a tangle connected with the names of Esau's wives. Two things must be kept in mind—Esau's unsuccessful compromise and Esau's unceasing carnality. Esau's parents were godly people, and his marriage to pagan women distressed them greatly. His marriage to Aholibamah, particularly, must have been especially abhorrent to them, for not only was she one of "the daughters of Canaan," she had a Horite ancestry. The Horites had a strong Anakim strain, that is, they were of a race of giants that so polluted the promised land. Those giants resulted from a further eruption of fallen angels into human affairs with a consequent advance in occultism and the appearance on earth of a semidemonic progeny. A similar eruption before the Flood led directly to that catastrophe; the latter eruption led to the conquest of Canaan by the Israelites and explains the stringent command of God that the entire Canaanite race be eradicated.

The names of Esau's wives in Genesis 36 are their real, or original, names. When Esau first introduced the Canaanite women to his parents and broke the news to them that they were now his wives, Isaac and Rebekah were horrified. To think that such women as those should be introduced into a camp made sacred by the divine covenant! Even Isaac, weak and careless of spiritual things as he had become, and indulgent of Esau as he was, bestirred himself at last. The names of the pagan women, at least, must be changed. He could not have names like theirs bandied around his camp. He could not hope to change the natures of the women, for that matter he had never been able to change Esau's, but, at least, their flagrant, pagan names must be changed.

There was Adah. She is called "the daughter of Elon the Hittite" (36:2). The name Adah was utterly repugnant to Isaac for another reason. The family records, handed down from Noah, preserved the memory of Adah, the wife of Lamech the great arch-rebel before the Flood. Isaac was not going to have *that* name mouthed constantly in his ears. The woman's Hittite origin, in itself, was offensive enough, for Isaac had not forgotten the care Abraham had taken to make sure no such lineage polluted the genealogy of the chosen race. Faced with his father's unexpected opposition, Esau, ever easygoing, settled for a compromise; he called her Bashemath instead. There! That was a nicer name, a name already associated with his father's half-brother Ishmael. Did not Uncle Ishmael have a daughter named Bashemath? Probably Esau already knew that cousin of his. So Adah became Bashemath—that should silence his father's strange scruples.

But the constant use of the name Bashemath kept bringing to Esau's mind visions of his delightful cousin. So off he went and married her as well. But now he had two wives by the name of Bashemath. Although it was a pleasant enough name and apparently acceptable to his father, polygamy was complicated enough without having two wives with the same name. It would be too much to ask the long-suffering Adah to change her name again, so Esau resorted to the obvious solution. He would have his cousin Bashemath change her name to Mahalath (Genesis 28:9). After all, what's in a name? A rose by any other name would smell as sweet.

That brings us to that remarkable young woman Aholibamah. She seems to have been Esau's favorite wife despite her somewhat colorful past. Her name means "tent of the High Place" from which we infer she could have been a temple priestess, in other words, a temple prostitute, for Canaanite worship was climaxed in ritual fornication with the professionals who served the temples and the groves. It is likely Esau met the woman in her official capacity when participating himself in the filthy rites of her religion. No wonder Esau's parents were outraged when he brought that girl home and introduced her as his wife. Always willing to oblige, Esau changed Aholibamah's name as well. What about Judith? There, that was a good, respectable name with a fine, Hebrew ring to it.

So, as long as he remained in the vicinity of his father's covenanted camp, Esau made shift with those new names for his wives, but as soon as he moved away he dropped them at once. He typifies the young person today, brought up in a Christian home, hardened to the gospel, yet, for the sake of peace, willing enough to mouth the proper phrases when around his parents, but only too glad to shed all such pretense when he finally moves away from home. Esau's heart never warmed to spiritual truth, and his intellect was never enlightened to what it was all about.

Aholibamah's parentage is important, too, in understanding Esau's moves. Her service as a temple "priestess" was no disgrace in Canaanite eyes. On the contrary it was probably looked upon, in the warped Canaanite view, as adding distinction to her father's house. Had he not devoted one of his daughters to the gods? Her father was Anah, an outstanding man among the Horite chieftains. He had attained fame and rank by achievement rather than through inheritance. His wife's connections gave Esau entrance into the Horite community and helped him to ultimately gain complete ascendancy over all the clans.

Aholibamah was Esau's favorite wife. The fact that she had been a temple girl suggests she was a very attractive and seductive young woman, just the kind who would appeal to a carnal, lustful man like Esau. Adah and Bashemath each had only one son; Aholibamah had three, which suggests she was Esau's chief wife and the one with whom he spent the most time. Probably Esau found her more attractive than the other two. When it came to grandsons, however, the other two wives completely outshone the favorite, who, so far as the record goes, had none at all. She made up for that deficiency in other ways, as we shall see.

So much, then, for Esau's immediate family. The wives of Esau are kept prominently before us throughout the chapter, but it was the Horite wife who predominated. The Edomite race thus contained three elements, one Canaanite, one Horite, and one Ishmaelite. No wonder as a race the Edomites settled down to a granite-hard hostility toward Israel.

Next we are told of *Esau's immense fortune* (36:6-7). By that time it had probably dawned even on Esau's spiritually sluggish mind that all the land of Canaan had been irrevocably deeded over by God to Jacob. Jacob's return to the promised land and his evident intention of remaining there dispelled whatever lingering illusions Esau might have had of obtaining the promise by default. Because he and his twin brother both had enormous holdings in livestock, because the available pastureland was obviously unable to support them both, because he saw no future for himself in Canaan, because he was at spiritual odds with Jacob anyway, and because he had a roaming spirit and was an incurable opportunist, Esau decided to move out. He would make a name for himself in the world somewhere else. He could get along fine without either Jacob or Jacob's God. In any case, Aholibamah had been whispering in his ear of late that there were good pickings for a bold man in her homeland of Seir. She herself, she told him, held rank down there and, besides, her father was one of the more eminent Horite dukes. Esau could be assured of a welcome in Seir. So, like Lot before him, Esau moved away from the place of fellowship with the people of God persuaded he could find more congenial company in the world.

Thus it was that Esau packed his bag, struck his camp, said a final farewell to Isaac and Jacob, and headed for the home of the Horites. It is strange that all of Esau's sons were born in Canaan, but turned their backs upon it, whereas all of Jacob's sons but one were born out of the land of promise but found their place in it at last. Esau's decision was typical of the flesh, which always finds the world a more congenial place than the meeting place of the people of God.

Then we are told of *Esau's impregnable fortress* (36:8). "Thus Esau dwelt in mount Seir; Esau is Edom." Genesis 36 is a tantalizing fragment of history. How and when did Esau finally wrest the impregnable fortress of Petra from the Horites? Control of Petra and its environs guaranteed a stranglehold on the great east-west trade routes, and its rocky fastnesses guaranteed virtual invulnerability. He who held Petra could defy brigands and invaders alike and impose whatever toll he wished on passing caravans. Moses tells us that Esau "destroyed" the Horites (Deuteronomy 2:12). He also tells us that like the Zamzummim and the Anakim, the Horim were a race of giants (Deuteronomy 2:20-22). It was doubtless through Aholibamah that Esau first gained acceptance and then a measure of ascendancy over the Horites. But what happened after that? The sons of Anak never were a match for those who had contact, however cursory, with the living God. In the mysterious providence of God, unbeknown to him, Esau brought the shadow of the Almighty with him into the Petra defile.

B. EDOM'S POLITICAL HISTORY (36:9-43)

The narrative that now opens before us is patchy and sparse. It is inclined to be repetitious and wholly lacking in matters of gripping interest such as arrest us constantly in the stories of the patriarchs. The chapter is set down in Genesis in deliberate contrast with the history of the patriarchal family. Whole chapters are devoted to Abraham, Isaac, and Jacob. A quarter of the book of Genesis is devoted to Joseph, who was not even in the Messianic line. Esau had a seemingly small role in the divine purpose; therefore his history and the history of the Edomites is of but sparse interest. On the other hand, God does record all those names for, dull as they may seem to us, each one represents a living, breathing, human being over whom the Spirit of God yearned as much as over any privileged child of the chosen race. God loves all men regardless of their disregard of Him.

1. ESAU'S PROGENY IN EDOM (36:9-19)

Space is given first to Esau's grandchildren through Eliphaz, the one son of Adah. The names of those grandchildren are written down twice, first as descendants (36:11-12) and then as dukes (36:15-16). Esau seems to have been very proud of those budding dukes of his. Eliphaz himself was not a duke, but all his sons attained that rank. Moreover he had a concubine who was a duke—not a duchess, the wife of a duke, but a duke (36:40). There is a hint here of a matriarchal society among the Horites. That woman duke, Timna by name, the concubine of Eliphaz, became the mother of another duke—*Amalek* (36:12, 16). From him came the Amalekites, the inveterate enemies of Israel against whom God Himself declared unending war. It was for befriending their king that Saul lost his throne. Amalek is the outstanding type of the flesh in the Old Testament.

Little of note is recorded about Esau's grandchildren through Reu, the son of Bashemath. There were only four of them (36:13), and, thanks no doubt to Esau's growing influence, each of the four attained royal rank (36:17) for each became a duke. In the context of that day and age, each became a tribal head or a sheikh, the equivalent of royalty today.

Astonishingly enough, no record is given of any grandchildren born to Esau through the sons of his favorite Aholibamah. But to make up for that each of that woman's *sons* attained the ducal rank denied the sons of Adah and Bashemath (36:18). Probably they attained that rank by virtue of their mother's ducal title. It is worth noting too that whereas the descendants of the other two wives are grouped together (36:10), the sons of Aholibamah are given in a separate list (36:18). It is another of the clues in the chapter to the special place that woman held over Esau's affections and his fortunes.

2. ESAU'S PREDECESSORS IN EDOM (36:20-30)

The Horites were the original inhabitants of the land that Esau was now about to make his own (Genesis 14:6). Their pedigree is traced back to Seir the Horite. The name Horite is derived from *hor* signifying "a hole" or "a cave"—an obvious reference to the caves and holes hollowed in the sandstone cliffs by those rockdwellers. The elaborate carvings and tunnels of Petra remain an object of wonder to tourists even today.

Seir's descendants, listed here, numbered seven sons and one daughter; the seven became nineteen in the next generation. Esau's descendants intermarried with those people. The list, for instance, gives the origin of Timna, who became the concubine of Eliphaz and the mother of Amalek. It also pays special attention to the lineage of Aholibamah, Esau's favorite wife (36:24-25). The list reveals too how quickly Esau's descendants became utterly pagan. The original Edomite ancestry, mixed and almost wholly heathen as it was, soon became diluted to the point of extinction. How quickly those who leave the fellowship of God's people pride themselves in their new worldly connections! Esau was no "stranger and sojourner" amongst the Horites. He settled right in and soon took over their spheres of interest entirely.

To the various names listed of those pre-Edomite settlers in Seir one interesting note is appended, and again it has to do with Aholibamah (36:24-25). It tells how her father leaped to fame. He is the only one of the Horites of whom we know anything beyond the mere listing of his name. He is said to have discovered some "mules" in the wilderness. That hardly seems a claim for fame. The Revised Version gives the rendering "hot springs," which certainly seems better. His discovery seems to have created a stir among his contemporaries and, indeed, throughout the country. Anah, Aholibamah's father, seems to have been so impressed himself by his discovery that he actually changed his name to Beeri (meaning "my well"), by which name he was known in Genesis 26:34. In other words, he boasted about his discovery for the rest of his life.

We should note too that not only in Aholibamah's father the only one who assumed anything like prominence, but the whole list given in verses 20-28 is at once repeated in verses 29-30, where the principal heads are now listed as dukes. Esau keeps on repeating and emphasizing his wife's social position. It did not disturb him that she was an utter pagan. It did impress him that she was of royal blood. It seems to have gone to his head.

3. ESAU'S PREEMINENCE IN EDOM (36:31-43)

First we are given a list of "the kings that reigned in the land of Edom, before there reigned any king over the children of Israel" (36:31). Those "kings" presumably were men of outstanding ability or power who had been able to combine several lesser clans under their rule. Esau's descendants seem to have taken the lead in that. Eight names are given; little is told about any of them, although two appear to have distinguished themselves. One gained a notable victory over the Midianites and another carried his victories as far as "the river" (36:37). Whether that is a reference to the Nile or to the Euphrates is not certain.

Finally we are given another list of Edom's dukes (36:40-42). It is from that final list that we learn that Timna, the mother of Amalek, and Aholibamah, Esau's favorite wife, were both dukes.

She must have been an impressive woman, that Aholibamah. Sprung from an illustrious father, she made quite a name for herself. She served as a temple priestess, met and married Esau, and ruled him as well as any woman could rule a man as wild and wayward as he. Through her influence he cast off, finally and forever, all family ties, to throw in his lot with her people. Through her he was introduced into high society in which, thereafter, he moved and advanced. Through her his sons and grandsons achieved positions of power in Seir and, through her, there can be little doubt, that remarkable list of Edomite notables came into being.

Such was the history of Esau. Before leaving the man to work out his sad destiny, we should take one final look around the chapter in which his history is found. For here, after all, are some sad but pertinent spiritual lessons that make the chapter relevant for us even today. Here we have the pedigree of the flesh.

We learn, for example, that the flesh is *very prolific*. How many names intrude themselves upon our notice as we run our eye down the chapter. The flesh belongs to a very large family. Self manifests itself in scores of ways.

The flesh is *very pious*—when it serves its turn, that is. Esau was quite willing to change the names of his wives to accommodate the narrow requirements of the patriarchal faith. After all, Abram's name was changed, Jacob's name was changed, why not the names of his wives? That the change of a name marks the change of a nature meant nothing to Esau, so long as outward appearances were preserved.

The flesh is *very prosperous* (36:6). In the Old Testament, prosperity was a mark of divine favor. The flesh can imitate that.

The flesh is *very persuasive*. The reference to Eliphaz and to Teman brings to mind Eliphaz the Temanite who, doubtless, was descended from the Edomite strain. He could argue religion by the hour, and had poor old Job up in arms more than once and hard put to defend his faith.

The flesh is *very pernicious* (36:13), thus Amalek, the treacherous and inveterate foe of Israel, springs from the same brood. After Israel had sheltered behind the blood, taken up a position of separation, and drunk the water from the riven rock—"then came Amalek." It took Joshua in the valley, sword in hand, and Moses, Aaron, and Hur on the mountain engaged in intercession to defeat that deadly foe.

The flesh is *very powerful*. Edom had his stronghold at Seir, the most impregnable fortress of the ancient world.

The flesh is *very persistent*. "In his stead" rings like a refrain throughout one section of chapter 36. Get rid of one aspect of the flesh and another is instantly ready to take its place.

Finally, the flesh is *very proud* (36:31). It will boast that it had its kings long before Israel.

What a pedigree! With relief we turn from Esau and all his tribe to Joseph, who dominates Genesis from here to the end.

II. JOSEPH'S BOYHOOD (37:1-11)

One quarter of Genesis is devoted to Joseph. God dismisses the creation of the universe in five words—"He made the stars also"; but He devotes chapter after chapter to the story of a man who was not even in the Messianic line.

We must remember that *Moses* wrote Genesis. The other books of the Pentateuch, Moses wrote out of his experience, but not Genesis. Genesis he learned at his mother's knee, for Genesis contained the oral traditions of his people, whispered from generation to generation in those slave camps on the Nile. But why twenty-five percent of Genesis for the story of Joseph? Why not more space, for example, to the development of the Cainite civilization dismissed in a chapter or two; or why not more space to the colonization of the earth by the scattered tribes marching outward from Babel, each with a confounded tongue?

We picture Jochebed with Moses on her knee, his wondering eyes fixed on her face, his bright, young mind open to her words. What should she teach him? She would have him for such a short time. Soon, all too soon, a demand would come from the palace and Moses would be torn from her and put to school in the courts of Pharaoh. She could imagine what he would learn there. But she had him for that little while, so she taught him the truths that form the sum and substance of Genesis. And, in view of the fact that soon the courts of Pharaoh must swallow him up forever, she devoted a disproportionate amount of space to the story of Joseph. For in those selfsame courts a Hebrew boy named Joseph had been subjected to the identical pressures and temptations that soon would face her son. With true spiritual insight, godly Jochebed drilled Moses in the story of Joseph. When Moses came to write Genesis, the Spirit of God endorsed Jochebed's view and led Moses to write with the same emphasis.

Of all the people who come and go on the busy, crowded pages of the Word of God, where can we find a life that more beautifully portrays the life of Jesus than the life of Joseph? Touch the life of Joseph at any point, and instantly this or that aspect of the person or work of Christ will be revealed. It was that characteristic that gave Joseph the right to occupy such a prominent position in Genesis. The great goal of the Holy Spirit in the life of any person is to make him like Christ, and when he does at last exhibit the beauties of the Lord Jesus, he becomes a trophy of grace worthy of deathless display.

A. JOSEPH'S SPIRITUAL DRIVE (37:1-2)

Joseph must have been one of the loneliest boys in history. The family into which he was born was a family in almost total disarray. With Jacob's favoritism for Rachel, and Leah's frustrations and disappointments, with the other two wives nagged in their souls by their inferior status in the family, with grandfather Laban's tricks and wiles, with Uncle Esau's mercurial temperament and just resentments, and with the motley crowd of older brothers he had, Joseph must often have felt that he was more *ambushed* than born.

He lost his mother in his middle teens, he was regarded by his brothers as father's pet and accordingly cordially detested, he was looked upon as a "goody-goody" and "Mama's little darling." Joseph, as a boy, was as much maligned by his brothers as he has been since by his commentators.

The boyhood of Joseph divides into three parts, one having to do with his spiritual drive, one with his splendid dress, and one with his special dreams. It seems an odd assortment of things to bring together. Suppose the only information Americans had of George Washington were the story of the cherry tree, a passing reference to his campaign vest, and a dream or two he might have had about leading the colonies to statehood—that would be about the equivalent of what we have of Joseph here.

Had we been entrusted with writing the story of Joseph, we would have described the town where he was born, given examples of his precocious ways as a youngster and his prowess at school, described his sweet disposition and his blossoming personality. We would have discussed his early bent toward management, we would have illustrated his relationship to his parents and brethren and found instances of his growing interest in spiritual things. The Holy Spirit passes over such material of which biographies are made and focuses on three incidents.

There was Joseph's spiritual drive, illustrated by two incidents of surpassing interest. Joseph's father was a shepherd with vast herds and flocks. One by one, as soon as they were old enough, his sons were packed off to learn the tricks of the trade. The four sons of the slave women formed a natural team. It would not have been desirable in those rough-and-ready days for a shepherd to work alone on those hills. There were not only wild animals and bandits on the prowl, but unscrupulous sheikhs as well. So Dan and Naphtali, Gad and Asher were banded together as a team.

When the time came, Joseph too was sent off to learn Jacob's business secrets. Favorite he might be, but if he was ever to have the preeminence his father secretly planned for him, then he must know the family business through and through. He must know how to tend sheep, how to breed them for the best results, how to lead them from pasture to pasture, how to locate the watering holes, how to ward off predators, how to tend the lame, the sick, the weak. So Jacob weighed the characteristics of his various sons and sent Joseph off with that particular band.

Almost at once Joseph faced the first temptation of a boy away from home. It is against the background of that temptation that Joseph's spiritual integrity is first seen. He was *tempted to conform.*

"Be not conformed to this world," says Paul (Romans 12:2) or, as Phillips renders it, "Don't let the world around you squeeze you into its own mold." The world maintains a constant pressure upon us, and we feel it first when we start a new job or make new friends. Joseph was about seventeen years old and he was away from home. For the first time in his life, he was about to have a rival in his mother's affections, for within the year, Benjamin would be born. He desperately needed to belong, so the pressure was on to conform.

When Augustine was about Joseph's age, his father sent him to Carthage to further his education. He was to stay in the home of a wealthy magnate by the name of Romanianus. In A.D. 369 Augustine found himself in one of the most glamorous cities of the world. He arrived a month before his studies were to begin so he could acclimatize himself to his new surroundings.

In the house of Romanianus he met Marcus, the magnate's pampered nephew. Marcus offered to initiate Augustine into the brawling life of the vice capital of the world, and Augustine, willing to conform, agreed. After a magnificent dinner the two sallied forth for an evening's revelry. First they went to Harbor Square where, like the Greeks of old, the idlers spent their time hearing and telling anything novel or new. Then, off to a booth for a round or two of wine, and that despite young Augustine's inbred distaste for alcohol. Next came a look at a lusty, brawling parade. Then past the Baths of Maximinianus with a promise to come back later and enjoy its delights and on past the lewd temple of Tanit with its obscenities and provocative dancing girls in full view. Then to a house of ill repute. There Augustine drew back. "We're not going in there?" he cried.

"Where else?" demanded his new friend.

"Have you been here before?"

"Been here! I come here all the time."

"Oh!" said Augustine.

"Come on," cried Marcus. "What are we waiting for?"

So, like a lamb led to the slaughter, Augustine ventured inside. Once inside he thought of his father who cared not a scrap for God's laws. He had a fleeting vision of his saintly mother, her beautiful face, her anguished tears. Then, prodded by the sneers of Marcus, he abandoned himself to sin.

Joseph, alone with his brothers, away from home, jostled and elbowed and shoved, the butt of their jokes and under constant pressure to conform, refused to do what Augustine did. Genesis drops sufficient hints about Jacob's sons for us to recognize their characters. Their names, the things actually recorded about them, the kinds of things Jacob said about them, all provide us with hints. Careful reconstruction shows us what Joseph was up against with those older brothers of his, each of whom resented him, for they were sons of slave women and he was the son of the favorite wife. Their dislike of Joseph could be vented to the full now, for they had him away from Jacob's watchful eye.

There was clever Dan, for example; Dan with his incisive, lawyer's mind, his sarcastic skill at summing up a situation, his ability to cut a person down to size, and his skill at asking questions that skewered the very soul. Dan had a clever way of passing judgment on others. He could make a fellow feel as small as a grain of sand. He would bore in with his incessant questions, his cutting jibes, his clever twisting of facts. Poor young Joseph was with Dan.

Then there was Naphtali, flighty, wild, carefree, "a hind let loose." There was always something graceful and fawnlike about him. He was hard to hold, hard to restrain. He had a passion for the wild and the untamed, a hatred of restriction, a scorn of law and order. He had to "do his own thing." With his wild ways he could make Joseph feel like a prude. If there was anything Naphtali could not stand, it was the kind of boy who was a namby-pamby, Daddy's pet. Joseph was with Naphtali.

There was Gad. His name means "troop." Perhaps there was something about Gad that savored of the gang. He was the bully type, perhaps, the kind who would pick a fight when it was safe, when numbers were on his side. "Here kid, drink this or me and the boys'll punch the tar out of yer." Was that Gad? Joseph was with Gad, and Gad was with the boys.

And what about Asher? As we would put it today, Asher liked to live "high off the hog," or, as the idiom of his day put it, he liked to "dip his foot in oil." What Asher wanted was life's luxuries, the extravagant things, life's riches and pleasures. He wanted to "live it up," indulge himself. He would have scant sympathy with Joseph's austerity, scruples, and conscience. "Eat, drink, and be merry," would be Asher's philosophy. Joseph was with Asher.

So we read, "Joseph, being seventeen years old, was . . . with his brethren; and the lad was with the sons of Bilhah, and with the sons of Zilpah, his father's wives." He was with Dan the cunning, with Naphtali the carefree, with Gad the coward, and with Asher the connoisseur. He was there with them, alone and unwanted in the far country away from help and home.

Anyone who has been in a similar situation can sympathize with Joseph's predicament. Violence was always a possibility, but apart from that his life would be made a living hell unless he lowered himself to their standards, conformed to their practices, and made himself an accomplice in their misdeeds.

Next came the *temptation to conceal.* It is at that point many commentators do Joseph a grave injustice. They picture him as a tattletale, running home to Daddy to tell stories about his brothers, a sneaky family spy. He was nothing of the kind. There is nothing in the text to warrant such an interpretation and, from all we know of Joseph's character, such meanness and littleness was foreign to him. Most likely he was instructed by his father to report on his sons' behavior, for Jacob felt very strongly his insecurity in Canaan, an insecurity aggravated by the behavior of his boys. It was part of Joseph's stewardship, as his father's agent, to report on the wild doings of those boys. Their behavior imperiled the whole clan. Certainly Joseph must have been under considerable pressure to conceal.

Mark Twain captures the situation. Tom Sawyer and Huckleberry Finn were accidental witnesses to the murder of young Dr. Robinson by the half-breed, Injun Joe. They saw the whole thing, and how the Indian planted the murder weapon on his unconscious partner, Muff Potter. When the coast was clear the two frightened boys ran for their lives and then held a hasty council of war. "Huckleberry, what do you reckon'll come of this?"

"I reckon hanging'll come of it."

Tom thought for awhile, then said, "Who'll tell? We?"

Huckleberry was alarmed at the very thought. "What are you talking about? S'pose something happened and Injun Joe didn't hang? Why he'd kill us sometime or other, just as dead sure as we're alaying here."

So Tom and Huckleberry made a solemn pact. Tom said, "Huck, you sure you can keep mum?"

"Tom, we got to keep mum. You know that. Now look-a-here Tom, less take and swear to one another, that's what we got to do, swear and keep mum."

Joseph was made of sterner stuff. The Bible says there is "a time to keep silence and a time to speak." So far as Joseph was concerned it was a time to speak. For him to tell Jacob what he had seen was an act of high courage. "See here, kid," the four of them might well have said, "you go preaching to the old man about what you've seen and we'll get ya some dark night. You keep yer mouth shut, understand?" It is often much easier to hold one's tongue than to stand up as a witness to a wrong we have seen.

The first glimpse we get of Joseph, then, reveals his spiritual drive. We see a teenage lad who not only had some well-grounded convictions concerning integrity and morality and practical godliness, but also a young man with the courage of his convictions.

B. JOSEPH'S SPLENDID DRESS (37:3-4)

"Now Israel loved Joseph more than all his children, because he was the son of his old age: and he made him a coat of many colours." Of all the things the Holy Spirit could have recorded about Joseph, he records that. The coat was a special coat, the coat worn by an eastern chieftain, the kind of coat given to the son destined to be the father's heir. It marked Joseph out as the one to whom Jacob intended to bequeath rulership of the clan and the lion's share of his property. It set him apart from his brothers and put him on a plane of equality with his father.

The other brothers eyed that coat with undisguised jealousy. Reuben, the firstborn, eyed it and read his own second-rate future in it. Judah eyed it, cruel Simeon eyed it, and so did his buddy Levi. The four sons of the slave wives eyed it, and the sight of it added fresh venom to their hatred. Joseph drew that robe around his youthful shoulders and wore it frankly and easily as his by right. After all, was he not his father's firstborn son? Was he not the firstborn of Rachel, the true bride of Jacob's heart? The robe was his and his by right, no matter what the jealous brothers might think. And so it was. It was his by virtue of his unique relationship to the father and by virtue of his blameless life, a life that threw into black relief the chronic misbehavior of his brothers. The robe of position, priesthood, and privilege was his.

Three things were wrapped up in the robe that Jacob presented to Joseph that day. As Joseph unwrapped the gift and saw it lying there before him he saw, at once, all that it implied. His jealous brothers saw it too.

That robe spoke of *priesthood*. The family priesthood should have gone to Reuben, but Reuben's basic instability was well known to Jacob. So, for the time being, the custodianship of the priesthood was given to Joseph. That robe spoke of *progenitorship*. That, too, should have gone to Reuben—the right to be the one from whose descendants the promised Seed would come. Within the year Reuben would forever disgrace himself in a night's lustful passion. Again, for the time being at any rate, only Joseph qualified to be Jacob's heir in the matter of progenitorship. That robe spoke of *priority*. It was the custom for the oldest son to receive a double portion of the father's estate, that is, he received twice as much as any of the other sons. The double portion was to go to Joseph; the robe proclaimed it and history assured it.

The splendid dress given to Joseph, then, spoke volumes of the special place Joseph held in his father's heart and of Jacob's determination to see his beloved son lifted high. Old Jacob acted with eternity's values in view, for his act was typical in significance and scope. Beyond the story of Jacob and Joseph we catch a glimpse of God delighting in that unique and beloved Son of His, His firstborn. Beyond Jacob and Joseph we see the Father in communion with His Son, finding all His delight in Him, determining that even though, by virtue of His coming into the world, He would have kinsmen according to the flesh, yet He would be distinct from them all and lifted up on high, above and beyond them all. The priesthood, the property, and the power were to be His. Thus Jacob acted in such a way that, through him, God could display in some measure His own great, eternal thoughts. We would pray He could do the same through us.

C. JOSEPH'S SPECTACULAR DREAMS (37:5-11)

We know Joseph's dreams by heart. He dreamed twice. The first time he saw the harvest field and the sheaves standing in orderly rows. There stood his sheaf and there the sheaves of his brethren. But what was that? Their sheaves bowed down to his! He dreamed again and saw the sun, the moon, and eleven stars bow down to him. He told his dreams to his family as, indeed, he was duty bound to do, for those dreams were not for him alone. So obvious was the meaning of those dreams that they needed no interpreter. His brethren were enraged at the bare recital of them, just as later the Jews were enraged at Christ for telling them the truth about Himself.

There was the dream of *the sheaves*, a dream of position and power, but of position and power relating to earth. The harvest field was a symbol of the world's resources, its bounty, prodigality, and wealth. The sons of Jacob were seen reaping the riches of the world, but Joseph outdid them all. In the end, his brethren would be forced to acknowledge him. It was a dream of the control that Joseph was to have over *the resources* of the world. The dream was fulfilled in Joseph's ultimate control over the resources of Egypt.

Then there was the dream of *the stars*. It likewise was a dream of position and power. From Genesis 1 we learn that the sun and the moon are symbols of rule—they symbolize those set on high to control the destinies of men. In a coming day Joseph was to be given command over *the rulers* of the world. That was literally fulfilled in the high position of authority Joseph attained in Egypt, an authority so great that even the pharaoh bowed to his will.

Those dreams did not exhaust themselves in the personal history of Joseph. They go beyond Joseph to Christ. And has not God given His Son a position of absolute supremacy over this planet? In a coming day Jesus will be exalted and every knee will bow to him "of things in heaven and things on earth and things under the earth." Then all the *resources* and all the *rulers* of the planet will be His to command. Israel, too, will own Jesus as Lord, just as Joseph's brethren finally owned their hated brother.

So Joseph told his brethren of his dreams. He had tasted their jealousy and spite already, but they had to know the truth of God, even if that truth spurred them on to violence. After Joseph told of his dreams, his brethren could no longer speak peaceably to him. Soon they seized their opportunity to rid themselves of him finally and forever, but they reckoned without God just as do people who imagine they can rid themselves of God's Son.

III. JOSEPH'S BETRAYAL (37:12-36)

Typology has fallen on hard times. There is a school of thought that grudgingly states that only those people and places, events and objects specifically named in the New Testament as types can be legitimately regarded as types. There is another school of thought that sees typology here, there, and everywhere in the Old Testament. Exponents of that belief sometimes exhibit as types things that simply are not so. Both extremes are wrong. Sound exegesis will forbid the importing into an Old Testament incident of wild and fanciful ideas in the name of typology, but it will not forbid, surely, our pointing out obvious parallels between Old Testament happenings and New Testament truth.

Types are a species of prophecy. The church, for example, was not *revealed* in the Old Testament but it is most certainly *concealed* in the Old Testament—in types. With the New Testament in our hands we can see it concealed in a score of places. We can see it in some of the Old Testament brides, in various aspects of Levitical ritual and in some parts of the tabernacle. We should not be surprised that Joseph is a type of Christ, even though it is not specifiically stated in the New Testament that he is. Parallels between Joseph and Jesus are going to constantly surface in our study.

A. HOW JOSEPH WAS SENT TO HIS BRETHREN (37:12-17)

On the human and historical level, we have described here the natural concern of an anxious parent for his wayward sons. They had been away for some time, and no word had reached Jacob about them. The concerned father, knowing something of the dangers that could befall his boys, and aware of their lawless tendencies, decided something had to be done. Somebody had to be sent to find them, and who better than Joseph? So the *mission was discussed* (37:12-14). "And Israel said unto Joseph, Do not thy brethren feed the flock in Shechem? Come and I will send thee unto them. And he said to him, Here am I. And he said to him, Go, I pray thee, see whether it be well with thy brethren . . . and bring me word again. So he sent him out of the vale of Hebron."

Joseph was about eighteen years old. Probably he would have preferred to stay at home at Hebron—the word means "fellowship"; it suggests Joseph's fellowship and communion with his father. The delights of home were at Hebron, but there was no hesitation, no word about difficulties, about distance, about dangers. His father knew about those things as well as he. His father was willing to make the sacrifice and Joseph was willing to do those things that pleased his father. His immediate response was, "Here am I." One can almost hear old Jacob saying to himself as his beloved Joseph responded so freely, *Surely they will reverence my son.*

The scene takes us back into eternity past and to the heavenly Hebron, the eternal city of God. There the Father and the Son had enjoyed communion as the eternal ages rolled. They had shared together the creation of a planet named Earth, the creation of man, made in the image and likeness of God, the entrance of sin into the world and death by sin, the expulsion of the race from paradise, and the consequent redemption of man. As old Jacob knew the dangers that lay ahead for his son, so Father and Son foresaw all the perils of a way that led via Bethlehem to Golgotha's tree. "Come," said the Father, "I will send thee."

"Here am I," was the instant reply.

The *mission was discharged* (37:15-17). It was a long way from Hebron to Shechem in those days. Hebron was in the south, Shechem sixty miles away in the hill country of central Canaan. Dothan was further yet, twelve miles north of Samaria toward the Plain of Esdraelon on the caravan route running from the north down to Egypt. Dothan was a small, oblong plain containing some of the best pasturage in the country. All that long way Joseph went seeking those who were wandering from home. The boys had not lingered at Shechem; it was a place of evil memories. There Simeon and Levi had massacred the Shechemites. The surrounding sheikhs would like well enough to rid themselves of that troublesome brood.

On Joseph went, guided by the counsel of an unnamed man, bearing the burden and heat of the day, the chill and cold of night. Wild beasts and brigands lurked in the path and ahead were his brethren. Joseph knew what kind of reception he could expect from them. But he was doing his father's will, ever his joy and delight, so on he went.

Hebron! Shechem! Dothan! The place names tell of a people wandering from home, and of moral and spiritual blindness besides. *Hebron* means "fellowship," but those boys had long ago left that place. Hebron suggests the loss of the *spiritual* side of things. What cared those boys for their father's will? for his fellowship and love? They were rebellious and self-willed, wanting their own way, heedless of his care for them and filled with bitterness toward his beloved son. Man's first loss was spiritual, and consequently he is out of fellowship with God, separated from Him by sin and wicked works, and maintained in that estrangement by hostility toward Christ.

Shechem means "strength." The boys had left the place of strength as well. Shechem was the place where Dinah their sister had lost her moral innocence and Simeon and Levi their moral integrity. An ill-omened place was Shechem, the place where human passions were displayed in sordid ugliness. Now they had left Shechem altogether. Man's second great loss was *moral.* Adam brought out of Eden with him a moral sense, a knowledge of good and evil, but he brought no strength to do the right or to shun the wrong. Man left the place of moral strength as soon as he arrived at it. God says, "There is none that doeth good, no not one" (Romans 3:12). He also says, "When we were yet without strength . . . Christ died for us" (Romans 5:6-8). One might as well tell a dead man to write an opera as tell a sinner to produce a life morally acceptable to God.

Dothan means "The Two Wells," and there the boys had settled down to enjoy the material comforts of the neighborhood. Perhaps one of the wells had already run dry, for a dry well later served as a convenient prison for Joseph. Dothan was the place that emphasized the *physical* side of life. They were far from home. Drifting from one place to another they had settled down to enjoy what creature comforts they could.

And there Joseph found them. His mission was discharged, he had come where they were and brought them tidings from home, good news indeed—the father loved them and longed for their return. He was at once rejected, sold for the price of a slave, handed over to the Gentiles, and his disappearance glossed over with a lie.

All of that speaks of Christ. Out of the ivory palaces He came, into a world of woe, to tread the path of obedience. He was guided by the Holy Spirit, for who else could direct the Son of God? The Spirit came upon Him at His anointing, the Spirit of wisdom and understanding, counsel, might, and knowledge. Like Joseph, the Lord Jesus "came unto his own, and his own received him not" (John 1:11). He too was sold for the price of a slave and handed over to the Gentiles, and His final disappearance, His empty tomb, glossed over by the Jews with a lie.

B. HOW JOSEPH WAS SEEN BY HIS BRETHREN (37:18-27)

The brethren saw him coming. The narrative draws attention to their *conscious wickedness* (37:18-23). There they were, lolling out on the grass near the wells, with the sheep dotted over the pasture. They were laughing perhaps at some lewd joke of Reuben's, plotting some new villainy in the neighborhood, or eating their midday meal. One of them, like as not, was a lookout keeping sharp watch for bandits or wolves. "Hey!" he called, "Guess who's coming! It's Daddy's little darling." And instantly the brothers closed ranks, for the Spirit of God records their *combined enmity* for Joseph (37:18-19). Whatever squabbles they might have had among themselves, they were united in their dislike of him. "And when they saw him afar off, even before he came near unto them, they conspired against him to slay him. And they said one to another, Behold, this dreamer cometh."

That was what galled them most—his dreams. If there was one thing they were determined they would never do, it was to bow the knee to Joseph. No matter that God Himself had destined Joseph for preemience and power, they would never accord it to him.

It is remarkable how the Jewish people have closed ranks in their opposition to Christ. Jewish histories that find it necessary to make mention of Jesus categorically deny Him His deity.[1]

Having described their combined enmity toward Joseph, the narrative next describes their *consuming envy* (37:20, 23). They said, "Come now therefore, and let us slay him, and cast him into some pit, and we will say, Some evil beast hath devoured him: and we shall see what will become of his dreams." Their first act was to strip him of his coat, the robe that gave focus to their hate.

As Joseph drew near we can almost hear his cheerful hail, "Shalom, my brothers! Peace be unto you." But with a howl of rage they leaped upon him. One twisted his arms, another rent off his robe, another spurned it savagely in the mud, another flung the young man on his back, another kicked him in the ribs. "Now then, dreamer! tell us one of your dreams!" Like a pack of dogs they snapped and snarled at him, all their passions aflame. In like manner their descendants, strong bulls of Bashan, gored the Son of God.

Having shown the conscious wickedness of them all, the narrative next describes the *criminal weakness* of Reuben (37:21-22, 29-30). Reuben, the oldest, a man marked by instability, wavered now between a sense of responsibility and a sense of his own lack of influence. He did not wish Joseph to be killed, but he did not dare to stand up for him in the face of the sneers and hostility of the rest. He decided to try compromise and, as usual, compromise did not work. Active wickedness is always stronger than halfhearted goodness. A bold stand for Joseph was needed, not a wishy-washy suggestion that they put him in the pit with the vague hope that later he could free him and send him home. Pilate, vacillating between right and wrong when confronted with Jesus, was another Reuben.

Charles Darwin was also a "Reuben." He was a ne'er-do-well in youth, a college dropout at Shrewsbury, and a failure at Edinburgh Univer-

1. Even so renowned and articulate a spokesman as Abba Eban, one time brilliant Israeli ambassador to the United Nations, cannot tell the truth about Jesus. In his book *My People,* he makes Him out to be a Pharasaic Jew, spokesman for a robust Galilean patriotism, a man who never considered Himself a Prophet, One who merely articulated the ideas and manners of the masses. Abba Eban blames Christianity on Paul.

Max Dimot, who has written a number of Jewish histories, invariably speaks sarcastically about Jesus. He says there is not enough historical material about Him to write a decent obituary. He dismisses the virgin birth, the visit of the wise men, the genealogy traced to David, and the Egyptian episode as pious theological license designed to prove that in Jesus the Old Testament prophecies were fulfilled. He sneeringly maintains that the gospel accounts of the trial and its aftermath abound with what he calls contradictions, improbabilities, and impossibilities.

The Jews have done with *Jesus* what Joseph's brethren did with *Joseph.* First they conspired against Him, rejected His claims, and insisted on His crucifixion. Then they concocted a childish tale to account for the empty tomb. Finally they settled down to a centuries-long pretense that Jesus is totally irrelevant. But just as God brought Joseph's brothers, at last, to the place of contrition and repentance, so God has decreed that one day all Israel will acknowledge Jesus to be both Lord and Christ.

sity. His wealthy father put the pressure on; Charles must do something worthwhile or the funds would be cut off. Young Darwin decided to be a clergyman, so to Cambridge he went to study for the ministry. There too he wasted his time, made bad friends, lived a life wholly inconsistent with the calling to which he was pledged. But he was caught! Twice he had failed his father; he did not dare write home and say he now regretted his choice. It was characteristic of his instability and double-mindedness that he continued his theological training, hoping for the best.

He graduated from college but, anxious to postpone the evil day when he must begin his profession, he signed on as a naturalist on the *Beagle.* It was on that voyage that he decided to collect evidence to prove the theory of evolution and, before long, he was convinced of its truth. But now he had another problem. Evolution had been proposed before, but it was highly unpopular with the masses. So Charles seesawed back and forth between a desire to win fame and a fear of the scorn of the world. Then, as happened with Reuben, circumstances took over. He received a letter from a colleague asking advice on a manuscript enclosed. A horrified Darwin discovered his correspondent had stolen a march on him. The manuscript stole his thunder on evolution. He stuffed it in his drawer, trying to make up his mind what to do. At last, after several agonizing months, he decided to let Wallace have the credit for discovering evolution, only to change his mind again the next day. In the end he coauthored a work with Wallace then pushed ahead with his own *Origin of the Species.*

The academic community was wholly against his work, and Darwin began to hope he had not fallen between two stools—the church on the one side and the scientific world on the other. Then circumstances took over with a vengeance. Huxley and Hooker, militant atheists and materialists both, slapped Darwin on the back and began such a thoroughgoing promotion of Darwin's ideas that, before long, all opposition was bullied and browbeaten into silence.

But now Darwin was assailed by fresh doubts. His belief in the Old Testament gone, he could no longer accept the miracles of the New, so he ended up stripped of even the vestige of faith. In revenge for his malingering and double-mindedness, ill health leaped upon him. A robust and athletic man with a sound constitution, he was forever sick. His malady? Nothing but guilt! His physical symptoms were brought on by chronic anxiety. So he paid for his vacillation with his health and for his apostasy with his soul. His compromise and indecision had simply made him a tool for more forceful men. So did Reuben's.

Reuben tried to please his brothers at the expense of his conscience and became guilty of criminal weakness. Indecision, in the end, is a decision after all. Having given us a glimpse of Reuben's criminal weakness the narrative now tells of Judah's *calculating worldliness* (37:25-27). "And they sat down to eat bread: and they lifted up their eyes and looked, and, behold, a company of Ishmaelites came from Gilead with their camels bearing spicery and balm and myrrh, going to carry it down to Egypt. And Judah said unto his brethren, What profit is it if we slay our brother, and conceal his blood? Come, and let us sell him to the Ishmaelites, and let not our hand be upon him."

Judah saw a chance to kill two birds with one stone. They could get rid of Joseph without violence, and they could pick up some cash in the process. It would be hard to find a more cold-blooded crime, but it was exceeded by the crime of Judas, a lineal descendant of Judah, who sold one greater than Joseph for an equally paltry sum.

C. How Joseph Was Sold by His Brethren (37:28-36)

The band of Midianites approached and reined in their camels as Judah hailed, "Shalom! Are you going to Egypt?"

"Peace be upon you," came the reply. "Yes, we are heading that way. Can we sell you some balm?"

"Maybe, maybe. Would you like to buy a slave? a bright, intelligent lad with a real head on his shoulders?"

The Midianites showed interest in making a deal, so Joseph was hauled out of the pit. He was made to stand before a merchant who poked and prodded at him, examined his teeth, inspected his feet, and looked him over as though he were a horse. "How about fifty pieces of silver?" said Judah.

"You must be crazy!" said the merchant. "He doesn't seem to have much spirit to me. Look at him sniveling. We'll pay you ten."

"Ten pieces of silver!" cried Judah. "Look how young he is. He's good for fifty years at least, and he's as clever as a fox. How about twenty-five?"

"Twenty, and that's our final offer," said the Midianite. "Ho, there, Eliphaz, get the camels moving."

"Twenty pieces of silver!" cried Judah. "Very well, my lords, the boy is yours."

Thus the cruel deal was closed and Joseph was led away, his cries and entreaties falling on deaf ears. What cared the Ishmaelites for a Hebrew's tears? What cared Judah and Simeon and Levi and the sons of the bondwomen? It had been their lucky day. They had rid themselves of a rival and lined their purses besides. It was a *fine bargain in cash.* But was it? Each of the ten pocketed a wretched two pieces of silver, and each inherited a conscience that would never rest again. There are some deals that are too expensive for the soul to permit, some moments of indulgence, some stolen pleasures it would be better to have shunned than to have shared.

It was not long before there came the *first bite of conscience.* The anguished cry of Reuben fell like a pall upon the spirits of the conspirators. Where was Reuben when Judah struck the deal? We do not know. When he came back, however, stopping at the pit to give Joseph a hail, he was horrified to discover the lad was gone. "The child is not," he wailed, "and I, whither shall I go?"

The others probably looked Reuben over with cold distaste and alarm. "Oh, shut up, Reuben. You're as guilty as we are. Here, put this in your wallet and be quiet. We only sold the boy, and that's better than slaying him, isn't it? Some softy in Egypt'll buy him and, like as not, he'll live in clover. What are we going to tell Father? Why, we can't help it if he sends the kid off on some wild goose chase! We'll tell him a wild beast killed him and that we found this coat and thought it looked like his. Here, fetch a kid and we'll soak it in blood. That'll make the story sound good."

And that is what they did. They deceived old Jacob with a kid as he, long years before, had deceived *his* father with a kid. They stained the garment in blood, concocted their lie, and thought they had forever concealed their sin. But a lie is a very poor refuge when dealing with the living God.

Conscience must have deepened its work when the boys arrived home and saw Jacob's inconsolable grief. They looked at one another and crept guiltily away as old Jacob, shaken to the core, his sobs sounding like the knell of doom throughout the camp, retired to the tent that once had been Rachel's to proclaim to God in heaven his unutterable grief.

IV. JOSEPH'S BROTHER (38:1-30)

Genesis 38 is one of those chapters of the Bible rarely read in public—rightly so perhaps, for it contains the record of deeds of darkest shame. The Bible does not shun telling the whole, sad truth about human nature. Human nature, as a result of the Fall, is raw.

The story is sandwiched between the record of Joseph's position at home and his piety abroad. The bright light of Joseph's high morals brings into even sharper relief the sordid nature of Judah's unprincipled behavior. Indeed, that God should pick a man like Judah and make him a prince in Israel, and then send His own Son into the world, not merely from Judah's line, but from the outworking of the very events recorded in that chapter, is nothing less than a miracle of grace.

A. JUDAH AND HIS SONS (38:1-10)

Joseph had been sold into slavery. Judah had pocketed his share of the loot, a paltry two pieces of silver, and had fallen heir to a nagging conscience. Day by day he looked upon his aging father's inconsolable grief, and night after night he would awaken with Joseph's despairing cry ringing in his ears. It made him so restless that he did what many people do when they can no longer stand the results of their misdeeds. He moved out.

We are told first of *Judah's wayward behavior* (38:1). "Judah went down from his brethren, and turned in to a certain Adullamite whose name was Hirah." The companionship of the unsaved seems a change for the better after contemplating the behavior of the brethren. Hirah, however, soon became Judah's evil genius. He turns up three times in the chapter. First he was Judah's acquaintance, then he became Judah's associate, and he ended up by becoming Judah's accomplice. It was while staying with his unsaved friend that Judah met the woman he married. One thing leads to another.

We are given some description of *Judah's worldly bride* (38:2-5). We are told about the family she represented and the family she raised. She was "the daughter of a certain Canaanite whose name was Shuah." That is to say, she was a raw pagan and a pagan of the very worst kind, a Canaanite pagan, a member of a sin-cursed race that practiced a religion of utter vileness. To make things worse, that unsaved wife of Judah's seems to have had no interest whatsoever in spiritual things and, worse still, his sons took after their mother.

The first son was Er ("the watcher"). His bright little eyes watched father and mother alike and took in everything—his mother's indifference to his father's mysterious, unseen God, and his father's neglect of spiritual things. Those bright eyes watched with interest and growing approval the licentiousness of his mother's religion.

The second son was Onan ("strength"). He was named by his mother. That, together with the name chosen, suggests the growing influence and family dominance of the pagan woman Judah had chosen for a wife. Onan himself grew up to be strong in wickedness.

Then there was Shelah ("he that breaks"). The mother named that boy too, a further indication that Judah had surrendered the headship of his home and was leaving the training of his sons to his wife.

With a pagan woman exercising increasing influence in his family affairs, it is not surprising that before long we are contemplating *Judah's wicked boys* (38:6-10). Er, the senior of the boys, had grown to young manhood, and Judah, stirring himself at last, decided the boy should be married. The woman he chose for his son was Tamar. Her name means "Palm Tree," suggestive of beauty, slenderness, grace, and usefulness. From the rest of the story, and from the position God gave that woman in the Messianic line, we conclude she must have been a woman of high character and noble aspirations despite her pagan birth and background. She seems to have entered into the Messianic hope of which, no doubt, Judah had spoken to her when negotiating the matter of her marriage to his oldest son.

Er, however, was not interested in his father's religious vagaries and he had no intention of cooperating in the matter of marriage. The mother's influence came through strong and sure in his life, a life that was very bad and very brief. It is summed up in a single sentence: "Er, Judah's firstborn, was wicked in the sight of the LORD, and the LORD slew him." Payday came very swiftly for that godless young man.

The second of the two boys was as bad as his brother. We are told what he did—he was guilty of an act of calculated insult both to his wife and to God. Following the custom of the time,[2] Judah told his second son to marry Tamar and raise up seed for his brother. Onan, like his brother, seems to have resented the marriage. Like Er he had no interest in matters pertaining to the Messiah, and he had no intention of cooperating with his father's wishes. He showed his contempt in a blatant, bestial way, and God simply slew him where he stood.

B. JUDAH AND HIS SINS (38:11-26)

Now whatever Judah may have preached to his family from time to time, his own example must have been deplorable. His perverted values, personal vileness, and pretended virtue must have been well marked by his wife and sons long before those marks of character were exposed to the world.

1. HIS PERVERTED VALUES (38:11-14)

Having buried his two sons, Judah tried to place the blame for their deaths on the innocent Tamar. "Remain a widow at thy father's house, till Shelah my son be grown," he said, "lest peradventure he die also, as his brethren did." Tamar seems to have had the makings of a spiritual woman, and a Messianic concept appears to have made an impression upon her. For Judah to insinuate that she was to blame for the death of his sons was not only unjust, it was a complete failure to recognize that he himself was really to blame. Had he not married a pagan woman, had he not left the training of his sons to her, had he been a more inspiring example of godliness, had he been more thorough in teaching the truth about the God of Abraham, Isaac, and Jacob to his wife and sons, things might well have been different. To blame Tamar simply revealed how perverted his sense of values had become.

Then that pagan wife of his, who had been the real source of his woes, died. God, in His mercy to Judah's soul, removed the woman and her baneful influence from the scene. Her death greatly affected Judah, who mourned her deeply. He could not see that her death was really a blessing in disguise.

It was at that point that his unsaved friend, the Adullamite, showed up again and instead of seeking comfort in the God of his father, Judah found comfort in his unsaved friend. Hirah knew how to cheer him up. "It's sheepshearing time at Timnath," he said. "That's always a barrel of fun, Judah. Why don't we go up and have a good time? It'll take your mind off things, my friend." Judah agreed to go. Instead of asking God why the disasters had come into his home, he did what so many do; he sought to drown his troubles in the amusements of the world.

All that time his youngest son, Shelah, had been growing up. He was now old enough to be married to Tamar as custom decreed, but Judah

2. One of the thirty-four laws of Genesis, later incorporated into the Mosaic Law.

had no intention whatsoever of fulfilling his promise to the widow. Not he! Sure, he had made her a solemn promise, but what is a promise made to one not strong enough to enforce its redemption? Judah, with perverted values, decided that Tamar, who by now he cordially disliked if not actually feared, could remain a widow. What a picture Judah presents. He was a man brought up in the home of one of God's giants; he stood directly in the Messianic line, but he was as crooked and as perverted in his values and in his dealings as the pagans he took for his friends.

2. His Personal Vileness (38:15-23)

Seeing that her father-in-law had no intention of fulfilling his promise, Tamar decided to take matters into her own hands. It was not just a desire to remarry that moved her. Her previous experiences with Judah's sons would surely have cured her from wanting further involvement with that family. But she seems to have understood and appreciated the spiritual significance of becoming a mother in the Judaic line. Her motives were good even if the means she adopted were bad.

She disguised herself as a temple prostitute.[3] The Canaanite religion not only employed vile symbols, but it also ministered directly to the flesh, consummating worship in an act of immorality with a temple prostitute. Tamar, therefore, set herself up by the highway as a priestess of the local temple. She knew her father-in-law well enough to know that he would be a likely candidate for the services such a woman would offer. Sure enough, before long Judah came that way. With the loose morals of the world to guide him, and with a total disregard for the calling of God, he stopped and propositioned Tamar, not knowing, of course, who she was.

Her price was a kid of the goats, something Judah obviously did not have with him. Knowing her man, Tamar demanded security in lieu of payment and asked for Judah's signet, bracelets, and staff. Judah was by now so hotly inflamed by lust that he parted with them readily.

The signet was his ring, used for impressing his signature into the clay tablets of the time; it represented his *person*. His "bracelets" were probably a valued chain of gold; they represented his *possessions*. His staff marked him out as a shepherd. In ancient times many people carried a staff, often carved with some identifying symbol such as an animal, a flower, or a bird. The staff represented his *position*. Judah could thus lightly forfeit person, possessions, and position for the sake of a moment of lust. He was well on his way to becoming a second Esau. Indeed, were it not for the fact that later he took his stand for Benjamin, it might well have been that he would have been as roundly

3. The word used for "harlot" literally means "the consecrated," which leads to the conclusion that Tamar did not simply set herself up as a common woman of the streets.

cursed by the dying Jacob as were Reuben, Simeon, and Levi (Genesis 49).

Judah indulged himself and went on his way minus his ring, bracelets, and staff, minus what was left of his good name, and minus what tattered shreds of his testimony he had left. Again his friend the Adullamite showed up. Hearing about the harlot, Hiram offered to act as Judah's go-between to take the kid to the woman and redeem the security Judah had left behind. Perhaps he wanted to meet the delectable young woman for himself.

But the temple call girl was nowhere to be found. The people from the neighborhood denied all knowledge of such a woman as Hiram described. Judah, of course, was upset, but not because he had transgressed against God, not because he had committed an act of immorality, but because he was afraid his reputation as a man of his word might be ruined. He fussed for awhile and then forgot the whole thing. Thus lightly do men sin. But he had ignited a fuse on a time bomb, and it was already beginning to burn down.

3. HIS PRETENDED VIRTUE (38:24-26)

Three months came and went, and the incident faded completely from Judah's mind. Then came startling news. It shook the whole neighborhood and gave the gossips something about which to really wag their tongues. Tamar was pregnant.

The news reached Judah. "Bring her forth and let her be burnt," was his harsh and hasty word. Of all the world's prating hypocrites, it would be hard to find a worse one than Judah. Talk about the double standard! The only difference between himself and Tamar was that Tamar was a woman and he was a man, that Tamar had been caught and he had not. "Let her be burnt!" he said, casting firebrands about like a madman, throwing the stones in the air which were to fall back on his head. We can imagine him continuing, "Get the stake, get the faggots, get the fire, fetch the woman. Where is she, the immoral wretch! She has disgraced my family, she has dishonored the Judaic line!" Was Judah still blaming Tamar for the death of his first two sons? Was he being nagged in his conscience because he refused to marry Tamar to Shelah? Well, here was a golden opportunity to get rid of a woman he had come to dread and dislike. "Let her be burnt!" he said.

As the executioners hurried off to Tamar's house, the news of a public burning spread throughout the town. Soon Tamar was dragged from her house and down the village street. "Hold it," she may have cried. "Hold everything. I have a confession to make. I should like to incriminate the partner to my crime." What a sensation that announcement must have made. She was probably hurried back home to get the evidence she said she had. Then she was dragged back down the street to the square. The stake may have been already set up and an excited crowd gathered to commiserate Judah and enjoy the sight of Tamar's death. The shameless woman was hauled up before Judah so that her death sentence might be ratified and her partner named. Then we can see Judah's swarthy face suddenly pale beneath his tan, his eyes stare in utter disbelief at what Tamar had in her hand. "By the man, whose these are, am I with child," she said. "Discern, I pray thee, whose are these, the signet, and bracelets, and staff."

Judah's sin had found him out. He vindicated Tamar, of course. What else could he do? "She has been more righteous than I. . . . Let the woman go," he said. She had simply taken what Judah should long ago have given. Then he whitewashed himself. "She hath been more righteous than I; because that I gave her not to Shelah my son," he said, carefully sidestepping the fact of his own immorality. There was no more talk of burning. The shoe was now on his foot and a very uncomfortable shoe it proved to be.

But God does not allow immorality to go unpunished. Judah might evade his embarrassing guilt, but the incident was not to be closed in that easy way. Moses was told by God to write up the whole story. It was incorporated into the Holy Scriptures, and has been read by millions of people down through all the ages from that day to this.

C. JUDAH AND HIS SEED (38:27-30)

Judah is not once named in the events that follow. He seems to have washed his hands completely of the woman who had shamed him so and seems to have been totally ignorant of the fact that one of the sons now to be born to him would stand directly in the Messianic line. Such a thought was beyond Judah in his backslidden condition. That God could be a God of such grace never occurred to him at all. That God should pick up the seed of a pagan woman, the seed of an act of shame, and make the resulting son to be a direct lineal ancestor of the Christ Himself was a knowledge of God too high for Judah in his sin.

Twins were born to Tamar. God had judicially taken away two of Judah's sons; now in grace He gave him two in return. But Judah was wholly indifferent. He wanted nothing to do with Tamar or her sons at all.

The first child can be called *the redeemed child.* It looked as though the one called Zerah was to be born first. When his hand appeared they tied a scarlet thread upon it—a beautifully symbolic act. Later in Scripture the scarlet thread became a symbol of salvation. It was a scarlet thread Rahab was to bind in her window on the wall of Jericho so that she and her house might escape the vengeace of God. Moreover, in the Bible, the one born first always had to be redeemed by sacrifice, under the Mosaic law. Thus Zerah was the redeemed child.

But Zerah did not fulfill the early promise and Pharez, *the royal child,* took his place. The midwife had never seen anything like it. She looked at the tiny little fellow in astonishment and held him up for his mother to see. "How hast thou broken forth?" she cried. "This breach be upon thee." So they called him Pharez and from that unusual child, ignored by his father, exclaimed over by a pagan midwife, the line to Christ was carried forward for another generation. Such was the grace of God to Tamar, yes, and to Judah too.

V. JOSEPH'S BONDAGE (39:1–40:23)

Like Paul arriving in Rome, Joseph arrived in Egypt in chains, his high hopes shattered, his life in ruins. The taunts of his brothers still rang in his ears, "'Bye, 'bye, Joey! Happy dreams!" What had become of those fine dreams of his? dreams of power, dreams of position, dreams of the resources and the riches of the world poured into his lap? He was a slave!

God draws the veil over the long, hot trek across the sands of Sinai, past the Egyptian forts, and into the land. We can picture the scene—Joseph being passed through the customs offices to be docketed and ticketed and stamped like so much baggage. "What's this?" the official sitting at the receipt of custom would demand. "One live body, value twenty pieces of silver. Here's the invoice and the receipt signed by one Judah of Canaan." We are told nothing of Joseph's awakened wonder, despite his chains, as the ancient glories of Kem burst upon his astonished sight. He had come to an amazing land with a history stretching back into the antiquity. When his great-grandfather Abraham had come to Egypt many years before, the Great Pyramid was already a thousand years old.

On down the Nile they went, Joseph's sharp eyes noting everything. There were the great camel caravans converging on Egypt with the wealth of the world, there the papyrus boats plying the placid waters of the Nile, there the great and thriving cities, and there the fabled pyramids and sphinx. For a moment the young man's sorrows would be forgotten in the wonder of the exotic new world into which he was being taken. Here was life as he had never dreamed it to be.

The caravan road arrived at last at the slave market where he was tagged and priced and put up for sale. There was something about his open good looks, perhaps, or his evident air of self-possession and general competence that attracted the eye of a buyer used to sizing up men. "How much for this stripling?" The speaker was a uniformed officer of Pharaoh's guard. In due course, Joseph was knocked down to Potiphar who, pleased enough with his bargain, took the foreign country boy home to his spacious suburban home.

Joseph entered Egypt at the age of eighteen. He left it at the age of one hundred ten for glory, and for eighty of the intervening years he was the highest lord of the land. What a success story! What was there about Joseph that marked him out for so incredible a career? What was there about him that lifted him on high when so many sold off the auction stand that day, simply sank into the morass and vanished on the rubbish heaps of time? What was there about Joseph that, be it in the prison or the palace, men instinctively trusted him and promoted him? It is no ordinary rags-to-riches tale. The years between the time he is seen with an *iron* chain on his wrist and the time he is seen with a *gold* chain about his neck were years of great testing for Joseph. From those years we can learn how faith can shine amidst the gloom and how hope's anchor can be fasted securely within the veil.

A. The Slave Man: Completely Trusted by a Prosperous Master (39:1-6)

The secret of Joseph's career at that stage of his life can be summed up in a single phrase—*boundless industry*. Not for Joseph was the long face, the sullen look, the resentful air. Not for him were senseless criticisms of fate and long, wasted hours plotting revenge. Not for him the futile cursing of God and the gnawing cancer of longed-for revenge. Not for Joseph the dull acquiescence with fate that would have turned him into a plodding brute. Evidently Joseph decided, once the initial stunning shock was absorbed, that God had some wise purpose in allowing him to be sold as a slave. "All things work together for good to those that love God, to them who are the called according to His purpose," he might well have assured himself. The will of God is "good and acceptable and perfect. I will therefore trust God in these dark circumstances. If God wants me to be a slave, I shall be the best slave in Egypt. I shall study my master until I know him better than he knows himself. I shall study his interests and make them my own, and I shall perform every task allotted to me, not as unto Potiphar, but as unto the Lord. Thus these bonds will no longer be the bonds of a slave, they will be the bonds of the Lord. I shall consider myself God's bondslave and in all my ways and words I shall endeavor to please Him."

So often adverse circumstances find us bemoaning our fate instead of looking for ways to glorify the Lord Jesus in them and through them. We have to learn life's adversities before we can be trusted with life's advancements.

Who would have thought that any good thing could have come out of the notorious Ravensbruck death camp of the Nazis? Surely when she was incarcerated there as prisoner 66730, Corrie ten Boom must have wondered at her fate. Yet, in that place of torment and horror, that devoted and courageous servant of the Lord Jesus decided if she had to live in that suburb of hell, where the only means of exit for a Jew or a Jew-sympathizer was up the smokestack of the crematorium, if death was to stare her in the face every day, if she must live daily with spine-chilling atrocities, if she must be subjected to indignity and intimidation, if she must be foul with vermin, whipped, forever hungry, terrorized day and night—why then, she would be the very best inmate

Ravensbruck horror camp had ever known. She would be a Christian. So there, in barracks number 28, she held clandestine Bible classes and taught her wretched fellow inmates how to face life and death with Jesus Christ.

As a result of her agony, God was able to open up for her in later years a worldwide ministry. Her story has been told in print and on the platform. It has been made into a major film and shown in movie houses around the world. It has thrilled and challenged and encouraged countless millions of people. Often she must have wondered why, after she had risked her life so often to rescue persecuted Jews, God should have allowed her to be piled into a boxcar with eighty other frightened human beings, packed in so tight that they could hardly breathe; why she should be forced to endure such thirst, such unspeakable filth, such naked horror, such sorrow over the death of her weaker sister. But now she knows! Through her life and ministry thousands upon thousands have been led to give their lives to the Lord. God meant it unto good.

So young Joseph gave himself to the task of becoming the very best slave Potiphar ever had, and Potiphar noticed, for he was a shrewd judge of men accustomed to command. He soon saw in that Hebrew slave of his all the traits of a good manager. Joseph was loyal, he could be trusted, he worked well with other people, he was a leader, he had creative talent, he had a knack for finding better ways to get things done. He was always willing to take on more responsibility. He did his own tasks well and was always on the lookout to advance his master's cause. He never lost an opportunity to educate and improve himself. He asked an endless stream of questions. He was enthusiastic, and infected others with his zeal. Moreover, he planned ahead and was always looking to the future. Such men were rare.

Potiphar noted other things as well about his strange slave; things that concerned Joseph's religious beliefs, for the young man made no secret of his ancestral faith. Perhaps Potiphar questioned Joseph about the strange Jehovah of whom he spoke, and learned how Joseph's ancestors had migrated to Canaan in the pursuit of the true and living God, and how a covenant relationship had been established between God and his fathers. Perhaps also Joseph told him how that eternal God had twice spoken to him in dreams. Something of Joseph's testimony left its mark, for "his master saw that the LORD was with him, and that the LORD made all that he did to prosper . . . and he made him overseer over his house, and all that he had he put into his hand. And it came to pass that from the time he made him overseer . . . that the LORD blessed the Egyptian's house for Joseph's sake; and the blessing of the LORD was upon all that he had in the house, and in the field."

The more Potiphar trusted Joseph, the more his business ventures prospered. One can picture Potiphar discussing the phenomenon in the officers' mess. "I cannot explain it," he might have said, "but it's ever since I made this fellow Joseph my manager. He's a Hebrew slave I picked up for a song from some Ishmaelites. But, what a prize! He's the finest manager I've ever set eyes on, and honest! I've never known an honest slave, few honest men, and no honest officials, but this fellow is the absolute soul of integrity. He attributes it to his God, some strange God named Jehovah. I wish all my slaves worshiped him!" Thus we see Joseph as a slave man, trusted by a prosperous master. We see a man marked by *boundless integrity*. In every situation Joseph behaved himself as a believer should.

B. THE SUCCESSFUL MAN: CONTINUALLY TEMPTED BY A PERSISTENT WOMAN (39:7-20)

The devil obviously could not leave a man like Joseph alone. He had tried to ruin him through the schemes of evil men and that had not worked. Now he used the shameless schemes of a woman. The secret of Joseph's life at that stage in his career may be summed up in a single phrase too—*blessed inability*. There was not much that Joseph could not do, but there was one thing: he could not lightly sin. He was "a goodly person and well favoured," we read. That means he was a good-looking fellow; Joseph had all his mother Rachel's good looks. Before long he caught the eye of his master's wife.

God has promised He will always provide a way of escape when temptation draws near, and that he will never allow us to be tempted beyond our ability to bear. There is always a way of escape—even if it is simply running away. Joseph could see the temptation coming long before it actually burst upon him in full force. First there was the way the woman looked at him. Then she would take pains to be where he was, especially when he was alone. She would probably do little things for him, try to make conversation with him, let him know that she liked him. The pattern is as old as the race. Joseph could see the thing coming, and he began to plot ways of his own, ways to avoid the woman. He was polite, but he saw to it that he was never cornered by her alone.

But by now the tigress had scented her prey. The more Joseph drew off, the more she drew on until it was obvious to everyone that the woman was infatuated with the good-looking slave—obvious to everyone, that is, except Potiphar. Joseph was a young man with all a young man's natural passions and desires. He was friendless, cast out by his brethren, a stranger and a slave in a foreign land. He must have been sorely tempted by the persistent woman. "After all," the devil would probably whisper, "Why not? Nobody knows you down here. Take what she offers. Morals are free and easy enough in Egypt—so long as you're not caught. After all, it's natural for a young man to flirt with an attractive woman."

Then, no doubt, the evil one would change his approach. He would paint pictures in Joseph's mind, evil, seductive pictures, the kind of pictures he has been painting in the minds of men and women ever since the Fall. "You're being accused of it anyway," he might well whisper, "so you might as well do it. People judge you by themselves. Most of them would long ago have taken advantage of what's offered if they had your chance. In their minds you're already guilty, so where does all your high and mighty morality get you after all?" Then he would come back to his favorite theme—the seductiveness, the availability of the woman. Joseph could see it coming and he was powerless to stop the thing from coming to a head. Any day now someone would get Potiphar's ear and then he would be scourged and slain.

We do not know how long the buildup lasted, but one day the stroke fell. Aflame now with her own passions, the woman caught Joseph alone. She threw aside all pretense, flung herself at him, urged and pleaded with him to accept her. "But he refused, and said, Behold my master wotteth [knows] not what is with me in the house, and he hath committed all that he hath to my hand; there is none greater in this house than I; neither hath he kept back any thing from me but thee, because thou art his wife: how then can I do this great wickedness, and sin against God?"

There it was, Joseph's *blessed inability*. He refused on two counts, one on the ground of simple justice, it would not be right so to defraud the master who trusted him, and he refused on the ground of his faith. He could not so sin against God. It was not "I *will not*" but "I *cannot*." It was an absolute moral and spiritual impossibility for him even to contemplate the kind of action she urged. It would have been imprudent socially; it was impossible spiritually. What the woman suggested was utterly repulsive to him as a believer. What a magnificent way to say no to temptation.

That is what John has in mind when he says, "Whosoever is born of God doth not commit sin; for his seed remaineth in him: and he cannot sin, because he is born of God" (1 John 3:9). I cannot do this thing! I cannot so grieve the Holy Spirit of God.

The woman, however, would not take no for an answer. She kept up her campaign and one day physically forced herself on him. The time for discussion and argument was past. Joseph did the only thing he could—he fled. How much temptation can be overcome simply by deliberately walking away from it. Is was not cowardice; it was courage and conviction of the highest order. The Bible says, "Flee youthful lusts," and so we should. That ungodly crowd that exerts such a godless influence, that book that so inflames the passions, that television program that so defiles the imagination—walk away from them.

The woman was enraged. As has been said, "hell hath no fury like a woman scorned." She stood there shaking with rage, Joseph's coat in her hand. The wheels whirled in her evil mind. If she could not have him then, by the gods, she would make him smart. She framed him. Her screams brought the servants running. Possibly her hands had been busy meantime and her disheveled hair and rent clothing would have told their own tale, adding up to irrefutable evidence of Joseph's guilt—at least so Potiphar thought. His servants might have been able to tell him otherwise had he cared to ask. Joseph, falsely accused and with no defense against the woman's lies, was branded an ungrateful scoundrel and flung headlong into prison.

C. The Slandered Man: Carefully Tested by a Patient God (39:21–40:23)

It was bad enough to have been sold as a slave—all because of his coat, but now to be branded as a seducer—all because of his coat; surely that was too much. The secret of Joseph's life at that stage may be likewise summed up in a single phrase—*beautiful integrity.* There in that dismal dungeon, Joseph learned faith, hope, and love. We do not know for sure how old Joseph was when he entered prison. He was eighteen when he entered Egypt. He had served Potiphar long enough for his affairs to prosper exceedingly, maybe for a couple of years. He was twenty, perhaps, when the doors of the prison slammed behind him with the hollow knell of doom. If so, he was in that prison for ten long years, for he was thirty when at last he stood before Pharaoh.

There in prison Joseph again quietly submitted himself to the will of God. We must consider *the faith demanded of Joseph.* Satan would whisper, "Now what about your God?" People who knew Joseph, who had heard his testimony, and who secretly believed in his innocence must also have wondered about his God. What kind of a God would so reward integrity and righteousness and moral purity with slander and prison? Like those of Job and Jeremiah, the sufferings of Joseph were for no apparent cause. Yet Joseph could say to himself, "I know whom I have believed, and am persuaded that He is able to keep that which I've committed to Him. I still have my dreams. This is a dreary path but it leads surely to the throne."

In His loving kindness, God gave Joseph little tokens to show that he was not forgotten. The jailor came to appreciate and trust him. For "the LORD was with Joseph, and shewed him mercy, and gave him favour in the sight of the keeper of the prison. . . . The keeper of the prison looked not to any thing that was under his hand; because the LORD was with him, and that which he did, the LORD made it to prosper." Potiphar's loss was the jailer's gain.

Next we consider *the love displayed by Joseph.* He won the confidence of the other prisoners. He cared for them and treated them as human beings. He was touched, as it were, with the feelings of their infirmities. Before long he not only had a position in that prison, he had a ministry there too, so much so that the two most notable prisoners in the cells were willing to share their anxieties with him.

First Pharaoh's *butler,* banished to prison for some trivial offense, shared with Joseph a dream that had disturbed him during the night. As Joseph listened he could tell at once that it was a dream full of promise. "Cheer up, man," he said, "Do not interpretations belong to God? In three days Pharaoh will restore you to your office. And then, my lord, please remember me. I was stolen away out of the land of the Hebrews: and here also have I done nothing that they should put me in this dungeon."

Encouraged by the butler's good news, Pharaoh's imprisoned *baker* took courage. He too shared with Joseph a dream he had received. Joseph's face grew grave as he listened, for well he read the portent. In three days the baker would be hanged. Sadly he told him to prepare for death and, no doubt, put his arm around the poor fellow's shoulders and sought to kindle in his pagan breast a knowledge of the true and living God.

Finally we read that *hope was deferred for Joseph.* In three days the prison gates opened and an officer of Pharaoh delivered two decrees. There was a pardon for the butler and a death sentence for the baker. We can picture Joseph hurrying along the dark corridors, key in eager hand, to open the gates for the butler. "And sir," he would say, "please remember me when it is well with thee." "Yet," we read, "did not the chief butler remember Joseph, but forgat him." To which Dr. G. Campbell Morgan appends the quaint note, "And his name is not always Butler!"

"Hope deferred maketh the heart sick," says God. The chief butler forgot Joseph. A few days went by, swift as a flash, Joseph expecting every moment to hear that Pharaoh had commanded his release. The days lengthened into weeks, and still no word. Undoubtedly the butler was busy and had much to do, but surely he would not forget. The weeks became months and the months became a year, then another and another and another. Joseph learned to hope no longer in man. All human help was now gone. Joseph's thoughts, however, did not creep down slimy stairways to grovel in base thoughts of suicide; instead they borrowed Jacob's ladder and lifted Joseph up to heaven's halls. Long, long centuries before ever the psalmist penned the words, Joseph had entered into their wondrous truth. "As the hart panteth after the water brooks, so panteth my soul after thee, O God. My soul thirsteth for God, for the living God. . . . Why art thou cast down, O my soul? and why art thou disquieted within me? hope thou in God; for I shall yet praise him for the help of his countenance" (Psalm 42:1-5).

VI. JOSEPH'S BLESSING
(41:1-44)

The man next to the king in Egypt was the grand vizier. Nowadays we would call him the prime minister, except his powers were derived directly from the king, not the people. He was the chief officer of state responsible for carrying on all the administrative functions of the kingdom, saving only matters relating to religion.

It was the grand vizier who appointed the men who, three times a year, reported on provincial affairs. The district inspectors reported to him. All matters having to do with provincial boundaries, land allocations, tax arrears, and internal security were his responsibility. A whole host of officials with high-sounding titles were his subordinates.

Egyptian tombs tell us much about the office. The grand vizier is shown, for instance, receiving envoys and viceregents from far-off lands. His chief function was to uphold the strong, centralized, authoritarian power of the throne. His tasks included keeping local princelings in check, their wings properly clipped so that they might never become a threat to the pharaoh. He was responsible for the appointment of those inspectors charged with keeping an eye on local governors. From time to time his duties would take him to various parts of Egypt. Tomb pictures depict him receiving the homage of local officials, who are shown prostrate before him in the dust. Scribes can be seen recording his decisions. He had to probe the status of the Nile; would it be a good Nile or a bad, that is, would there be a plentiful inundation or a meager one? How were the dikes and canals? how much forced labor must be drafted to effect repairs? He would cross-question his subordinates regarding census lists, expected agricultural yield, the well-being of the herds.

He is shown traveling in pomp, his haughty looks never deigning to notice the serfs, bending to their endless, arduous and thankless tasks. Always surrounded by guards, his way was cleared before him as humble laborers touched their foreheads to the dust before him. His chariot was of gold, his home a mansion in the gilded suburbs, his life one of opulence and power.

That was the position for which God, through twelve long years of suffering and silence, had been preparing Joseph. Truly God's schools are not like ours. To prepare a man for such a position we would send him to Princeton; God sent Joseph to prison. Joseph had passed some stiff tests, but he graduated at last with flying colors, having won honors in every difficult trial that had come his way. And now the moment had come when he was to be pulled from prison, hastily shaved, made presentable, thrust before Pharaoh, and then promoted to the lofty post of grand vizier of Egypt. All in the space of an hour! Little did Joseph dream that morning as he took the keys of the cells and began his daily, tedious rounds, that the sufferings were over and the glories were to begin. The years of adversity were finished, the years of advancement had come.

A. THE PROVIDENTIAL WAYS OF GOD (41:1-8)

William Cowper, who pioneered the awakening of England's literary genius, was much used to suffering. Cowper was a frail, shuddering bundle of nerves, a man with a pinched face and eyes constantly swollen from chronic inflammation. He attempted suicide. He spent time in a lunatic asylum where contempt and cruelty were the order of the day.

Yet, out of all those sufferings, God fashioned the grand vizier of English letters. It was William Cowper who wrote:

> God moves in a mysterious way,
> His wonders to perform;
> He plants His footsteps in the sea
> And rides upon the storm.
>
> Deep in unfathomable mines
> Of never failing skill,
> He treasures up His bright designs
> And works His sovereign will.

We see those "mysterious ways" exemplified in Joseph. The hour struck for the emancipation of that captive in Pharaoh's prison. God moved, moved providentially. Joseph pulled no strings. He had tried that once with no success. The butler forgot him. The days, the weeks, the months, and the years came and went with monotonous regularity, and Joseph was buried alive. He was forgotten by his brothers, forgotten by the evil woman who had lied away his character and career, forgotten by Potiphar who had owed him so much, forgotten by the butler, forgotten by all except his father who thought of him, no doubt, but thought him long since dead. Forgotten by all but God!

And now God made His move. He began with neither baker nor butler but with the king. *The king's dreams* were what started it. There were two of them. First he fell asleep and dreamed about cattle, then he fell asleep again and dreamed about corn. In his first dream he saw seven fat, flourishing cows emerge from the life-giving waters of the Nile. Pharaoh looked on with approval. That is how cows ought to look! He would have to appoint a new grand vizier soon to look into the condition of his cattle throughout the land. Then, suddenly, to Pharaoh's horror, from the same river emerged seven more cows. But what mangy, bony, starved, ill-kempt cows those were! May he never live to see their like! The dream had turned into a nightmare. But worse, the lean and hungry cows, made fierce by famine, turned upon their sleek and shining kin and devoured them, hoof and hide, before the pharaoh's astonished gaze.

He awoke in horror, stared about him, and fell asleep again, only to dream the same thing all over again. He saw the golden fields of corn. He examined the nearest stand, seven delightful, magnificent, golden, prize-winning ears tossing proudly in the breeze beneath a smiling sun. But then up sprang seven blotched and blighted ears, spindly, nightmare ears. Those turned upon their flourishing neighbors and devoured them stalk and stem. Pharaoh awoke in fresh horror, convinced now that the dreams were a portent. But what could they mean?

We are told of *the king's distress.* "And it came to pass in the morning that his spirit was troubled; and he sent and called for the magicians of Egypt, and all the wise men thereof: and Pharaoh told them his dream; but there was none that could interpret them unto Pharaoh." What a scene! There the wise men stood in their distinctive robes, embroidered with mystical signs, the scholars, the sages, men learned in the lore of dreams. They listened intently as Pharaoh told his tale.

It was the turn of the god Thot to speak to his priests so that they might make known to the majesty of the Pharaoh the meaning of his dreams. Thot was the god of all magical arts. It was Thot who knew the mystic names of all the other gods, what it was that made the other gods afraid, and with what mystic rites they could be subdued. Thot could give his worshipers power to dominate Osiris, Anubis, or Set. He was the god of inspiration. With the incantations and prayers taught by Thot, one god could be frightened by the terror of another. The magicians of Egypt, therefore, turned to their magical tricks to conjure from Thot the secret of the pharaoh's dreams. But they were up against the true God now, a God who could not be coerced, cajoled, or cowed. Pharaoh, himself an initiate into the mysteries, watched anxiously as his ministers went through their consultations and incantations. His spirits fell as with embarrassment and bewilderment they confessed themselves defeated. "O King," they cried, with the ritual formula of the Pharonic court, "O King! Life! Prosperity! Health! We confess ourselves baffled. Thot gives no answer. The Pharaoh must seek elsewhere for the meaning of his dreams."

Thus, in the providential ways of God, the ground was prepared for the coming of Joseph. Pharaoh's distress must have been evident to all. His dreams. Who could interpret his dreams?

B. THE PERFECT WISDOM OF GOD (41:9-13)

Standing near Pharaoh's throne was a high official of the court, the king's cupbearer, Joseph's old friend the butler. He had listened keenly to the story of the dreams and watched with curious eye the self-assurance, then the bewilderment, and finally the outright fear and embarrassment of the magicians. Suddenly it all came back to him! He saw himself back in prison, perhaps shuddered at the thought and shied away from it, but the thought persisted. He remembered his dream and the dream of the baker, and he remembered the nice-looking Hebrew slave who had run the prison and who had ministered once to him in his need. What was the fellow's name?

Stepping forward he made his obeisance before Pharaoh and told his royal master of that incident from the past. "The young man was at one time, my lord, slave to Potiphar, captain of your majesty's guard." Perhaps Potiphar was there that day. If so his eyebrows must have shot up and a sudden chill gripped his heart. He too owed much to Joseph. He had, perhaps, been too hasty in heeding the story of his wife. His face would have been a study to behold.

What an exhibit we have here of *the perfect timing of God.* What an apologetic could be written on the timings of God in the affairs of men.

If one had the historical perspective and sufficient mastery of the facts, what a book could be written to challenge agnosticism. One would begin, perhaps, with Galatians 4:4. "But when the fulness of the time was come, God sent forth his Son, made of a woman, made under the law, to redeem them that were under the law."

So it was that God displayed His perfect wisdom in the perfect timing of the events of Joseph's life. Not a moment too soon, not a moment too late, but in the very fulness of time, God acted. Pharaoh was ready, his dreams saw to that; Joseph was ready, twelve years of iron discipline in a very hard school saw to that; the butler was ready, enough time had passed for him to speak of his imprisonment without fear. Twelve years is a long time to us, but it is nothing to God. "A thousand ages in Thy sight are like an evening gone, short as the watch that ends the night, before the rising sun." He had not forgotten Joseph; He was working to a timetable, that was all.

What an exhibit we have too of *the perfect tactics of God.* First He awakened in Pharaoh a tremendous sense of the supernatural of impending doom, of coming disaster, all tuned up to a fine pitch by the failure of his magicians. He awakened thus in Pharaoh dissatisfaction and disillusionment with the "experts," the magicians, and made him receptive to whatever Joseph might have to say. By the time those preliminaries were over, the stage was fully set for the entrance of Joseph. The atmosphere was right for him to carry everything before him, both Pharaoh and the court. And it was all done so smoothly and naturally. What is more natural than a dream? God works behind the scenes and, in seemingly ordinary ways, works out His sovereign will.[4]

C. THE PEERLESS WILL OF GOD (41:14-44)

It was God's peerless will to elevate Joseph to a position of great power in the world. He had shown that will to Joseph many years before in those boyhood dreams. The long years of discipline and development had been designed to prepare Joseph for the high post now to be his.

4. Miraculous displays of power are used very sparingly by God in His dealings with men. There are only four biblical periods when such miracles are prominent. There are the *emancipating miracles* that in the days of Moses smashed Egypt's power and led to the liberation of the enslaved Hebrew people, and that in the days of Joshua facilitated the conquest of Canaan. There are the *educational miracles* that, in the days of Elijah and Elisha, were intended to recall an apostate nation back to God and set the stage for the dawning of a complete prophetic era. There are the *evidential miracles* by which the Lord Jesus substantiated His claims to be the Son of God and by which the early church attested its message to a reluctant Jewish world. There are the *eschatologocal miracles* of the Apocalypse, those mighty miracles by which Satan will popularize the Beast and the counter miracles of the two witnesses by which God will expose Satan's messiah as false. Apart from those there are hardly any other miracles in the Bible at all. God usually brings His purposes to pass by such normal and natural means that only the eye of faith can see that He has been at work at all. It was in that way God prepared for the coming of Joseph.

It was, therefore, the peerless will of God to *present Joseph to Pharaoh* (41:14-37). Once his name was brought before Pharaoh, things moved very quickly. We can picture the scene. There was Joseph in his prison garb, bustling to and fro on his many errands as righthand man of the prison governor. Perhaps he was inducting a new convict into prison routine when the message came, or supervising perhaps the preparation of the noonday meal, or haggling with a supplier over the price of corn. But suddenly his name was called and the jailer was before him. "Quick, off with those clothes. Here, wash yourself, shave off that beard. Put on these robes. Hurry man, the pharaoh wants you!" "The pharaoh wants me, whatever for?" "I don't know, something about a dream. Hurry, man! Do you want me to lose my head?"

So Joseph, arrayed in court robes, was hurried off to Pharaoh. On the throne before him was a man with keen, penetrating eyes, bare, muscular arms, regal carriage and proud mein, a man wearing the double crown that for a thousand years had symbolized the union of Upper and Lower Egypt. On the imperial brow was the twin insignia of the two lands, the falcon and the serpent. In one hand was the crook for Upper Egypt, in the other the flail for Lower Egypt. The Pharaoh was probably arrayed in a long, fluted skirt made of priceless Egyptian linen. He had golden sandals on his feet. Such was the pharaoh, a man supposed to be god, the incarnation of Ra, a man whose functions were as much religious as political.[5]

Joseph looked at him as he sat there upon his throne, weighed down with his heavy crown and by the regalia of royalty. He saw before him a man occupying a position sanctified by over fifteen hundred years of unbroken tradition. Joseph, however, saw beyond the trappings of power. He saw a lost, lonely man with a soul to be saved.

"My dreams, young man, you can interpret them?" demanded the awesome king. The all-important moment had come. What a moment for Joseph to take the credit. How Satan must have whispered in Joseph's ear, "Now don't blow it, man! Don't be preaching to this fellow about God. Remember he's a god himself and a mighty powerful one. He'll have your head off as soon as look at you if you insult him before all these people." But Joseph had not been in God's school all those years for nothing. "Young man, can you interpret my dreams?" "And Joseph answered Pharaoh, saying, It is not in me: God shall give Pharaoh an answer of peace. . . . The dream of Pharaoh is one: God hath shewed Pharaoh what he is about to do—" First a word of Bible testimony, in which Pharaoh was dethroned and the true and living God put in absolute control, then the unfolding of Pharaoh's dream.

Having read to Pharaoh the meaning of his dreams, a meaning obvious to everyone the moment Joseph produced the key, Joseph went on

5. The pharaoh was essentially a priest-king, the mediator between the people and the spirits, the one who embodied in his own person the health and virility of the nation. His whole life was immersed in ritual, most of which had a religious significance.

to read Pharaoh a short lesson in economics. He advised the king to appoint a man "discreet and wise" and to set that man over the land of Egypt to husband the harvests of the plenteous years against the years of want and woe.

It was the peerless will of God not merely to present Joseph to Pharaoh but also to *promote Joseph through Pharaoh* (41:38-44). Pharaoh gazed at the young man standing before him and felt his heart strangely warmed and moved. He would make Joseph his grand vizier! Perhaps the post was vacant at the time, perhaps it was held by one of the courtiers standing confounded before him. We do not know. All we know is that Joseph was lifted then and there to the highest post in the land; that absolute power was placed in his hands, power second only to that of Pharaoh himself; that Joseph walked into Pharaoh's presence that day a condemned man, straight from prison, and walked out again the greatest man in the world.

Potiphar must have been there. Imagine what must have happened that night when he arrived home. He would look his wife in the eye at supper and say, "Do you remember that Hebrew slave we had around here some years ago, the one you accused of molesting you?" The woman's face would become a sudden mask. "Well, what about the wretch?" "I only hope your accusation was just, my dear, that's all. Pharaoh has just appointed him grand vizier of Egypt and I'm to report to him tomorrow morning."

"And Pharaoh said unto Joseph, Forasmuch as God hath shewed thee all this, there is none so discreet and wise as thou art: Thou shalt be over my house, and according unto thy word shall all my people be ruled: only in the throne will I be greater than thou. And Pharaoh said unto Joseph, See, I have set thee over all the land of Egypt."

Is that what Solomon had in mind when later, a great king himself, he wrote, "The king's heart is in the hand of the LORD, as the rivers of water: he turneth it whithersoever he will" (Proverbs 21:1)?

Most of us are still in God's school learning the lessons of life. How are we getting along? Are we preparing for graduation day? Or are we failing the tests He sends us from time to time?

VII. JOSEPH'S BRIDE (41:45-52)

The brides of the Bible speak of Christ and His church—not all of them (Sarah, for instance, is a type of Israel rather than the church), but many of them. We think for instance of Eve, of Sarah, Rachel and Rebekah, of Ruth and Abigail, and, of course, we think of Asenath.

In Eve we have a picture of the *formation* of the church. The story of Eve is the story of Adam's deep, deathlike sleep, of the opening of his side, of the taking from Adam that which was needed to form his helpmeet. Eve was a new creature, taken from Adam to be presented to

Adam, to share his life, to be the special object of his love. When we think of Adam and Eve, we think of Christ and the church.

Rebekah speaks to us of the *faith* of the church. How ignorant she was of Isaac until the servant came from the father with rich gifts and a call. We think of her prompt response to the invitation: "Wilt thou go with this man?" We think of the long journey, the many miles and days that lay between her meeting with the servant and her meeting with the son. It was time well spent in learning of Isaac and in preparing to meet him at his coming. When we think of Isaac and Rebekah, we think of Christ and His church.

Asenath sets before us the *future* of the church. Here was a woman taken from obscurity and made to share the high and lofty position of the one seated at the right hand of the majesty of the Pharaoh. When we think of Joseph and Asenath, we think of Christ and His church.

Some Bible teachers cannot see types in the Old Testament, others would restrict them to those so used in the New Testament. But what we have in the New Testament are mere *specimens;* they by no means exhaust the *species.* Asenath is nowhere mentioned in the New Testament as a type, nor for that matter is Joseph, yet a type she is and like it or not the type will intrude.

A. HER FAVORED PLACE (41:45-49)

To understand her favored place, we must first ignore her altogether. We must concentrate on the groom. Joseph's sufferings were over, and now for him there remained nothing but glory—a glory Asenath would share.

In the first place he was *highly exalted.* "And Pharaoh said unto Joseph . . . Thou shalt be over my house, and according to thy word shall all my people be ruled: only in the throne will I be greater than thou." Envious looks might well have been darted at Joseph by high officers of the court as Pharaoh took Joseph, the despised and rejected of men, and set him on high at his own right hand and invested him with power. That is where Jesus is today, seated at the right hand of the majesty on high. The jealousy and rage of men cannot alter His role.

The scene comes readily to view, the magnificent courtroom where the imperial pharaoh sat upon his great ivory throne and the pharaoh himself in regal robes. The steps to the throne would be of marble, a live lion would lie couchant at the pharaoh's feet. The pillars of the throne room would look like tall lotus plants, and their stately columns would picture ritual scenes from Egypt's religious codes. Behind the pharaoh would stand slaves with expensive ostrich feather fans richly trimmed with gold. Guards would stand around walls ablaze with scenes depicting the pharaoh's prowess of war. Around the king would stand his ministers of state and there, before him, stood the young man Joseph, his face pallid from prison and an ill-fitting robe flung hastily about his form.

The faces of the courtiers must have been a study. Amazement, admiration, fear, envy, resentment, gratitude, suspicion—all would be mirrored there according to their temperaments and ambitions. And, on the face of the pharaoh, a warm, welcoming smile. "Come here, Joseph! Ho, there, where's the keeper of the royal wardrobe? Fine linen for Joseph, a gold chain for his neck!" he might say. "Here, Potiphar, put this ring on Joseph's hand. This is Joseph. I have set him over all the land of Egypt."

Thus it was, too, that after His sufferings, our Lord was exalted on high. The gates of glory swung wide to receive Him, and in He went in triumph midst the wondering gaze of the angel hosts—a Man striding into heaven to take His place at the right hand of God! And on the faces of the cherubim, the seraphim, the highest archangels of glory, holy awe, wonder, worship, love.

Joseph was highly exalted; he was also *highly extolled.* "Pharaoh called Joseph's name Zaphnath-paaneah," and they cried before him, "Bow the knee!" Down on their knees they went before him, the whole vast assembly of Egyptian dignitaries, the guards, the military chiefs, the lords and ladies of the court, the attendants, the dancing girls, the aristocracy, the high and the low alike. From one end of the vast audience chamber to the other the word was whispered, like the rustling of a forest's leaves before the evening breeze, "Zaphnath-paaneah!" To the Egyptians the name would mean "Savior of the world," which is exactly what Joseph was to them. To the Hebrews the name would mean "Revealer of secrets," which is what he had been to his brethren in the days of his dreams and what he would be to Asenath in the days to come. In all this, of course, Joseph speaks of Jesus.

The unsaved man needs to know only one truth about Jesus—He is the *Savior of the world;* He came into the world to save sinners, and He can save from the wrath to come. He is God's answer to man's desperate need. The saved person needs to know Him in a deeper way as the *revealer of secrets,* the one who can unfold the thoughts of God's heart. We need to know Him as the twelve came to know Him in the upper room, as the two disciples came to know Him on the road to Emmaus, as Saul of Tarsus came to know Him in the solitudes of Sinai.

But we are being discourteous to a lady. We have kept Asenath, daughter of Potiphera, priest of On, standing far too long neglected and alone, and this her wedding day. We have digressed because only thus can her favored place be properly appreciated. Now that Joseph was exalted, Pharaoh chose a bride for him, one called by him to share the lofty seat of power that now belonged to the man of his right hand. "And he [Pharaoh] gave him to wife Asenath the daughter of Potiphera priest of On." She was brought in, wedded to Joseph, and exalted to share the position that was his. Such was her favored place.

Paul, speaking of the church, reminds us that we are to be "to the praise of his glory . . . that in the ages to come he might shew the exceeding riches of his grace in his kindness toward us through Christ Jesus . . . that now unto the principalities and powers in heavenly places might be known by the church the manifold wisdom of God" (Ephesians 1:12; 2:7; 3:10). That is our favored place. We have been chosen to be united to Christ in the seat of highest power, to manifest to an admiring universe the glory, the grace, and the genius of God.

B. HER FORGOTTEN PAST (41:45)

We know nothing about the woman beyond her name and the occupation of her father. Her father was Potiphera, a name that means "Given by the sun god." He was priest of On, the great city of Egypt later to be called Heliopolis ("City of the sun god"), located about nineteen miles north of Memphis in the Delta. It was the chief city of Egyptian science, the religious capital of ancient Egypt, and one of the four chief cities in the land. It was famous for the annual festivities held there in honor of the sun, of whom the pharaoh was believed to be the current incarnation. Asenath's father, therefore, was an important man in Egypt. He was a priest of On.

And what of Asenath herself? Her name means "One who belongs to Naith." The inference is that she was, herself, a priestess of the ancient Egyptian goddess Naith, the Earth Mother of the Delta. One tradition makes Naith the mother of Isis, Horus, and Osiris, three of the chief gods in the Egyptian pantheon. Naith was supposed to be the source of wisdom, a goddess consulted by the other gods when disputes arose between them.

On all that, however, Scripture is silent. Asenath was not introduced so that she might occupy the limelight, but rather to illustrate the high honor the pharaoh would bestow upon the man who had become the savior of the world.

How did Joseph react to marriage to a pagan priestess? Surely he and she must have had many a long talk on the veranda of their home as the brilliant stars looked down from a cloudless Egyptian sky. "And what of Ra?" Asenath might ask. "What of Naith, Mother of the Earth? What of all our great and illustrious gods, Joseph? Have you no thought for them at all? What of Osiris of the Nile on whom Egypt's life depends? What of Hathor, goddess of the sky? What of Isis the Enchantress, wife of Osiris? And what of Set, the dark slayer of Osiris? What of Horus and Harmahkis and Thot?"

Might not Joseph point her then to the true and living God of whom he had born such bold witness to the pharaoh himself? "I know not the gods of Egypt," he would say. "In Egypt I find a mixture of great wisdom and great folly. Egypt has the skill to build a pyramid or to make a sphinx; Egypt has the genius to rule the world. But Egypt worships cows and crocodiles and cats! Thot has the head of an ibis, Horus the head of a falcon, Anubis the head of a jackal. That strikes me as folly. In Egypt you understand astronomy, medicine, surgery, geometry, political science, and the craft of empire. Yet you worship mummified cats and snakes and fall down before a bull!"

Asenath would reply, "But Joseph, the falcon floating in the sky, the jackal flitting ghostlike along the desert's rim, the terrible crocodile lurking in the rushes of the Nile—these embody forces stronger than those possessed by man. Those creatures are different from us. They possess powers and functions we do not possess and therefore they are respected and reverenced as holders of superhuman powers. Thus have I been taught."

Joseph might say, "Not so, beloved! Lay aside those follies. Let me tell you of Elohim, of the Lord, of the true and living God of Abraham, Isaac, and Jacob, my fathers. Thus our traditions run: 'In the beginning God created the heavens and the earth, and the earth was without form and void and darkness was upon the face of the deep. And the Spirit of God moved upon the face of the waters. And God said, Light be! and light was—' "

Would not Asenath whisper, "What you say, Joseph, rings like the very word of God in my heart. Oh, tell me more." Thus Joseph would become to Asenath the revealer of secrets indeed.

But as for Asenath, God has blotted out her past. We are told nothing of her childhood days, nothing about her education in the follies of Egyptian religion, nothing of her desires and decisions, the whole story of her unregenerate days. All is blotted out. God remembers it no more, and He refuses to keep a record of it in His Book. All that mattered was that she had been brought to Joseph and had linked her life with his. Thus Joseph rightly fills the scene, for he was all in all. Thus it is with our heavenly Joseph too. The great work of the Holy Spirit is not to speak of Himself, not to focus our attention upon Himself and His gifts, not to keep on raking up our past, but to engage our thoughts and affections with Christ.

C. HER FAITHFUL PART (41:50-52)

It was Asenath's part to have a share in bringing sons into glory. "And unto Joseph were born two sons before the years of famine came, which Asenath the daughter of Potiphera priest of On bare unto him." The true and heavenly Joseph, too, in this age, is gathering in an elect family and when it is complete it will be followed by the years of famine, "the time of Jacob's trouble." Moreover, just as the famine of old was used to drive Joseph's brethren to him, so the coming Tribulation will be used by God to drive the Jews to Jesus.

Two sons were born to Joseph. The first was Manasseh, whose name means "*Forgetting.*" He has something to say to us. Jesus said concerning the communion feast, "This do in remembrance of me." Are we forgetting that? The Holy Spirit says, "I beseech you therefore brethren by the mercies of God that ye present your bodies a living sacrifice." Are we forgetting that? We are told, "Be filled with the Spirit." Are we forgetting that? We are commanded, "Study to show thyself approved unto God." Are we forgetting that? We are told, "Pray without ceasing"; we are told, "God loveth a cheerful giver." Are we forgetting? Need we extend the list? Are we marked by that which is suggested by Manasseh? Forgetting!

Ephraim, the name of the second son, means "*Fruitfulness.*" He has something to say to us too. Jesus said, "Herein is my Father glorified that ye bear much fruit." Are we fruitful? Paul says we are "married to another, even to him that is raised from the dead that we should bring forth fruit unto God." Are we fruitful? Paul says, "The fruit of the Spirit is love, joy, peace, longsuffering, gentleness, goodness, faith, meekness, temperance" (Galatians 5:22). Are we fruitful?

Manasseh and Ephraim speak to us of the things that characterize the people of God in this age. We will either be forgetful or fruitful. Am I being a Manasseh or an Ephraim?

VIII. JOSEPH'S BRETHREN (41:53–47:10)

A. THE MYSTERY PHASE (41:53–44:34)

There are thirteen famines in the Bible. This one was used of God to drive the chosen family to Joseph, just as in a coming day He will use the rigors of the great Tribulation to drive Israel to Christ. Joseph's dealings with his brethren in the long section now opening up to us may be divided into three phases. There is *the mystery phase* of his dealings (41:53–44:34), during which his brethren were at a complete loss to explain what was happening to them and during which their consciences were awakened to the wrongs they had done to Joseph years before. There is *the majesty phase* (45:1-24), during which Joseph made himself known to his brethren in all the glory that was now his. There is *the ministry phase* (45:25–47:10), during which he represented their interests at the court of Pharaoh, brought them to be with himself, and settled them in the best of the land. All three phases are rich in symbolic teaching and set before us phases of the Lord's future dealings with His people Israel. The story as it unfolds also contains many practical lessons for us today.

1. HOW JOSEPH'S BRETHREN WERE BURDENED (41:53–42:34)

The story begins with the clearly *predicted famine* (41:53-57). Its *severity* is first set on record. "And the seven years of plenteousness, that was in the land of Egypt, were ended. And the seven years of dearth began to come, according as Joseph had said: and the dearth was in all lands; but in all the land of Egypt there was bread."

There are few left today who can remember the terrible dust bowl era in the United States. John Steinbeck in *The Grapes of Wrath* has given us one of literature's most graphic pictures of it. He depicts Oklahoma as the sun flared down on the growing corn and withered it where it stood, the weeds flinching and succumbing to the heat, the dust tossed high as the fence tops by the passing of a wagon. He pictures the tantalizing rain heads appearing in the sky to gaze down at the tortured land below, dropping an infuriating drop or two on blistering fields and farms, and then moving on to other parts. He tells of the coming of the wind, a wind that picked up the topsoil and carried it away. He tells how the dust filtered back to earth to cover the land like a blanket and to settle like powder on fence posts and blasted corn.

Thus famine came to middle America, and thus famine came to Egypt and the lands about, the famine divinely foretold and against which God had raised up a Joseph and a wise and thoughtful pharaoh.

In Egypt the Nile failed, and when the Nile failed, Egypt died. Far away every year the waters of the Blue Nile thundering down from Ethiopia met the waters of the White Nile coming down from "Livingstone's Lake." The turbulent Nile from the Ethiopian highlands carried on its swell the rich treasure of fertilizing mud that, each year, brought life to the land. The ancient Egyptians knew little if anything of those things. Their world ended south of Nubia. The life-giving flood, the yearly miracle, was the gift of Ra. At Thebes and other towns along the serpentine length of the Nile, the priests with their gauges measured the floodwater and compared their findings with the records of other years. In a good year the river would begin to rise in August, and the Egyptians held the High Nile Festival in thanksgiving to the gods. It would reach its crest in September, and by late October the floods would begin to subside. Planting began in November.

For seven long and wonderful years the Egyptians rejoiced in their "good" Niles. There never had been such Niles. The prodigality of those years was so great that the twenty percent levy on grain imposed by Joseph and garnered into Pharaoh's barns was so abundant that it fed all of Egypt for the seven famine-stricken years with plenty left over for sale to stricken surrounding lands.

But now the seven-year drought had come. The bountiful Nile failed to rise, failed to provide its life-giving mud, failed as Joseph said it would. Year after year, for seven long years, the watchers along the Nile sent back the same gloomy report: "Another bad Nile." Four thousand miles away to the south, in the secret springs where the Nile had its source, the torrential rains that fed the lakes and tributaries ceased. Egypt and all the lands round about faced famine.

Not only its severity, but its *significance* is recorded. "And when all the land of Egypt was famished, the people cried to Pharaoh for bread: and Pharaoh said unto all the Egyptians, Go unto Joseph; what he saith unto you, do. And the famine was over all the face of the earth: And Joseph opened all the storehouses and sold unto the Egyptians; and the famine waxed sore in the land of Egypt. And all countries came into Egypt unto Joseph for to buy corn; because that the famine was so sore in all lands." There is the significance of it. Joseph! Joseph! Joseph!

The underlying purpose of the famine was to drive people to Joseph, and especially his kinsmen, the children of Israel.

Now look at the *perplexed family* (42:1-5). The spotlight swings from Egypt to Canaan. The patriarchal family was caught up in the widespread disaster that had overtaken the world. God's people have no unconditional guarantee they will escape the floods and the famines, the tornadoes and earthquakes, the horrors of war and rebellion that descend from time to time upon the world. When disaster does strike, we should not sit back and wring our hands and expect God to do some miracle on our behalf. We should look around for natural means for relief. At least, so thought Jacob. "When Jacob saw that there was corn in Egypt, Jacob said unto his sons, Why do ye look one upon another? . . . I have heard that there is corn in Egypt: get you down thither" (42:1-2). That was the sensible thing to do. There is no law that states that a spiritual person cannot also be a sensible person.

No doubt the chosen family was perplexed at the extent and severity of the famine. Why should it affect Canaan? Were they not in the promised land in obedience to the mind and will of God? Why did God allow such things? They looked askance at the beggars, at the starving children, at many a pitiful corpse. Why? They were soon to find out why. Their own sin, long since buried in their minds, long covered up, was about to be exposed and written up in banner headlines for all the world to read.

Thus the story tells us of the *pointing finger* (42:6-34). The finger of God kept pointing at the consciences of those men and, at the same time, at Joseph. The brethren first acknowledged Joseph, just as his dreams had foretold in *simple ignorance* (42:6-9). They simply did not know they were doing it. "And Joseph's brethren came, and bowed down themselves before him with their faces to the earth. And Joseph saw his brethren, and he knew them, but made himself strange unto them . . . and Joseph knew his brethren, but they knew him not. And Joseph remembered the dreams." Into Egypt they had come, to be directed at the frontier to the division of the Egyptian foreign office that dealt with the exporting of vital national resources to aliens and foreign powers. There they had been referred to Joseph and, awed by his magnificence, had fallen prostrate on the ground. The finger was pointing to him but, in their blindness, they did not recognize him for who he was. It is the same for the Jew today. The finger keeps pointing at Jesus, but most Jews fail to see in Him their long looked-for Messiah, Savior, and Lord. "Blindness," says Paul, "has happened to Israel" (Romans 11:25).

Then by *subtle implication* they acknowledged Joseph (42:10-17). Joseph accused them of being spies. "Nay, my lord, but to buy food are thy servants come. We are all one man's sons; we are true men, Thy servants are no spies." Because they had made no mention of him, Joseph taxed them again with being spies. That time they said,

"Thy servants are twelve brethren, the sons of one man in the land of Canaan; and behold, the youngest is this day with our father, and one is not." There it was! The reference to Joseph by subtle implication. They would not name him or acknowledge him; they would prefer not to think of him. But since they must, they would make only the slightest possible casual and passing reference to him. They would say nothing about what they had done to him, nothing at all about their rejection of him. Joseph was an awkward fact of history they would prefer not to face at all.

Joseph, however, had no intention of letting them off like that. He accused them a third time of being spies and locked them up in ward for three days. One can imagine their consternation. They were deathly afraid of that person, that mysterious Egyptian who was demonstrating what absolute power he had over them. And in adversity they began to think.

Their third acknowledgment of Joseph was in *self incrimination* (42: 18-23). After three days Joseph had his brethren released. "I am going to put you to the test," he said. "You say you have a younger brother at home? Then go and bring him here! True men are you? We'll see!" Then he stood back with a look of indifference on his face and listened to their further conversation.

And they, not knowing that he understood their Hebrew tongue, spoke freely. The pointing finger had found them out. They began to accuse themselves and each other for what they had done to Joseph long years before and then, out it came—their confession! "And they said one to another, We are varily guilty concerning our brother [conscience at work], in that we saw the anguish of his soul, when he besought us, and we would not hear [memory at work]; therefore is this distress come upon us" [reason at work]. Conscience, memory, and reason—God's three great hounds to bark and bay at the door of the soul. The pointing finger was doing its work. They were still blind as to who Joseph really was, but they were now thoroughly awakened to their appalling guilt concerning him. They would now mention his name, at least among themselves, and admit what they had done.

Their fourth acknowledgment of Joseph was under *sore intimidation* (42:24-34). Joseph turned aside and wept, for his heart bled for them and he wanted to make himself known to them then and there. But he was too wise for that. They were not yet ready to see him, in his glory, for who he was. They needed to taste more severe adversity so that their sluggish consciences might be further aroused.

To accomplish that, Joseph laid hands on Simeon, the cruelest of them all, and whisked him away. Simeon needed special discipline and, moreover, his sufferings would speak to his brethren. Minus Simeon, now detained as a hostage, the brothers left Egypt. Their sacks were full of corn indeed, but their thoughts were greatly troubled. Where would it all end? What would they ever say to their father?

At the first oasis they stopped for rest and food and opened their sacks. Horror of horrors! There in their sacks was the money they had brought with them and had paid over to the cashier in payment for their corn. They stared at it in utter disbelief. Where did that money come from? They picked up the coins as though they were red hot, counting them over and over again. A great loathing for the money surged up in their souls; it burned their fingers, it spelled trouble of the very worst sort.

These selfsame men had sold Joseph for cold cash years before. They were men who loved money. They had happily prospered financially during the long days of their rejection of him. Joseph must teach them to loathe the very sight of money.

When they arrived home they poured into their father's ears the whole amazing story, being careful to omit, of course, any mention of their betrayal of Joseph years before. They might whisper of that among themselves, but they were not yet ready to make a clean breast of it to their father. Remorse was at work, but not repentance. They acknowledged God's hand in those mysterious events ("What is this that God hath done unto us?"), but they were not yet brought low enough to pour out their hearts in bitter tears over Joseph.

All that goes far beyond the story of Joseph and his brothers. It reaches far down the centuries to Jewish people and their treatment of Jesus. For long centuries the Jews have persistently rejected Him. Their historians pass lightly over the story of Jesus. They cannot deny that such a man existed, but they hurry past Him as fast as they can. They dismiss Him lightly, flippantly, as one of the pseudo-Messiahs. Some will acknowledge His goodness, even His greatness, even own Him as an ornament of the Hebrew race—as a *man.* But not for a moment will they give Him His proper place or acknowledge Christianity. Many Jewish writers execrate Christianity.

The Jews have wandered the world for centuries pursued by their national guilt. They have the Midas touch, and invariably they prosper in the lands they adopt. They rise to the top in business, in the professions, in the arts and sciences, in politics. And they make money. But the day will come when they will loathe it. Their prosperity will bring down upon them the hatred of the world. It has happened before. It happened in Germany during the Nazi era, it has happened countless times in their long, tragic history, and it will happen again. Their sorrows will come to a head in that dreadful time known as "the time of Jacob's trouble." They will cry out like Joseph's brethren, "What is this that God hath done unto us?" They will find themselves gripped, as Joseph's brethren did, by circumstances beyond their control. The pointing finger will point at Jesus and at their rejection of Him and will continue to point until the scales fall away from their eyes.

2. How Joseph's Brethren Were Bewildered (42:35–43:34)

The story in the next section revolves around three people—Jacob, Judah, and Joseph—as it continues to tell of Joseph's dealings with his brethren, dealings designed to reveal to them the lawlessness that resided in their hearts and the love that reigned in his.

a. Jacob's Plight (42:35-38)

The old man listened to what his sons had to say, but he only half believed their tale. Where was Simeon? What was all the talk about taking Benjamin next time they went? Those boys of his were nothing but a source of sorrow and concern to him. Years ago they had come home with Joseph's coat, and he had fully believed their united testimony. "It is my son's coat," he had said. "An evil beast hath devoured him, Joseph is without doubt rent in pieces." The brothers had heaved a sigh of relief. But time had passed and shrewd old Jacob entertained second thoughts, had given more consideration to the jealousy and hostility the others had always shown to his favorite. Now they stood before him without Simeon and with the bald statement that the next time they must take his beloved Benjamin to Egypt with them. Their story was unbelievable; he demanded proof. "Open your sacks," he said. There, sure enough, was the cold cash that confirmed their tale. "All these things are against me," he groaned as his faith broke down. In reality, had he but known it, Joseph had been exalted on high and was working all things for his good.

Then Reuben spoke up, Reuben his firstborn, Reuben whose guilty secret in the matter of Bilhah was well known to the old man. "Slay my two sons if I bring not Benjamin to thee," he said. "Deliver him into my hand, and I will bring him to thee again." Jacob gave him a withering look. "My son shall not go down with you."

b. Judah's Pledge (43:1-15)

The supply of food from Egypt ran low and a new trip must be made. Judah knew that to go back to Egypt without Benjamin would be worse than useless, so he spoke plainly to Jacob. We observe *the sanity of Judah's pledge* (43:1-8). He simply set forth the cold logic of the situation. It was no use to put one's head in the sand; facts were facts. Either Benjamin must go, or nobody would go. We observe *the sincerity of Judah's pledge* (43:9-10). He did not do what Reuben did—offer his own sons as hostages. He put himself in pledge. "I will be surety for him . . . if I bring him not unto thee . . . let me bear the blame for ever."

When we saw Judah last he had married an unsaved woman, had been widowed, and was living a dissolute life. He had evidently retured home and come back into the fellowship of the patriarchal family. God had been working in his life. Perhaps the birth of his twins affected him more than it seemed. Moreover, he had been brought into the presence of Joseph and, unknowingly, had felt the power and the goodness of the man. Thus it was that a new Judah stepped forward, a Judah with a new heart.

We observe *the success of Judah's pledge* (43:11-15). Old Jacob was convinced. However, he insisted that if Benjamin must go, suitable preparations must be made to insure that he would be kindly received. That awesome, powerful man who held all their destinies in his hands must be properly approached. A present was prepared, the best fruits of the impoverished land, balm and honey, spices and myrrh, nuts and almonds, and the money that had so mysteriously appeared in the sacks must be returned. And, alas, Benjamin must go.

c. JOSEPH'S PLANS (43:16-34)

The story returns to Egypt and focuses on Joseph's plans. We can detect eight steps in Joseph's planned dealings with his brethren now. There was, first, the *undeserved feast* (43:16-17). "And when Joseph saw Benjamin with them, he said to the ruler of his house, Bring these men home, and slay, and make ready; for these men shall dine with me at noon. And the man did as Joseph bade; and the man brought the men into Joseph's house." The initiative was all with Joseph. He spread the feast, he bore its cost, he took care of the sacrifice upon which it was founded, he commissioned "the ruler of his house" to bring in the men. How like the gospel. It was all of grace.

Then there was *unconcealed fear* (43:18). "And the men were afraid, because they were brought into Joseph's house." Understandably so. Imagine the strangeness of it all. They were farmers, rough men, men of the woods and the wilds. The opulence that surrounded them in Joseph's house, his magnificence and luxury, the exotic artifacts he had culled from all over the civilized world, the air of unbounded wealth, the atmosphere of unlimited power—all those things struck fear into their souls. Moreover, they misinterpreted what was happening. "Because of the money that was returned in our sacks at the first time are we brought in," they whispered among themselves. Then, with an added note of alarm, "That he may seek occasion against us, and take us for bondsmen, and our asses." Nothing could have been further from the truth. It was a slander on the character of the unknown stranger who held their destinies in his hands. They simply did not know him; their thoughts were not his thoughts and their ways not his. They judged him by themselves.

Often, the unregenerate man's first contact with the gospel awakens feelings of guilt and unease. It must be so. Introduce an unsaved person into the house of God and you bring him into contact with another world, one wholly alien to his ways of thought and manner of life. Unsaved people are aliens, strangers, foreigners there, and, often as not, they misinterpret the gospel. It is some kind of trap; God delights in their discomforture. They do not know Him or his Son, nor can they understand His grace. Like Joseph's brethren they could well wish themselves anywhere but in the house of the Lord.

Next mention is made of the *unexplained find* (43:19-24). Panic-stricken, the brothers took Joseph's steward into their confidence, explaining to him about the money in their sacks and assuring him they had brought it back. The steward's reply was reassuring but not revealing. "Peace be to you," he said, "fear not: your God, and the God of your father, hath given you treasure in your sacks: I had your money." Then he brought Simeon out to them. Thus there was a deliberate attempt made by the steward to disarm their fears, develop their faith, and denote their future. The brethren were still as far from knowing Joseph as ever, but now they knew that it was grace at work, sovereign grace, grace in some way connected with the true and living God, the God they had ignored for so long in their worldly and wicked ways.

Then we have recorded the *understandable formality* that marked Joseph's entrance (43:25-28). High noon arrived, and the waiting brothers, no doubt eagerly questioning Simeon as to what had happened to him during their absence, heard the heralds announce the approach of the unknown lord of the land. They made ready their present, bowed low before him, offered their gift, and waited for what would happen. How formal it all was! Of course, they did not know Joseph; their dreadful crime still lay between them. That deed of shame had long since been forgiven by Joseph, but they had no knowledge of that, nor were they yet ready in soul for the full revelation of his grace he longed to make.

In all, Joseph acted with them as the Lord acts with a soul. God is never in a hurry; He never skimps. We would put the pressure on and seek to get people to make a hasty decision for Christ, but God allows the Holy Spirit to carry on a thorough work of conviction and to bring people to the point of genuine repentance. Then and only then He brings the sinner to the point of decision.

Next we have the record of an *unrevealed feeling* (43:29-31). "And Joseph lifted up his eyes, and saw his brother Benjamin, his mother's son . . . and he said, God be gracious unto thee, my son. And Joseph made haste; for his bowels [being] did yearn upon his brother: and he sought where to weep; and he entered into his chamber, and wept there. And he washed his face, and went out and refrained himself." How like our Lord! How often He yearns over a soul, longing to sweep aside all that stands between and overwhelm with His grace, but He refuses to ravish; He will only woo.

Joseph wept! Jesus wept! How easy it would have been for Him that day, when He stood on the heights over Jerusalem with tears running down His cheeks, then and there to have summoned His legions from the sky. How easy it would have been to march into the city at the head of an angel host, overthrow Rome, and set up a mighty, earthly kingdom. But it would have spoiled everything. It would have merely perpetuated things as they were without regenerating men. And how easy it would be for Him today to reveal Himself to men in flaming bursts of glory. But it would force the pace, and dazzle, and overawe, and compel, and such is not His way in the present age of grace.

The story next records the *uncanny familiarity* that the stranger lord had with them all (43:32-33). "And they set on for him by himself, and for the Egyptians," we read, "and they sat before him, the firstborn according to his birthright, and the youngest according to his youth: and the men marvelled one at another." How did he know them thus? There was Reuben at the head of the table and next to him Simeon, then Levi and Judah, followed in order by Dan, Naphtali, Gad, Asher, Issachar, and Zebulun, and there, last of all the youngest—Benjamin. The brothers stared at one another. They were known! What did the man not know? The arrow of conviction penetrated deeper.

Then came the *unusual favor* shown to Benjamin (43:34*a*). The food was brought in, and each was given his portion, bread enough and to spare, but what was this? Here came five men staggering beneath Benjamin's portion. His was five times that of Reuben or Judah or Gad. What a broad hint that was! The stranger lord had a preference for Benjamin. How blind they were not to put two and two together.

What was Joseph doing by giving Benjamin such a lion's share and doing it so openly and obviously, heaping slights upon the older men? Well, years before those same men had sold him because they were envious of him. Were they envious still? Would they eye Benjamin as once they had him? His dealings were bearing fruit, it seems, for there is not the slightest hint they showed resentment or jealousy at the preference shown to the youngest.

Finally the story tells of an *unrestrained fellowship* that prevailed (43:34*b*). "And they drank, and were merry with him." Not all of God's dealings are dark and threatening. True, there are times when He thunders, but He often sends the sunshine, and often as not, He paints the storm cloud with the rainbow's hues.

Thus it was that Joseph's brethren moved from being burdened to being bewildered. They were not the same hard, thoughtless men they had been when first they came under his hand. However, the mystery phase of his dealings was not over yet. There was to be one step more.

3. How Joseph's Brethren Were Broken (44:1-34)

The story that now unfolds is rich in typical teaching. It looks far beyond the actual dealings of Joseph with his brethren and mirrors the coming dealings of Jesus with the Jews. That phase of Joseph's dealings is unfolded in three stages.

a. THE CONSPIRACY (44:1-3)

The brothers had once conspired in hate against Joseph; now he conspired in love against them. He commenced by dealing with *their greed* (44:1). "And he commanded the steward of his house, saying, Fill the men's sacks with food, as much as they can carry, and put every man's money in his sack's mouth." They had once sold him for money, so let them have money. Let them have it until they loathe the very sight of it.

Most people like money, but few have been so successful in acquiring it as the Jews. As a race they seem to have an instinctive flair for getting rich. Their great natural talents, wedded to their tireless industry, business acumen and mutual cooperation have made the Jews the financiers of the world. During the Middle Ages they invariably rose swiftly to positions of affluence and power in all the lands into which they were driven by persecution. Kings, emperors, and popes appealed to them times without number for financial aid. And always those alluring riches, once acquired, made them the envy of their neighbors. It became an international game to fleece the Jews. They had used cold cash to buy Judas; money has become their snare.

Having dealt with their greed, Joseph dealt next with *their grudge* (44:2-3). "And put my cup, the silver cup, in the sack's mouth of the youngest, and his corn money," he commanded his steward. He had confronted them with *dangerous riches* in the first part of the gentle conspiracy; now he confronted them with *dreadful responsibility.* In Benjamin's sack was set a bomb timed to explode before the brothers left behind the final frontiers of the land. Benjamin was to become a threat to them all just as he, Joseph, had been to them (or so they had imagined) long years ago. What would they do with Benjamin? That was what Joseph wished to know.

b. THE CONFRONTATION (44:4-15)

As Joseph's brothers were heading toward the sands of Sinai, Joseph's steward and an escort of armed men came up behind. "Wherefore have ye rewarded evil for good?" the steward demanded as he reined in his horse and motioned to the escort to surround the brothers. "Where is my lord's cup, the cup he uses in his divining arts?" In ancient Egypt a goblet was frequently used as a means of communicating with the spirits. In some cases small pieces of gold or silver, together with precious stones, were cast into the goblet over which appropriate incantations were uttered. The cup then acted as a species of Ouija board. Sometimes the goblet would be filled with water and set in the sun so that the deeps and shadows cast in the cup could be read just as some people today read tea leaves in a cup. It is hardly likely that Joseph indulged in such practices, but he certainly must have known about them.

The magicians of Egypt made uses of such methods of divination and were held in great awe by the people in consequence. The brothers, already in awe of Joseph, were now terrified at his supposed ability to see into their very sacks.

To the last man they protested their innocence. So confident were they that none of them had tampered with the cup they swore a great oath. "With whomsoever of thy servants it be found, both let him die, and we also will be my lord's bondsmen." The steward smiled grimly and asked them to open their sacks. One by one the brothers passed inspection until the searchers came to Benjamin, then, there it was! The missing cup was in the mouth of Benjamin's sack.

The brothers had come to life's greatest crossroad. What would they do with Benjamin? Would they compound their wickedness and toss him to the wolves as once they had sloughed off Joseph? Or would they take their stand for Benjamin? It did not take long for the interested steward to see the result of the game being played out there on the desert sands. Without a moment's hesitation the stricken men cast in their lot with Benjamin and prepared to share whatever fate was in store for him. Little did they know it, but by that action they had turned the tide. The incident points forward to the day when the Jews, the Lord's kinsmen according to the flesh, will be put into the furnace of affliction, to be purified by the flame and be made ready for the revelation to them of Jesus in His glory, the one who has been active in their affairs all along.

Discernment was dawning, but not yet were Joseph's brethren ready for the moment of the "apocalypse," when Joseph would be unveiled before them. Greatly chastened, they rent their clothes in typical eastern fashion, for they had come to an end of all their cleverness and pride. Greatly changed, they came to Joseph and flung themselves before him.

At once Joseph made them face the fact of his greatness and his power. "What deed is this that ye have done?" he demanded. "Wot ye not that such a man as I can certainly divine?" He was forcing them to think of him in even bigger terms than any they had conceded before. Likewise, in a coming day, in the furnace of the Great Tribulation, the Lord Jesus will force the Jews to think of Him in far greater terms than ever they have been willing to do. Whatever current Jewish thought might be about Jesus, one thing is certain: the Jews, as a people, are not prepared to admit His Deity, that He is their Messiah and the Son of God, and that, as a nation, they committed the crime of crimes in forcing Pilate's hand by insisting on the crucifixion of Christ. "His blood be on us and upon our children," they had cried, crowning their guilt. The Tribulation, however, will smash right through their national and religious pride and will prepare them for the full and final unveiling to them of Jesus Himself.

c. THE CONFESSION (44:16-34)

Now Judah took the stage. First he offered to share the blame and then to shoulder the blame completely himself. "What shall we say unto my lord," he cried. "What shall we speak? or how shall we clear ourselves? God hath found out the iniquity of thy servants." In a vague and general way Judah confessed the guilt of the brothers in the rejection and sale of Joseph long years before. It was a great step forward, but it was still not enough. Joseph promptly rejected their offer to share the blame with Benjamin—for Judah evidently thought it possible that Benjamin, despite his cries of innocence, had actually stolen the cup. "Behold we are my lord's servants, both we, and he also with whom the cup is found."

Joseph rejected the suggestion out of hand; it was not what he wanted. "God forbid," he said, "that I should do so: but the man in whose hand the cup is found, he shall be my servant; and as for you, get you up in peace to your father." He was still forcing the issue—what would they do with Benjamin?

Judah rose to the occasion in one of the great intercessory prayers of the Bible, a prayer that demonstrated Judah's moral greatness and his supremacy over all his brethren. It was for that prayer, possibly, that the Messianic line was finally settled on Judah. As a result of his prayer all the barriers to Joseph's complete revelation of himself were removed. In his prayer Judah took his stand, on behalf of all his brethren, with Benjamin the father's beloved.

He appealed to the stranger-lord's *patience* (44:18). "Oh my lord, let thy servant, I pray thee, speak a word in my lord's ears, and let not thine anger burn against thy servant: for thou art even as Pharaoh." He gave Joseph his proper position and appealed to him on the ground of grace. He appealed to the stranger-lord's *purposes* (44:19-23), telling Joseph how the famine had affected the family and how Joseph's heart must have warmed as Judah rehearsed all Joseph's dealings with them. He reminded the stranger-lord of his inflexible demand that he be approached only through Benjamin. He appealed to the stranger-lord's *pity* (44:24-31), speaking to him of the father's great sorrow that Benjamin must go. "And thy servant my father said unto us, Ye know that my wife bare me two sons: and the one went out from me, and I said, Surely he is torn in pieces; and I saw him not since: and if ye take this also from me . . . ye shall bring down my gray hairs with sorrow to the grave."

How that must have touched Joseph's heart! Here was Judah talking to him about the father's sorrow, telling of the agony that had gone through the father's soul at the tidings of Joseph's death. As Judah spoke of the father's broken heart, Joseph's heart overflowed.

What a lesson concerning intercession is embodied here. If we would be intercessors, let us tell our Lord about His sufferings and what those sufferings meant to the Father. Let us talk to Him about Calvary. Let us tell Him how Calvary broke the heart of God. Let us tell Him that Calvary can never be allowed to happen again—once for that kind of sorrow is enough for all eternity. Such pleading cannot go in vain.

In concluding his plea, Judah appealed to the stranger-lord's *power* (44:32-34). To return to his father without Benjamin was out of the question; it would be the last straw, it would bring down the final curse. Far better to be dead than that. It was a plea that melted Joseph's heart into hot, gushing tears. The mystery phase was over. The majesty phase of Joseph's dealings could begin.

B. THE MAJESTY PHASE (45:1-24)

Genesis 45 anticipates the day when the Lord will reveal Himself fully and finally to the nation of Israel at the close of the Great Tribulation. At the same time it speaks of the way the Lord Jesus reveals Himself to those today whose hearts have been prepared to own Him as Lord. And, of course, it chronicles for us the continuing drama of Joseph's own, personal dealings with his brothers.

1. THE REVELATION OF JOSEPH (45:1-16)

a. THE REVELATION OF HIS PERSON (45:1-3)

Any true appreciation of Christ must begin with an appreciation of who He really is. The professing church sometimes misrepresents Him to men. For instance, the Roman Catholic church presents Him as a babe in the arms of the virgin Mary, a helpless little child overshadowed by a woman, or as a man nailed to and still hanging on a cross. Both concepts are inadequate, for both present Him in weakness. He is no longer in the cradle, no longer on the cross; He is the Lord of Glory, exalted Son of the living God.

Joseph's revelation of his person to his brethren was *a sudden revelation* (45:1). "Then Joseph could not refrain himself before all them that stood by him; and he cried, Cause every man to go out from me. And there stood no man with him, while Joseph made himself known unto his brethren." It was sudden. One moment their eyes were holden that they should not know him, the next he stood fully revealed before them. What a stunning moment it must have been. What guilty memories were suddenly raging rampant in the souls of those men. They had known him only as Zaphnath-paaneah, the savior of the world, a great and terrible lord of Egypt; now they knew him as Joseph.

In just that way the Jews will one day have their eyes opened to Jesus. They will have come to know Him in a general sort of way as Savior during the closing years of the Tribulation, calling upon Him by His Old Testament name. Then, suddenly, He will be unveiled before them at His coming and they will see in a flash that the Lord-God of the Old Testament and the Jesus of the New Testament are one and the same. Like the man born blind, like many an awakened sinner today, the testimony of the suddenly enlightened Jew will be: "Once I was blind but now I can see! How could we ever have not recognized the truth concerning this Person?" will be their wondering cry.

It was not only a sudden revelation, it was *a sobering revelation* (45:2). "And he wept aloud: and the Egyptians and the house of Pharaoh heard." The initial moment of revelation was packed with emotion and drenched with tears and the tidings of it were carried up to the throne. For when a person (or, as will be the case with the remnant of Israel in a coming day, a people) comes face to face with Jesus and realizes at last who He really is, there should be emotion. It is an emotion-packed experience in heaven as the tidings are carried up to the throne, for Jesus says there is "joy in the presence of the angels of God over one sinner that repenteth" (Luke 15:10). Joseph's tears were tears of joy, joy that the long estrangement between himself and his brethren was over. The news spread swiftly throughout the land, just as when a person truly comes to Christ the impact of it will always be felt in the world.

Then too it was *a simple revelation* (45:3*a*). "And Joseph said unto his brethren, I am Joseph; doth my father yet live?" "I am Joseph!" That was all. How very simple it was. The gospel is so simple in its essence that a little child can grasp its truth.

Many centuries after that simple revelation of Joseph to his brethren, a fiery Jew was posting north along the Damascus road from Jerusalem as fast as his goaded camel could go. His armed escort, trailing behind, were hard put to it to keep the pace. In Damascus there lived apostates who were daring to proclaim that Jesus of Nazareth, a crucified man, was actually the Messiah of Israel and the Savior of the world. *That dangerous cult must be stamped out,* thought Saul of Tarsus as he urged his camel on that day, hurrying north as the official agent of the Sanhedrin to root heresy out of Damascus. Then came a blinding light, and Saul of Tarsus, smitten from the beast, lay prostrate on the ground. "Who art thou, Lord?" he cried. Back came the simple answer: "I am Jesus." That was all. One moment Saul was a sinner, the next he was a saint; one moment a blasphemer, the next a believer.

"I am Joseph." "I am Jesus." We often make conversion such a difficult business. We arm ourselves with proof texts, with "the four spiritual laws," with arguments, with proved methods. But with God it is all so simple: "I am Jesus." When the time is ripe, the Holy Spirit reveals Christ to the sinner's soul in such a simple way, and the work is done.

Furthermore, Joseph's revelation was *a successful revelation* (45:3*b*). It quickened a sense of sin in his brethren. They had rejected him, sold him, done their best to forget him. The word "troubled" in that verse means "terrified." Well might they be terrified! They had fallen, in all their guilt, into the hands of the one they had so dreadfully wronged, one now armed with absolute power. Turning back from Joseph to Jesus we see the parallel, for well might the sinner be terrified when conviction comes home to his heart—when he realizes the enormity of his sin as a Christ-rejector, guilty of the crime of Calvary, and guilty of persistent and stubborn rejection of Christ over so many years. The same, of course, applies to Israel as a nation at the end of the Tribulation.

The revelation of Jesus to a human heart is bound to awaken thoughts of sin. The first work of the Holy Spirit in a human soul is the work of conviction (John 16:7-11). Salvation is not a matter of raising one's hand in a meeting for prayer, or walking down an aisle; it is a matter of facing up to personal guilt expressed in a lifelong rejection of Christ. There can be no true conversion without conviction.

The revelation of his person by Joseph was very successful; it smote the consciences of his brothers as nothing done before had been able to do.

b. THE REVELATION OF HIS PURPOSES (45:4-16)

His purpose in *pardon* was instantly revealed (45:4-5). Not for a moment would he keep those stricken brothers in doubt about his grace. "Come near to me, I pray you. And they came near. And he said, I am Joseph your brother, whom ye sold into Egypt." He could not gloss over their sin, but it was mentioned only so it could be pardoned. No hint is given as to the tone of Joseph's voice, but surely it was in a tender tone he spoke. Here was no peremptory command, but persuasive invitation. "Now therefore be not grieved, nor angry with yourselves, that ye sold me hither: for God did send me before you to preserve life." It was not only pardon he offered, but pardon couched in terms that made their very wickedness seem like a blessing.

"You sold . . . God did send." Thus Joseph underlined the fact that God sovereignly overrules the actions of men and makes the wrath of man to praise Him. The greatest manifestation of that, of course, took place at Calvary. Calvary represents the greatest possible *tragedy* in man's dealings with God and the greatest possible *triumph* in God's dealings with man. Joseph's dealings with his brethren illustrate God's dealings with us.

Then Joseph had a purpose in *provision* (45:6-12). He told them something of the future. "There are five years, in the which there shall be neither earing nor harvest."[6] His brethren were not able to read the future, but he could; they could not see the dark days that lay ahead for the world, but Joseph knew, and he knew what was best for them. He assured them he would make every provision for them, come what may. "God did send me before you to preserve you a posterity in the earth, and to save your lives by a great deliverance," he said, backing up his

6. Nine years had come and gone since Joseph's exaltation to Pharaoh's right hand.

assertion by revealing to them something of the position he occupied in Egypt. "God . . hath made me a father to Pharaoh, and lord of all his house, and a ruler throughout all the land of Egypt" (45:8).

God's plan of salvation, so perfectly illustrated in the story of Joseph, not only included the rejection of Christ but also His subsequent exaltation to the highest seat of power in the universe. The great and eternal fact is that there is a Man in heaven, seated at God's right hand in a human body, a Man who is also God.

Being reconciled with Joseph meant that the brethren, long estranged from the father, could be reconciled with him as well. "Haste ye, and go up to my father, and say unto him, Thus saith thy son Joseph, God hath made me lord of all Egypt: come down unto me, tarry not." Joseph sent them back to the father, forgiven, restored, and with a message from himself. That is exactly what grace does for us. It sanctifies us, sets us apart for God, and sends us to the Father to tell Him about His Son.

Moreover, Joseph planned that they should be with him, where he was. "Thou shalt dwell in the land of Goshen," he said. "There will I nourish thee . . . lest thou, and thy household, and all that thou hast, come to poverty." His grace took in all their needs, physical, moral, and spiritual; it was the kind of grace Jesus extends to His own, all-sufficient grace!

Thus Joseph's purposes for his brethren included pardon and provision; it also included *praise* (45:13). "And ye shall tell my father of all my glory in Egypt, and of all that ye have seen; and ye shall haste and bring down my father hither." Joseph wanted his brethren to talk to the father about him.

Where can we find a more expressive description of worship than that? "Tell my Father of all my glory." So might the Lord Jesus speak to us. What volumes those brothers had to tell their father about Joseph! We can imagine what they said. "Father we have come to tell you about your beloved. First we confess that once we hated him, cast him out, rejected him, and sold him for the price of a slave. We saw his woe and agony, Father, and turned our backs upon him. But we have seen him! He has been raised on high and given a name above every name. The world is at his feet, he controls all things, people are coming to him from the ends of the earth! Father, your beloved is altogether lovely, the chiefest among ten thousand. We did not see beauty in him before, but now we do, such beauty as takes our breath away! And what can we say of his grace? He has forgiven all our sins; he even said God meant it unto good! He has made our very guilt minister both to his glory and to our good. And his desire is that where he is, there we might be also." Joseph's brethren, talking to their father about him, might also be us, talking to our Father about Christ.

Joseph's purpose included *proximity* (45:14-16). He wanted to be near his brothers, and for them to be near to him, not just in physical terms but in terms of communion and love. Thus we read, "He fell upon his brother Benjamin's neck, and wept; and Benjamin wept upon his neck. Moreover he kissed all his brethren, and wept upon them: and after that his brethren talked with him." For that is what he was after all the time—their fellowship. His promise of pardon and provision seemed too good to be true, but after Joseph opened up the way for close fellowship, they talked with him.

Talking with the Lord, of course, is the privilege of every one of His own. We can be sure Joseph's brethren did not emphasize their own wants and needs when talking with him. They communed with him of the things that were on his heart. They talked to him about their father and about their wives and children. They brought to him all sorts of odds and ends of information, mere trivialities, we might suppose, but dear and precious to a heart hungry to know all they had to tell. Could such a great lord as he be interested in the humdrum affairs of their little, parochial lives? Of course! He was their brother. The little things interested him most. And does not our Lord want to hear from us about everything—about that flat tire, about the upset in the kitchen, about that overdue bus? Of course He does.

2. THE RESOURCES OF JOSEPH (45:17-23)

Joseph had already hinted to his brethren that vast resources were his to command. The Holy Spirit now emphasized *their source* (45:16-20). "And the fame thereof was heard in Pharaoh's house, saying Joseph's brethren are come: and it pleased Pharaoh well, and his servants. And Pharaoh said unto Joseph, Say unto thy brethren, This do ye; lade your beasts, and go, get you into the land of Canaan; And take your father and your households, and come unto me: and I will give you the good of the land of Egypt, and ye shall eat the fat of the land. . . . Also regard not your stuff; for the good of all the land of Egypt is yours."

Joseph made no mention to Pharaoh of the guilt and misbehavior of the men. That was not only forgiven, it was forgotten, blotted from his mind, dismissed so that it existed no more. He owned, instead, his relationship to his own.

Joseph's resources were derived directly from the throne. What he had promised to his brethren in grace, Pharaoh confirmed by decree. The resources of the throne were laid at their feet, for Joseph's sake.

And note what is said about the "stuff." "Regard not your stuff," said Pharaoh. How stuff gets in our way of doing God's will! We have so many things and we want more things, bigger things, better things. "Never mind your stuff," said Pharaoh. It was a wise word to them and to us.

A young man once came into my office to discuss a matter of mutual interest. He was an interesting person, one whom God has since greatly used around the world. He was wearing a gold watch, and in the course of conversation he said, "Do you need a watch?"

I said, "No thanks! I have one already."

"Do you know of any brother who needs a watch?" he continued. "I have this gold watch, worth well over a hundred dollars. Somebody gave it to me. I'll tell you how it is—people give me things, this watch for instance. Sooner or later I'll meet a needy Christian who doesn't have a watch. I'll give him mine. Then, someone will see I don't have a watch and will give one to me!"

What a way to regard "stuff!" No wonder that man heads one of the most dynamic and thrilling ministries for God in the world today.

The Spirit of God not only points to the source of Joseph's resources, but He points also to *their sufficiency* (45:21-23). Joseph gave wagons to his brothers and changes of raiment—ever an item of wealth in Bible lands and times. To Benjamin he gave an additional 300 pieces of silver and five changes of raiment. It was a test of the cupidity of the brothers and, so changed were they they never seemed to notice Benjamin had more than they. To his father Joseph sent ten asses laden with the good things of Egypt and ten she-asses laden with bread and meat and corn. The whole list illustrates how rich Joseph was and how prodigally he was willing to give. He gave them sufficient provisions for every step of the way until they were brought finally to be with him.

3. THE REQUEST OF JOSEPH (45:24)

"So he sent his brethren away, and they departed: and he said unto them, See that ye fall not out by the way." They were on their journey home. It was to be a long, tiresome road. Perhaps they would squabble among themselves, even become envious, after all, of Benjamin's unique gifts. For though they had all been recipients of Joseph's grace, goodness, and gifts they were not yet safely home. Thus Joseph bade them guard well their tempers and their testimony. "See that ye fall not out by the way," he said. It was good parting advice—for them, and for us.

C. THE MINISTRY PHASE (45:25–47:10)

The Bible next deals with the migration of the Hebrew people into Egypt and their settlement in the land of Goshen. Prophetically, it anticipates the time when the Hebrew people will be not only fully reconciled to Christ but will, in the fulness of the Father's favor, be given high administrative posts in the coming Kingdom. The section can be summarized in four words—proposition, propagation, preparation, and presentation.

1. PROPOSITION (45:25–46:7)

The section begins by setting before us *Jacob's fears* (45:25-28). The brethren had arrived safely home. Jacob's heart was set at ease by the sight of his beloved Benjamin and by the presence of Simeon as well. The brothers could not wait to break the news gently. "Joseph is yet alive!" they blurted out, "and he is governor over all the land of Egypt." Jacob nearly had a heart attack, and, recovering from shock, took refuge in unbelief. "I don't believe it! I simply don't believe it!" he gasped. How difficult it is to convince a person of the *truth* concerning Christ. The devil can deceive people with religious lies, and they will accept them readily enough; but tell them the truth and at once they will set it aside.

Mary Baker Eddy, for instance, can tell people that pain and death are not real, mere errors of mortal mind, and people will believe it—all common sense evidence to the contrary notwithstanding. Joseph Smith can invent a fantastic story about an angel, about being given magic glasses with which to read Egyptian hieroglyphics, so that he can translate a great deal of historical and religious nonsense into pseudo-King James English—and people believe it. The Jehovah's Witnesses can claim that Christ came in 1914, and people believe it. Urban VIII can pontificate that the sun revolves around the earth, in the name of papal infallibility—and people believed it even though Galileo proved the dogma false. But tell people the simple truth as it is in Christ, and, like Jacob when told that Joseph was alive, they simply will not believe it.

"And they told him all the words of Joseph, which he had said unto them: and when he saw the wagons which Joseph had sent . . . the spirit of Jacob their father revived: and Israel said, It is enough; Joseph my son is yet alive: I will go and see him before I die." How true that is to human nature. Joseph's *word* did not convince Jacob, but Joseph's *wagons* did. He had to have a sign before he would believe. Thus Jesus said to his doubting disciple, "Thomas, because thou hast seen me, thou hast believed: blessed are they that have not seen and yet have believed" (John 20:29).

Jacob's fears being dissolved, *Jacob's faith* took over (46:1-7). Once his eyes were opened to the truth, the Jacob in him gave place to the Israel. "When he saw the wagons the spirit of *Jacob* revived and *Israel* said, It is enough . . . and *Israel* took his journey—"

Acting on the spur of the moment, Jacob set out for the south and continued until he came to Beersheba. There he paused. When Abraham had gone down to Egypt he had done so out of the will of God; the result had been disastrous. Now, much as Jacob longed to see his son, he did not dare take another step lest he too step out of the will of God. So there, on the southern edge of Canaan, he "offered sacrifices unto the God of his father" (46:1). What an important principle. Just because something looks like the right thing to do, just because all the circumstances point that way, just because one's own desires affirm the move, and just because everyone else urges it as the sensible thing to do, it does not necessarily follow that it is the will of God. The important thing to ask is, "What does God have to say?" We had best inquire of Him.

Thus Jacob paused before taking the final plunge. "And God spake unto Israel in the visions of the night, and said, Jacob, Jacob. And he said, Here am I. And he said, I am God, the God of thy father: fear not to go down into Egypt: for I will there make of thee a great nation." Thus we learn that Jacob did fear to go to Egypt in spite of the fact that his son was now the greatest lord of the land. After all, his father had been forbidden by God to go to Egypt (26:2), and his grandfather had made spiritual shipwreck there. Mere natural affection must not be allowed to sway decision.

God told him to go. How often people have the idea that God always says no to the things they would like to do, the things that accord with their natural desires. We imagine that serving God and walking in His will always entails doing distasteful things. Not so! God's will is good, perfect, and acceptable (Romans 12:2), and as often as not it coincides with our own natural preferences and legitimate desires.

So "Jacob rose up from Beersheba . . . and came into Egypt, Jacob and all his seed with him." Once assured of the mind of God, he put it into immediate effect. As a result the family migrated to Egypt, to remain there for four centuries until grown into a mighty people.

2. PROPAGATION (46:8-30)

Jacob's family had begun to multiply before ever the move was made to Egypt. With Abraham, the seed had been restricted to Isaac, with Isaac it had been restricted to Jacob, but now it had already swollen to seventy souls.

The list of Jacob's dependents contains a number of interesting facts. The migrating family consisted of Jacob and his wives, twelve sons and one daughter, fifty-two grandchildren, and four great-grandsons. Dan had the fewest number of children (he had only one son), and Benjamin had the most (he had ten sons, a fact that wipes out any notion we might have that Benjamin was a mere child).

The historian makes several comments. He lists the names of Simeon's first five sons, then adds "And Shaul, the son of a Canaanitish woman." It was typical of Simeon's spiritual hardness that he should have married a member of a cursed race. Unlike Judah, Simeon continued on in oblivion of his offense. The Spirit of God, however, makes note of it for it is another sidelight on Simeon's carnality. Perhaps that "Canaanitish woman" was one of the women seized as a captive at the sack of Shechem.

The children of Judah are listed thus: "And the sons of Judah; Er, and Onan, and Shelah, and Pharez, and Zerah: but Er and Onan died in the land of Canaan. And the sons of Pharez were Hezron and Hamul" (46:12). The vileness of Judah's first two sons is passed over lightly and the fact that their mother was a Canaanite is ignored. Likewise the shameful story of Tamar and the circumstances of the birth of the last two sons is ignored. Judah had redeemed himself and God, who ever delights to cover sins when He can, passes on to Pharez and from him to Hezron to show that the royal march into the future, toward the coming of the Christ through Judah's line, had begun.

The list of Benjamin's sons (46:21) seems to go on and on. If Benjamin, as some believe, was about twenty-two years of age at the time of the migration, he must have married quite young. Or perhaps he had several wives, or perhaps his wife had a number of multiple births. He was young to have ten sons. Whichever way we look at it, old Jacob must have been astonished at the size of Benjamin's family, for sons were what counted in those days. The other brothers must have been astonished too. If it went on like that, Benjamin would have the largest tribe in Israel. As it happened, the tribe of Benjamin ended up as the smallest of them all, for the promise of those early days was ruined by tribal sin.

When we come to Issachar we stop and take a hard, long look, for the name of his third son arrests us right away. "And the sons of Issachar," we read, "Tola and Puvah and Job and Shimron" (46:13). Could that possibly be the Job who so suffered that a whole book of the Bible is devoted to his experiences and trials? Some have thought so.[7] There is at least a possibility that Job, the grandson of Leah, the unwanted wife, was none other than that mighty Job whose book was the first book of the Bible to be penned.

None of the names are given of the wives of Jacob's sons. The only one whose name we know is Asenath; the others are totally ignored. The wives lost their identities in that of the husbands. They became channels of blessing to the world by their union with the heads of the patriarchal family. They typify the vast, anonymous throng who make up the rank and file of the faith who through virtue of their union with Christ become a blessing to mankind. The names of such may not be

7. Job's friends were all descendants of Esau and contemporaries of Job the son of Issachar. We are given details concerning two of them. Eliphaz was a son of Esau. He is called a Temanite, that is, he was associated with Teman in Idumea, Esau's adopted homeland. The son of Eliphaz was Teman from whom, presumably, the surrounding country took its name (Genesis 36:10-11). Teman, as a country, was later fabled for its wise men.

Bildad the Shuhite was the sixth son of Abraham by Keturah (Genesis 25:2) and is mentioned in connection with Esau, Edom, and Teman (Jeremiah 49:8).

Issachar was about forty when the family migrated to Egypt. His son, Job, must have been about twenty. Job lived 140 years after God restored him double for all he had lost. If the double blessing included length of days then, of course, he would have been 70 at the time the double blessing was given and must have lived until he was 210. If that is so, he was born the year after Joseph was sold into Egypt and was 91 when Joseph died.

Probably Job left Egypt to live in Uz. Moses was 55 when Job died and had himself been a refugee in Midian for 15 years. Thus Moses might have known Job well and might have been personally acquainted with the events the book of Job records. Moses might even have been the human author of the book of Job.

recorded here but we can be sure they are written over there, and that they will be recognized in the crowning day that is coming by and by.

Having talked thus about Jacob's *family*, the narrative draws our attention to Jacob's *favorites* (46:28-30), telling us how Judah came to Joseph and how Joseph came to Jacob. Thus the two great names of Judah and Joseph are brought significantly together. Judah and Joseph were the giants among the children of Israel. The tribes of Judah and Ephraim dominate Old Testament history. There was always a measure of Ephraimite tribal jealousy toward Judah but that sad development lay in the future. Here we simply see Judah as he hurried ahead of the others, to appraise Joseph of the soon arrival of the rest of the clan.

What a scene it must have been when Jacob and Joseph, father and son, finally met. Can we not detect in that scene a picture of the even greater reunion that took place in heaven, when the heavenly Joseph was reunited with His Father after His years of suffering on earth? We can enter into the feelings that ran so deep between Joseph and Jacob as they were reunited. So, in some measure, we can enter into the joy with which Father and Son met together when the work of redemption was done.

3. PREPARATION (46:31-34)

Joseph was now going to arrange for his brethren to settle in Egypt. The matter was of great importance, for where they settled would have a lasting influence on them. It was important they be situated so that although *in* Egypt they would not be *of* Egypt.

First we see Joseph as *the successful mediator* (46:31-32), appearing before Pharaoh on behalf of his brethren. "And Joseph said unto his brethren, and unto his father's house, I will go up, and shew Pharaoh, and say unto him, My brethren, and my father's house, which were in the land of Canaan, are come unto me." He was not ashamed to call them brethren. Just as our Lord first ascended into heaven and appeared in the presence of God for us, before all the hosts of heaven to own us for His own and to urge our interests before the throne, so Joseph did for his brethren in Egypt.

"The men are shepherds, for their trade hath been to feed cattle," he said to Pharaoh, "and they have brought their flocks, and their herds, and all that they have." It was Joseph's intention to prepare Pharaoh for the meeting with his brethren just, as a little later, he was going to prepare his brethren for the meeting with Pharaoh. The distance between a divine Pharaoh and a rough and ready farmer was vast indeed. Joseph had to be the mediator to bridge that great gulf. As *Joseph,* born and brought up in the family of Jacob in the land of Canaan, he was one with them, knew their way of life, their natures, strengths, weaknesses, needs. He could put one hand upon them. As *Zaphnath-paaneah,* seated at the right hand of Pharaoh, at home amid the pomp and splendor of the court, he could place his other hand upon the Pharaoh. He understood his thoughts and ways. Joseph was a perfect mediator. Without Joseph, the brothers would have had no access to that throne, no means of approaching it, and no hope of making a successful appeal to Pharaoh at all. Without Joseph they had nothing; with him they had everything. In all there is a direct parallel between Joseph and his brethren, and us and our mediator. The Lord Jesus, both God and man, brings us to the throne and negotiates for us in a way we never could.

We are next shown Joseph as *the successful minister* (46:33-34). He began by explaining to his brethren something of his work at Pharaoh's right hand, and explained its practical significance to them. They must cooperate with him; there could be no self-seeking, no independent action; they must do exactly as he told them. He had their future good in mind and knew, far better than they, what pitfalls lay ahead for them in Egypt. He could see things they could not see, and his wisdom was far greater than theirs. He was their mediator before the throne so that he might be their minister in their daily lives. Again, the parallel between Joseph and Jesus is inescapable.

We note Joseph's *plain instructions* to his brethren (46:33-34*a*). "And it shall come to pass when Pharaoh shall call you, and shall say, What is your occupation? That ye shall say, Thy servants' trade hath been about cattle from our youth even until now, both we and also our fathers." In other words, the brethren were to confess to Pharaoh their shepherd character. They were to confess it before him and all his splendid court. Unlike the Egyptians who were a settled, agricultural people, shepherds were a nomadic, migratory people, ever on the move, never sending their roots down deeply into any one spot. That was of vital importance. Unless the brethren held onto their shepherd character, pilgrim character all would be lost. The Lord would also have us be pilgrims and strangers on the earth and take our stand before the throne above in that character.

We note also Joseph's *plain intention* for his brethren (46:34*b*). "That ye may dwell in the land of Goshen," he explained, "for every shepherd is an abomination to the Egyptians." That is what he was after. He wanted to keep a clear line of demarcation between the chosen family and the Egyptians. Goshen would secure their separation from Egypt even though they must live in that land. Goshen was on the Canaan side of the land, so settling there would make it that much easier for them to leave Egypt when the time came.

Moreover, the Egyptians despised cattlemen, one of the seven castes, or guilds, into which the Egyptians were divided. They were held in such contempt by other Egyptians that they were not allowed to enter the temples or to marry any other Egyptian outside their caste. Joseph's intention, therefore, in insisting that his brethren confess their shepherd character was obvious. He did not want them to get involved with the Egyptians either in the matter of worship or marriage; spiritually and socially they were to be separate from the Egyptians. His concern illustrates what the Lord expects of His people in the world today. The world's attractions are not for us; its religious systems are anathema to us. This world is not our home.

4. PRESENTATION (47:1-10)

Joseph's ministry to his brethren was successful. They took the stand before Pharaoh and his court that Joseph had instructed them to take. "And he took some of his brethren, even five men, and presented them unto Pharaoh." Out of the election there was a selection, not all of his brethren being taken in before Pharaoh. Five is said to be the number of grace in the Bible. It was saving grace that led Joseph to forgive and embrace and royally accept all the brothers; it was special grace that enabled some of them to be confessed before Pharaoh in a unique way. It is grace alone that puts us in the family of God, forgives our sins, and makes us accepted in the Beloved. But, beyond that, some will be confessed before the Father and before the angels of heaven in a special and unique sense and will win a special place in the Kingdom. Positions of great honor and responsibility are to be bestowed in the coming Kingdom age. Although those posts of splendor are available to all, they will be given only to those who have earned the right to them.

On what grounds did Joseph make his selection? We are not told. We can be sure, however, that, being Joseph, he did not necessarily choose the handsomest, the strongest, the cleverest, the wealthiest of his brethren. Moral and spiritual considerations doubtless played the highest part in his choice. One thing is sure, only five of the eleven were selected for that special honor to hear, as it were, Joseph's "Well done!"

"If thou knowest any men of activity among them," said Pharaoh as he surveyed Joseph's brethren, "make them rulers over my cattle" (47:6). The words "men of activity" mean "men of strength." The phrase comes from a root meaning "to twist" (the idea is that of a cord being twisted to make a strong and reliable rope). Those who had proved themselves could be given places of responsibility in Pharaoh's kingdom. Our place in the coming Kingdom of Christ will depend on whether we are "men of activity" now.

So, Joseph brought his brethren to Pharaoh. Then comes a most enlightening incident; Jacob bestowed his blessing on Pharaoh (47:7-10). Moreover, he blessed him twice, once as he came into Pharaoh's presence and once as he left. Jacob was a far greater man than his renowned grandfather, Abraham. Abraham had been a curse to Pharaoh; Jacob was a blessing. Jacob was not being pretentious, for he confessed both his inferiority as compared with his forebears and his inflictions along the pilgrim way.

We can picture the gnarled, weather-beaten old shepherd whose hard life on the hills had etched its lines on his face. We can picture him dressed in the best raiment Joseph could find for him and wearing it as uncomfortably as one might expect. In contrast we see the immaculate, sophisticated, aristocratic courtiers standing in the audience chamber of the king. We picture the imperial guards in their splendid robes, the ministers of state in their impressive robes, and Joseph standing before Pharaoh wearing his court attire like a man of noble birth. And there stood old Jacob, all out of place, it would seem, amid the flaunted finery of the court.

We see him walking slowly down the long line of guards and officials, halting on his thigh and leaning on his staff. We see him making his way up to Pharaoh's throne and there, to the astonishment of all the court, raising himself erect instead of falling prostrate on his face. We see him raise his sunburned hand in blessing, and we hear the benediction fall from his lips.

"Without all contradiction, the less is blessed of the better," says God (Hebrews 7:7). So, in blessing Pharaoh, Jacob was saying, "You, my lord, may be a prince among men and have power on earth. I am a prince with God and have power in heaven. Therefore, as greater than you, I bless you, Pharaoh, in the name of my God."

Never, except perhaps on his deathbed, did Jacob rise higher. What a lesson for us! Are we being a blessing? When we come into the presence of people, do we bring for them a blessing from God? When we leave, do we leave a blessing behind? Are we princes with God and therefore a blessing to men? Jacob was.

IX. JOSEPH'S BOUNTY (47:11-26)

The incidents recorded in Genesis 47 anticipate the day when the Lord Jesus will set up His Kingdom on earth and rule over all the world. It gives a prophetic glimpse of the Lord's coming dealings with the Jewish people and with all nations. Joseph was the greatest benefactor Egypt ever had. In a single stroke he broke the power of the feudal system, set up one master and one lord in the realm, and made the throne supreme. In a coming day the Lord will bring the empire of the world directly under God, and will establish a true theocracy, with God as its head and Himself as its administrator, and will sovereignly deal with man's natural tendency to rebellion and independence.

A. JOSEPH'S GRACE (47:11-12)

Observe, first, how Joseph dealt with his brethren on the principle of grace. We are told of *the position* he gave them. "And Joseph placed his father and his brethren . . . in the land of Egypt." We know from Genesis 46:34 that he placed them in the land of Goshen, later called

Rameses. The name *Goshen* means "to draw near." In other words, his brethren were put in a place where they could have access to him. The name *Rameses* ("the thunder that destroys") suggests they were given access to him as the one who spoke with a voice of authority. The scene anticipates the day when Jesus will reign, when the nation of Israel will be given a privileged position in His Kingdom, one of special access to Himself, and when His voice will be like thunder on the earth. The Jewish people will draw near to Him and will be His viceroys to the ends of the earth, and His edicts will be like thunder.

We are told next of *the possessions* Joseph gave his brethren. "And Joseph . . . gave them a possession in the land of Egypt, in the best of the land, in the land of Rameses, as Pharaoh had commanded." He gave them the best. That was grace, but it was grace cooperating with the throne, for Joseph never acted in independence. Those brethren of his who had done their worst to him in the bad old days had been forgiven and were now lifted on high by grace.

We note also *the portion* Joseph gave them (47:12). "And Joseph nourished his father, and his brethren, and all his father's household, with bread, according to their families." He met their needs and took care of each and every one, right down to the youngest child. Not a need was overlooked.

To teach us His care for us, Jesus said, "Are not five sparrows sold for two farthings, and not one of them is forgotten before God?" (Luke 12:6). "Are not two sparrows sold for a farthing? and not one of them shall fall to the ground without your Father" (Matthew 10:29). Two sparrows, one farthing; five sparrows, two farthings. In other words, for two farthings an extra sparrow was tossed in to make a bargain. The one sparrow had no value at all. That one sparrow, the sparrow the dealer was willing to toss in just for the sake of a sale—*that* sparrow does not fall to the ground without the Father's knowledge. That is, God attends the funeral of even such a valueless thing as that. That is how detailed is His care. That is grace.

B. JOSEPH'S GOVERNMENT (47:13-22)

The focus now turns to Joseph's dealings with the Egyptians. The famine having reached its height, the Egyptians realized that there was no hope apart from Joseph. The famine brought them to the place where they were willing to submit to him, at all costs and on any terms. They had come to an end of themselves. Egypt was bankrupt and its condition hopeless. There was no future except in Joseph.

The story foreshadows the return of Christ. He will come back to an exhausted, impoverished, bankrupt earth. The terrible ecological disasters described in the Apocalypse will have taken their toll. Earthquakes, wars, famines, pestilences, natural disasters of global magnitude will have bereft the world of its resources. The persecutions of the beast will have decimated the world's population. By the time Christ returns, the earth will have exhausted itself and men will have come to an end of themselves. Apart from Him there will be no hope. His word will be absolute law on the planet, gladly accepted by all who enter the millennial Kingdom. His reign, like Joseph's, will be rigorous, the reign of a rod of iron. Drastic conditions will call for a drastic cure.

Joseph's solution to Egypt's ills was very simple. He brought all things under the authority of the throne as the only way to safeguard the future. First, he demanded *the purses* of the Egyptians (47:13-14). "And there was no bread in all the land; for the famine was very sore, so that the land of Egypt and all the land of Canaan fainted by reason of the famine. And Joseph gathered up all the money that was found in the land of Egypt, and in the land of Canaan, for the corn which they bought: and Joseph brought the money into Pharaoh's house." People could no longer put their trust in money, for the simple reason that they did not have any. The love of money, a root of all evil, was taken away from them. All men, rich and poor alike, were reduced to the same level. The economy of the land was in Pharaoh's hands alone.

Little or nothing is revealed about the monetary policy Christ will pursue during the Millennium. It will be perfect, equable, and unsurpassed, for, as the prophet puts it, every man will dwell under his own fig and his own vine. There will be no more secret bank accounts in foreign lands where ill-gotten wealth can be hidden. No longer will money talk. The Marxist dream, "from each according to his ability, to each according to his need," will come true, for Christ and not sinful man will administer the resources of the world. The state will be supreme in Christ. The world's wealth will be dispensed by the throne for the blessing and benefit of all.

Next, Joseph demanded *the possessions* of the Egyptians (47:15-17). "And when money failed in the land of Egypt, and in the land of Canaan, all the Egyptians came unto Joseph, and said, Give us bread: for why should we die in thy presence? for the money faileth. And Joseph said, Give your cattle; and I will give you for your cattle, if money fail. And they brought their cattle unto Joseph." That made sense. What use would it be to control and centralize the monetary system if people could barter with their other liquid assets? The problem of the love of money would remain. So Joseph concentrated the liquid assets of Egypt under the control of the throne. The very wealthy might have been able to hold out longer than others but, eventually, all gave in and the power of the throne was advanced for the good of all.

Then Joseph demanded *the property* of the Egyptians (47:18-20). "And when that year was ended, they came unto him the second year, and said unto him, We will not hide from my lord, how that our money is spent; my lord hath also our herds of cattle: there is aught [nothing] left in the sight of my lord, but our bodies and our lands . . . and Joseph bought all the land of Egypt." Now all fixed as well as liquid assets were in the hands of Joseph. The Egyptians, indeed, were brought to an end of themselves, brought to the place where total and unquestioning trust had to be placed in him. Just so, in a coming day, all sources of power will be concentrated in the capable and kindly hands of Jesus. We would have cause to fear if the hands to wield such power were any other than the hands of a Joseph or Jesus, but those hands were completely dependable and could be trusted to the full. Joseph wanted an end to divided loyalties and human rivalries, and the blessing of a beneficent, efficient, and centralized rule. The flaw in Joseph's case lay in the fact that sooner or later he would die and lesser, more greedy hands would seize the reins, but when all such power is concentrated in the hands of Jesus it will be for the lasting good of mankind.

Finally, Joseph took control of *their persons* (47:21). "And as for the people, he removed them to cities from one end of the borders of Egypt even to the other." He exercised his right to redistribute the population of the land so that the manpower resources of the land could be utilized in the future for the good of all. No doubt he cleared out the slums and resettled people in the cities or on the land for their own immediate and future good. The millennial reign will begin in a similar way. Only a few people will be left after the judgments of the Tribulation era and after the judgment of the Valley of Jehoshaphat. They will be appointed their places of residence by the Lord in keeping with His wisdom, love, and power. What He originally planned for mankind when at Babel He commanded and enforced a distribution of the world's population, will become fact.

In Joseph's case we find that there was one area where even his power, vast as it was, was curbed. "Only the land of the priests bought he not: for the priests had a portion assigned to them of Pharaoh, and did eat the portion which Pharaoh gave them: wherefore they sold not their lands" (47:22). What a golden opportunity Pharaoh threw away to smash the tremendous power of the priesthood throughout Egypt. Joseph's power was limited because Pharaoh's nerve failed, or perhaps because Pharaoh's heart inclined toward the sacerdotalism of the land.

But in a coming day the Lord will not be limited by a weak throne. With all the power of Deity behind Him He will smash the power of false religion. No longer will dark, Satanic creeds hold empire over human souls. Temples, raised at incalculable cost and dedicated to the propagation of error will vanish from the earth. A magnificent temple will be built in Jerusalem to direct the thoughts of all mankind to God upon His throne.

C. JOSEPH'S GOODNESS (47:23-26)

Joseph now enunciated the basic law for the new age that had dawned in Egypt. The basic principle was first of all *explained* (47:23-25). It was *worded very simply* (47:23-24). "Then Joseph said unto the people, Behold I have bought you this day and your land for Pharaoh: Lo, here is seed for you, and ye shall sow the land. And it shall come to pass in the increase, that ye shall give the fifth part unto Pharaoh, and four parts shall be your own . . . for your food, and for them of your households, and for food for your little ones." Concentration of power in the throne was intended to be a means of blessing, not a means of oppression. It meant that the resources of Egypt could be managed for the good of all.

During the years of plenty Joseph had been empowered by Pharaoh to tax the land owners a fifth of their produce against the years of need. Now he made that tax a permanent institution in the land in order to finance the centralized administration. It was a wise move as well as a demonstration of Joseph's goodness. He was under no obligation to give the people anything. He could have simply reduced the people to serfdom, but instead he dealt with them bountifully out of the goodness of his heart.

The principle was *welcomed very sincerely*. "And they said, Thou hast saved our lives: let us find grace in the sight of my lord, and we will be Pharaoh's servants." It is thus the millennial age will begin. A grateful people, saved by the Lord Himself, glad to be the Lord's bondsmen, their future assured and their happiness guaranteed, will be conscious that grace reigns on earth at last.

The basic principle, having been explained, was then *established* (47:25). "And Joseph made it a law," we read. The principle was made a precept. Thus God's grace and His government were wedded and a new age began.

Surely there is a lesson in all this for us. "Thou hast saved our lives. Let us find grace in the sight of my lord, and we will be thy servants." The principle of a 20 percent annual tithe for the throne is interesting. *Jacob* promised the Lord 10 percent (Genesis 28:22), the *Egyptians*, saved and sustained by Joseph were to give 20 (Genesis 47:24), the saved tax collector, *Zaccheus* promised 50 percent (Luke 19:8), the *widow* with her two mites gave all (Mark 12:41-44). How much should we give to God? A saved soul with a thankful heart cannot possibly do less than its best to express its gratitude for the person and work of Christ.

Chapter 9

CONCLUSION

(47:27–50:26)

I. The Death of Jacob (47:27–50:21)
   A. Jacob's Foreknowledge (47:27–49:27)
      1. The Chosen Favorite (47:27–48:22)
      2. The Chosen Family (49:1-27)
   B. Jacob's Funeral (49:28–50:21)
      1. The Pledge (49:28-33)
      2. The Preparation (50:1-3)
      3. The Permission (50:4-6)
      4. The Procession (50:7-14)
      5. The Pardon (50:15-21)

II. The Death of Joseph (50:22-26)
   A. Joseph's Dwelling (50:22)
   B. Joseph's Descendants (50:23)
   C. Joseph's Discernment (50:24)
   D. Joseph's Demand (50:25)
   E. Joseph's Decease (50:26)

9

CONCLUSION

I. The Death of Jacob (47:27–50:21)

A. Jacob's Foreknowledge (47:27–49:27)

The Genesis road now turns its final bend. Joseph is on the throne, the days of his rejection are over, and the long day of his glory has come. The story could well end there. But, as Moses looks over his manuscript, the Spirit of God tells him to write an appendix. The appendix deals with two notable deaths—the death of Jacob (47:27–50:21) and the death of Joseph (50:22-26).

The book of Genesis is one vast graveyard, one great handbook of funeral sermons, one long obituary. We have stood by the mutilated corpse of Abel. We have read the register of births and deaths in chapter 5 and attended the burial of a race in the Flood. We have been to the funeral services of Abraham, Sarah, Isaac, and Ishmael, and we have wept with Jacob at Rachel's tomb. We have missed this one and that. "Where's Rebekah? Where's Terah? Where's Lot?" And always the answer comes, "They're dead." Now we come to the last two funerals in the book.

The record of Jacob's death is lengthy. We shall therefore view it in two stages—his foreknowledge (47:27–49:27) and his funeral (49:28–50:21).

As with Abraham and Isaac, the Spirit of prophecy descended now on Jacob and enabled him to see with great clarity the future of his people. The prophecies that now poured from Jacob's lips are among the most remarkable and detailed in the entire Bible. There was no hesitation. The poetic but prophetic stanzas flowed steadily from Jacob's lips as his eyes moved from son to son. His foreknowledge focused first on his *chosen favorite* (47:27–48:22) and then on the *chosen family* (49:1-27).

1. The Chosen Favorite (47:27–48:22)

Jacob's chosen favorite was Joseph. As a lad he had been his father's pride and joy, and the rejoicing of his heart. Not one of Jacob's other sons had been worth a thought. Even Benjamin brought with him the sad memory of Rachel's death, but Joseph had brought nothing but bliss.

Simeon and Levi were cruel, Reuben was contemptible, Judah was carnal, the sons of the slave women were corrupt. But Joseph was a prodigy. Joseph as a *lad* was all that Jacob ever wanted in a son; Joseph as a *lord* vindicated everything he had ever thought or said about him.

a. JACOB'S BURIAL (47:27-31)

We are told first where Jacob's *home* was. "And Israel dwelt in the land of Egypt, in the country of Goshen; and they had possessions therein, and grew, and multiplied exceedingly. And Jacob lived in the land of Egypt seventeen years: so the whole age of Jacob was an hundred forty and seven years." For seventeen years he had been surrounded by pomp and splendor as the honored father of Egypt's greatest lord. For seventeen years everything the world has to offer had been made available to him. He had seventeen years in which to lose his testimony by succumbing to the world, the flesh, and the devil. Seventeen years in Egypt! Seventeen years for the world, in its most alluring form, to set its seductions before him. But it was *Israel* who was in Egypt—not just Israel the person, but Israel the people. It is the first time the prospective nation is so called. What does the world have to offer the Israel of God? Nothing.

We notice too where Jacob's *heart* was. "And the time drew nigh that Israel must die: and he called his son Joseph, and said . . . Bury me not, I pray thee, in Egypt: but I will lie with my fathers, and thou shalt carry me out of Egypt and bury me in their buryingplace" (47:29-31). Jacob was in Egypt for seventeen years, but not for a moment was Egypt in him. He was in the world, but not of the world, for he had thoroughly learned separation. If he must live in Egypt he would keep his heart in Canaan, the land of promise, the place where God had put his name. Jacob's earthly affairs were in Egypt; his heart was in Canaan.

b. JACOB'S BEDSIDE (48:1-6)

The news came to Joseph one day, "Behold thy father is sick." At once affairs of state were laid aside and Joseph, with his sons in tow, hurried off to see the patriarch. As soon as Jacob heard that Joseph was coming, he sat up in bed. "Israel strengthened himself," we read. The work before him was of the utmost importance, for it concerned the structure and composition of the tribes for the rest of time.

Joseph, Ephraim, and Manasseh entered the bedroom and gazed on the venerable old shepherd. Joseph's heart was full. Ephraim and Manasseh were there, dressed no doubt like the young Egyptian courtiers they were. They had been brought up in Pharaoh's court, so their appearance, manners, education, and outlook must have been more Egyptian than Hebrew. Perhaps that is why Joseph brought them along. He wanted them to feel the full weight of the old patriarch's dying presence and wanted too for his father to give them a spiritual blessing before he died.

Jacob peered at them and began by making a statement about *the past.* "And Jacob said unto Joseph, God Almighty appeared unto me at Luz in the land of Canaan, and blessed me" (48:3-4). God had appeared to Jacob twice, once after his own deception of Isaac, with the wrath of Esau still ringing in his ears, and once after the disaster at Shechem, with the wrath of all Canaan ringing in his ears (28:10-19; 35:6-13). Both times God had reconfirmed to Jacob His promises to Abraham and Isaac. Probably Jacob had both occasions in mind when he spoke about the past.

Next, Jacob made a statement about *the present.* "And now thy two sons, Ephraim and Manasseh, which were born unto thee in the land of Egypt before I came unto thee into Egypt, are mine; as Reuben and Simeon, they shall be mine." Jacob officially adopted Joseph's two sons into his family as *his* sons, to stand on equal footing with his own twelve boys.[1]

c. JACOB'S BEREAVEMENT (48:7)

"And as for me, when I came from Padan, Rachel died by me in the land of Canaan in the way . . . and I buried her there in the way of Ephrath." The passing of the years had not softened that blow. Jacob's voice still choked when he thought of his one true love. Thinking of Joseph's sons made Jacob think of their grandmother. Had circumstances not been too strong for him, doubtless he would have married none of the others. Rachel was all the wife he had ever desired. All his sons would have been Rachel's sons if he had had his way. It was fitting, therefore, that Joseph, Rachel's firstborn, be given the inheritance rights of the firstborn. So Jacob gave the double portion to Joseph by bringing in Ephraim and Manasseh as full sons; it was his last tribute to a memory that would not die.

d. JACOB'S BLINDNESS (48:8-12)

"And Israel beheld Joseph's sons, and said, Who are these?" He had been talking about adopting Joseph's two boys, but evidently had either not noticed them standing quietly in the room, or had seen them only dimly and failed to recognize them. The old patriarch's physical sight failed him (48:10) just as Isaac's had done. Jacob's decision to adopt Joseph's two sons was not done, therefore, on the spur of the moment under the prompting and impulse of their presence in his room. He had not even seen them. His act was the result of premeditated and careful thought under the direct leading of the Spirit of God. "I had not thought to see thy face!" the old man said, beaming upon Joseph, "and,

1. That meant, of course, that there would actually be thirteen tribes, although God invariably only counts twelve in any given list.

lo, God hath shewed me also thy seed." He peered hard at the two boys as Joseph brought them forward to his bedside.

e. JACOB'S BLESSING (48:13-16)

Joseph now realized his father intended to bestow his patriarchal blessing on the boys he had just adopted as sons. Joseph wanted the older boy to get the superior blessing, so he set Manasseh directly in front of Jacob's right hand. The old man, however, deliberately crossed his hands so that the right hand rested on Ephraim and the left hand on Manasseh. It was God's will that the tribe that would spring from Ephraim would be superior to the tribe that would come from Manasseh. Natural preference had nothing to do with it. Jacob was being moved by the spiritual man, not the natural man.

f. JACOB'S BEHAVIOR (48:17-20)

Joseph was agitated by his father's action. "Not so," he cried. "Not so my father: for this is the firstborn; put thy right hand upon his head." He thought Jacob's shortsightedness accounted for his action, and he certainly did not want his father to preempt his own preferences. Manasseh was his older boy, and by all natural standards Manasseh should get the prime share of any material or spiritual benefits Jacob might bestow.

Jacob knew what he was doing. "I know it, my son, I know it," he said. Thus Jacob's faith overcame *the will of man* (Joseph's will) just as Isaac's faith had overcome *the will of the flesh.* "And he blessed them that day, saying, In thee shall Israel bless, saying, God make thee as Ephraim and as Manasseh: and he set Ephraim before Manasseh." That was not just the stubbornness of an old man used to having his own way. It was not a personal preference but a prophetic pronouncement.

Jacob was a true prophet, for Ephraim certainly became the greater of the two tribes. Ephraim became so dominant that, after the ten tribes broke away to set up its rival kingdom, it was Jeroboam, an Ephraimite, who led the rebellion (1 Kings 11:26). As time wore on the tribe of Ephraim gave its name to the entire Northern Kingdom.

g. JACOB'S BELIEF (48:21-22)

"And Israel said unto Joseph, Behold, I die: but God shall be with you, and bring you again unto the land of your fathers. Moreover I have given to thee one portion above thy brethren, which I took out of the hand of the Amorite with my sword and with my bow." The double portion in Ephraim and Manasseh was confirmed, but its fulfillment would be in Canaan, not Egypt. Jacob's words about the Amorites are puzzling. But we must remember the spirit of prophecy was still upon him. He was speaking of himself as the embodiment of the nation and speaking of the future as though it were the past—as though the conquest of Canaan and the slaying of the Amorite were already an accomplished fact.[2]

2. THE CHOSEN FAMILY (49:1-27)

We now come to a prophetic utterance that can be compared for scope and detail only with Daniel 11. The long and intricate prophetic pronouncement can be viewed either *dispensationally* or *dispositionally.* That is, the various dispensations of time in God's dealings with mankind were foreseen by Jacob insofar as those dispensations had a direct bearing upon his people.[3] Here we are going to view the prophecy dispositionally.

As Jacob looked at his sons, their traits of *disposition* gave him the clue to their destinies as tribes. He had closely observed those boys for many years. He knew their histories, their strengths and weaknesses, their characters. Now the Holy Spirit enabled him to project the lines of their personalities into the future and predict their future as tribes. Each tribe would expand, amplify, and inherit the dispositional traits seen in its founder.

a. INTRODUCTION (49:1-2)

"And Jacob called unto his sons, and said, Gather yourselves together, that I may tell you that which shall befall you in the last days. Gather yourselves together, and hear, ye sons of Jacob; and hearken unto Israel your father." The expression "the last days" is used here for the first of fourteen occurrences in the Old Testament. The expression has al-

2. There is no record in Jacob's life of any such expedition against the Amorites. Certainly Jacob would not be referring to the destruction of the Shechemites by Levi and Simeon, for his righteous soul would recoil in horror from every remembrance of that deed of shame. His words were prophetic words, and Israel would leave Egypt; Israel would conquer Canaan now in the grip of the Amorites. Jacob's belief was based solidly on God's promises. He was banking on God's promise to Abraham (Genesis 15:13-16)—"*Thy seed shall be a stranger in a land that is not theirs*" (that part of the prophecy to Abraham could not refer to *Canaan* for Canaan was his; it had been given to him and to his seed by God. It referred to the sojourn in Egypt. Jacob had lived to see that part of the prophecy partially fulfilled) "*and they shall afflict them four hundred years . . . and in the fourth generation they shall come hither again: for the iniquity of the Amorites is not yet full.*" Jacob believed that. He would not live to see the final fulfillment of the prophecy, nor would Joseph, nor would Ephraim and Manasseh, nor would the sons of Ephraim and Manasseh. But their grandsons would. Jacob staked everything on that. In the days of Ephraim's grandchildren the iniquity of the Amorites would overflow and then *he* (Jacob representing the nation) would take the land with sword and bow out of the hand of the Amorites. It was as good as done. So he spoke of it as a past event. Such is the absolute integrity of God's Word.

3. *Reuben, Simeon, and Levi* give the history of the nation down to the first advent of the Messiah. *Judah* gives a sketch of the Messiah's appearing and rejection. *Zebulun and Issachar* set forth the dispersal of Israel and the long subjection of the race to the Gentiles. *Dan* foreshadows the appearing and kingdom of the Antichrist. *Gad, Asher, and Naphtali* depict the moral character of the elect in the last days—victorious, royally nourished, and witnessing. *Joseph and Benjamin* foreshadow the second coming and triumphs of Israel's Messiah.

ways been taken by the rabbis to be Messianic. It is an eschatological expression referring, generally, to "the end time" of Daniel 12:4, 9. In its ultimate fulfillment Jacob's prophecy focuses on the climax of the ages, on that terminal point in time to which all history leads. But the viewpoint of the speaker must be kept in mind. So, although the prophecy refers to Messianic times it begins with that particular era of consummation that would begin with the conquest of Canaan—an event to which Jacob had already prophetically referred.

So we see Jacob's sons gathered about his bed. We view the scene as *the judgment seat of Jacob,* and it prefigures the judgment seat of Christ. Lives are brought up for review and rebukes and rewards are meted out. What has been sowed must be reaped. Hidden things are exposed and judged; open things are praised or punished. There is a place in a Kingdom at stake for each one, and each one is weighed in the light of that.

Jacob's style of speech was not the usual conversational style. It was a declamation couched in poetic, symbolic, and exclamatory phrases such as would cause a deep hush of awe, fear, and expectation to grip each heart. It was, indeed, a judgment seat.

b. REUBEN (49:3-4)

As he peered with his failing eyes into Reuben's face, Jacob saw pride, weakness, lust, and guilt mirrored there, all struggling for the mastery. He began with a word about *Reuben's unique position* (49:3). "Reuben, thou art my firstborn, my might, and the excellency of dignity and the excellency of power."

Reuben had once been his father's pride and joy. As he heard his father's opening words his heart expanded and his face glowed. The anxious, haunted look vanished, pride triumphed. He was going to get his rights after all! "My firstborn!" He was going to get the double portion of the property; his father must have remembered he had tried to save Joseph when the others were for killing or selling him. He must have remembered how he had pledged his own sons for Benjamin's safety. "My might, the beginning of my strength." He must be going to get the preeminence, too. He was to be the royal, the dominant tribe. Perhaps the Messiah would come from him. "The excellency of dignity and the excellence of power." That must mean he was to get the priesthood. He was going to get it all. The possessions, the preeminence, the priesthood. The land would be called after him. They would call it "Reuben." That was his unique position, that was his birthright. Nothing could ever change that. Reuben's shoulders went back and his head went up.

But he was premature. His father was still speaking. He was talking now about *Reuben's unstable personality* (49:4*a*). "Unstable as water, thou shalt not excel." It came like a douche of ice-cold water, like a paralyzing shock to his soul. Unstable. Like water! Like water that always seeks its own level no matter how low that might be, water that when spilled upon the ground cannot be gathered again. "Thou shalt not excel." All Reuben's rosy daydreams exploded in his face. There was nothing in his character that could fit him to be leader of the tribes; he simply did not have what it would take. He lacked character, he lacked courage, he lacked conviction, he lacked everything.

And he never did excel. His tribe never rose to prominence in Israel. None of the tribe ever ruled, ever rose to prominence except in a negative sense. Not one of the judges was a Reubenite. Reuben was the first tribe to demand its inheritance and, careless of consequences, rashly chose the wrong side of Jordan. Reuben could not wait for the best (Numbers 32). Barred from the priesthood, the Reubenites were all too ready to assist a disaffected Levite, Korah by name, in his attempt to seize what had been denied him by divine decree. And Reuben was the first tribe to be carried into captivity by Tiglath-pileser the Assyrian (1 Chronicles 5:26). The Reubenites excelled in nothing.

But there was worse to come. As Reuben stood there, his ambitions in ruins, he heard Jacob's last words and they smote like a lash, for Jacob was speaking now of *Reuben's unscrupulous passion* (49:4*b*). "Thou wentest up to thy father's bed; then defiledst thou it: he went up to my couch." It had taken a long time to come, but now that axe, poised unseen over Reuben's unsuspecting head all those years, fell with all the weight of divine wrath. The sin had taken place forty years ago. There had been plenty of time for repentance and confession. There had been twenty-two years in Canaan and seventeen years in Egypt—time enough for Reuben to weep out his sorrow and shame to his father. But there had been nothing, nothing but a big cover-up and a furtive look in his eye every time he looked either at Bilhah or Jacob. So Reuben reaped what he sowed. Here at the judgment seat unconfessed sin was exposed and dealt with, and Reuben, left with no space for repentance, looked forward to the coming kingdom with his hopes of glory in broken fragments at his feet.

c. SIMEON AND LEVI (49:5-7)

Old Jacob saw the two as one as he peered at them standing by his bed. What God had *not* joined together as he was now going to rend asunder. The two brothers shifted uneasily under his gaze. It was evident that promiscuous blessings were simply not being handed out at that judgment seat. They must have thought of their past as it rose up, unbidden, specterlike, from the grave of forgotten memories. Way back then, when it had happened, Jacob had been swift to express his displeasure and to disassociate himself from their deed, but they had never confessed themselves wicked and wrong. Now their behavior must be publicly reviewed and judged.

Seeing the two as one, Jacob began by mentioning their *close brother-*

hood (49:5*a*). "Simeon and Levi are brethren." Well, that was not so bad! It seemed an auspicious start. Brethren! The word spoke of fellowship and felicity. The brothers stole a furtive look at each other. Perhaps the old patriarch had come to see the Shechem affair in its proper light. After all, they had only been defending his honor in avenging their sister's disgrace. Brethren. Yes, it was a very good start.

Then, with Jacob's next breath, they froze where they stood, for he was speaking now of their *criminal behavior* (49:5*b*-6). "Simeon and Levi . . . instruments of cruelty are in their habitations. O my soul, come not thou into their secret; unto their assembly, mine honour, be not thou united: for in their anger they slew a man, and in their selfwill they digged down a wall." Their sin was not one of weakness like the sin of Reuben; it was one of downright, deliberate wickedness. Jacob had disassociated himself from it at the time; he wanted no part in their craftiness and cruelty and in the sack of Shechem. At the time he had been forced to content himself with a reprimand; now the time had come for retribution.

The atmosphere grew tense. The bedroom had become a courtroom, and the old patriarch's deathbed a judgment seat indeed. The shrewd old man, with all his senses keyed and quickened by the Holy Spirit, was weighing his sons. Positions in the coming kingdom were being assigned. Character and career were the determining factors, the past was determining the future. Issues of vast future significance were being decided by deeds long since hammered into history.

Jacob's next words emphasized Simeon's and Levi's *continuing blame* (49:7). Did they think that all would be whitewashed and forgotten by their father? If so, they were very much mistaken. Just because they were in the family did not absolve them from responsibility for their behavior. "Cursed be their anger," cried Jacob, "for it was fierce; and their wrath, for it was cruel: I will divide them in Jacob and scatter them in Israel." For the *sin*, Jacob had a curse, for the *sinners* a cure. Their places in the coming kingdom were not so fixed that recovery, during the kingdom age, could never be effected. On the contrary one of the brothers, Levi, profited from the judgment and his tribe rose to fame.

Of all the tribes, Simeon alone had no inheritance in the land. "Out of the part of the children of Judah was the inheritance of the children of Simeon," we read (Joshua 19:9). Even at that, some of Simeon's towns reverted to Judah, for Beersheba is said to belong to Judah (1 Kings 19:3). The tribe itself was scattered. Some of its members migrated to Gidor and others wandered off to Mount Seir (1 Chronicles 4:39-43). In the days of Josiah, the Simeonites were counted with the people of Ephraim, Manasseh, and Naphtali (2 Chronicles 34:6). They were indeed divided and dispersed in Israel. At the time of the second census in the wilderness, the tribe of Simeon had shrunk to the smallest (Numbers 26:14), and it was no doubt because of weakness that Simeon had to rely on his stronger brother Judah to get even so much as a ghost of an inheritance in Canaan. Truly Simeon lost out in the kingdom. Nor was the verdict of Jacob reversed. When Moses came to bless the tribes, he transformed Jacob's judgment of Levi into a blessing, but Simeon he passed over in silence (Deuteronomy 33).

The scattering and dividing of Levi was the same, but with a very important difference. Levi took a stand for God at Baal-peor when Israel sinned with the daughters of Moab (Exodus 32). When Moses raised his standard and cried: "Who is on the Lord's side?" it was the tribe of Levi that responded. The Levites received no actual territorial grant in Canaan; instead they received forty-eight cities scattered up and down the kingdom among the tribes. The tribe of Levi was thus judicially dismembered but, because of its bold stand for God in the wilderness, the priesthood and the religious service of the nation was given to it. The very scattering was to become a blessing, for Levites were found in all the coasts of the kingdom.

d. JUDAH (49:8-12)

Judah had some shady things in his background as well, and it must have been with real apprehension that he sensed his father's eyes upon him. What would Jacob say now, at the judgment seat, about that pagan woman he had married? Would he say anything about his parental slackness that had resulted in the vileness of Onan and Er? What would he say about the wretched business with Tamar?

Interestingly enough, Jacob said nothing about any of those things. Judah had apparently repented of them and so they were forgotten. He had declared himself fully when he had put *himself,* not his sons, in pledge for Benjamin and when he had poured out his soul before Joseph. Jacob's judgment seat was not convened to rake up confessed and forgiven sin.

Looking at Judah, Jacob saw *the leader* (49:8). "Judah, thou art he whom thy brethren shall praise: thy hand shall be in the neck of thine enemies; thy father's children shall bow down before thee." Judah had prevailed and had become a godly man. Lordship was bestowed upon him over three classes of people—his brethren, his enemies, and his father's children. Looking beyond Judah we think at once of the Lord Jesus and the three classes who will one day acknowledge His supremacy—the Jews (His kinsmen according to the flesh), the Gentiles (in their end-time hostility toward Himself), and the church (the Father's children).

Then Jacob saw *the lion* (49:9). "Judah is a lion's whelp: from the prey, my son, thou art gone up: he stooped down, he couched as a lion, and as an old lion; who shall rouse him up?" Judah would be the royal tribe, as the lion was king among beasts. No one would tamper with Judah in the day of his power. Be it the young lion raising its massive head from its prey, or the mere cub feeling the first flush of its strength, or the old lion stretched out at peace in its den, Judah was to be king. From beginning to end sovereignty was his. Jacob, of course, had no means of knowing by natural inference that Jesus would be the Lion of the tribe of Judah. The Spirit of God was speaking through his lips. The sovereignty Reuben had tossed away for a half hour's unholy passion was now bestowed on Judah. In the coming kingdom he would reign.

Looking yet at Judah, Jacob saw *the Lord* (49:10). "The sceptre shall not depart from Judah, nor a lawgiver from between his feet, until Shiloh come; and unto him shall the gathering of the people be." The name *Shiloh* comes from the same root as the Hebrew word *shalom*—peace! In Jacob's prophecy it refers not to a place but a person, and points to that true Prince of Peace into whose almighty hand the sceptre of absolute and universal dominion is yet to be placed. He would come from Judah's line. What more could Judah have than that, for by giving Him the Messianic line, Jacob gave him everything. The natural man in Jacob would have greatly desired to bestow that sovereignty on Joseph; the spiritual man bestowed it on Judah.

But he had not yet finished with that son. Still looking at Judah, the old patriarch saw *the land* (49:11-12), the land as it will be when Judah's Lion comes to reign. He saw millennial blessings flowing from that. "Binding his foal unto the vine, and his ass's colt unto the choice vine; he washed his garments in wine, and his clothes in the blood of grapes." The whole poetic idiom is one of peace and plenty.

Little had Judah known, when he stood before that great and dreadful lord in Egypt, the unknown Joseph, and pleaded Benjamin's cause, that such lavish praise and reward would one day be his. At the judgment seat of Jacob nothing was forgotten, just as at the judgment seat of Christ no stand taken for Christ will go unrewarded in the Kingdom. As Jacob looked at Judah all he could see was Jesus. All Judah's faults and failings were blotted out in that glorious vision of Christ. That is what will count at the judgment seat.

e. ZEBULUN (49:13)

Zebulun was the youngest of Leah's sons. Genesis tells us nothing about him beyond the fact he was one of those who sold Joseph—but that was the common guilt of all in those dark, unregenerate days. Zebulun stood at the foot of the bed next to his mighty brother Judah. He was probably a somewhat silent, ordinary, unassuming, and anonymous person. He had never been a very bold man like Judah nor yet a very bad man like Reuben. What would Jacob say to him?

Jacob's far-seeing prophetic eye saw Zebulun's future *coastal interests*. "Zebulun shall dwell at the haven of the sea." The exact territory assigned to Zebulun in the kingdom is not known for sure. We do not know, for instance, whether his borders actually touched either the Galilee or the Mediterranean, but, if they did not do so during the past kingdom age, they certainly will during the one that is to come, for Jacob saw Zebulun with coastal interests.

He would also have *commercial interests.* "And he shall be an haven of ships." The fulfillment of that is vague. So far as we know, and as most maps show, Zebulun's land-grant in the kingdom did not reach to the Mediterranean. It could have touched the Sea of Galilee, but such a small inland body of water, however important it might have been to Palestine, hardly exhausts the magnificence implied in Jacob's words. Minor fishing concessions along a lake or even profit resulting from the intersection of trade routes there seems only a minor fulfillment of what Jacob saw.

For Jacob went on to depict Zebulun's *continental interests.* "And his border shall be unto Zidon." Again, there is no proof that Zebulun's borders ever reached that far, but the prophecy certainly implies great enlargement for Zebulun and vast, continental interests. For Zidon (Sidon) was one of the world's mightest cities with maritime interests to the ends of the earth. It was the mother of mighty Tyre, one of the greatest cities of antiquity. The ultimate fulfillment of Jacob's words must surely be in the Millennium.

The *millennial* interpretation of Jacob's words, however, does not exhaust their meaning. There is a *mystical* interpretation that needs to be considered. Zebulun's tribal inheritance included Nazareth and Cana of Galilee. Who can think of places like that without thinking of Jesus? Was He not frequently called simply "Jesus of Nazareth"? It was there He spent His boyhood days, grew to full manhood, and labored at the bench. In New Testament times the borders of Zebulun may have reached as far as Capernaum on the shore of Galilee. It was in favored Zebulun that the Lord Jesus performed many of His mightiest miracles (Matthew 4:15-16). Thus Zebulun cradled that mighty movement in history that resulted, on the Day of Pentecost, in the advent of the church—the church that soon thereafter set out to conquer the world. Little did insignificant Zebulun realize what great honor was being bestowed upon him that day as he stood silent at Jacob's judgment seat.

f. ISSACHAR (49:14-15)

Issachar was also one of Leah's sons, the son born when Leah hired away Jacob from Rachel. The circumstances of his birth may have colored Issachar's character, for he does not seem to have been an active and aggressive person but one quite content to take a humble place. Yet Jacob, looking at Issachar, spoke of *his strength* (49:14). "Issachar," he said, "is a strong ass." It was a characterization of which most would be ashamed but that many are content to assume just the same. It was not flattering to be likened to a strong but somewhat stupid animal. How much better to be a lion like Judah, a hind like Naphtali, a wolf like Benjamin, or even a serpent like Dan! The very picture of a donkey is one of dumbness and of an inability to appreciate higher things. Yet, at the same time, it is a picture of usefulness and strength.

It was Issachar's strength that was first mentioned by Jacob. He was a strong man—not strong in the sense of explosive leadership but in the sense of dependability. He was not a man easily moved, but you knew where you stood with him. He was a plodder, but solid.

Jacob next spoke of *his satisfaction* (49:15*a*). "And he saw that rest was good, and the land that it was pleasant." Issachar would prefer the comforts of home to glory. He inherited a very fertile strip of land in the kingdom; it was in the north, fronting on the Jordan, a territory much coveted by raiders. Issachar would yield up dignity and freedom so long as he could continue to farm his fields and be at ease. When the book of Judges recapitulates the sketchy achievements of the tribes in taking hold of their possessions in Canaan, Issachar is not even mentioned (Judges 1). The tribe was such a failure along military lines it did not deserve a place among those who at least made some effort to possess their possessions.

But Jacob saw even more. The indolent, easygoing disposition of Issachar pointed to *his servitude* (49:15*b*). "And he bowed his shoulder to bear and became a servant unto tribute." There was no blame, simply a lack of achievement. But here again, the judgment seat was to produce salutary results for in later years, in the kingdom, Issachar did amount to something after all.

When the tribes were camped or on the march, Issachar was placed next to Zebulun and Judah at the head of them all (Numbers 10:15). Association with those vigorous members of the kingdom was intended to inspire sluggish Issachar, and that is just what happened. In the days of the judges, Issachar came forward to fight with Barak and even marched in the van to bear the brunt of battle (Judges 5:15). Deborah, whose name means "the bee," stung lazy Issachar into activity at last. Later on, Issachar gave four kings to the northern kingdom. But, best of all, in David's day the men of Issachar were men who had understanding of the times, men who knew what Israel ought to do. They took the lead in welcoming David back to the throne (1 Chronicles 12:32, 38-40).

g. DAN (49:16-18)

Dan was the first son to be born by proxy to Rachel. He was a son of Bilhah the maid. Nothing is said about Dan in Genesis beyond the fact that Joseph gave Jacob an evil report about the boy and his three closest brothers. But that was years ago. Would Jacob bring that up now? What would he say to Dan, a man who felt keenly his inferiority as a son of a bondwoman? What would Jacob say to him?

The first thing Jacob saw as he gazed at Dan was *position* (49:16). "Dan shall judge his people, as one of the tribes of Israel." We can see Dan suddenly stand up straight and square his shoulders. That was better than being called an ass like Issachar. And Jacob's prophetic vision was accurate, for out of Dan came the mightiest of all the judges—great Samson whose exploits later became a legend in the land.

But there was more; Jacob had not finished with Dan. He could see serious flaws in Dan's disposition. The next thing the old prophet saw as he looked at Dan was *poison* (49:17). "Dan shall be a serpent by the way, an adder in the path, that biteth the horse heels, so that his rider shall fall backward." Dan's inheritance in the kingdom was a rich one territorially, for it bordered on the Mediterranean and included the great seaport of Joppa. It was a tribal territory, however, that fronted on Philistine country and one that was constantly threatened by those warlike neighbors.

The Danites, dissatisfied with such a portion, migrated north. They fell with serpentlike cunning on the city of Laish and established themselves in the far north of Israel. There, however, they had to face constant pressure from the hostile northern powers such as Syria. It was Dan that first introduced idolatry into Israel as tribal religious policy (Judges 18:30-31), and it was in Dan that Jeroboam set up one of his golden calves (1 Kings 12:2-30). Many think that the Antichrist will come from the tribe of Dan. There was poison in Dan's cup.

But Jacob could see something else, something better, something worth mentioning at the judgment seat. He could see *pardon* (49:18). "I have waited for thy salvation, O LORD!" he exclaimed. For suddenly, peering down the future ages, taken up with coming events as they were suggested to his mind by Dan, the old patriarch saw far, far beyond Dan and his treacheries. He saw the Lord, the covenant-keeping Jehovah, bringing salvation to his sons—even to Dan with his serpentlike ways. There was a grace even in the midst of judgment. At the judgment seat of Christ, too, grace will triumph, for nothing can rob God's people of their salvation. It is worth noting too that the reference here—"I have waited for thy salvation, O LORD"—is the very first reference to salvation in the Bible. And it occurs in connection with Dan!

h. GAD (49:19)

Gad was the first son born to Leah's maid, and we know no more about him than we know about Dan. He, too, was included in Joseph's ill report to the father along with Asher and Napthali. Looking at Gad, Jacob saw him in two lights. He saw him as *vanquished*. "Gad," he said, "a troop shall overcome him." But he also saw him as *victorious*. "But he shall overcome at the last."

Gad chose his inheritance on the far side of Jordan. His territory was under constant attack from warlike, nomadic tribes, which swooped down upon his fields from the deserts. All the tribes that settled east of Jordan were vulnerable and, indeed, were the first to be carried away when Assyrian hordes came down on the fold.

The tribe of Gad was not without its notables. Jephthah, beloved Barzillai, and Elijah—that prince among the prophets—were all from the tribe of Gad. Gad could take a beating from the foe and come back in triumph. It is in that character that he was owned at the judgment seat of Jacob. He was an overcomer—a great thing to be in the day when actions are weighed.

i. ASHER (49:20)

Asher was another of the bondwomen's sons, like the others, a seeming nonentity. Those undistinguished sons of Jacob represent the crowd, the rank and file of the faith, the great mass who fill out the ranks of the redeemed. At the judgment seat of Jacob all were present; all had to appear. There was no difference. The review was not just for those outstanding either in sin or sanctity; it was for all. Looking at Asher, Jacob again saw two things. He saw *life's routine rewards.* "Out of Asher his bread shall be fat," he said. He saw also *life's royal riches*—"and he shall yield royal dainties." How Asher's face must have glowed at the note of praise and reward and of promised honor in the coming kingdom.

Asher's inheritance in Canaan was that amazingly fertile strip that ran along the foot of Carmel, up the Mediterranean coast past Tyre. Asher was never strong enough to dispossess the tough and tenacious Phoenicians of Tyre, but then even Nebuchadnezzar and Alexander the Great had trouble subduing Tyre. Surely, though, the God who could vanquish the Egyptian army at the Red Sea could have uprooted Tyre for Asher. Instead, Tyre lingered on, a veritable stronghold of Satan in Canaan, all through the years of Joshua and the judges and through the reigns of David, Solomon, and the northern kings.

Asher was to "dip his foot in oil." Commentators are taken up with the rich oil-producing olive groves that flourished so abundantly in Asher's territory. But there is more to it than that. The great modern port of Haifa is situated in Asher's territory today and there, at Haifa, the giant pipelines from the great Iranian oilfields terminate. Asher literally dips his foot in oil today.

j. NAPHTALI (49:21)

The remaining bondwoman's son was Naphtali. Jacob put his finger, first, on his son's *natural wildness.* "Naphtali is a hind let loose," he said. The hind, the female deer, is a timid, swift, and graceful creature of the woods and wilds. In those early days, before he was regenerated with the help of Joseph, Naphtali had apparently been a wild and ungovernable young fellow, hard to tame, imbued with a passion for freedom and unrestraint. That love for freedom was now to be turned to good account, for it was a dispositional trait capable of development for better or for worse. At the judgment seat, the Lord is going to look at what we have done with natural traits. Have we simply developed them along ungoverned, natural lines? Or have we brought them to the altar and allowed them to be put to death in the death of Christ and resurrected in the Spirit's power to new and nobler ends?

Jacob saw also, in Naphtali, his *notable wisdom.* "Naphtali," he said, "giveth goodly words." That is, he was an eloquent man, and God's kingdom has always been able to use such. The suggestion has been made that, when the brothers returned from Egypt with the news that Joseph was alive, Naphtali ran on ahead to tell his father that not only was all well with Benjamin but also that Joseph lived. The sight of Naphtali, perhaps, awakened some such memory in Jacob. The hind let loose was one that gave goodly words. Naphtali's swiftness of foot and eloquence of tongue was held up for praise at Jacob's judgment seat. At the judgment seat of Christ may we too find that our walk and our talk can be held up for warm commendation before all.

k. JOSEPH (49:22-26)

Then Jacob's eye fell on Joseph, and his own eloquence took wings. He had much to say about that eminently godly man. For that is what is going to count most at the coming judgment seat. Courage, strength, and wisdom will all have their rewards, but it is Christlikeness in us that will make the very vaults of heaven ring.

With so much to say to Joseph, Jacob focused his thoughts in four areas. First he extolled *his fruitfulness* (49:22). "Joseph is a fruitful bough, even a fruitful bough by a well; whose branches run over the wall." Jacob had just given Joseph a double portion in Israel by adding Ephraim and Manasseh to the tribes. He now foresaw how fruitful that addition would be. After the second census in the wilderness those two tribes, taken together, were by far the most populous in Israel. Joseph was a fruitful bough.

Then Jacob made mention of *his foes* (49:23). "The archers have sorely grieved him, and shot at him, and hated him." The hostility of Joseph's brethren was a faint picture, a mere type, of the larger hostilities Ephraim and Manasseh would have to face in the world. It was Ephraim who gave the tribes their Joshua, the great military leader who wrested Canaan from the massed might of the foe. Thus it was Joseph who conquered the foe.

Next, Jacob reviewed *his faith* (49:24). "But his bow abode in strength, and the arms of his hands were made strong by the hands of the mighty God of Jacob; (from thence is the shepherd and stone of Israel)." By the vigor of his faith Joseph had triumphed in his adversities and testings and had been made so strong that there was not a man his equal in all of Egypt. It was faith that had carried him through. That personal truth gave rise to prophetic truth. Jacob could see in Joseph a type of the promised Messiah. He would be both a *Shepherd* (that relates to His first coming), and a *Stone* (that relates to His second coming). The dying Jacob dimly grasped the truth of the two comings of Christ as they were typified in the personal history of his own beloved son.

Words seemed to fail Jacob in seeking to describe all the blessings he could see in Joseph. The word "blessing" simply came to his lips and there it stayed—one blessing after another poured out of his mouth as, looking at Joseph, he described *his fulness* (49:25-26). He blessed him with the blessing of heaven above and of the deep that lieth under; he blessed him with sufficiency, with security, and with sovereignty. "The blessings of thy father," he cried, "have prevailed above the blessings of my progenitors." I have been blessed above Abraham and Isaac; you will be blessed above me! "Blessings," he cried as he warmed to his work. "Blessings unto the utmost bound of the everlasting hills: they shall be on the head of Joseph, and on the crown of him that was separate from his brethren."

Jacob's words leaped far beyond mere tribal blessings into total blessing. That was Joseph's reward at the judgment seat of Jacob—a blessing that reached out and beyond all intervening kingdom ages to the furthest reaches of eternity. And it was Christlikeness in Joseph that opened up that floodtide of blessing—that and that alone.

l. BENJAMIN (49:27)

Benjamin was the son of Jacob's old age, born in the same hour that Rachel died, and the son of his right hand. As he looked at Benjamin he underlined *his character*. "Benjamin shall ravin as a wolf." The wolf, the largest member of the canine family, oftens weighs as much as a hundred pounds and is a powerful predator. It was in that character that Jacob saw Benjamin. Benjamin would become a warrior tribe.

The territory allotted to Benjamin was small (only about four hundred square miles) but rugged and placed in a most strategic position for the defense of the whole land. His holdings were often under attack from invading powers. But Benjamin had the character for that. It would have been a great mistake to give to an Issachar what belonged to a Benjamin—a wolf, not an ass, was required to hold the terrain that would later contain Jerusalem, the capital city of Israel.

As Jacob continued to look at Benjamin he saw also *his conquests*. "In the morning he shall devour the prey, and at night he shall divide the spoil." Two illustrious Benjamites are found in Scripture—both Sauls, one in the Old Testament, the other in the New. In the morn-

ing Saul, the son of Kish, leaped to the throne to become Israel's first king; in the evening Saul of Tarsus seized the reins of the church and became the greatest of all the apostles, with a message that hammered at the very gates of Rome.

One and all the sons had now stood before Jacob as he opened the books and rendered accounts. The judgment had been searching but fair, and, above all, it had been *private*—the world had been shut out from that bedchamber. It had been *pointed*, too. Jacob had seized the salient dispositional trait of each son; he had weighed the highlights of each one's history, and he had seen the whole person, the whole tribe, the very mountain peaks of unborn time. The judgment-seat experience had been painful for some, pleasant for others, but the verdict had been *perfect* in each case. Not a voice was raised in protest, each individual knew he had been fairly dealt with, and that the judge had been without bias. As the men trooped out of the room to face their respective futures in the coming kingdom, they could not help but see that they had reaped just what they had sown.

B. Jacob's Funeral (49:28–50:21)

As God took Moses to the heights of Pisgah just before his death to show him the promised land, so He took Jacob to a lofty spiritual peak, just prior to his death, to show him the future history of his sons and the destiny of the nation which would come out of Egypt. Having chronicled Jacob's foreknowledge, the Spirit of God now tells of Jacob's funeral.

1. The Pledge (49:28-33)

The review of his family was over, and Jacob prepared for death. Before finally crossing over Jordan, however, he had three last things to accomplish. We have *his last words*. "All these are the twelve tribes of Israel." Moses adds: "And this is it that their father spake unto them and blessed them; every one according to his blessing he blessed them." The thought is that, in blessing his sons, he was blessing the tribes that would spring from them. Jacob had no doubt that the promise of a great seed, made to Abraham and confirmed to Isaac, was now being fulfilled in his sons. Already in Goshen the family was "multiplying exceedingly" (47:27). Thus, prophetically, in his very last words, Jacob made mention for the first time in Scripture of "the twelve tribes of Israel."

Then he published *his last will* (49:29-32). "I am to be gathered unto my people," he said. "Bury me with my fathers in the cave that is in the field of Ephron the Hittite." Jacob did not want to be buried in Egypt. His heart was in Canaan, and there he wished to lie. God had promised him Canaan, and in Canaan, dead or alive, he intended to be when God made good the promise. Perhaps he suspected something more, for Jacob was a prophet in his last hours. The Messiah was coming to

Canaan, and he may have wanted to be there when Christ came. Who could tell what wonders the Messiah would perform![4]

Jacob had something else to say about his will. His thoughts were centered now on that cave in the field of Machpelah. Abraham's body was there, and so was Sarah's. Isaac's body was there; Rebekah's was too. Leah was buried there along with the others—the first intimation we have of her death. Jacob wanted his mortal remains to be at rest with theirs. They would be the first ones he would see on the resurrection morn.

There remained only one thing more. Having given his last word and his last will, Jacob gave *his last witness* (49:33). "And when Jacob had made an end of commanding his sons, he gathered up his feet into the bed, and yielded up the ghost, and was gathered unto his people." He had ordered his body to be buried with his loved ones, and now he departed to be with them himself. He summoned what was left of his strength, hauled his feet into bed, let fall his staff, and smiled into the face of God. He was dead.

There he lay upon his gilded couch in that gorgeous chamber in the land of Egypt. The painted walls gazed silently down. The echo of the old man's voice died away and all was still. The awed family gazed at the mortal remains of one of God's great worthies. There it lay, stiffening now in death—that old, weather-beaten form, its struggles over, its battles won. He was with Abraham and Isaac. He was with his mother, Rebekah, and his grandmother, Sarah. He was with Leah. And, oh the bliss of it—he was with Rachel. He was at home with God.

2. THE PREPARATION (50:1-3)

Arrangements were now made for embalming Jacob's body. Joseph took care of all that. "And Joseph fell upon his father's face, and wept upon him, and kissed him. And Joseph commanded his servants the physicians to embalm his father, and the physicians embalmed Israel."[5]

4. Matthew 27 records a significant event that took place at the time of Christ's death and resurrection. "The graves were opened: and many bodies of the saints which slept arose, and came out of their graves after his resurrection, and went into the holy city, and appeared unto many." Is that why the patriarchs coveted burial in Canaan? Could it be that Jacob had an inkling of that and wanted to be where it would happen? Did he hope to be part of that wondrous and mysterious wave-sheaf to be snatched from the grave at the great Feast of Firstfruits on Christ's resurrection morn? We do not know, but the possibility exists.

5. Burying the dead was big business in Egypt. Embalming and coffin-making, painting and constructing funeral furniture and all the accompanying religious ritual kept whole guilds forever busy. It took about two months to complete the process of embalming a body. First the brain was drawn out of the skull through the nostrils. Then, through an incision made in the flank, the vital organs were extracted. The body was then cleansed with palm wine and purified with pounded incense. The hollowed-out body was filled with spices and perfumes—pure myrrh and cassia—and similar items, and soaked in nitron for weeks on end. After the proper period of saturation, the corpse was washed and wrapped in strips of fine linen, smeared with gum the Egyptians used for glue. The embalming being thus completed, the corpse was placed in a wooden case fashioned in human shape and taken to the sepulchre.

Little had Jacob thought in those distant days when he had been bickering with Laban that he would end his days being given a state funeral in Egypt. Jacob's death had such an effect on Joseph and through Joseph on all Egypt that the whole land was plunged into mourning. It gives us some idea of the extent of Joseph's power and influence in Egypt.

3. The Permission (50:4-6)

"And when the days of his mourning were past, Joseph spake unto the house of Pharaoh, saying, If now I have found grace in your eyes, speak, I pray you, in the ears of Pharaoh, saying, My father made me swear, saying, Lo I die: in my grave which I have digged for me in the land of Canaan, there shalt thou bury me. Now therefore let me go up, I pray thee, and bury my father, and I will come again. And Pharaoh said, Go."

Joseph was a born diplomat. He knew he was indispensable to Pharaoh even though the years of famine were long a thing of the past. If he and all his kin were to have left for Canaan it would have alarmed the Egyptians and prompted restrictive measures. He needed permission to leave. Should he approach Pharaoh himself? Joseph knew enough about the whims of autocrats not to risk that. He therefore urged his friends to make the first approach for him along with his promise to return. That was enough for Pharaoh. There was not a soul in Egypt, highborn or low, who did not know the value of Joseph's word; it was worth millions. What a testimony Joseph had.

4. The Procession (50:7-14)

Nowhere else in Scripture do we have such a full description of a funeral. Jacob was buried with full military honors as though he had been commander-in-chief of Egypt's armed forces instead of a nomadic shepherd who had wandered into the land late in life. There was a mourning entourage and a military escort. Joseph was there, the other brothers and their households were there—all except the little children who were left behind either as proof of Joseph's good faith or because their presence would have been a hindrance. High officials of the court went along to represent Pharaoh at the funeral. There were supply wagons and servants and sufficient cavalry to discourage attack.

The route was similar to that taken later during the Exodus. The procession followed the line of the Red Sea, struck out across the Sinai Peninsula, and reached the southern bank of the Dead Sea. It followed the coastline of the Dead Sea along its eastern bank and then on up the Jordan to "the threshing floor of Atad." There the whole great host camped for seven days, and there was enacted a ceremonial mourning for Jacob.

The local peoples were astonished. "When the inhabitants of the land, the Canaanites, saw the mourning in the floor of Atad, they said, This is a grievous mourning to the Egyptians." And Moses adds the note: "Wherefore the name of it was called Abelmizraim ("the meadow of the Egyptians"), with a play on the word for "mourning." The Egyptians were a very demonstrative people and vehement in their public lamentations for the dead. They rent their clothes, smote their breasts, threw dust and mud on their heads, called on the deceased by name, and chanted funeral dirges to the sound of the tambourine. The local peoples concluded that it was the burial of a very high Egyptian official and could not understand why it should take place so far from Egypt.

The ceremonies over, Joseph and his brothers carried Jacob's mummy over Jordan and on to the cave in the field of Machpelah in accordance with their father's command. Then they rejoined the waiting escort and returned, as promised, to Egypt.

5. THE PARDON (50:15-21)

One more incident is recorded in connection with Jacob's death. It is a sad addition because it shows how terribly the brothers misjudged Joseph. "And when Joseph's brethren saw that their father was dead, they said, Joseph will peradventure hate us, and will certainly requite us all the evil which we did unto him" (50:15). What a slander on the character of Joseph after all the kindness he had shown them. Their suspicions must have been an arrow in his soul. Yet how often we misjudge our own glorious Lord in the very same way. What a grief our unbelief must be to Him.

However, God overruled the sad event, for it was at that time the brothers gave the first forthright and outright confession of their sin. They had hinted at it before; they had shown that they were sorry. But either fear or pride had kept them from being thoroughly honest and making a clean breast of it. But now they did.

They selected a messenger to represent them before Joseph—probably Benjamin or Judah: Benjamin because he had not been involved in the betrayal, or Judah because of his former success as an intercessor. "Forgive, I pray thee now, the trespass of thy brethren," the messenger said, "and their sin; for they did thee evil: and now, we pray thee, forgive the trespass of the servants of the God of thy father."

The appeal broke Joseph's heart. As the brothers to a man prostrated themselves before him, he said: "Fear not: for am I in the place of God? But as for you, ye thought evil against me; but God meant it unto good . . . now therefore fear ye not: I will nourish you and your little ones." He comforted them, we are told, and spake kindly unto them. Such is grace. Such was Joseph. Such is Jesus our Lord. We can fail him and disappoint him as Peter did, but His love is always the same.

Thus, on that note of grace, the story of Jacob ends. All that remains is to record the death and burial of Joseph.

II. THE DEATH OF JOSEPH (50:22-26)

The story of Joseph's death and burial is told in five short verses, and with that death the book of Genesis ends. It was a significant death. In Hebrews 11, the Holy Spirit passes over scores of things He could have said about Joseph and fastens on the incident mentioned here—the fact that Joseph, when he died, made mention of the departing of the children of Israel and gave commandment concerning his bones. It was the greatest and most illuminating act of faith in a life that was ablaze with faith.

A. JOSEPH'S DWELLING (50:22)

"And Joseph dwelt in Egypt, he, and his father's house: and Joseph lived an hundred and ten years." He was fifty-six when Jacob died, and he lived on in all the pomp and splendor of his high position for another fifty-four years. The commandment concerning his bones was fulfilled only after the lapse of centuries. There had to come another pharaonic dynasty and "a new king of Egypt which knew not Joseph" (Exodus 1:8) and the great oppression of Israel before Joseph's command could be fulfilled.

So we picture Joseph living out his days in a splendor known by only a few. His contemporaries at court were spending fortunes on their tombs, but not Joseph. They would say to him: "Joseph, don't you think it's about time you started work on your tomb? Do you think you're going to live forever?" And Joseph would bear testimony to his faith and to his God. For though he had success and influence, majesty and power, children and grandchildren, wisdom and wealth, and all that this world could offer, he never once forgot the true values of life and death. And those values did not include a tomb in Egypt. One suspects he would have traded Egypt with all its magnificence any day for a tent in Canaan. His heart's affections were in the promised land, not Egypt. His heart was in safekeeping in the hands of God. No wonder God could trust him with such wealth and power. It is not money that is a root of all evil; it is the love of money. Joseph, then, dwelt in Egypt but desired Canaan.

B. JOSEPH'S DESCENDANTS (50:23)

"And Joseph saw Ephraim's children of the third generation: the children also of Machir the son of Manasseh were brought up upon Joseph's knees." What a delightful grandfather Joseph must have made! Somehow it adds a delightfully human touch to the story of Joseph to picture him, as the Holy Spirit does, as a grandfather with little ones on his knee.

Joseph would have been a very human kind of a grandfather after all. He would have told those little ones exciting stories, as grandfathers are supposed to do. He would have pulled little surprises out of his pockets, because that is what grandfathers are for. He would have taken them on walks and spoiled their suppers with unauthorized treats. For after all, he was not just the grand vizier of Egypt, he was a grandfather. And, of course, he would have told them about Cain and Abel and the Flood, about the Tower of Babel, how Abraham came into the promised land and how he once visited Pharaoh. He would have told them about the offering up of Isaac at Mount Moriah and about Jacob's ladder reaching up to heaven. He would have filled the young hearts of his grandchildren with those exciting stories later on to be written by Moses into a book we call the Bible. For that is why God invented grandfathers. They are intended to form a living link, not just with the past out of which they have emerged, but with the eternal future on the threshold of which they stand.

C. JOSEPH'S DISCERNMENT (50:24)

Then, when he was one hundred ten, Joseph realized his time had come to make his exodus from Egypt. His time had come to die. He summoned his brethren to his mansion on the Nile. "I die," he said, "and God will surely visit you, and bring you out of this land unto the land which he sware to Abraham, to Isaac and to Jacob." That was his discernment. He took his stand on that.

For the aged diplomat saw beyond his own approaching death. He saw the days of tribulation that would surely come. He saw Israel crushed and broken beneath a conquering pharaoh's heel. He saw the coming of a kinsman-redeemer. He could see so far ahead because he was so rooted and grounded in the past. His faith was anchored to the word of God, to God's infallible promise to Abraham.

Joseph did not spiritualize and allegorize the promises of God. He took them literally and at their face value. God said what He meant and meant what He said. Joseph did not call Canaan "heaven" and dissolve the promises of God into mystical fantasy. God's promises dealt with cold, hard facts, and Joseph took them thus. "God will surely visit you," he said. It was the right way to handle the word of truth. Joseph needed no divining cup, no magicians and soothsayers to make a statement like that. He simply banked on the literal integrity of the word of God. God had spoken, that was enough for him.

D. JOSEPH'S DEMAND (50:25)

"And Joseph took an oath of the children of Israel, saying, God will surely visit you, and ye shall carry up my bones from hence." It was his last command.

Look at that old man. He was a man well used to being obeyed. For the best part of a century he had been issuing commands and seeing them instantly done. He was about to leave all that behind him forever.

He had something to bequeath to his brethren—the most valuable thing, potentially, in Egypt—his bones! How eagerly the brothers must have gathered around him when he told them he was about to leave them something in his will. But what he left was not a mansion on the Nile, or a stable of Arabian racehorses, or jewels worth a king's ransom. Such things would be worthless to a people soon to be reduced to slavery. He left them something worthless to the Egyptians but priceless to them—his bones! In other words, he left them *a memorial body.*

Moses knew the value of that box of bones. On the great night of the Exodus, every Hebrew in Egypt was carrying something—the spoil of a nation was theirs to be carted away. Moses "took the bones of Joseph with *him*" (Exodus 13:19, italics added). Those bones, that memorial body, had a message for Israel just as our Lord's memorial body has a message for us. Joseph's body pointed back to the past, to the fact that God had kept His word and it pointed on—all through the wilderness way and wilderness wanderings—it pointed on to Canaan. "God had brought them out; God would bring them in." Joseph's memorial body spoke to Israel as the Lord's body does to His church. It was the last and final point in which Joseph typified Jesus. "This do in remembrance of me," said Joseph as he spoke of his body.

E. JOSEPH'S DECEASE (50:26)

"So Joseph died, being an hundred and ten years old: and they embalmed him, and he was put in a coffin in Egypt." But he did not stay there. Moses carried his bones across the sands of Sinai, and Joshua carried them on into Canaan. Genesis ends with a reference to the bones of Joseph, and so does the book of Joshua. "And the bones of Joseph, which the children of Israel brought up out of Egypt, buried they in Shechem, in a parcel of ground which Jacob bought of the sons of Hamor the father of Shechem for an hundred pieces of silver: and it became the inheritance of the children of Joseph" (Joshua 24:32).

Joseph could have done what all the grand viziers of Egypt before him had done—spent a fortune and half a lifetime building and gilding a tomb in Egypt. And like as not, his tomb would have been plundered by grave robbers long since. Or perhaps it would be an exhibit in the Cairo Museum! Joseph knew better than that. He wanted burial in Canaan.

Had we been able to stand there that day as Joshua, one of Joseph's lineal descendants, lovingly and loyally lowered Joseph's sarcophagus to rest at Shechem, we might well have heard a chuckle from that box of bones. Nor would we need degrees in theology or anthropology to know what those bones had to say. "God will surely visit you," the knee bone would be saying to the thigh bone, the back bone to the neck bone! "God will surely visit you and carry up these bones from hence. He has brought us up out of Egypt into *this* land, but one of these days He will visit us again and carry us up to *His* land. We shall be raised, incorruptible, and forever glorified!"

"So Joseph died being an hundred and ten years old: and they embalmed him, and he was put in a coffin in Egypt." Thus ends Genesis. It begins with creation and ends with a coffin. It begins with the glory and ends with a grave. It begins with the vastness of eternity and ends with the shortness of time. It begins with the living God and ends with a dead man. It begins with a blaze of brightness in heaven and ends with a box of bones in Egypt. That is the Holy Spirit's final comment in the book on the nature and tragedy of human sin. That is the final exposure of the devil's lie, "Thou shalt not surely die." "So Joseph died" (Joseph, the most Christlike man in all the Bible), "Joseph died . . . and they embalmed him, and he was put in a coffin in Egypt."